Neolithic Scotland

Neolithic Scotland

Timber, Stone, Earth and Fire

Gordon Noble

Edinburgh University Press

Transferred to digital print 2012

Edinburgh University Press Ltd
22 George Square, Edinburgh

Typeset in Minion by
Servis Filmsetting Ltd, Manchester and
printed and bound by CPI Group (UK) Ltd
Croydon, CR0 4YY

A CIP record for this book is available from the British Library

ISBN-10 0 7486 2337 X (hardback)
ISBN-13 978 0 7486 2337 2 (hardback)
ISBN-10 0 7486 2338 8 (paperback)
ISBN-13 978 0 7486 2338 9 (paperback)

Contents

List of figures vi

Preface x

Introduction 1

1. Scotland in the Neolithic: an introduction 7
2. Islands in the fast lane: the Mesolithic-Neolithic transition 24
3. Burning down the house: the destruction of timber structures 45
4. Planting trees, planting people: long and round barrows in eastern Scotland and beyond 71
5. Megalithic architecture in Atlantic Scotland 102
6. The emergence of monument complexes 139
7. The architecture of monumental landscapes 194
8. The Early Bronze Age: deconstructing and rebuilding the past 219

Conclusion: timber, stone, earth and fire 233

Bibliography 238

Index 260

Figures

1.1	The 'agricultural frontier'	8
1.2	Scotland in Europe	10
1.3	Areas and regions mentioned in the text	11
1.4	The geographical zones of Scotland	11
1.5	The composition of the woodland in Earlier Neolithic Scotland	13
1.6	The regional monument traditions of Earlier Neolithic Scotland	16
1.7	The changing forms of Neolithic pottery	18
2.1	The tides and currents of the sea	25
2.2	The island chains of the western British Isles	27
2.3	The major sea-routes in the Irish Sea zone	30
2.4	The brooding presence of the Isle of Man	31
2.5	Glecknabae chambered cairn	34
2.6	Machrie North	38
2.7	Earlier Neolithic field boundary and agricultural area near Brodick	39
2.8	Shetland: a Neolithic landscape	41
3.1	The distribution of pit-defined cursus monuments in Scotland	46
3.2	The radiocarbon dates for timber structures in lowland Scotland	47
3.3	The enclosure at Holywood North	48
3.4	Kirkburn, Lockerbie	49
3.5	The timber halls at Balbridie and Claish	50
3.6	The enclosure at Inchtuthil	50
3.7	The enclosures at Bannockburn	51
3.8	Douglasmuir	52
3.9	House 2, Coolfore, Co. Louth	53
3.10	Cloghers, Co. Kerry	53
3.11	Enagh Townland, Co. Derry	54
3.12	Ballyharry, Co. Antrim	54
3.13	Drummenny Lower, Co. Donegal	55
3.14	Chapelfield Cowie	60
3.15	Lamb's Nursery Structure A	60
3.16	Deer's Den, Aberdeenshire	61
3.17	Kinbeachie Farm	62
3.18	The pits at Blairhall Burn	63
3.19	Boghead mound	63

3.20 Radiocarbon dates for Neolithic settlement sites in lowland Scotland 65
3.21 The pits to the southeast of Douglasmuir 67
4.1 The distribution of long and round mounds and cairns in Scotland 72
4.2 Radiocarbon dates for timber structures 73
4.3 Aldwincle I, Northamptonshire 74
4.4 Fussell's Lodge 75
4.5 Exposure platforms: Scott's interpretation 76
4.6 A section through the mound at Fussell's Lodge 77
4.7 The sequence at Pitnacree 79
4.8 Pitnacree: detail 80
4.9 The sequence at the Slewcairn 81
4.10 The sequence at Lochhill 82
4.11 The primary phases of Dalladies long barrow 84
4.12 The full sequence at Dalladies 85
4.13 Sections through Dalladies long barrow 86
4.14 Wayland's Smithy 87
4.15 Detail of the split trunks at Wayland's Smithy 88
4.16 Street House 89
4.17 Nutbane 91
4.18 Dooey's Cairn, Co. Antrim 92
4.19 The forest 95
4.20 Trees of the past and the future 97
4.21 The trunk 98
4.22 Decay 100
5.1 The regional traditions of megalithic architecture in Scotland 103
5.2 An idealised Clyde Cairn 104
5.3 (a, b, c) Radiocarbon dates for chambered cairns in Scotland 106–8
5.4 The primary cairns at Mid Gleniron I 109
5.5 The cairn at Mid Gleniron I after enlargement 109
5.6 Mid Gleniron II primary cairn 110
5.7 Mid Gleniron B 110
5.8 Mid Gleniron II after cairn enlargement 111
5.9 Isometric drawing of Cairnholy I 112
5.10 A section through Cairnholy I 113
5.11 Phase 1 Achnacreebeag 114
5.12 Phase 2 Achnacreebeag 115
5.13 Calf of Eday 116
5.14 Papa Westray North 117
5.15 Anderson's sketch of Camster Long 119
5.16 Tulach an t'Sionnaich 120
5.17 Embo 122
5.18 Balvraid 122
5.19 Vementry 123
5.20 Craonaval 124

5.21 Oban nam Fiadh 125
5.22 Rudh' an Dunain 125
5.23 Notgrove 126
5.24 Ty Isaf 127
5.25 Pipton 128
5.26 Dyffryn Ardudwy 129
5.27 Trefignath 129
5.28 Primary cairns from across Britain 130
5.29 Camster Long forecourt 131
5.30 Midhowe, Orkney 135
6.1 The monument complex at Balfarg 142
6.2 Radiocarbon dates for Balfarg and Balfarg Riding School 143
6.3 Balfarg Riding School 144
6.4 Balfarg henge 145
6.5 Balbirnie stone circle 146
6.6 The location of North Mains henge 147
6.7 Radiocarbon dates for North Mains 148
6.8 North Mains henge and timber circle 149
6.9 The location of Cairnpapple Hill henge 150
6.10 Cairnpapple Hill henge 151
6.11 The Upper Clyde Valley 152
6.12 Blackshouse Burn 153
6.13 Radiocarbon dates for Blackhouse Burn 154
6.14 Meldon Bridge 155
6.15 Radiocarbon dates for Meldon Bridge 156
6.16 Dunragit (site) 157
6.17 Dunragit 158
6.18 Radiocarbon dates for Dunragit 159
6.19 Droughduil mound 159
6.20 Twelve Apostles, Holywood North and South and Holm 160
6.21 The relationship between Holywood and Twelve Apostles 161
6.22 Machrie Moor 162
6.23 The Earlier Neolithic features at Machrie Moor 163
6.24 Radiocarbon dates for Machrie Moor 164
6.25 Machrie Moor timber circles 165
6.26 Machrie Moor stone circles 165
6.27 Kilmartin Glen 166
6.28 Upper Largie 167
6.29 Temple Wood 167
6.30 Temple Wood as it survives today 168
6.31 Carvings at Achnabreck 169
6.32 Callanish 170
6.33 Callanish I 171
6.34 Radiocarbon dates for Callanish 172

6.35 The Stenness-Brodgar complex 174
6.36 The Stones of Stenness 175
6.37 Radiocarbon dates for the Stenness-Brodgar complex 176
6.38 Maeshowe 177
6.39 Howe 179
6.40 The Ring of Brodgar 180
6.41 Leadketty, Perthshire 182
6.42 Rectangular timber structures from the fourth millennium BC 183
6.43 The location of the Upper Clyde Valley 189
6.44 Henges and motorways 191
7.1 The layout of one of the houses at Barnhouse 199
7.2 House 7 at Skara Brae 201
7.3 House 2 at Barnhouse 202
7.4 Beckton Farm 203
8.1 An Early Bronze Age cist burial 220
8.2 Forecourt blocking at Cairnholy 223
8.3 Blocking at Mid Gleniron I 224
8.4 Auchategan, Cowal: Neolithic settlement 225
8.5 Early Bronze Age phase at Auchategan 226
8.6 Early Bronze Age reuse of Pitnacree mound 227
8.7 Embo 228

Preface

My first excavation experience was at a stone circle in Aberdeenshire. At the time I was studying the History of Art at the University of Aberdeen. I remember phoning the excavation director and asking if I could come and dig. He said, 'Hold a minute, I just have to lie behind the spoil heap so that I can hear you!' At that stage I didn't really know what a spoil heap was and was rather confused by the whole event, so much so that I thought about not going after all, as I was unsure of what to expect. After two weeks of digging on top of a hill in freezing conditions, occasionally having to clear snow off the trench before we could dig, I was hooked. I was hooked because I loved the excitement of trying to imagine the past and loved handling objects that people had touched and used thousands of years previously. On the last day of my time there I found a beautiful flint blade that was one of the best finds of the whole excavation. After that there was no turning back. The same year, I went to Orkney and after visiting sites like Skara Brae and Maeshowe I realised that archaeology was something I'd like to pursue further. Subsequently I wrote my final year History of Art dissertation on the architecture of Neolithic chambered cairns in Orkney and after a year in London, a Ph.D. in Reading and now this book, it is safe to say that I am still enamoured by the whole process of archaeological investigation.

The director of the Tomnaverie excavation was Professor Richard Bradley of Reading University and his unwavering support has been the main reason for my successful transition from art historian to archaeologist. I now know very well what a spoil heap is and I would like to thank Richard for allowing me to contribute to the one at Tomnaverie and for all his help and guidance in the completion of this book and for his excellent supervision in my Ph.D. research. This book would not have been possible without your inspiration.

The research for this book has also benefited from conversations and pints of Tennent's with the following: Amanda Brend, Martin Carruthers, Martin Goldberg, Tessa Poller, Meggen Gondek, Kylie Seretis, Fay Stevens, Kenny Brophy, Steve Timoney and Gavin MacGregor. Meggen and Tessa also read large chunks of the manuscript. Most of all, thanks and love should be expressed towards my family who have always supported me: Mum, Dad, Graeme, David, Marie-Anne and Luke (Luke . . . Luke . . . I am your uncle), the Davidsons, Helen, Doug and Megan.

Marianne, I've dug a lot of sites now, but you are still my best find . . . .

Introduction

Themes and structure

The research undertaken for this book draws on a number of current themes in Neolithic archaeology. One of major themes is the idea of regional variation. There has been a growing awareness of the diversity of the Neolithic archaeological record in Scotland in recent years. The need for regional interpretation has been promoted and this book attempts just such an undertaking (Ashmore 1996; Barclay 1997, 2000, 2001a).

As well as looking at regional sequences, it is also important to account for the ways in which regions interacted to make up Neolithic society as a whole. Julian Thomas has highlighted the continuing need for wider considerations of 'how we conceive broader historical trajectories' (Thomas 1998: 38). In this book regional considerations of monument and settlement traditions have been linked to wider considerations of Neolithic society in Scotland. The study employs differing scales of focus throughout. There are few archaeology books that now attempt to consider larger geographical regions that incorporate a number of regionally distinct archaeologies. Academic studies in recent decades have focused on regional sequences of change. While this is a valid approach, there is little consideration of how local lifestyles and social traditions interacted with one another to create the wider Neolithic world. This often produces a sense of isolation, both in the past and in the present. Archaeologists who work on regional material often loose sight of wider trends in prehistoric archaeology and their interpretations often fail to consider how regional communities understood and reacted to the wider Neolithic world.

The second major theme of this book is an attempt to remedy an imbalance in the Scottish and British Neolithic by moving the focus away from well-studied areas such as Orkney that have dominated considerations of the Neolithic in Scotland. The Orkney Islands have been extensively studied since the early days of archaeology; Gordon Barclay terms Orkney one of British prehistory's 'core areas', not necessarily due to its importance in the past, but due to the prominence of this area in current and past archaeological fieldwork (Barclay 2000, 2001a). Orkney's prominence has led to a disparity in accounts of the Neolithic where large areas of Scotland are ignored in major syntheses. In this book regions not widely considered in the past are studied in detail. Good syntheses and studies of Orkney are already available (Davidson and Henshall 1989; Fraser 1983; Hedges 1984; Renfrew 1979; Richards 1988, 1992a, 1992b, 1996b, 1998). The shift in focus is designed to incorporate lesser known sites and traditions of monuments into wider considerations of the Neolithic. The remains of timber structures in eastern Scotland, while not as spectacular as some of those surviving in the north, can provide as rich a resource for understanding the past as their more famous stone counterparts.

Each chapter of this book considers different aspects of Neolithic Scotland, from the earliest traces of the Neolithic to the transformation of society in the Early Bronze Age. The following chapter considers the issue of the Mesolithic-Neolithic transition. Early archaeologists such as Gordon Childe and Stuart Piggott thought that farming and associated material culture was brought to the islands by incoming settlers (Childe 1935; Piggott 1954), however more recent writers have argued for a greater contribution to change by the local Mesolithic population, through the adoption of aspects of a farming lifestyle in traditional hunting and gathering lifestyles (Bradley 1993, 1998; Thomas 1988, 1991, 1999a; Whittle 1996). Interpretations in the 1990s focused on the importance of changes in ideology and world-view in indigenous society during the transition to farming, but opinion in the last few years has since begun to swing in the opposite direction, with some archaeologists now arguing that some form of population movement may have been involved after all in the onset of the Neolithic (Richards 2003; Schulting and Richards 2002; Sheridan 2000). This is, in part, driven by advances in archaeological science and in particular the development of stable isotope studies where ancient diets can be reconstructed through the analysis of particular chemical signatures in human bone (Schulting and Richards 2002). This has revealed a much greater reliance on land-based, most probably domesticated, resources from the Earlier Neolithic onward than had hitherto been supposed. Chapter 2 is inspired by this debate and attempts to examine the nature of the transition through a detailed consideration of the archaeology of Scotland and the adjacent islands. Here it is argued that ideas about the transition have been overly simplistic and that it is essential that regional differences are accounted for in interpretations of this major process of change. I argue that critical to an understanding of the transition in the British Isles is a consideration of maritime culture and sea travel. Boats and seamanship were amongst the most complex technologies and skills in prehistory. The expertise involved in maritime activity is restricted and certain communities are often better placed to develop technologies of the sea. Small island communities in Scotland and Ireland utilising the Atlantic seaways may have been crucial to the adoption of Neolithic lifestyles. The archaeological record of the island communities of the west contains significant differences from adjacent mainland areas during the period of the Mesolithic-Neolithic transition. The Atlantic sea-routes that led up the west coast of Britain may have been instrumental in enacting change at the beginning of the Neolithic and there may have been significant differences in the nature of the transition in eastern and western Scotland.

Chapter 2 acts as a further introduction to the archaeology and geography of Scotland. In particular it develops the distinction between Atlantic Scotland in the west, made up of a pattern of islands, and eastern, lowland Scotland. This distinction is crucial to the next three chapters, where the major regional traditions of Earlier Neolithic monuments are outlined in detail and their form and characteristics examined. Differences in the nature of the Mesolithic-Neolithic transition seem to have aided the creation of very distinct Neolithic worlds, where different styles of monumental architecture, artefact style and lifestyle were found in eastern and western Scotland. The regional traditions of monuments symbolised diverse ideas about the world, inspired by the different environments and lifestyles present in these areas. The geography of the British Isles allowed contact with markedly divergent areas of Europe and the monument traditions of Earlier Neolithic Scotland reflect this. In western Scotland the chambered cairns are part of an Atlantic tradition of megalithic architecture concentrated in areas to the south in France and Iberia. In eastern Scotland a series of timber monuments are related to styles of monument found in northern and central Europe and the history of these monuments can be traced back to the very core origins of the Neolithic in Europe (Bradley 1998: chapter 3; Bradley 2002: chapter 2; Childe 1949). These separate traditions require different approaches in interpretation and this is the purpose of Chapters 3 to 5.

Chapter 5 examines western Scotland and the construction of megalithic tombs. Excavations at chambered cairns in western Scotland have shown that these monuments are the result of a number of distinct periods of construction. Through detailed analysis of the altering nature of the architecture of these monuments it is possible to link these changes with a transformation in the relationships between the living and the dead in Neolithic society. The secondary phases of many of these cairns involved increasing the capacity of these monuments and adding areas for public display. These changes can be seen as being related to the growing importance of remembering the dead, aided by drama, performance and concepts of ancestry.

In Chapter 4 the focus shifts to eastern Scotland, where timber was the main medium through which ideas about the world were symbolised. Split tree trunks placed under long and round barrows has often been explained in functional terms, but I argue that the tree may have been used as a symbol in rituals that highlighted processes of life and death. Cursus monuments in eastern Scotland also involved the manipulation of timber and natural symbols (Chapter 3). However, the rituals and performances at these monuments involved building post enclosures that were then burnt down, creating a dramatic spectacle. In Scotland, these pit-defined cursus monuments and other associated traditions seem to be related to Neolithic settlement patterns and the building of such structures may have been intended as memorials to past inhabitations and the use of significant places.

Chapters 6 and 7 move the discussion onto the Later Neolithic period. In the Later Neolithic many of the regional traditions of architecture present in the earlier period ceased to be built, and in their place styles of architecture and material culture reflecting larger and more long-distance contacts can be identified. In the Later Neolithic, the locations of earlier monuments were augmented by the construction of further monumental structures, creating what has been defined as 'ceremonial' or 'monumental' complexes, landscapes where a wide range of structures, of more than one period, are found in close proximity. Chapter 6 outlines the major ceremonial complexes of Scotland, focusing in particular on landscapes where there are reasonable levels of contextual information on the monuments themselves and their surrounding environment. Chapter 7 then proceeds to interpret the ways in which monumental complexes functioned in Neolithic society. It is argued that economy and monument building were intertwined at monument complexes, with complexes at the centre of a network of paths that led across the landscape and across the sea. In this respect, Neolithic society was maintained and renewed through community interaction at these places. Chapter 8 completes the discussion of Neolithic Scotland by looking at the ways in which the Neolithic society was transformed in the Early Bronze Age, examining how the material traces of the Neolithic were manipulated and reused at this time.

This book is a synthesis and interpretation of countless excavations and previous interpretations of the Scottish Neolithic and draws too on wider European traditions of prehistoric studies. Its inspiration draws on the sentiments of Gordon Childe expressed as long ago as 1935 in his landmark study *The Prehistory of Scotland*:

> This book, which must appeal to a wider public, cannot take the place of such detailed technical studies which can only appear in learned periodicals. The data it presents are accordingly incomplete, the conclusions it tentatively offers are provisional or even premature. Its aim is to stimulate interest among the mass of Scottish people, to suggest lines for more intensive and systematic research and to reveal the significance of Scottish prehistory to students abroad. To that end it is essential to attempt a synthesis in the light of the new knowledge and new conceptions that intensive research and international co-operation have established. (Childe 1935: xi)

The Scottish Neolithic presented in this book would be barely recognisable when compared to the one Childe studied in the 1930s, yet I hope he would have approved of the aims of this book which were to produce a volume that considers the entirety of the Scottish Neolithic, no matter how tentative, general or provisional the conclusions may be. The Neolithic communities of Scotland left some of the most spectacular archaeological remains in Western Europe; I hope this book conveys some of the interest and understanding of the past that can be gained through their study.

A brief history of Scottish Neolithic studies: a fragmented Scotland

Scotland formed an important arena for some of the pioneering research into the study of the European Neolithic and prehistoric archaeology in general in the nineteenth and early twentieth centuries. Archaeologists like Wilson, Abercromby, Munro and Anderson, working largely on Scottish material, promoted new forms of European prehistory that provided important frameworks for the study of the past (Childe 1935: xi; Kinnes 1985; Piggott 1983).

Joseph Anderson in particular considerably advanced the study of prehistory and set out a manifesto for the study of archaeology as a discipline: 'It may be possible, from purely scientific materials, by purely scientific methods, to construct a logical, though not a chronological, history of culture and civilisation' (Anderson 1886: 386–7). Anderson emphasised the importance of interpreting material culture as a method for studying the past. As he recognised himself, he was hampered by the lack of an absolute chronology, but this did not prevent him from constructing a coherent narrative about Scottish prehistory. Anderson completed a number of important excavations on chambered cairns in Scotland and the discussion of the results of this fieldwork formed much of his discussion of the Neolithic in *Scotland in Pagan Times* (1886). Anderson's work at times was almost purely descriptive, but he recognised many of the important features of the Scottish Neolithic: the successive nature of burial in chambered cairns; the close relationship between houses and tombs; the regionally distinct nature of the Neolithic; and the links between forms of material culture found in widely dispersed areas. Throughout Anderson's account his wonderment and amazement at the achievements of the prehistoric communities of Scotland was obvious. His admiration for the past was much more admirable than many of his contemporaries' accounts of prehistoric 'savages'.

Anderson's book on the Scottish Neolithic was largely based on the remains of chambered cairns that due to their constituent materials have survived well into the present. Consequently, Anderson's account had a western focus; the Neolithic in the eastern lowlands was poorly recognised and represented largely by artefacts found during agricultural activity with little context (Anderson 1886: 306).

The study of Scottish prehistoric archaeology in the early twentieth century was dominated by Gordon Childe and Stuart Piggott, both of whom held the prestigious Abercromby Chair of Archaeology at Edinburgh University from 1927 to 1946 (Childe and Piggott from 1946 to 1977). Childe saw Scotland as a 'theatre of prehistoric migrations and settlement' and his narratives drew on the principles of culture history that explained change through reference to successive waves of migrants (Childe 1935: 3). Like Anderson, Childe's account of the Scottish Neolithic was mainly concerned with the chambered cairns of western Scotland and before the advent of radiocarbon dating, Childe's chronological understanding was confused. Childe thought the chronologically later Early Bronze Age burials of eastern Scotland were contemporary with the chambered cairns and consequently the Neolithic of lowland Scotland was largely unaccounted for (Barclay 2001a: 10). Childe proposed that the Neolithic in Scotland had been introduced by Iberian colonists in boats coasting up the Atlantic western coast, their boats crewed by English crew members, laden with all the elements of the Neolithic 'package': domestic animals and cereals, pottery and stone axes (Childe 1935: 77–8).

Stuart Piggott's work was also concerned with the origins and diffusion of incoming settlers (Piggott 1954, 1958). Eastern Scotland was also a 'virtually unknown territory' to Piggott (Barclay 2001a: 11). Piggott's Neolithic was condensed into five centuries, rather than the period of at least 1,500 years that we recognise today, and consequently Piggott's account of the period was one thought to consist of rapid change (Piggott 1954: 380–1). The monuments that represented the Scottish Neolithic were thought to be late, adopted at a later stage of the Neolithic from more advanced cultures to the south (Piggott 1958: 30).

It is only with the work of the Royal Commission since the Second World War and the use of aerial photography in archaeology that a more balanced view of Scottish prehistory been possible (Barclay 2000, 2001a). The identification of crop mark sites from the air (the remains of decayed timber and earth monuments and sites) has revolutionised our understanding of the Scottish Neolithic. Numerous sites have been identified in eastern Scotland using this technique and the excavation of these sites has revealed a previously unrecognised wealth of information about Neolithic lifestyles. In particular the excavation of lowland sites such as North Mains, Balfarg and Dunragit has significantly extended the range of material that we can use in accounts of Neolithic Scotland (Barclay 1983; Mercer 1977–8; Thomas 2001b). It is only in more recent years that a more comprehensive view of the Scottish Neolithic has been possible. This is an exciting era for Neolithic studies.

CHAPTER ONE

Scotland in the Neolithic: an introduction

Introduction

After the end of the last Ice Age, some 12,000 years ago (c. 10000 BC), the first human societies started to move into the area of what is now modern Scotland. These peoples were hunter-gatherers who lived a largely mobile existence following herds of animals. They moved around the landscape to obtain food, resources and to maintain social contacts. These hunter-gatherers belong to the archaeological era called the 'Mesolithic' or Middle Stone Age (c. 9000–4000 BC in Scotland). They shared much in common with hunter-gatherer communities spread across the British Isles and beyond in Western and Central Europe (Wickham-Jones 1994; Saville 2004).

Mesolithic Scotland was a very different place to that of modern Scotland. The initial post-ice, tundra-like landscape was soon transformed into a forest world; most of the landscape was cloaked with trees. Within this forest environment Mesolithic communities lived, their world governed by pathways through the forest, linking families and individuals in dispersed social ties. These communities, like many hunter-gatherer societies today, had close relationships with the surrounding natural world. The exact nature of Mesolithic life is difficult to ascertain. Finding information on such ancient communities is a hard task and one which archaeologists have only recently begun to tackle. The hunter-gatherer communities of Scotland left few traces of their lifestyle that are still evident today without excavation. Settlement structures tended to consist of light wooden windbreaks or tent-like structures (Wickham-Jones 2004), the organic elements of which have long since rotted away, leaving only traces in surrounding soils.

Mesolithic life continued for some 5,000 years in Scotland, before a significant transformation occurred in the centuries leading up to the fourth millennium BC. Around this time (c. 4000 BC), the British Isles and the fringes of western Europe came in contact with new ways of life associated with communities that practised the agricultural routines of crop-growing and animal husbandry. This period of prehistory is known as the Neolithic or New Stone Age and in the British Isles this era lasted for over a millennium and a half (4000–2500 BC or between 4,500 and 6,000 years ago). The Neolithic in Britain and Ireland is generally recognised as the period when domesticated resources (cattle, sheep, cereals and so on) and new technologies (such as pottery and different forms of stone tool) were introduced to the British Isles. Farming had originally spread from its origins in the Fertile Crescent (an area in the Middle East where the origins of agriculture are to be found) to southeast Europe through population movement or through the movement of ideas and material culture (Bradley 1998; Childe 1935; Sherratt 1990; Thomas 1991; Whittle 1996). The British Isles were amongst the last locations in Europe to become Neolithic. A few centuries previous to 4000 BC, Britain and Ireland lay to the west of an 'agricultural frontier', part of an increasingly smaller area of Europe that was not in direct contact with farming societies (see Figure 1.1).

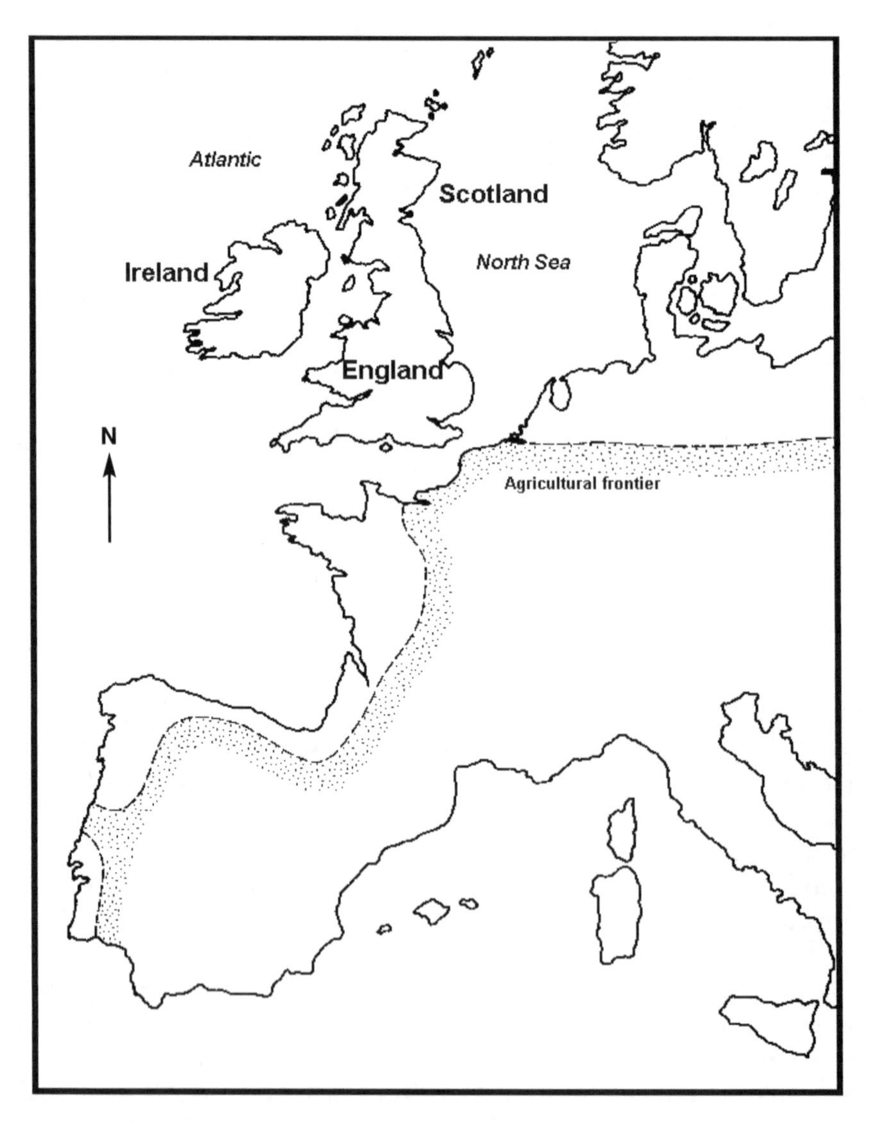

FIGURE 1.1 *Britain and Ireland around 4500 BC situated to the west of an 'agricultural frontier' (Source: Bradley 1998: figure 4)*

The Neolithic is not merely about the spread of agrarian technologies, but also documents the spread of new ideas about life, death and the world around. In western Europe the onset of the Neolithic, as well as being associated with the introduction of domesticated resources, was also associated with the construction of elaborate timber and stone monuments, monuments which often incorporated remains of the dead. These monuments were associated with a range of beliefs concerning the natural world, death, the regeneration of life and human-animal relationships. Monuments have characterised the ways in which the Neolithic has been studied as these remain the most visible elements of Neolithic life. In order to understand the spread of agriculture in western Europe we must also understand the ways in which monument construction and heightened levels of ritualised activity became an integral part of life in this part of the Neolithic world.

SCOTLAND DEFINED

Physical geography

Scotland is a northern part of the British Isles, an island chain situated off the western coast of the European mainland (Figure 1.2). Scotland is divided from its neighbour England to the south by the Cheviot Hills, a range of uplands that run northeast to southwest across northern England. That is not to say that Scotland was a recognisably discrete and bounded area of the Neolithic world. As we shall see in the following chapters, the area that is now Scotland was always connected to its neighbours, England, Ireland and Wales, and at times to the European mainland, through a complex network of contacts. This study often strays beyond the modern borders of the present Scottish nation to examine the ways in which traditions of monuments and material culture related to their wider distributions and contexts. Scotland itself is a country of varying topography, landscape and climate and different areas of Scotland have distinct characters that reflect contrasting relationships with the land and sea.

Scotland is at the junction of a number of seaways: the Irish Sea, the Atlantic and the North Sea. Hence, the area of Scotland has always been open to a variety of contacts with a range of geographically distant lands. In particular, there are distinct differences between the Atlantic areas of western Scotland and the North Sea areas of the eastern coast. Contacts, historical and ancient, in the west have been predominantly across the Irish Sea and through the Atlantic sea-routes to the south and north, whereas in the east, links with England to the south and areas across the North Sea to the lowland countries of Europe have been predominant. These distinctions have important implications for the way in which the Neolithic was introduced to these areas and its subsequent development. Scotland is split into a variety of administrative, historical and political areas to which reference will be made in the text. The main regions and areas mentioned in the text are shown in Figure 1.3.

Scotland can be divided into three main geographical zones: the Highlands and Islands, the Southern Uplands and the Central Belt (Figure 1.4). The Southern Uplands are a series of gently rolling hills, which, while a significant feature in their

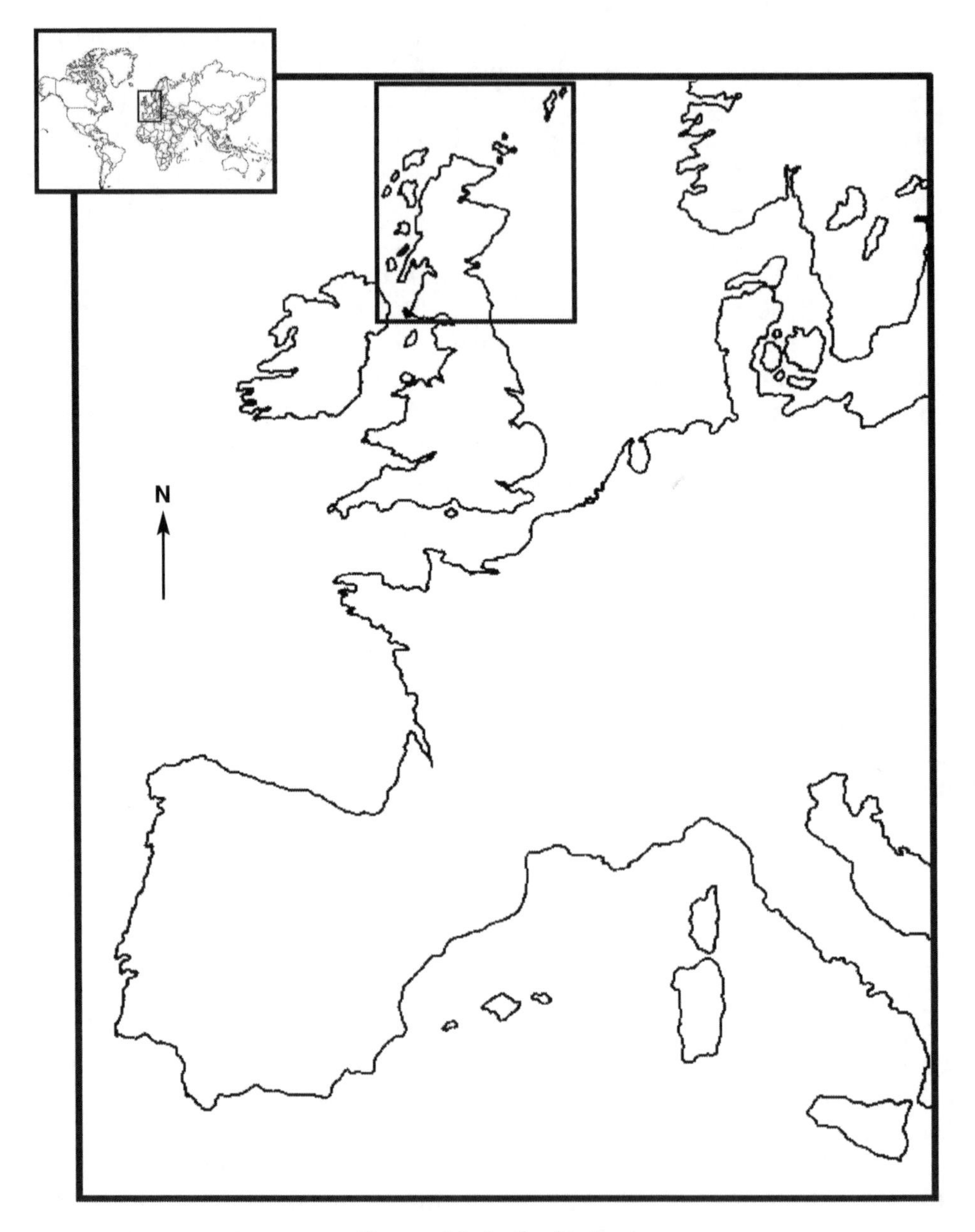

FIGURE 1.2 *Scotland in Europe*

own right, are much less formidable than the taller and more rugged Highland and Grampian mountains which cover large parts of northern and western Scotland. Settlement is severely restricted in the higher mountainous areas. In the north and west of Scotland settlement today is mainly on the coastal fringes and on the islands. The land of Scotland is of a higher average elevation than any other area in the British Isles, consequently low-lying land in Scotland is restricted and in mainland Scotland

FIGURE 1.3 *Areas and regions mentioned in the text*

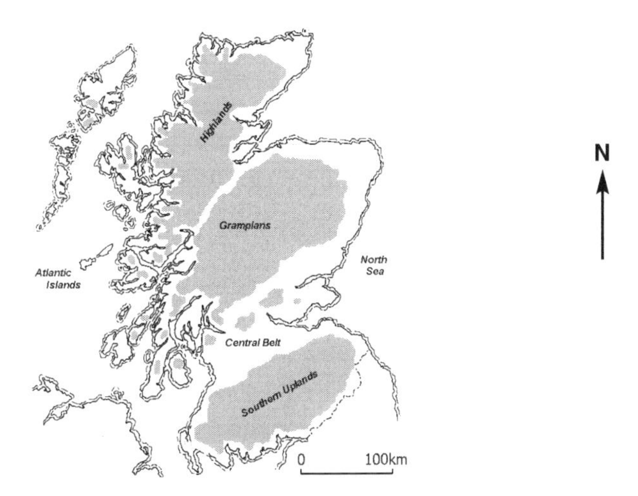

FIGURE 1.4 *The geographical zones of Scotland*

the largest tracts are found in the Central Belt, on the coasts of Dumfries and Galloway, in the Borders around the Tweed river, and in Aberdeenshire and Caithness. This is not to say that settlement and agriculture was restricted to these areas. Today the central lowlands are the most productive areas for agriculture in Scotland, but in the past the differences between the coastal areas of western Scotland and the islands, and the eastern lowlands may not have been as marked, especially in the more favourable climatic conditions of the Neolithic (Coppock 1976: 10; Turnock 1974; Whittington and Edwards 1997). The landscape of Scotland probably had greater implications for movement and contact than it did for agricultural potential. The upland areas form important barriers to movement; routeways across the landscape would probably have followed the paths that were easiest to traverse, following the major valley systems and rivers.

Environment

Scotland's environment in the Mesolithic and Neolithic has been reconstructed through the work of palynology, the analysis of pollen remains from lake and peat deposits. The techniques of palynology can give us a generalised picture of the natural distribution and composition of Scotland's woodlands after the ice retreated (Tipping 1994; Edwards and Whittington 1997; Edwards 2004). The last major glaciation in northwest Europe is known as the Weichselian. At its peak the Weichselian covered the entirety of Scotland and large parts of England; the ice almost a kilometer thick in places (Wickham-Jones 1994: 45). The Weichselian withdrew from Scotland around 10000 BC (around 12,000 years ago). The reprieve was brief, however. Soon after, the climate became cold again in a period known as the Loch Lomond Stadial, and a number of mini glaciers formed. While not as extensive as the earlier glaciation, it is likely that few large plant species survived this latest period of glaciation (Tipping 1994: 9). After a short period, conditions improved and the ice finally disappeared and trees and larger plant species returned to the area of modern Scotland. Tree species migrated from England and the adjacent Continent, attracted by the warming climate (Tipping 1994: 9). Birch and hazel were the first tree species to colonise the area on a large scale, in the ninth millennium BC (9000–8000 BC). Some considerable time later, elm and oak also began to appear in Scotland and by the fifth millennium BC, all of the major tree species of Scotland were extensively distributed across the landscape (Figure 1.5). Woodland reached its fullest distribution shortly before the beginnings of the Neolithic and at the beginnings of the fourth millennium BC forest dominated much of the landscape, except perhaps in the north and west where there may have been lighter cover (Tipping 1994; Edwards 2004). In southern Scotland oak, elm and hazel were the main woodland species, whereas in northeast Scotland, birch and hazel trees were the main constituents with only a small proportion of oak and elm. In the west and north, woodland was less dense in composition with open stands of birch and hazel; the more recent colonisers of oak and elm made little impact on these areas. All of these woodlands would have contained a range of other tree and plant species including meadowsweet, poplar, plantain, fern, cherry, willow, ash, and myrtle (Tipping 1994: 11).

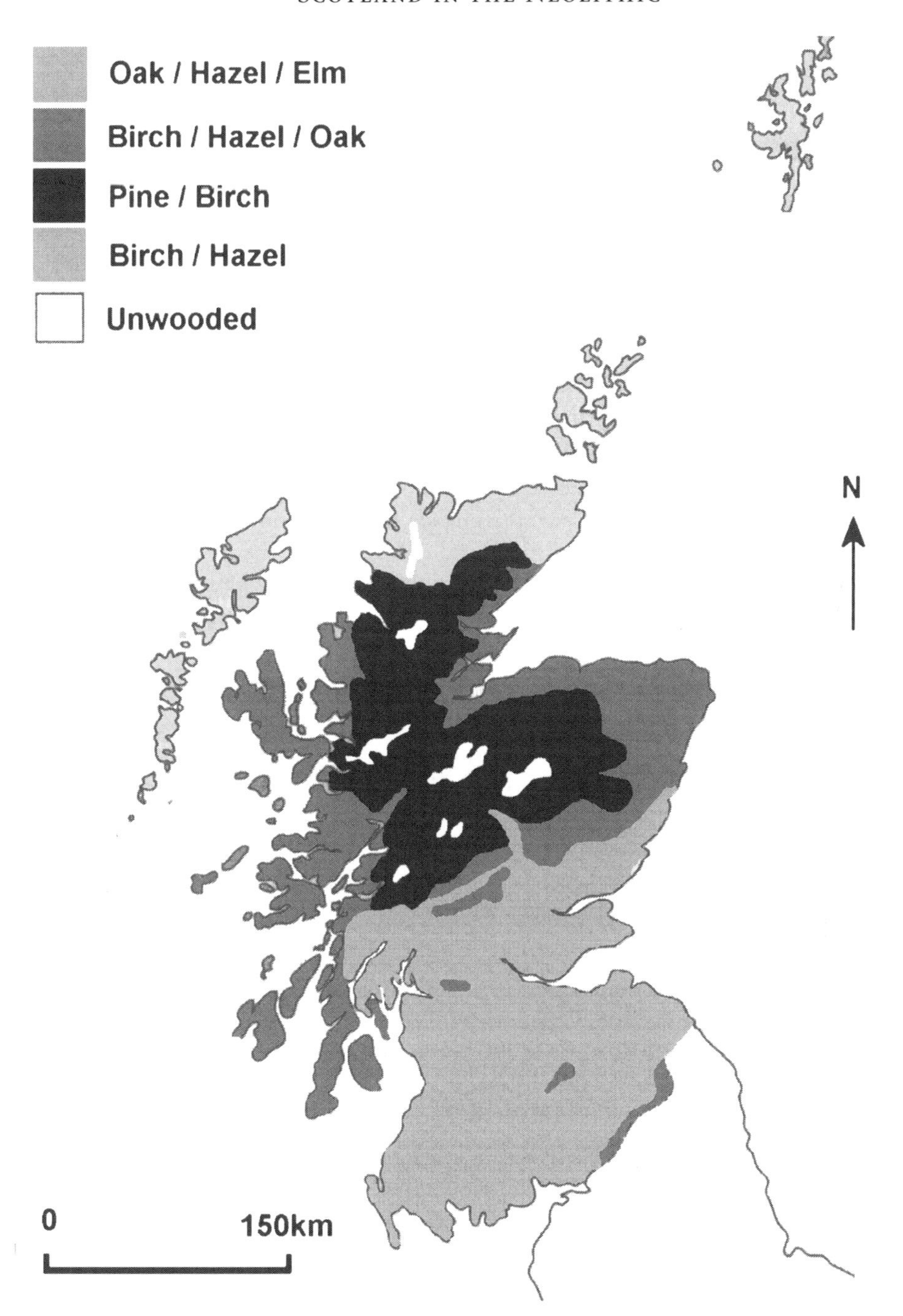

Figure 1.5 *The composition of the woodland in Earlier Neolithic Scotland (Source: Edwards 2004)*

Human impact

There has been tentative and not entirely unambiguous evidence for human impact on the natural woodland in the Mesolithic (Edwards and Hirons 1984; Edwards and Ralston 1984; Tipping 1994). The difficulty has been differentiating between possible human impacts and more natural causes. In some locations, however, there are possible indicators that woodland was burnt by Mesolithic people perhaps to encourage the development of areas of grazing for animals. In the Neolithic, evidence for clearance becomes more common, widespread and less ambiguous. The Neolithic in Scotland, and western Europe generally, was formerly thought to be marked by a phenomenon in palynological records known as the elm decline. The elm decline was a period c. 4000 BC, around the generally recognised beginnings of the Neolithic, that was marked by a sudden and widespread reduction in elm trees. The exact causes of this reduction is now hotly debated and a range of causal factors have been suggested from climate change to tree disease to soil deterioration, along with more traditional accounts of human impact (Tipping 1994: 22; Edwards 2004: 57). Human impact on the woodland in the Neolithic is generally thought to be associated with clearance for the growth of cereal crops and to provide grazing areas for domesticated animals. Whether the elm decline can be associated with the beginnings of the Neolithic or not, many pollen diagrams do seem to show impacts on the tree cover from the Earlier Neolithic onwards (Edwards 2004: 57). This can be accompanied by a rise in the numbers of pollen indicators for species such as *Plantago lanceolata* (ribwort plantain) which probably indicates some form of associated pastoral activity. Loch deposits also often show increased rates of soil erosion in the centuries after 4000 BC across Britain and Ireland (Edwards 2004: 60). This too may be associated with the onset of agricultural practices, but natural causes could also have contributed to the increased rates of erosion. Cereal-type pollen should be a less ambiguous trace of early farming, but cereal pollen is difficult to identify in the pollen record and can be confused with wild native grasses (Edwards and Hirons 1984; Tipping 1994). Cereal-type pollen has been identified in a number of pre-elm decline and hence possibly pre-Neolithic instances, but the interpretations and identifications of this are not always secure. Earlier Neolithic clearance of woodland may have been most effective in the north and west where there was only light woodland in the first instance and soon after the beginnings of the Neolithic some of the islands and northern areas of Scotland may have been relatively treeless (Tipping 1994: 24). Destruction would have been exacerbated by use of the cleared land for crop growing and animal grazing, inhibiting forest regeneration.

THE NEOLITHIC DEFINED

Chronology

The Neolithic for the purposes of this study has been divided into two major periods: the Earlier Neolithic and the Later Neolithic. Each period is characterised by different forms of monumental architecture and material culture. The Earlier Neolithic

(4000–3300 BC) includes the period of transition from the Mesolithic to the Neolithic and is characterised by a series of regionalised monument traditions and forms of pottery and stone tools. The Later Neolithic (3300–2500 BC) can be identified by a series of innovations in material culture and architecture, primarily the construction of massive-scale circular enclosures of various forms and the use of Grooved Ware pottery, which replaced the more regional traditions of pottery available in the earlier centuries.

Further divisions of the Neolithic period are possible, but difficult in Scotland. Radiocarbon determinations are few in number and only broad chronologies are available. A further division of the Neolithic is possible with reference to pottery styles. Early plain carinated bowl pottery associated with the very beginnings of pottery production in Neolithic Britain was transformed in a matter of centuries into a series of more regionally distinct traditions of Impressed Ware pottery (Herne 1988; Thomas 1999a: chapter 4) (see below). These later styles of decorated pots were themselves replaced by Grooved Ware traditions. While in pottery terms the Neolithic can be divided into at least three periods, these divisions seem overly complex. Impressed Ware is occasionally found at settlement sites in Scotland, but rarely at other site types. In northern Scotland local styles of Impressed Ware, known as Unstan Ware in Orkney, are associated with some forms of chambered cairn, but elsewhere the links are rare. Sherds of Impressed Ware were found at a chambered cairn at Cairnholy, Dumfries and Galloway (Piggott and Powell 1948–9), and under a ring cairn at Balfarg, Fife (Barclay and Russell-White 1993), but these are unusual occurrences and many later styles of monument are not associated with any form of pottery.

Since analysis of monumental architecture structures the contents of this book, the broader Earlier-Later division was thought sufficient to demonstrate the main trajectories of Neolithic development. With these developments in mind it is now time to outline the main changes that occurred in monumental and domestic architecture and material culture throughout the duration of the Neolithic in Scotland.

Monumental architecture

Earlier Neolithic

Monument traditions in the Earlier Neolithic were distinctly regional in construction and character (Figure 1.6). There seems to have been a general east-west divide in Scotland, with timber and earth forming the main constituents of monuments in the east, whereas in the west, stone-built chambered cairns dominated. In the east a series of differing forms of timber structure were constructed during the fourth millennium BC. These included structures classified by archaeologists as cursus monuments, mortuary enclosures and timber halls. Cursus monuments are named after Roman chariot racing tracks as they were originally thought to be Roman in date, but excavation has since shown these were in fact Neolithic monuments (Barclay and Harding 1999). Cursus monuments were massive timber and/or earthen enclosures that at times covered vast areas of landscape (Brophy 1999a). The role of these structures is not immediately apparent and much debate has centred on their interpretation. In

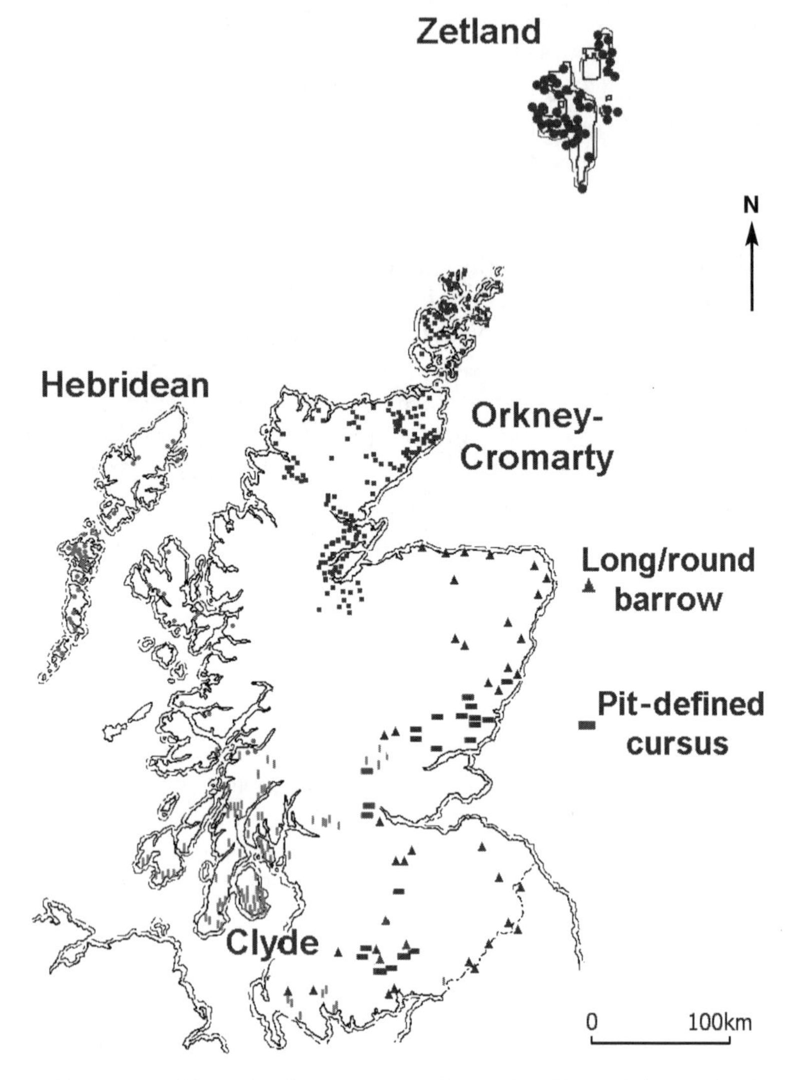

FIGURE 1.6 *The regional monument traditions of Earlier Neolithic Scotland (Sources: Brophy 1999a; Davidson and Henshall 1989, 1991; Henshall 1963, 1972; Kinnes 1992a; Ritchie 1997).*

the south of England, where most of the 'classic' site-types exist and where they were first identified, cursus monuments generally consist of two parallel ditches and internal banks often with some form of terminal feature. These are typically between 770 and 4,000 metres in length (Barclay and Harding 1999: 1). In contrast, in Scotland cursus monuments were usually defined by settings of timber posts rather than earthen banks or ditches. These tend to be smaller than their English counterparts and share more in common with monuments classified as long mortuary enclosures (Loveday and Petchey 1982). In Scotland, cursus monuments and other forms of enclosure are difficult to differentiate; in the past classifications have been based mainly on size, with the cursus monuments identified as the larger examples. In Scotland there seems to be little distinction between larger and smaller enclosures other than the scale at which they were constructed. All of the structures were made of oak timber and all enclosed space and shielded views from the outside. These buildings also shared similar endings, with almost all being burnt down at the end of their lives. The similarities between these different structures suggests that similar purposes may have lain behind their construction and eventual destruction. Cursus monuments and mortuary enclosures may also be related to a less common site-type. These are called 'timber halls' and have only been found in Scotland to date. The timber halls were massive roofed buildings made of oak. The role of these buildings in Neolithic life has been fiercely debated and their interpretation is fundamental to how we interpret Earlier Neolithic society. At times these buildings have been seen as regular farming homesteads of Neolithic families (Rowley-Conwy 2002). Others see these as being more specialised in nature and related more closely to a series of monumental constructions (Barclay et al. 2002; Bradley 2003; Topping 1996). One of the most significant aspects of these buildings was their destruction. Again, like many of the Scottish cursus monuments and mortuary enclosures, these were burnt down.

Another recurring monument type in eastern Scotland was the earthen long or round barrow. All of these excavated in Scotland have been found to overlay timber structures, which formed the first phases of activity on these sites. Under nearly all of the barrows in Scotland, large postholes, which held split tree trunks, have been found. Unlike the monuments considered above, these were not burnt down, but were allowed to decay *in situ*. In the past the trunks have been considered as functional parts of some form of mortuary structure, but the trees may have been significant in their own right, drawing on the symbolism of the forest that surrounded Neolithic life. The distribution of these monuments coincides with the burnt timber traditions, but concentrated in different areas, suggesting that these may have represented different ritual practices associated with different interpretations of the world around.

In western and northern Scotland the Neolithic landscape was dominated by large burial monuments, known as chambered cairns, made of stone. These have been classified into various regional categories that reflect different styles of architecture (Henshall 1963, 1972; Davidson and Henshall 1989, 1991; Henshall and Ritche 1995, 2001). In the early days of archaeology these traditions were often thought to relate to different cultures of people (Childe 1935; Piggott 1954). This association is now thought to be problematic, but undoubtedly these traditions do indicate spheres of contact in the Neolithic world and at the very least shared traditions of burial architecture. While these chambered cairns can be classified into differing styles of architecture, the traditions underwent similar development cycles that suggest the significance of these locations increased over time.

Later Neolithic

Most of the Later Neolithic monument traditions were circular enclosures of some form (Bradley 1998). These included sites classified as stone circles, henges, palisaded enclosures and timber circles (Barnatt 1989; Burl 1976; Gibson 1998). These sites may have essentially been for the same purpose as both have strongly similar layouts, dimensions and at times similar construction methods (Gibson 1998). However, each type tends to be associated with different deposits. For example, funerary remains are more common at stone circles than timber sites (Parker Pearson and Ramilisonina 1998). In Scotland timber circles tend to be found more commonly in the east of Scotland than in the west, where stone circles dominate, but excavation has shown that many stone circles overlie timber circles and timber circles in the east may have been superseded by stone (Haggarty 1991; Mercer 1977–8; Scott 1989–9). Elsewhere in Britain, stone and timber circles are located in most areas, with a broad east-west divide between the distribution of the two (Bradley 1998: fig. 38).

Henges were earthwork enclosures defined by large interior ditches with banks thrown up on the outside and entered by one or more entrances (Atkinson et al. 1951; Harding 2003; Wainwright 1989). These are concentrated in eastern Scotland, with only a handful of examples in the west. They are, however, found further to the west in Ireland and across England and Wales to the south (Malone 2001: fig. 124). Palisaded enclosures were continuous barriers of timbers arranged in circular or oval shapes, often enclosing very large areas. These are a relatively recently recognised element of the Later Neolithic and have been identified in southern Scotland, England, Wales and Ireland (Gibson 2002). With a few exceptions many of these Later Neolithic enclosures were built on a much larger scale than the majority of the Earlier Neolithic traditions of monuments.

Neolithic pottery

The earliest pottery in Scotland coincides with the widespread appearance of many other forms of material culture associated with the Neolithic. These include the Earlier Neolithic monument traditions outlined above, new forms of stone tool production and domesticated plants and animals. The earliest pottery included a restricted range of vessel forms, the most widespread being shallow, round-based bowls with simple rims and often displaying some form of carination below the rim. These vessels are known as 'traditional carinated bowls' (c. 4000–3800 BC) (Herne 1988; Sheridan 2000) (Figure 1.7). Pottery in the Neolithic may have at first been special-purpose artefacts associated with new forms of preparing and serving food (Herne 1988). Earlier Neolithic vessels were of high-quality materials, their surfaces often burnished and were often deposited in a deliberate, structured manner in pits at settlement sites or at monuments (Herne 1988; Sheridan 2000; Thomas 1999a; Warren 2004: 93). Traditional carinated bowls and some of the other forms of the earliest

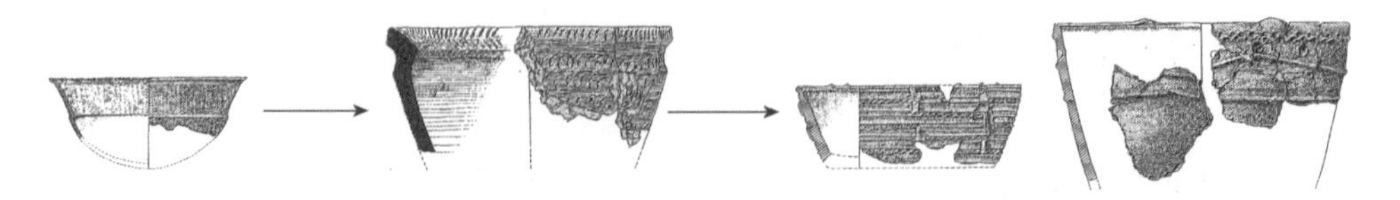

FIGURE 1.7 *The changing forms of Neolithic pottery*
(Sources: Henshall 1983: figure 2; Speak and Burgess 1999: figure 35; Barclay and Russell-White 1993: figures 28 and 30).

pottery traditions in Britain and Ireland have parallels with traditions found on the Continent (Herne 1988). In western Scotland and Ireland in particular, Sheridan has proposed that some of the decorated pottery found in megalithic tombs (known as Beacharra Ware) is specifically related to forms of pottery found in Brittany (Sheridan 2000). Only the earliest forms of Neolithic pottery were geographically homogenous; soon more regionalised traditions of pottery were created. Within a few centuries of the beginning of the Neolithic, regional traditions of 'modified carinated bowls', vessels with greater levels of decoration, replaced the more widespread plain-bowl traditions (c. 3800 BC onwards) (Herne 1988; Sheridan 2000). It is tempting to link these developments with growing regional identities after a period of widespread and far-reaching change.

Modified forms of carinated bowl have a number of names and various regional traditions have been identified. In England pottery known as 'Peterborough Ware' dominates assemblages from sites after the first half of the fourth millennium BC (Thomas 1999a: 106). Peterborough Ware is often highly decorated, with heavy rims. The Peterborough traditions were also mainly round-based and the earliest forms have clear parallels with decorated traditional carinated bowls (Gibson 1986). In Scotland, Peterborough-style vessels are known as 'Impressed Ware', which simply refers to the forms of decoration often present on these vessels, made by impressions of bird bones, cords and other materials (see Figure 1.7). In northern and western Scotland two distinctive forms of Impressed Ware are known as 'Hebridean Ware' and 'Unstan Ware' (Sheridan 2000). Hebridean traditions are characterised by baggy, deep round-based vessels, while Unstan Ware assemblages tend to consist of shallower but wider bowls with incised decoration on the rim.

One of the most frequently recurring and distinctive finds on Later Neolithic monumental sites is a style of pottery known as Grooved Ware (c. 3300–2000 BC). Grooved Ware vessels are highly decorated flat-bottomed vessels, found across the British Isles (Thomas 1999a: chapter 5). These, like the Impressed Ware traditions, were also highly decorated, the vessels often divided into separate panels with different forms of decoration on each. Grooved Ware came in a much greater variety of sizes and volumes, seemingly indicating changes in the ways in which food was consumed, perhaps now organised on a much grander scale (Thomas 1999a: 114). Grooved Ware is found across Britain and Ireland, though there were also more regionalised yet overlapping styles (MacSween 1995: 47; Thomas 1999a: 113). In many areas the adoption of Grooved Ware represents a significant break in the ceramic forms of Neolithic Britain (Sheridan 1995: 18; Thomas 1999a: 113) as Grooved Ware has few parallels in Earlier Neolithic pottery, with the possible exception of areas in northern Scotland (MacSween 1992; Cowie and MacSween 1999). The designs on Grooved Ware vessels can be paralleled in a range of media, such as carved stone balls, maceheads, and in designs found in passage graves and on open-air rock art sites found across Britain and Ireland (Thomas 1999a: 119). The adoption of Grooved Ware in the Later Neolithic seems to herald a period in Neolithic Britain and Ireland when longer-distance, inter-regional contacts were renewed and became increasingly important to the maintenance of social structure (Bradley and Chapman 1986).

At the end of the Neolithic a new form of pottery was introduced from the Continent in the Early Bronze Age (2500–1800 BC). These vessels are known as 'Beakers' (Clarke 1970; Burgess and Shennan 1976; Shepherd 1986; Thorpe and Richards 1984). Beakers are small, well-made pots with S-shaped profiles. These are very distinctive vessels and are often found in cist graves accompanying the burial of single individuals. Their introduction was associated with the first evidence of metal-working in the British Isles and their deposition are in many cases associated with the closure of Neolithic monuments. In this way, the introduction of Beakers and the practices of single burial and metalworking associated with these forms of material culture are thought to mark a major transition in prehistoric society when the British Isles became more closely linked to Continental Europe and when new cultural practices superseded Neolithic ways of life.

Lithics

The types of stone tool technology used in Neolithic Scotland remain uncertain. Traditions of stoneworking in the preceding Mesolithic are also only vaguely understood. Later Mesolithic lithic types may have included microliths – small finely worked pieces of flint, or other material, often used in composite tools (Warren 2004: 94). In the Neolithic there are few diagnostic tool types in comparison to stoneworking traditions further south where the changing characters of lithic types are much better known (Edmonds 1995). One commonly used indicator of Earlier Neolithic activity in Scotland is the presence of leaf-shaped arrowheads (Kinnes 1985). Other tool types in the Earlier Neolithic included plano-convex knives and a range of scraper forms, comparable to artefacts found in the rest of Britain and Ireland, but not as well documented (Warren 2004). These tools were used for a variety of tasks, including food processing, preparing animal hides and for hunting.

The sources of raw materials for stone tools were restricted in Scotland (Wickham-Jones and Collins 1977–8). Flint was the main material used, but in Scotland there are no *in situ* deposits of flint, only deposits of flint gravels, found most abundantly in the Buchan area in Aberdeenshire (Wickham-Jones and Collins 1977–8: 7). Pitchstone from the island of Arran was also extensively used and is found across Britain and Ireland, many miles from its source (Simpson and Meighan 1999; Thorpe and Thorpe 1984). Other more localised deposits were also utilised including bloodstone from Rhum and chert deposits which are found in a number of locations (Wickham-Jones 1990a; Wickham-Jones and Collins 1977–8). Flint was also imported from Ireland and Yorkshire. In England, Later Neolithic lithic types are associated with a move to broader-flake industries and an increase in the number of tool types (Edmonds 1995). In Scotland the changes in tool forms and working traditions in the Later Neolithic are less well known.

One of the most important and significant forms of material culture in the Neolithic was the stone axe. Many thousands of stone axes have been found across Britain and Ireland and analyses of the sources of these axes has shown that these were moved over vast distances (Clough and Cummins 1988). Many different sources of stone were used, but two of the most significant were the sources of tuff in the

Langdale Pikes, Cumbria, and porcellanite sources in northeast Ireland. Axes made from these sources were extensively used in Scotland, augmenting more localised sources of raw materials (Edmonds et al. 1993). Axes were used in tree clearance and in cultivation, as well as being powerful symbols and ritualised objects in their own right (Bradley and Edmonds 1993).

Subsistence

Assessments of both the Mesolithic and Neolithic economies are hampered by the generally acidic nature of soils in Scotland, detrimental to the survival of bone (McCormick and Buckland 1997). Sampling of archaeological deposits for plant remains has also only recently become routine. Hence our understanding of the Neolithic economy in Scotland is fragmentary. Stable isotope studies of Mesolithic and Neolithic human bone have revealed an apparent dramatic shift in diet around the time of the Mesolithic-Neolithic transition from a primarily marine-based diet to a terrestrial diet (Richards and Hedges 1999; Richards 2003; Richards 2004; Schulting and Richards 2002). This may represent the widespread and rapid adoption of domesticated resources at the beginning of the Neolithic. In the Mesolithic, aurochs (wild cattle), wild boar, fox, lynx, brown bear, red and roe deer and a range of birds would have been amongst the species found in the woodlands (McCormick and Buckland 1997). Mesolithic sites such as Morton on the east coast also show that Mesolithic people extensively exploited the sea, catching cod, haddock, turbot and sturgeon – species that would probably have necessitated some form of deep-sea fishing (Coles 1971). Shell middens on the west coast and elsewhere show that shellfish were extensively used (Mellars 1987), while hazelnuts and other plants also formed a significant part of the Mesolithic diet (Mithen 2000; Wickham-Jones 1990a).

In the Neolithic there was some movement away from a diet based on hunted and gathered resources to one based on domesticated resources. As noted previously, clearance of woodland is documented in the Neolithic in many pollen diagrams (Tipping 1994; Edwards 2004). At times this was associated with cereal agriculture and animal grazing. However, clearings were also made to create open spaces for monument construction and for the raw materials for monuments themselves. Soil sampling at Neolithic sites has recovered a variety of plant remains including cereals, most spectacularly at a timber hall at Balbridie, Aberdeenshire, where over 20,000 cereal grains were recovered (Fairweather and Ralston 1993). The main varieties were emmer wheat and naked barley, with smaller amounts of bread wheat and other types. Much smaller amounts of cereal have been found on most other Neolithic sites, including monuments, and given the difficulty in recovering cereal remains in comparison to other plant types, we may be underestimating the extent to which Neolithic communities relied on domesticated cereals (Tipping 1994: 35; Edwards 2004; Rowley-Conwy 2004). Possible traces of clearance and cultivation have been recorded under a number of the barrows in Scotland including Pitnacree, Perthshire and Dalladies in northeast Scotland (Coles and Simpson 1965; Piggott 1971–2).

Good assemblages of animal bone on Neolithic sites in Scotland are few in number and generally restricted to sites on Orkney and the Western Isles where survival conditions are better. Domesticated animals dominate all Neolithic assemblages on Orkney, where present (McCormick and Buckland 1997). Sheep and cattle are the most common species found, with smaller numbers of pig and red deer. Earlier and Later Neolithic sites in Orkney have similar bone assemblages and no discernible changes through time can yet be demonstrated. Bone assemblages from mainland sites are almost non-existent (McCormick and Buckland 1997: 99). Evidence from Knap of Howar and Skara Brae show that fishing was an important element of the Neolithic economy at least in the Orkney Isles (Sturt 2005). Overall, fragmentary as the evidence is, it increasingly suggests that domesticated plants and animals were quickly adopted in the Neolithic and were the mainstays of the economy from the earliest stages of the Neolithic onwards.

Settlement

In the preceding Mesolithic period few substantial domestic structures have been found in Scotland. A largely mobile lifestyle did not often warrant the investment of labour and resources in particular places. The structures that have been found tend to be slight timber structures, possibly some form of windbreak or light timber hut, although some larger structures have been excavated in more recent years (Wickham-Jones 2004). Since the early days of Neolithic archaeology it was often assumed that the Neolithic and farming would be associated with sedentary communities (Bradley 2003). This idea has been extensively critiqued in more recent times with some archaeologists suggesting that Neolithic life continued to be largely mobile in nature (Thomas 1991, 1999a). This idea has, in turn, since been critiqued itself, with some arguing that Neolithic communities *were* sedentary farmers and that the evidence for domestic structures has simply been difficult to recover due to preservation issues (Cooney 1997, 2003; Barclay 1997). A more balanced view is possible by recognising the regionalised nature of the Neolithic in Britain and Ireland (Bradley 2003). Neolithic houses have been found in large numbers in Ireland (Armit et al. 2003; Grogan 1996, 2002) and were common in the Orkney Isles and Shetland (Barclay 1996; Whittle 1986), but have not been found in large numbers in England (Bradley 2003). It seems clear that the Neolithic of Britain and Ireland may have been highly variable and that both mobile and sedentary lifestyles may have been present in different areas of the country. Even where houses were present a level of mobility in settlement strategies may still have existed.

In Scotland, numerous substantial stone-built houses have been found on the Orkney Isles (Ritchie 1983; Childe 1931; Childe and Grant 1938–9, 1946–7; Clarke 2003). Earlier Neolithic houses on Orkney tend to be long sub-rectangular structures, while later houses are round and more closely clustered together in 'villages' (Richards 1991, 1992b, 1993a, 1993b). In Shetland extensive field systems with associated houses have been found; some of these are undoubtedly Neolithic in date (Fojut 1993; Whittle 1986). In the Western Isles stone-built rectangular structures have been found at Eilean Domhnuil, but the exact role of these structures is disputed (Armit 1996). While a settled, organised domestic landscape is easily identifiable in Orkney and Shetland, on mainland Scotland the picture is much more confused (Barclay 1996,

2003). Large timber buildings such as the 'timber halls' at Balbridie and Claish have been identified, but their everyday role is disputed (Barclay et al. 2002; Ralston 1982; Rowley-Conwy 2002; Topping 1996). At present the identified number of timber halls are too few in number to be thought of as typical of domestic settlement in lowland Scotland. Moreover, these structures share much in common with timber monuments found in the same general areas. Other possible settlement sites in mainland Scotland tend to be much slighter in nature (Barclay 2003). These may indicate that a greater level of mobility in Neolithic lifestyles was common in this part of Scotland in contrast to the more settled and organised landscapes of the Northern Isles.

CHAPTER TWO

Islands in the fast lane: the Mesolithic-Neolithic transition

Introduction

In discussions on the beginnings of the Neolithic, little consideration has been given to the actual mechanisms of change. Critical to an understanding of the Mesolithic-Neolithic transition is an understanding of maritime culture. Boats and seamanship were the most complex technologies and skills in prehistory. The expertise involved in maritime activity is restricted and certain communities are often better placed to develop technologies of the sea. This chapter emphasises the importance of small island communities and the western seaways to the beginnings of the Neolithic in Britain and Ireland.

If we examine the archaeological record of the island communities of the west it is possible to identify significant differences between these places and adjacent mainland areas during the period of the Mesolithic-Neolithic transition. The western parts of the British Isles consist of a series of island archipelagos and an indented coastline that favours the development of maritime activity. There is evidence to suggest that the Atlantic sea-routes that led up the west coast of Britain were instrumental in enacting change in the Neolithic period. The processes that led to the adoption of Neolithic traditions from the European mainland may have been very different in the west and east and the processes of Neolithicisation seem to be reflected in the nature of the ensuing Neolithic period, where marked regional differences can be identified in monument styles and settlement.

Boats, seamanship and Neolithic transformations

The Mesolithic-Neolithic transition, the period when Continental resources such as cereals and domesticated animals were introduced to Britain, has been discussed in a number of ways. Debate in recent archaeological literature has focused on the nature of the transition: whether crops and animals were introduced by settlers from Continental Europe or whether these were adopted by indigenous communities, with little or no population movement involved. The dominant interpretation in recent years has been that Mesolithic people in the British Isles gradually adopted aspects of Neolithic culture found on the European mainland, while maintaining a lifestyle on the move and relying predominantly on wild resources (Bradley 1993; Thomas 1988, 1991, 1999a; Whittle 1996). In contrast, others see the changes as more rapid and wholesale, involving some form of population movement (Ashmore 1996; Cooney 1986; Richards 2003; Richards and Hedges 1999; Schulting and Richards 2002; Sheridan 2000). Many of these views have taken extreme positions with little common ground.

Very few of these hypotheses ever explicitly discuss the actual mechanisms and means of change involved in the beginnings of the Neolithic. Britain by the beginnings of the Neolithic had been separated from the European mainland for some millennia and thus any animals or cereals had to be moved by boat, whether by indigenous hunter-gatherer or seafaring farmer. Cereals are not found in the wild in Britain and although wild cattle did exist in parts of the islands (with the notable exception of Ireland) the first domesticated cattle found on Neolithic sites in Britain are very different in size and form from these wild ancestors (Clutton-Brock 1979; Tresset 2003; Woodman and McCarthy 2003: 36).

Another important part of the transition was the introduction of monumental architecture (Bradley 1998). In Britain the first monuments built are closely related to Continental forms and parallels between nearly all types of monument in Britain and mainland Europe are widely documented (Bradley 1998; Cooney 1986; Kinnes 1992a; Sheridan 2000; Whittle 1977). The ideas behind such constructions must have been the outcome of contact between the European mainland and Britain. Again the medium of these contacts must have been maritime in origin. Lifestyles at the beginning of the Neolithic were changed through the activities of those who were able to harness the power of the sea (Figure 2.1). However, as Fraser Sturt notes (2005), the sea is notably absent in accounts of the Neolithic period. Neolithic interpretations are generally based on landscapes and the monuments and activities found there (although see Phillips 2003) and the critical importance of the sea in the Mesolithic-Neolithic transition has rarely been noted. However, maritime traditions are essential

FIGURE 2.1 *The tides and currents of the sea*

in understanding the transition between early farming and hunter-gatherer societies in Britain and Ireland.

The lack of consideration given to maritime traditions in accounts of the Neolithic is perhaps due to the fact that boats and travelling across water play a relatively minor role in modern life in Britain; both our concepts of and means of travel have changed radically over the last few centuries. Roads and land transport figure so highly in our everyday lives that it is difficult to imagine alternative means of travel. The landscape has also changed in radical ways. Vast numbers of roads, pathways, drainage systems and bridges have dramatically altered the landscape that we inhabit, making it more predictable, easier to traverse and lessening the time it takes to travel over land. In these circumstances it is easy to forget how the landscape would have looked before these revolutions in land transport even though this is a relatively recent change. For example, when Dr Johnson visited Scotland in the late eighteenth century he found it impossible to ride in parts of the country and some journeys were only passable by foot (Scott 1951: 24).

In order to understand maritime activity it is imperative that we understand the tides, currents and other factors which govern seafaring. The log boats which survive from the Mesolithic and Neolithic give a very poor impression of boat technology at this time. It is unlikely that such craft were ever used on anything other than inland waterways (McGrail 1998: 53). The most common craft are likely to have been hide boats which are still built in parts of Britain and Ireland today and are effective and stable, capable of carrying large loads (Bowen 1972: 36). In comparison with plank-built boats, the earliest of which are dated to the Early Bronze Age (Gifford and Gifford 2004), hide boats can be built relatively quickly (McGrail 1998: 184). Nevertheless, it should not be assumed that seafaring and the use of boats were undertaken by all. Constructing boats, seamanship and navigation are highly skilled activities that would not have been part of everybody's daily life. Muckelroy (1978) argues that the boat was the most complex machine in the pre-industrial world. A Neolithic seafarer undertaking long-distance sea journeys would have needed the skills to: 'observe and forecast the weather, observe and forecast tidal conditions, make simple astronomical observations, recognise coastal landscapes and retain . . . a good estimate of his constantly changing position relative to point of departure and destination' (McGrail 1998: 277). Seafarers need constantly to adjust their movement in relation to 'the *flow* of waves, wind, current and stars' (Ingold 2000: 237). Such skills would have been of even more vital importance in the difficult seas of northwest Europe and would have been gained only through generations of maritime activity.

Depending upon their environment, certain social groups have a heightened degree of orientation to the sea, and form maritime communities that spend as much time at sea as they do on land (Broodbank 2000: 34; Lethbridge 1952). Communities that live close to the sea and need to use the sea as a means of securing essential resources often have strong maritime cultures. Examples of places with particularly strong maritime cultures are islands, particularly small islands. Britain itself is of course an island, but the great size of the mainland often limits contact with the sea and most people today do not see themselves as islanders. Small island communities on the other hand are highly aware of their island status and many of them have strong links with the sea. For example, Orcadians are often been described as 'farmers with boats' and Shetlanders 'fishermen with crofts' (Sturt 2005). The short distances between the individual islands of these archipelagos encourages the development of maritime societies (Broodbank 2000: 131).

Broken coastlines and island archipelagos are conducive to island- and coast-hopping, the development of long-distance contacts and maritime economies based on the resources of the sea (Kinnes 1984). A favourable configuration of islands and coast encourages expansion of settlement and the development of maritime cultures (Broodbank 2000: 131; Erdoğu 2003: 8). The west coast of the British mainland comprising Ireland, the Irish Sea and the islands to the north and south is one such area, consisting of an indented coastline and a 'maze of lochs, inlets, small islands and skerries' coupled with a number of island archipelagos (Henshall 1972: 20). Combined with the strong tidal streams in this area, this part of the British Isles is very much conducive to the development of maritime activities (Clarke 1977). The Atlantic sea-routes channel movement up and down the west coast of Britain (Cunliffe 2001). Kinnes and Mercer, amongst others, have highlighted the importance of the west coast route in prehistory, pointing out that the tidal currents around the British Isles, essential to seafaring in prehistory, lead north and west, not eastwards, meaning that the west coast route was an important contact route between the British Isles and the European mainland (Kinnes 1984: 367; Mercer 2003: 69).

If we return to the Mesolithic-Neolithic transition in Britain and Ireland and the means of actually transporting cereals and animals across water, then it is clear that not all groups would necessarily have had the skills essential to achieve such feats of seamanship. It can be argued that western Britain with its favourable configuration of islands and coasts is more likely to have developed maritime societies and that the importance of the Atlantic route might suggest that the west had an important role in the Mesolithic-Neolithic transition (Figure 2.2). The islands of the west have rarely featured in discussions of the Mesolithic-Neolithic transition. This is not due to a lack of fieldwork on these islands (although some of these areas have been under studied), islands such as Orkney have seen intensive archaeological excavation and survey in recent years. However, the lack of interest in the western and northern islands of

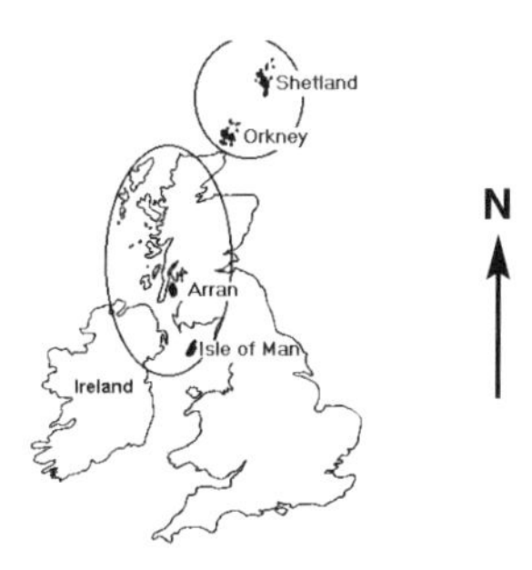

FIGURE 2.2 *The island chains of the western British Isles and specific islands that form the main topic of Chapter 1*

Britain when discussing this issue has mainly to do with how the modern cultural and political history of the United Kingdom has affected the way we write about the Neolithic (Barclay 2001a). Concepts of core and periphery based on modern society have biased our views of the west and north in prehistory meaning that many of the interpretative syntheses of the Neolithic are based on evidence from southern England alone (Barclay 2001a). When areas such as Orkney and Shetland and even Ireland are incorporated into these syntheses these places are often seen as exceptions or the evidence only partly considered (Barclay 1996: 62, 2000: 278; Cooney 1997). This is mainly to do with how we view islands and the west in contemporary British society. Modernity has brought 'chronic social, economic and ecological disintegration' to many island communities and recent historical changes have left many parts of western Scotland sparsely populated (Broodbank 2000: 6; Turnock 1974).

These changes have been dramatic and should not be underestimated. Urbanisation in recent centuries instigated major changes in the United Kingdom and the growth of the major mainland cities led to great population movements to the industrial parts of the lowlands. In the Scottish Isles the expulsion of people from their lands during the Clearances exacerbated the problem and resulted in a great population differential between the islands and mainland. For example, in 1801 almost 20 per cent of Scotland's population lived in the Highlands and Islands, dropping dramatically to around 5 per cent in 1971 (Turnock 1974: 6). Differences in economy between parts of western Britain and the eastern mainland have also been aggravated by modern farming practices based on intensive cattle rearing and crop growing. This has been possible in much of mainland Britain, after intense agricultural improvement, but in the west and on the islands this is more difficult (Turnock 1974: 7). Yet it is clear that traditional agriculture in the Highlands and Islands was successful and the economy of these places would not have been significantly impoverished in comparison to lowland areas in the past (Turnock 1974: 7). In Scotland, images of the west have also been tarnished by Walter Scott's romantic reinvention of the Highlands and the painting traditions that grew up around this vision, which show vast expanses of wilderness almost entirely devoid of human presence (Barclay 2001a: 5). The changes to the west, real and imagined, have led to a landscape sparsely populated in terms of actual population and contemporary imagination. 'Dreams of a virgin paradise' have lead many to assume that these areas were always relatively sparsely inhabited (Broodbank 2000: 7). For example, Schulting and Richards describe the west coast of Britain as the 'periphery of Britain' when considering Neolithic society in Britain and Ireland (Schulting and Richards 2002: 149) and Telford has recently asserted that the potential for agriculture in western Scotland was limited in the Neolithic, an idea presumably based on modern land capability maps without accounting for over 6,000 years of environmental and landscape change and the excellent evidence for successful agricultural systems in many of these island locations in the Neolithic (Telford 2002). Before the nineteenth century, lowland and highland areas would have had relatively similar levels of population and would not have been blighted by a lack of agricultural land. Concepts of core and periphery are clearly subjective and open to bias and should therefore be avoided as they may result in misleading analyses of prehistory (Cooney 1997; Barclay 2001a).

In discussing islands it is also necessary to get beyond a number of stereotypes that have grown up around island communities. Often seen as 'places apart', islands have in the past been seen as bound and closed systems where change only happens slowly and always subsequent to that on larger landmasses (Evans 1973). Ideas of what island life entailed in the past are often grossly distorted by the current peripheral status of islands (Broodbank 2000: 6). The current standing of these islands has a number of causes, all of which can be traced back to recent historical processes. Before the introduction of major road systems the islands occupied important positions in the Atlantic seaways and the communication routes of Britain and Ireland (Cunliffe 2001). Thus, the Western Isles of Britain have been contested by a number of different countries throughout history. The status of these places as islands mattered little in the past; indeed the very fact that they were islands has meant that they have had a much more dynamic history than many parts of mainland Britain. However, in recent times the islands have fallen out of mainstream culture and their place amongst the powers of Western Europe is no longer contested.

THE MARINE HIGHWAYS: TIDAL CURRENTS, VISIBILITY AND NAVIGATION

In Britain and Ireland there are important reasons other than the possible presence of a maritime culture for believing that small islands may have had an important part to play in the Mesolithic-Neolithic transition. From a landscape perspective it might be expected that the first areas to make contact with Neolithic communities on mainland Europe would be those closest to that area. Thus, people in southern England might be likely to adopt domesticates and cereals first as they are closest to Continental Europe. However, this was not the case: radiocarbon dates in southern England for the Neolithic are not earlier than elsewhere (Schulting and Richards 2002; Richards 2003). Furthermore, as we shall see, important early dates are found at some distances away from the southern mainland. Boats allow major landmasses to be 'leapfrogged' and instead of proximity, it may be more important in seagoing terms to assess where a place is in relation to the major tidal streams and how visible that place is from the sea (Broodbank 2000; Davies 1946: 42; McGrail 1998: 278). For example, in terms of tidal streams and currents the Isle of Man occupies a central position in the Irish Sea and many routes converge on the island (Davies 1946) (Figure 2.3).

The tidal flows in the Irish Sea region favour north-south movement, allowing journeys from Cornwall to County Antrim in Ireland, the Isle of Man acting as a conduit to travel in the Irish Sea basin (Darvill 2003: 112). The Isle of Man is dominated by the peak of Snaefell, making the island a highly visible place from the sea, a major factor in traditional sea navigation (Bowen 1972: 40; Darvill 1999: 1; Davies 1946: 42; McGrail 1998: 278) (Figure 2.4). From the Isle of Man itself, Scotland, Ireland, England and Wales are visible and before the invention of modern navigation equipment the Isle of Man was one of the most important navigation points in western Britain (Burrow 1997: 2).

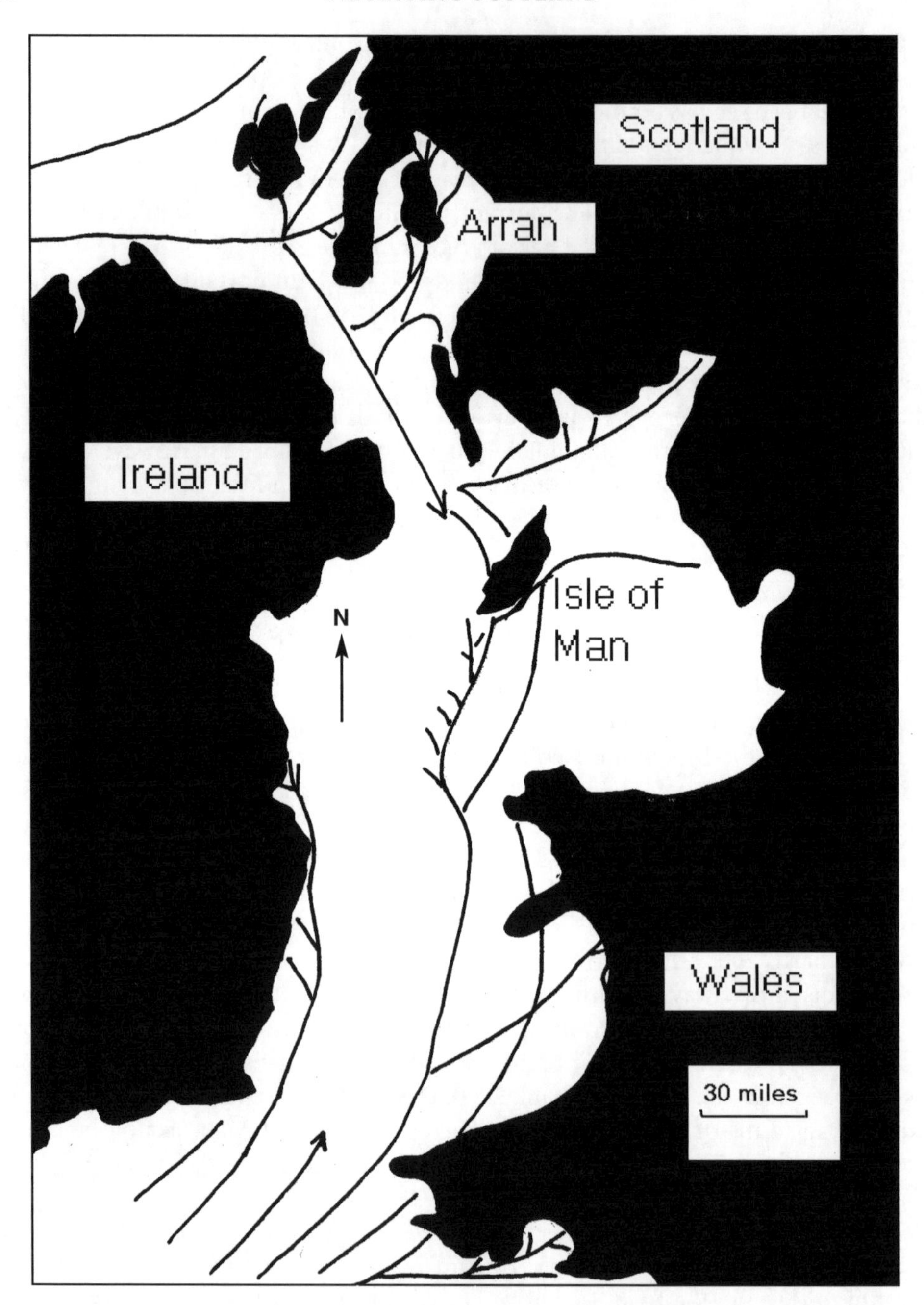

FIGURE 2.3 *The major sea-routes in the Irish Sea zone. Davies calculated the main sea-routes by studying Admiralty pilots of the area. The routes are based on the directions of the major tidal currents, which would need to be utilised in order to make a sea journey in a small boat. The tidal circulation in the Irish Sea zone is likely to have been similar in the Neolithic as the coastal configuration has changed only slightly in the last 6,000 years (McGrail 1998: 259) (Source: Davies 1946: figure 2)*

Figure 2.4 *The brooding presence of the Isle of Man as seen from the southwest coast of Scotland*

If small-island communities were more likely to have a maritime culture and if tidal streams and visibility were important in early navigation, then it might be possible to suggest that some of the islands of western Britain were particularly significant places in the adoption or introduction of Neolithic ways of life. Moreover, if it can be shown that our modern conceptions of core and periphery are flawed and that the relegation of island societies in modern life is due to a number of circumstances that have arisen only in recent centuries, then it might be possible to show that these islands had an important part to play in social change. The evidence is fragmentary, but it is possible to suggest that the island communities of the west were indeed instrumental to the changes that occurred around the beginning of the fourth millennium BC.

The Isle of Man: continuities and change

As I outlined at the beginning, theories on the Mesolithic-Neolithic transition in the last few decades have generally been dominated by the idea that the period was one of gradual change where the indigenous hunting and gathering groups adopted some of the aspects of farming from communities on mainland Europe into traditional lifestyles. However, evidence of continuity between the two periods is meagre. Radiocarbon dates for Late Mesolithic and Earlier Neolithic sites rarely overlap (Schulting and Richards 2002). Neolithic material and Mesolithic material is rarely found in close proximity on mainland Britain and rarely in areas suggesting continuous occupation (Bradley 2003). A number of fieldwork projects in recent years have found little evidence for overlap between the Mesolithic and Neolithic in Britain. In the Tyne Valley in northern England, for example, Christopher Tolan-Smith found that Mesolithic and Neolithic materials were found in the same area in only 8 of the 221 blocks of land surveyed in the valley (Tolan-Smith 1996). Similar results have been gained in northeast Scotland. Fieldwalking in Inverness-shire by Richard Bradley and Aaron Watson of Reading University found that Neolithic and Mesolithic artefacts were found in very different parts of the landscape (Bradley 2000b: chapter 9). It seems difficult to reconcile these patterns with ideas of Mesolithic-Neolithic continuity.

On the other hand, the evidence obtained from the mainland may not be relevant to all areas of Britain. There is more widespread evidence for links between the Mesolithic and Neolithic in areas further to the north and west. On many of the islands of western Britain (see Figure 2.2) the connections between the Mesolithic and Neolithic are more evident. On the Isle of Man, for example, Mesolithic and Neolithic material regularly occurs on the same sites (Darvill 2000: 373; McCartan 1999: 6; Woodman 1978: 120). At a causewayed enclosure at Billown on the Isle of Man, Later Mesolithic flintwork and dated features were found in direct association with Neolithic features (Darvill 1995: 48, 2000, 2002). The nature of the activity at Billown suggests activity across the divide we traditionally associate with the Mesolithic and Neolithic (Darvill 2003: 118). For example, a tradition of pit digging at Billown began in what would traditionally be termed the Later Mesolithic, in the middle of the fifth millennium BC, but continued throughout the Neolithic period and throughout the use of the causewayed enclosure. As Darvill states, Billown was not a Late Mesolithic site followed by an Earlier Neolithic site, but indicates continuity of practice over significant periods of time (Darvill 2003: 119). Overlap between the Mesolithic and Neolithic at Billown is further suggested by the nature of the finds. Although cereals were found, the amounts tend to be very small. In the early levels, wild plant remains dominated the pollen assemblages (Darvill 1998: 16). The evidence at Billown fits well with models proposed for Mesolithic-Neolithic continuity developed by Thomas (1988) and Armit and Finlayson (1992) where cereals and domesticates only gradually replaced wild resources and where Mesolithic and Neolithic activities were closely associated.

However, the evidence is contradictory. As well as evidence for continuity, the Isle of Man also potentially has some of the earliest recorded traces of cereal-type pollen found in the British Isles in deposits that may well date to before the main adoption of domesticates across the British Isles. A number of pollen records in Britain and Ireland over the last few decades have recorded possible Mesolithic impacts on the vegetation (Edwards and Hirons 1984; Edwards and Ralston 1984; Tipping 1994). However, the number of sites where early disturbances are recorded are small in number. In a review of the evidence for Scotland, for example, Edwards and Ralston concluded that although impacts could be identified at site level there were no broader-scale changes occurring in the Later Mesolithic (Edwards and Ralston 1984). One of the few places in Britain where early disturbances are recorded is on the Isle of Man (Darvill 1998: 15; McCarroll et al. 1990) and more recent work has increased the evidence substantially for pre-Neolithic activity (Davey and Innes 2003). A number of pollen cores carried out on the island have indicated pre-elm-decline activity. The elm decline occurs in many pollen cores across Britain and Ireland in the fourth millennium BC and has often been linked to the beginnings of the Neolithic (Edwards and Hirons 1984). On the Isle of Man a few of the cores have some slight traces of cereal-type pollen before the elm decline (Davey and Innes 2003: 121). The most interesting core is undoubtedly that at Ballachrink, where disturbances in the vegetation are recorded as early as the first half of the sixth millennium BC (Davey and Innes 2003: 122). A second series of impacts are recorded in the fifth millennium BC at around 4950–4670 BC when reductions in tree pollen were accompanied by cereal-type pollen and high values for agricultural weeds and other signs of disturbance. The core was located close to a number of Late Mesolithic sites, including a concentration of heavy-blade, Late Mesolithic-type lithics (Davey and Innes 2003: 125). In the same valley, a site at Rhendoo has been excavated which provides radiocarbon-dated occupation traces that span the period from the late sixth millennium BC to the Earlier Neolithic (Burrow 1997: 9; Davey and Innes 2003: 122).

Tipping (1994) has highlighted the difficulties in differentiating between cultivated cereals and natural wild grasses, but the evidence at Ballachrink is accompanied by all the indicators that might be expected in an area of cultivation and the core is located in relation to archaeological material that extends back to the period in which the cereals were detected. The results are compelling and suggestive and are part of a group of pollen cores with traces of early cereal-type pollen from around the northern Irish Sea basin (Davey and Innes 2003: 126). The early cereal-type pollen suggests that parts of the Isle of Man may have been the focus for pioneering cereal cultivation, well before the recognised beginnings of the Neolithic elsewhere. At the same time the evidence for continuity of land use, as suggested by lithic scatters and sites such as Billown, suggests a closer relationship between the indigenous hunter-gatherers of the island and the novel resources that were introduced from Continental Europe than has been identified elsewhere.

Evidence from other islands off the west coast of Scotland also hints at a close relationship between the Later Mesolithic and ensuing Earlier Neolithic. At Kinloch on the island of Rhum, for example, environmental evidence appears to indicate continuous human activity through the Late Mesolithic and Earlier Neolithic periods (Wickham-Jones 1990a: 135). The same sources of raw materials for lithics and the same basic reduction techniques for stone tools were used throughout the two periods (Wickham-Jones 1990a: 84). The evidence from this area seems to indicate significant continuities across the Mesolithic–Neolithic divide (Armit and Finlayson 1992; Bradley 2003: 220). On the island of Islay, too, many of the lithic scatters located during a recent large-scale fieldwalking project were found to contain Mesolithic and

Neolithic material indicating continuity of activity zones across the Mesolithic-Neolithic divide, much like on the Isle of Man (Mithen 2000: chapter 3.5). Mesolithic shell middens on the west coast of Scotland also often have Neolithic levels that include pottery, stone tools and human bone (Armit and Finlayson 1992: 669; Bonsall et al. 1994; Schulting and Richards 2002). In some cases the evidence of Neolithic use of shell middens is more dramatic. On the island of Bute, a Clyde-style chambered cairn was constructed on top of a shell midden at Glecknabae, from which a microlithic core of Mesolithic date has been recovered (Bryce 1908–9; Cormack 1986) (Figure 2.5). Some Mesolithic middens may also have been cultivated in the Neolithic and on the island of Jura the few indications of Neolithic activity found are also stratified in the upper layers of Mesolithic sites (Guttmann 2005; Mercer 1967–8, 1972–4, 1978–80). The evidence is fragmentary but suggests that some aspects of traditional lifestyles were continued in the Neolithic period in parts of western Scotland. Similar evidence on mainland Britain is not as common, which may suggest that the nature of the transition there may well have been different and perhaps more abrupt.

Like the Isle of Man, some of the islands of western Scotland also contain evidence for early impact on the environment, in some cases in direct contrast to that found on the adjacent mainland. On the island of Arran, Mesolithic lithics are closely associated with areas of Neolithic activity and lithic scatters are often multi-period (Barber 1997: 92; Gorman et al. 1993a, 1993b). The evidence for activity across the Mesolithic-Neolithic divide is supported by pollen evidence. In a pollen core from Machrie Moor, in the western part of the island, evidence of unusual activity occurring long before the beginnings of the Neolithic has been obtained (Robinson and Dickson 1988). The Machrie pollen core indicates disturbances and changes in the natural vegetation from as early as the eighth millennium BC (8000–7000 BC). At this time the development of heather heathland was accompanied by charcoal increases and in the seventh millennium BC, pollen indicative of small-scale clearances of

FIGURE 2.5 *Glecknabae chambered cairn on the island of Bute. The cairn overlies a shell midden from which a Mesolithic-type flint core has been found*

woodland, suggestive of human activity, appeared. Recurring decreases in both birch and oak pollen and an increase in open-condition indicators occurred from the Later Mesolithic into the Neolithic period, strongly suggesting episodes of forest clearance throughout, some lasting up to 200 years. In the last three or four centuries of the fifth millennium BC, before the main elm decline, cereal-type pollen grain was identified at this site and at a nearby site at Machrie Farm (Edwards and McIntosh 1988). Tipping (1994: 19–20) has disputed whether the cereals were of the cultivated variety and whether they were really pre-elm decline, but combined with the extensive evidence for clearance and human activity as demonstrated by the weeds and other indicators of open conditions, it is evident that this part of the island was the focus for some form of sustained activity. Robinson and Dickson marvelled at the incompleteness of the forest canopy at Machrie throughout prehistory and the 'duration and intensity of human activity on the island' and linked these two phenomena (Robinson and Dickson 1988: 233). It was only after the end of the Bronze Age that agricultural activity decreased and blanket peat began to develop and Machrie Moor began to resemble the marginal landscape that exists today.

The activity on Arran is remarkable when it is contrasted with that on the surrounding mainland (Hughes 1988). At locations such as Airds Moss and Kipplemoss in Ayrshire, pollen diagrams indicate that woodland dominated the vegetation around these locations until recent centuries (Durno 1956, 1976). At Snibe Bog and Loch Dungeon, both in Galloway, the elm decline was associated with some pastoral activity, but this was not intensive in nature, nor long-lived (Birks 1972). Pollen cores from Bloax Moss, Kennox Moss and Loch Cill an Aonghais, in Ayrshire, also show little indication of woodland reduction or human activity until later phases of the Bronze Age (Switsur 1981: 93; Turner 1965). Only one pollen core from the mainland surrounding Arran has recorded substantial activity around the beginnings of the Neolithic. This is at Aros Moss, Kintyre, where similar impacts on the vegetation to that at Machrie Moor occurred (Hughes 1988: 46; Nichols 1967; Tipping 1994: 19). The archaeological record for this area of southwest Scotland again suggests that the nature of the Mesolithic-Neolithic transition was varied. It also suggests that some of the islands of western Britain have distinctive evidence of both early traces of domesticates and/or evidence of an apparently closer relationship between Mesolithic and Neolithic lifestyles than other places.

Ferriter's Cove and the introduction of domesticates

The distinctiveness of the islands of the west is highlighted by the fact that the earliest examples of domesticated animals found in the British Isles are not in the areas closest to the European mainland, but located on the west coast of Ireland. At Ferriter's Cove, Co. Kerry, in southwest Ireland, a number of cattle and sheep bones have been found within a series of Late Mesolithic occupation levels (Woodman et al. 1999; Woodman and McCarthy 2003: 32). Two of the cattle bones have been radiocarbon dated to the mid fifth millennium BC (4500–4220 BC and 4800–4540 BC). These bones are many centuries earlier than the earliest examples from southern

England (Tresset 2003: 19). The animal remains were accompanied by a number of human bones, two of which have been dated to a similar date range of 4530–4240 BC and 4550–4330 BC. The people associated with this site may have consumed the cattle and domesticates only as dietary supplement as analysis of the human bones suggested that they had consumed mainly a marine-based diet (Woodman and McCarthy 2003: 33). However, these individuals may have been amongst the first to bring into or receive domesticated resources in Britain and Ireland, many centuries before the first traces of the Neolithic on mainland Britain. The environment of Ireland was very different to that of Britain, with an almost total lack of large mammals prior to the Neolithic (Tresset 2003: 24; Woodman 2000: 237). This may have meant that the introduction of cattle and sheep to Ireland may have been more desirable and their introduction enacted at an earlier date than elsewhere.

While the Ferriter's Cove bones indicated that these individuals consumed a largely marine-based diet, other Late Mesolithic bones in Ireland show a more varied use of marine resources (Woodman and McCarthy 2003: 33). This is in contrast to the few Mesolithic humans analysed in Britain, who seem to show a total reliance on marine resources, in contrast to Earlier Neolithic human remains (Richards and Hedges 1999; Schulting and Richards 2002; Richards 2003). This may indicate that in Ireland the shift in dietary basis across the Mesolithic-Neolithic transition may not have been as abrupt as that suggested for southern England and parts of mainland Scotland (Richards and Hedges 1999; Schulting and Richards 2002; Richards 2003). Radiocarbon dates for the Late Mesolithic and Earlier Neolithic in Ireland also overlap. This is again in contrast to southern Britain where more sudden change is indicated (Tresset 2003; Williams 1989). The evidence for the early introduction of domesticates to Ireland is also supported by pollen evidence. While pollen analysis is always likely to be more ambiguous, Edward and Hiron's 1984 survey of pre-elm decline occurrences of cereal-type pollen found that five of the eight recorded instances were located in Ireland, a high proportion considering the excellent history of environmental analysis elsewhere in the British Isles (Edwards and Hirons 1984). Again this may indicate divergent histories for places like Ireland and more land-bound mainland locations.

THE NATURE OF THE NEOLITHIC IN THE WEST

As well as thinking about the Mesolithic-Neolithic transition, it is also important to outline the nature of the Neolithic once it was established. For example, general models of the Earlier Neolithic period based on evidence from southern England have, over the last decade or so, suggested that the Neolithic population did not practise fully developed, formal agriculture. Instead the Neolithic is said to be a period when Mesolithic people adopted some of the material symbols and the ideas of the Neolithic without fully embracing an agricultural lifestyle. The major transition to an agricultural lifestyle may have occurred at a much later date, during the Middle Bronze Age (Thomas 1988, 1999a; Barrett 1994; Bradley 1998; Whittle 1996). The role of domesticated resources, domestic architecture and the material traces associated with the maintenance of agricultural systems, such as field systems, have been downplayed in these models. Domesticates, intensive agricultural systems and field systems were, however, very much part of the earliest Neolithic in places such as Ireland and parts of western and northern Scotland (Barclay 1996, 1997; Cooney 1997, 2003). This is not to argue that agriculture was not practised on mainland Scotland. As Rowley-Conwy has recently argued (2004), we have probably seriously underestimated the impact and uptake of domesticated resources in Neolithic Britain and Ireland. Cereals are a consistent find on Neolithic sites across Scotland and it seems likely that they were a common part of Neolithic subsistence. However, the evidence for substantial domestic structures on mainland Scotland is not common and the range of pits and fragmentary architectural traces found (Barclay 2003) certainly suggests some level of mobility was retained in Neolithic lifestyles in this part of Scotland (see Chapter 3).

In contrast, in Ireland large numbers of substantial rectangular Earlier Neolithic buildings, associated with a range of domestic debris, have in the last decade or so been found. These provide an increasingly convincing picture of permanency in the settlement pattern, for at least the first centuries of the fourth millennium BC, and seem to be part of an intensive uptake of the Neolithic of the type that has been downplayed for southern England (Armit et al. 2003; Grogan 1996, 2002). Field systems for the management of domesticated plants and animals have also been located at the Céide Fields in Co. Mayo, an extensive system of Neolithic field enclosures, and similar systems have been found elsewhere (Cooney 1997, 2003). This seems to contrast with the more fragmentary evidence in much of mainland Britain (Bradley 2003; Thomas 1999a).

Like in parts of Ireland, Neolithic field systems have also been identified on the islands of western Scotland. On Arran, for example, excavations by John Barber in the late 1970s and early 1980s found a series of features that were of Neolithic date at Machrie North, including field systems, stone structures, lithics, pits and a rectangular stone structure, which Barber compared to Earlier Neolithic rectangular houses in Ireland (Barber 1997: 81–3, 128–9; O'Kelly 1989: 57). The structure was not accurately dated, but was partly sealed by a layer of hill wash, into which a pit with Grooved Ware and Beaker pottery had been cut higher up the hillside, suggesting activity in the earlier phases of the Neolithic. The stone structure appeared to be contemporary with a gridiron field system, which lay to the north and west (Figure 2.6). The fields consisted of small rectangular strips, around 200 metres long by 50 metres wide, running down the hill, defined by stone banks (Barber 1997: 144). The rectangular structure itself was built over a deposit of field clearance, which was partly covered by hill wash, deriving most likely from cultivation upslope. Many of the stone field walls had evidence of long-term use that included a number of phases of rebuilding (Barber 1997: 131). Further Neolithic field systems may also be located in the southern half of the island where extensive pre-peat field walls have been found at Kilpatrick (Barber 1997: 144). The evidence at Machrie North is supported by recent excavations by Glasgow University Archaeological Research Division at Brodick, in the eastern part of the island, where excavations in advance of a water pipeline found a large linear feature

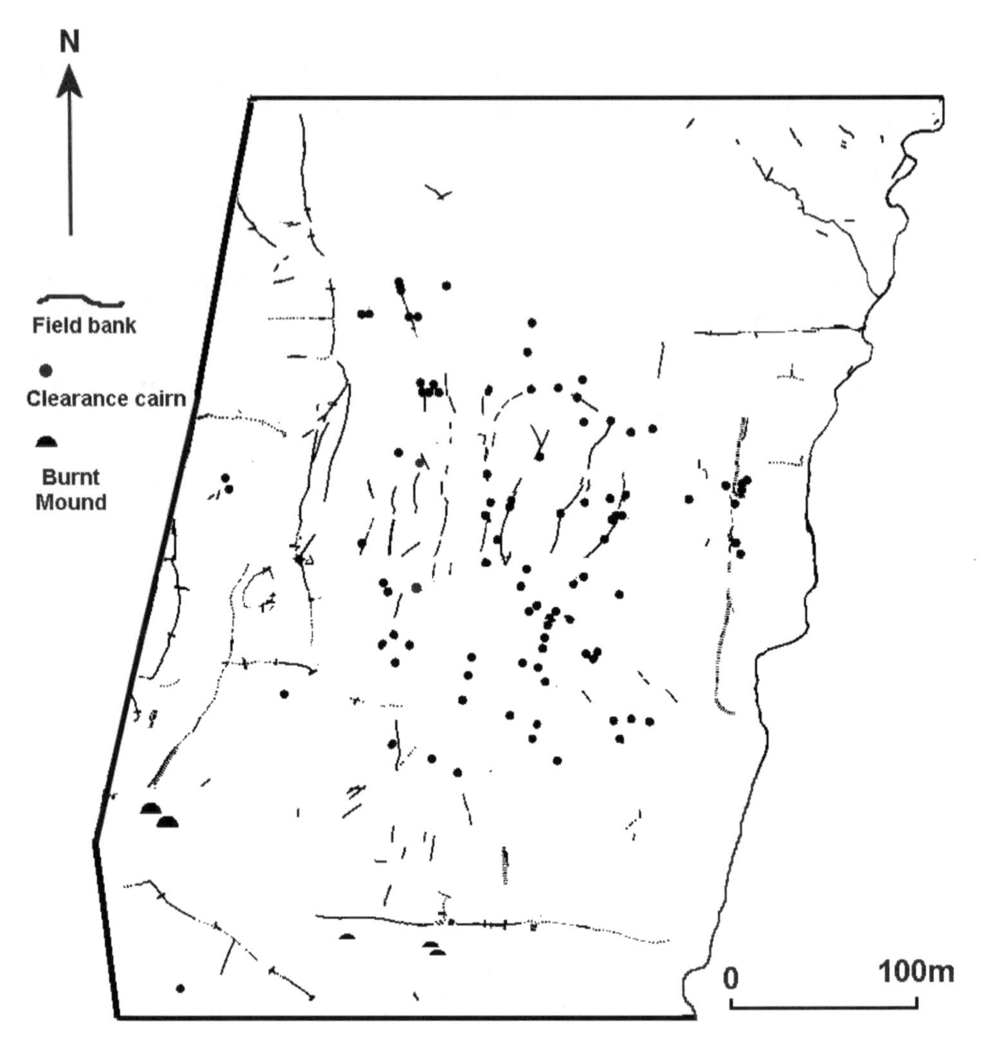

FIGURE 2.6 *Machrie North – schematic diagram showing field boundaries and clearance cairns (Source: Barber 1997: figure 41)*

aligned northeast to southwest that contained pitchstone, flint and Earlier Neolithic pottery (Donnelly et al. 2000: 18–26) (Figure 2.7). The linear feature has been interpreted as a field boundary as preserved cultivated soils and ardmarks were contained within its limits (Donnelly et al. 2000: 25). A small rectangular timber structure and a group of stake and postholes were also found within the boundary.

Like Ireland, the Earlier Neolithic in Orkney and Shetland in northern Scotland were also inhabited by Neolithic communities who invested large amounts of labour in the construction of substantial, permanent house architecture and consisted of communities that might be described as 'house societies' (Carsten and Hugh-Jones 1995). In Orkney large rectangular houses were constructed from the Earlier Neolithic onwards and small clusters of houses formed larger settlements often referred to as

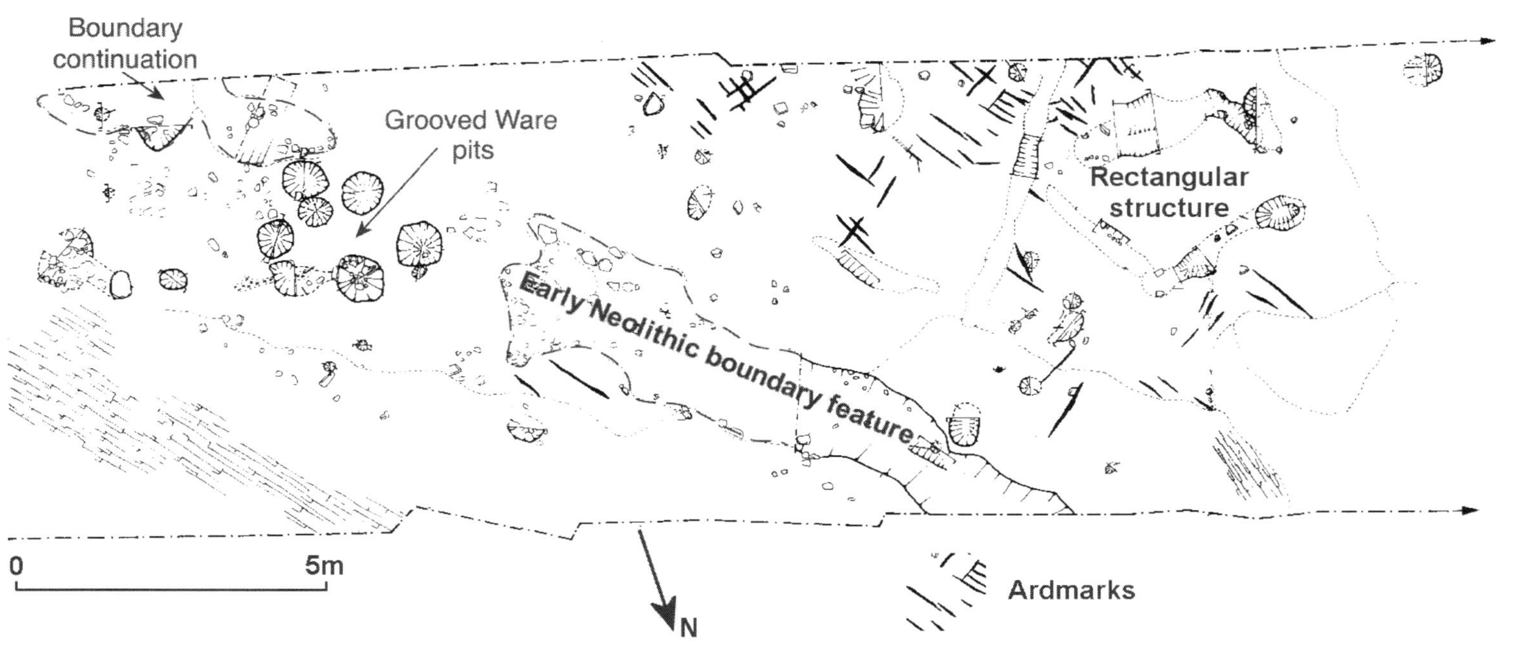

FIGURE 2.7 *Earlier Neolithic field boundary and agricultural area near Brodick, Isle of Arran. Excavated by GUARD in advance of redevelopment. The boundary was associated with a timber rectangular structure and ardmarks*
(Source: Donnelly et al. 2000: figure 3)

'villages' (Ritchie 1983; Carruthers and Richards 2000; Richards 2005). Fully developed mixed agricultural systems were also utilised here. Cereals and quern stones are found in the earliest Neolithic contexts and cattle and sheep were also kept, while fishing remained an important part of the economy (Barclay 1996; Ritchie 1983; Sturt 2005; Clarke and Sharples 1985). In Shetland over 180 prehistoric house sites are known, some of which date to the Neolithic, and some also have associated field systems (Calder 1949–50, 1955–6; Fojut 1993; Whittle 1985, 1986) (Figure 2.8). At Scord of Brouster, in Shetland, the dated houses belonged to the second half of the fourth millennium, but settlements of a similar nature were undoubtedly in use at an earlier date (Whittle 1986: 146). A mixed economy was present at Scord of Brouster including the ard-cultivation of barley, the maintenance of cattle and sheep and the hunting of wild animals. The fields at Scord of Brouster were manured with seaweed and domestic refuse and the wider landscape of Shetland appears to have been divided at an early date as massive boundary walls, some of which are likely to be Neolithic, run for long distances across the islands indicating widespread division of the land (Turner 1998: 26). The evidence from Shetland points to an intensive and extensive use of the landscape during the Earlier Neolithic. Despite the perceived marginality of these places today, it is clear that developed agricultural systems were present in these island landscapes from a very early date.

THE UPTAKE OF FARMING

The abundant evidence for mixed farming, defined by field boundaries, the evidence for substantial domestic architecture and the evidence for rapid change at the beginning of the Neolithic on the islands of western Britain seems difficult to reconcile with models that argue for a gradual transition (Barrett 1994; Thomas 1999a; Whittle 1996). Despite the evidence for earlier links between hunter-gatherer and Earlier Neolithic landscape use it is clear that by the beginnings of the fourth millennium BC, the Neolithic on many of these islands heralded a period of radical change that involved a settled lifestyle, widespread division of the land and the use of new resources (Barber 1997: 144–5; Darvill 2002). These patterns are also found on islands such as Orkney and Shetland, where the Mesolithic is unidentified or only poorly recognised (Saville 2000; Turner 1998). The Neolithic on these islands heralded a period of radical change (Barber 1997: 144–5; Darvill 2002). The evidence of tentative contact with farming communities at sites like Ferriter's Cove was superseded a number of centuries later by a more wholesale adoption of domesticated resources (Tresset 2003: 24). During the first centuries of the fourth millennium, Neolithic lifestyles were more fully embraced and the changes at this time appear to have been rapid and extensive, affecting all parts of the British Isles (Tresset 2003: 24).

The early focus of the Neolithic in the west and the differences between these areas and much of the mainland has important implications for how we study the Mesolithic-Neolithic transition. The evidence outlined here suggests that many different processes may have been at work during the transition. Early, gradual indigenous adoption with a significant availability phase of domesticates in parts of

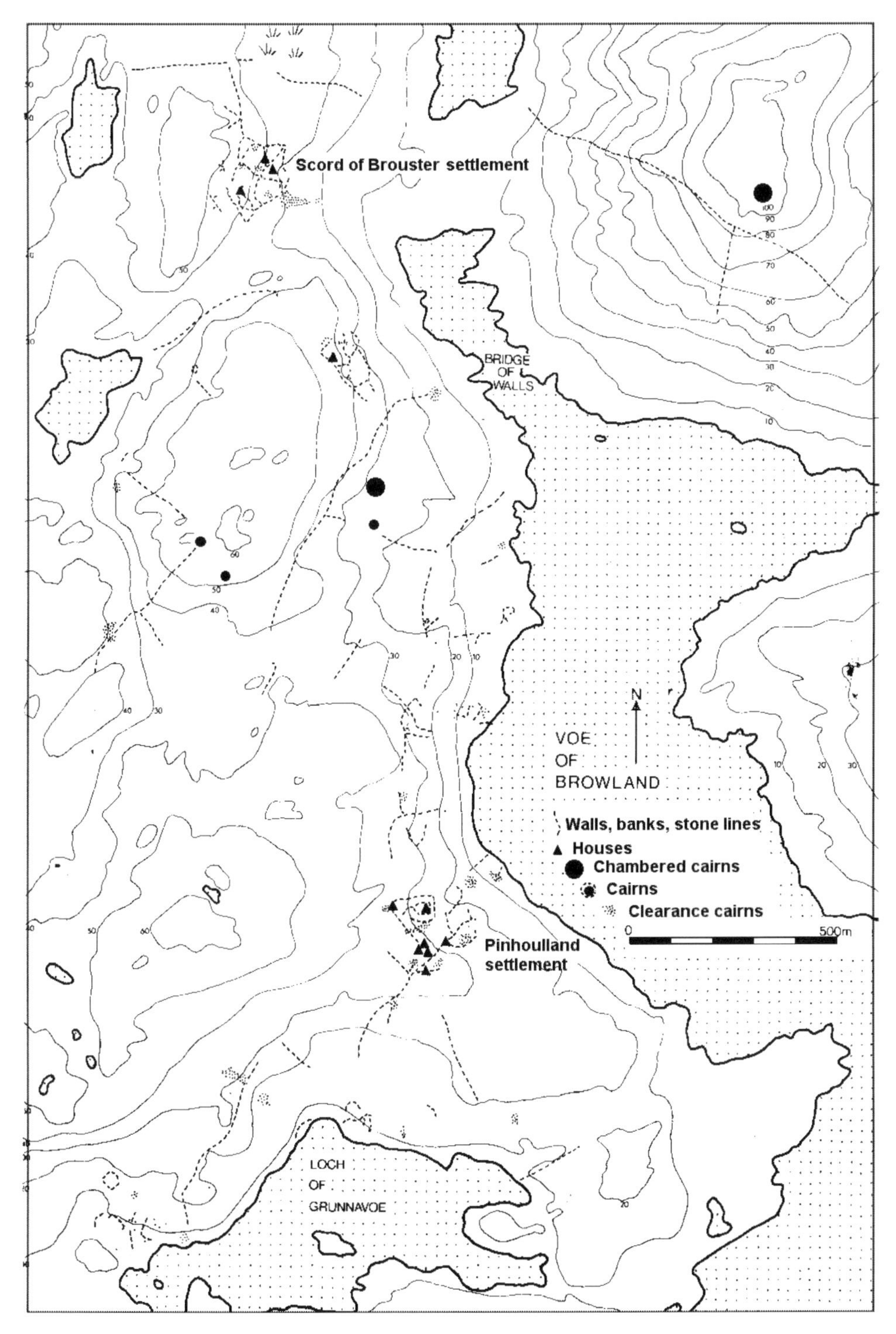

FIGURE 2.8 *Shetland: a Neolithic landscape defined by fields, stone walls, houses and tombs (Source: Whittle 1986: figure 47)*

Ireland and western Britain may have occurred before the beginnings of the Neolithic elsewhere in Britain. At the beginning of the fourth millennium BC all areas seem to have undergone more rapid transformations. In areas where there is little evidence of links between the two periods, these changes may have resulted from some form of population movement. Indeed the rapidity of the uptake of the Neolithic that seems to have occurred at this time has led some to suggest that population movement of farmers from Continental Europe was the main instigator of change (Richards 2003; Schulting and Richards 2002; Sheridan 2000). Schulting and Richards compare the transition to an 'event', suggesting that the onset of the Neolithic was sudden and wholesale (Schulting and Richards 2002: 177). However, migration is never event-like; migration is a *process* that almost always depends upon contact with, and knowledge of, the destination (Anthony 1990). If any population movement did occur (and migrations of farming populations can be long-distance, highly-directed processes) (Anthony 1990: 902), early contact with the west may have been the catalyst. Whether the later transition was caused by indigenous processes or incoming farmers, the evidence from the island communities of the west points to the importance of these places in the Mesolithic-Neolithic transition. The very islands which tend to be seen as peripheral places today may have been the places where a farming lifestyle was first experimented with and then first fully embraced. Indeed, a process of change, which happened at an early date in the islands, may not have taken place for a further 2,000 years or more on parts of the mainland (Barrett 1994; Bradley 1998; Thomas 1988, 1999a; Whittle 1996).

The variability of the evidence indicates that the Mesolithic-Neolithic transition may have been complex. Differences in the nature of the Mesolithic-Neolithic transition may explain why distinct regional traditions of architecture can be identified in Early Neolithic Britain and Ireland, traditions often based on differences between east and west (Barclay et al. 2002; Henshall 1963, 1972; Malone 2001; Whittle 1977). In Wales, Cummings and Whittle have highlighted the differences between east and west in relation to the megalithic tombs of Wales (Cummings and Whittle 2004a). The portal dolmens of west Wales have no direct antecedents in continental traditions of megalithic architecture whereas traditions further to the east relate more closely to styles of Neolithic architecture found in northern France, the Low Countries and the Rhineland. Cummings and Whittle argue that this may relate to different processes of Neolithicisation, with greater levels of colonisation through the fissuring or filtering of the populations of the adjacent continent in the east than in the west (Cummings and Whittle 2004a: 91). In the west the traditions of architecture may relate more to indigenous belief systems. Sherratt highlighted some time ago how the Atlantic traditions of round mounds and chambers of the first megalithic monuments had little precedent in the long house and causewayed enclosure traditions of the LBK of Central Europe, the first agricultural communities in this part of the world (Sherratt 1990). In contrast the traditions of the east, found in most areas of mainland Britain, share a much stronger resemblance to those found on Continental Europe (Kinnes 1984: 367, 1992a; Whittle 1977; Hodder 1990, 1994). These differences strongly suggest variations in the nature and mechanisms of change in eastern and western

Britain and Ireland. The presence of more strongly maritime-based communities in the west and the importance of the Atlantic sea-routes in enacting change through indigenous action may help explain the regional differences present in Early Neolithic society in the British Isles. Monument traditions in eastern and western Scotland were distinctly regional and the divergent processes of social change may explain why the Neolithic assumed different forms in different regions.

As well as having implications for how we view the transition in the islands the evidence outlined above also highlights the need for islands to be rehabilitated in terms of how we think of them in archaeological terms. The state of many island communities today need not be a model for how islands were in the past. Islands *were* affected by rapid change and island communities were rarely closed communities (contra. Evans 1973). The traditional use of islands as a means of assessing wider processes must be rejected. Island and mainland histories are interlinked, but are rarely ever identical in nature (Broodbank 2000: 9). Islands are not suitable laboratories for the study of wider cultural processes (Evans 1973; Darvill 2000; Whittle 1985: 2) but must instead be assessed on their own terms, in relation to, but not dependent upon, mainland histories.

CONCLUSIONS

Our view of the Mesolithic-Neolithic transition is fragmented and incomplete, and this topic will remain a matter of debate for some time to come. It is clear that the Mesolithic-Neolithic transition was complex and we are only beginning to understand the major changes that occurred at this time. Some of the evidence from Neolithic Scotland indicates relatively little continuity between hunter-gatherer lifestyles and Neolithic lifestyles at the beginnings of the fourth millennium BC. This suggests that indigenous hunter-gatherers may have had relatively little input into the introduction of new forms of material culture, plants and animals. Evidence from elsewhere, particularly in the west, suggests a different picture. Some of the islands in the western seaways, such as Ireland, the Isle of Man and Arran, may have been the scene of early introductions of domesticates some centuries before similar changes occurred elsewhere. Many of the islands in this part of the British Isles were also the areas in which Neolithic lifestyles were first fully embraced and became places demarcated by field systems and substantial domestic architecture from the earliest centuries of the fourth millennium BC. In this chapter I have suggested that the early traces of domesticates in these places may relate to the position of these places in the western seaways and be due to the presence of maritime cultures on these islands. The early traces of the Neolithic in the western islands of Britain and Ireland mirror the situation in the Aegean, where distinctive islands, important landmarks for sea travel, have earlier traces of the Neolithic than larger and possibly more productive locations (Erdoğu 2003). Our understanding of prehistoric maritime capabilities is vague, but we must not assume they were simple. The feat of carrying domesticated animals across a stretch of water must not be underestimated. This was a skill that brought new species of animal and plant across dangerous seas as far north as the

Shetland Isles. It is also essential not to assume the direction of contact. While contact across the English Channel seems eminently sensible to us today, the western seaways and routes from Scandinavia may have been as important. The people who piloted the vessels that brought the plants and animals that characterise the Neolithic were responsible for some of the most significant transformations in the history of the British Isles. These led to a Scotland that transformed quickly from the one that had existed previously. The resulting Neolithic was a mosaic of lifestyles and traditions, represented perhaps most obviously by a series of regional styles of monumental architecture. These form the subject of the three following chapters.

CHAPTER THREE

Burning down the house: the destruction of timber structures

Ritual focuses attention by framing; it enlivens the memory and links the present with the relevant past. In all this it aids perception. (Douglas 1966: 65)

Introduction

A whole series of different types of timber monument were built in Earlier Neolithic lowland Scotland at the beginning of the fourth millennium BC. These timber constructions included cursus monuments, mortuary enclosures, timber halls, cremation pyres and other forms of enclosure. They have been interpreted in different ways. Cursus monuments, for example, have been related to the symbolism of water (Brophy 2000). Other types, such as the mortuary enclosures, are assumed to have had some role in mortuary rites, as the name implies (Barclay and Maxwell 1991). While these structures assumed many different forms and were markedly different in scale, they also had much in common. All were rectangular in shape and constructed of massive oak timbers and nearly all were burnt down at the end of their lives, whether it was a timber hall or cremation pyre. In this respect, they are part of a wider European tradition of burnt Neolithic structures that includes many of the sites identified as Earlier Neolithic houses in Ireland and some of the structures under long barrows in England. The crucial aspect of these sites may have been the burning, which may have been associated with creating memories of people, places and events. In lowland Scotland it is argued that the timber structures may have been related to the Neolithic settlement pattern and were structures that added notions of permanency to a lifestyle that involved a large degree of settlement mobility. Drawing on images of the house, these structures were aimed at creating social unity at times when this was threatened. With the exception of cursus monuments, they have not been catalogued, but the distribution of pit-defined cursus monuments gives an impression of the general distributions of timber enclosures in eastern and southern Scotland (Figure 3.1). These are found spread across the area, but are concentrated in Tayside in the east and around the River Nith in Dumfries and Galloway. The radiocarbon dates for these structures indicate a consistent dating clustering between 4000 and 3600 BC (Figure 3.2).

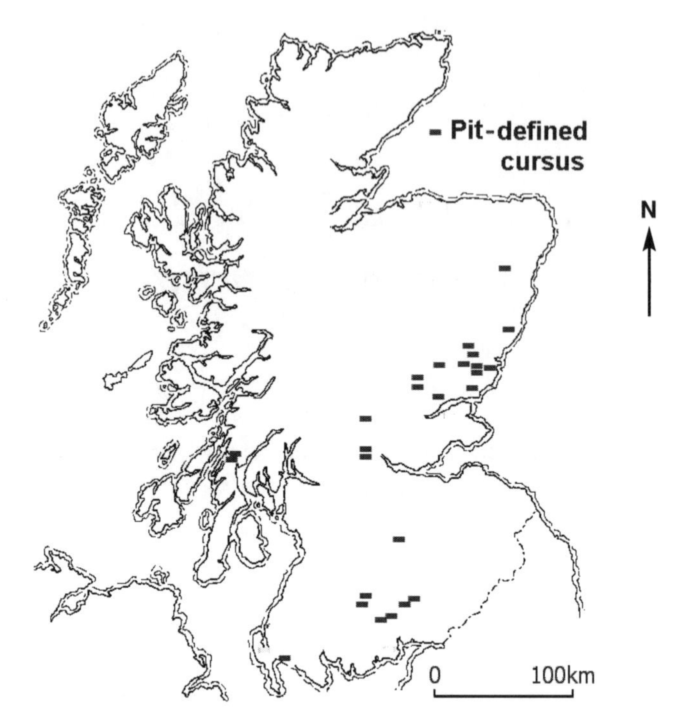

FIGURE 3.1 *The distribution of pit-defined cursus monuments in Scotland (Source: Brophy 1999a: figure 11.1)*

THE BURNING OF ENCLOSURES

Recently, Julian Thomas has highlighted the burning of a number of Neolithic timber monuments in the southwest of Scotland (Thomas 2000). At Holywood North, timber posts revetted a bank that had been made inside a substantial ditch (Thomas 2000: 81) (Figure 3.3). Soon after completion the posts of the enclosure were set alight and the structure burnt. The firing resulted in the complete destruction of the monument. Burnt posts were also found inside the nearby cursus at Holywood North (Thomas 1999c: 113). At Holm Farm, a series of alignments of posts were also burnt down (Thomas 2000: 86). Here at least eight phases of post erection and destruction were detected. The same basic structure seems to have been built and used on each occasion and each was probably destroyed soon after use.

The burning of timber structures in the Neolithic is not a practice restricted to this region or even to Scotland, but is part of a much wider phenomenon. In Scotland many of the excavated Earlier Neolithic post-built structures seem to have been burnt down. At Kirkburn, Lockerbie, two large trenches which held oak stake and post structures were burnt down (Cormack 1962–3) (Figure 3.4). Traces of cremated bone were found in one of these structures. At Claish Farm, Stirling, a massive timber building was also burnt down on at least one occasion (Barclay et al. 2002) (Figure 3.5). Traces of intense burning were found in many of the post-pipes of the building, the burning having penetrated to the very bases of the posts in some instances. Most of

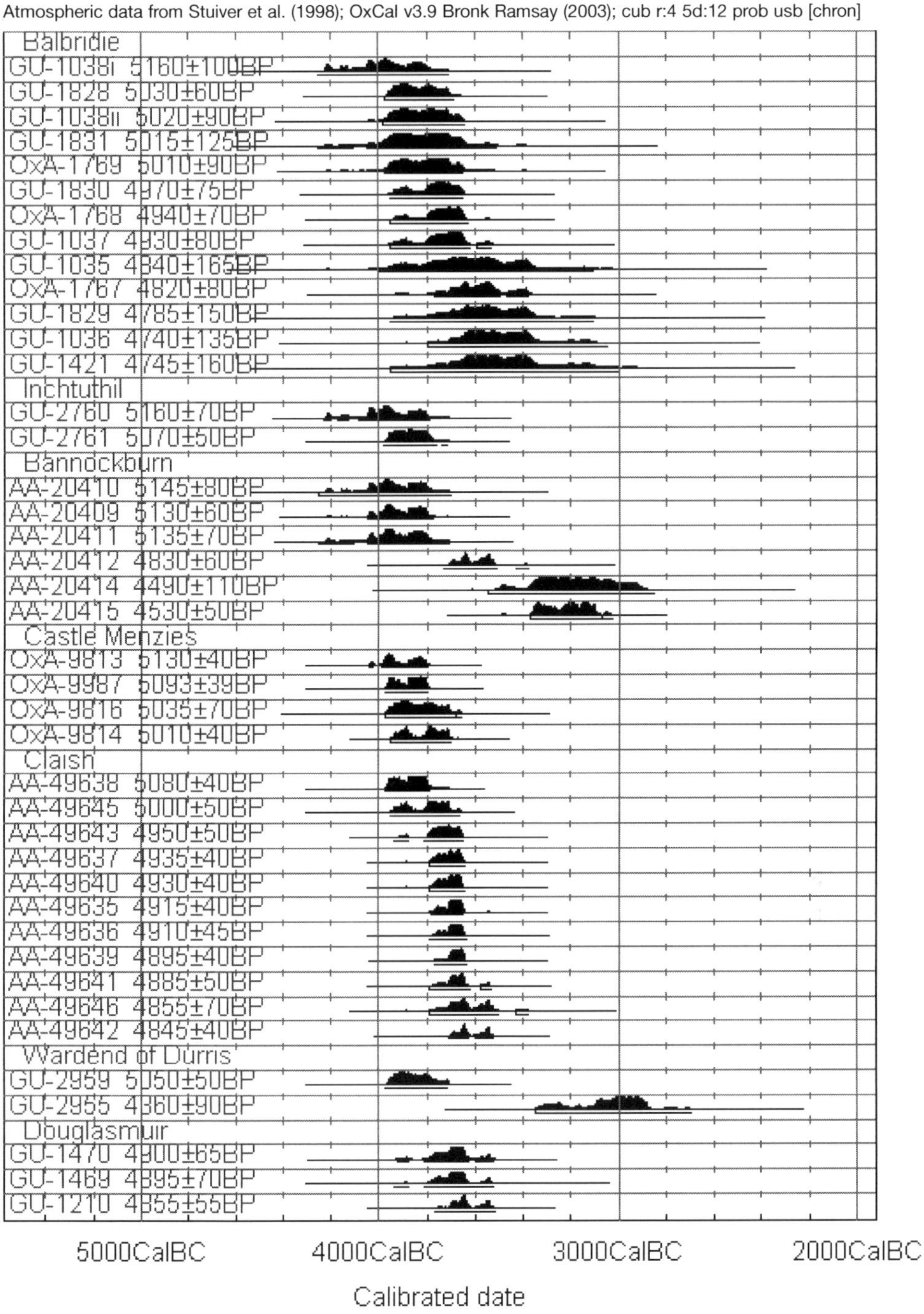

FIGURE 3.2 *The radiocarbon dates for timber structures in lowland Scotland. These cluster around the centuries at the beginning of the fourth millennium*

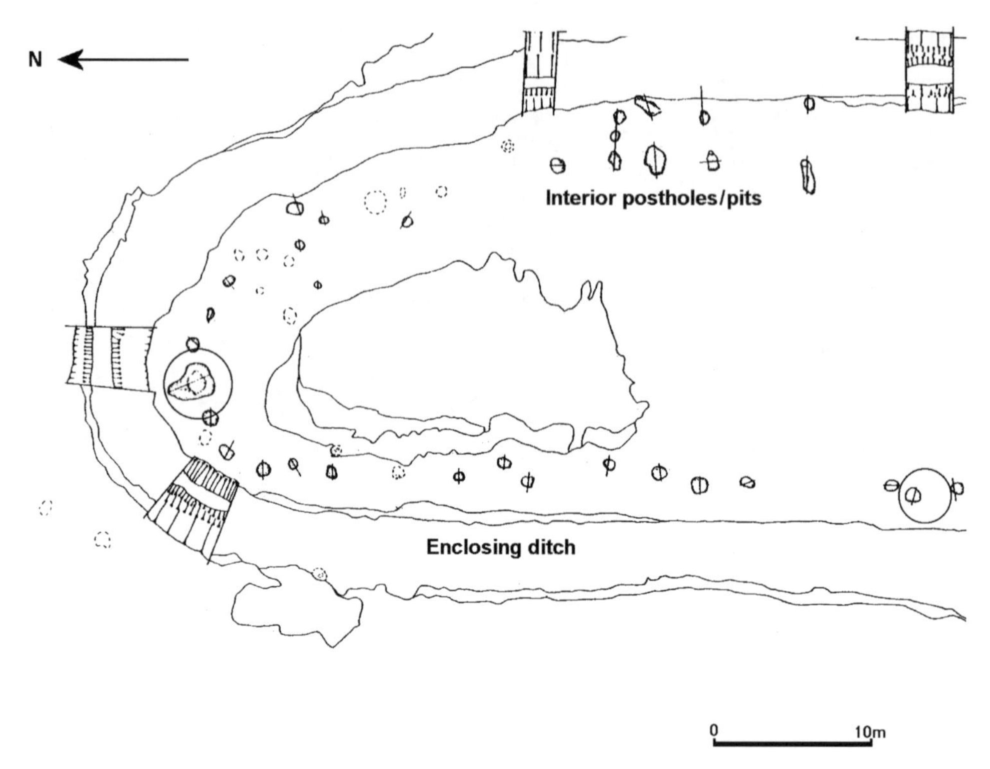

FIGURE 3.3 *The enclosure at Holywood North. A ditch and a setting of posts defined this site. Circles enclose some of the features that were probably earlier than the enclosure (Source: Thomas 1999c: figure 10.1)*

the postholes indicated two phases of burning, suggesting the structure was burnt, rebuilt or repaired and burnt again. The intensity of the burning seems to indicate that the structure was a roofed building, the roofing and walling providing fuel for the fire (Barclay et al. 2002: 98). The posts of the building were all made of oak (Miller and Ramsay 2002: 95). At Balbridie, Aberdeenshire, a very similar building to that at Claish was also burnt down. Like Claish, Balbridie has also been interpreted as a timber hall of massive proportions (Ralston 1982: 239) (see Figure 3.5). The contents of the hall were also burnt, preserving an assemblage of over 20,000 cereal grains (Fairweather and Ralston 1993). Like Claish, the main part of the Balbridie structure was built from squared oak timbers or beams (Ralston 1982: 240). Planking may have joined the timber uprights. The walls could have been around 2 metres high with a central ridge beam over 8 metres high, creating an enormous roofed space carefully divided by a series of screens (Ralston 1982: 243).

At Inchtuthil, Perthshire, the second phase of a Neolithic enclosure was also burnt (Barclay and Maxwell 1991) (Figure 3.6). The first phase of construction on the site involved the erection of a rectangular enclosure around 50 metres long defined by a timber fence, with a small entrance in the southeast corner. This was allowed to decay *in situ* or was later removed. A second fence of similar form, made of oak, was then

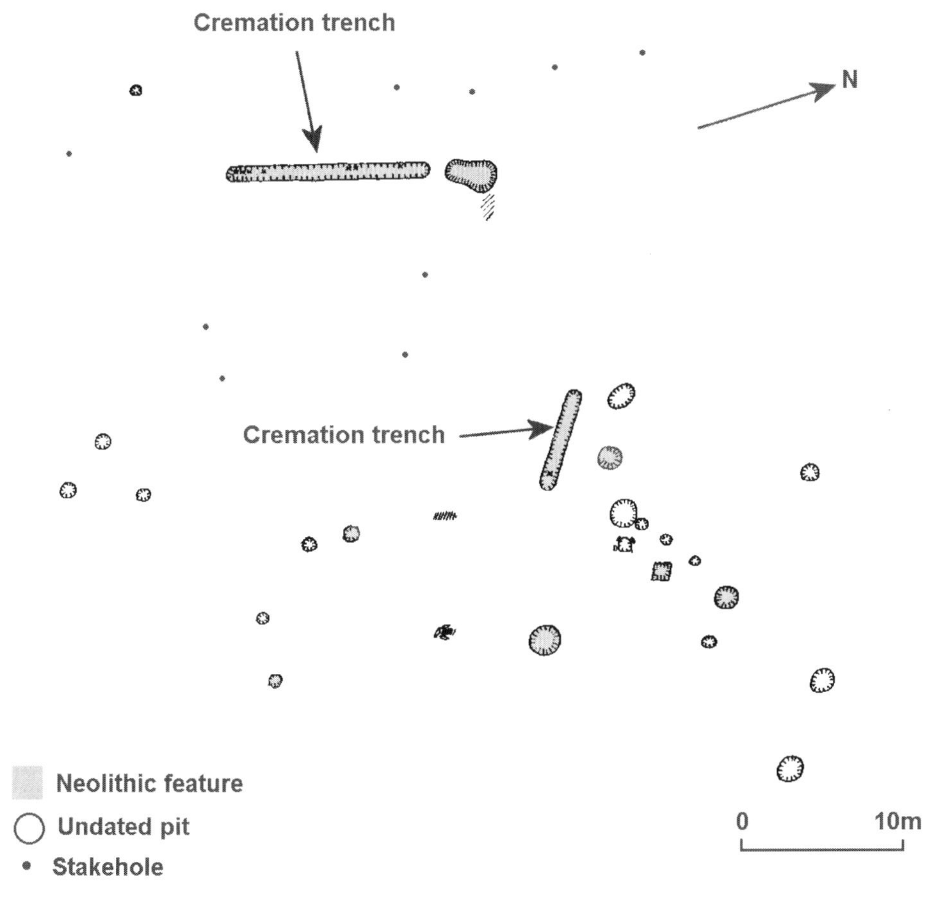

Figure 3.4 *Kirkburn, Lockerbie*
(Source: Cormack 1962–3: figure 3)

erected in the same bedding trench (Mills 1991: 37). Once built, the second fenced enclosure was burnt and soil was thrown on the timbers as they burnt (Barclay and Maxwell 1991: 33). The intensity of the burning was great and the surrounding soils were burnt a bright orange/red and the burning penetrated to the very bases of the posts.

At Cowie Road, Bannockburn, Stirling, two further Neolithic enclosures have been excavated which may have been burnt (Rideout 1997) (Figure 3.7). Some of the multiple phases of use of the pits of the enclosures included the *in situ* burning of oak timber in the lower levels of the pits (Cressey 1995: 51). The excavator, Rideout, argued that there was no clear evidence that the pits held posts, however it is clear that the burning of oak timber was a significant part of the activities carried out at the enclosure, whatever the exact nature of the structure (Cressey 1995: 51; Rideout 1997: 52, 56). At Douglasmuir in Angus another Neolithic enclosure, measuring 65 by 20 metres, was also destroyed by fire (Kendrick 1995) (Figure 3.8). Here, timber posts (0.5 to 1 metre diameter) defined a rectangular, unroofed enclosure that was divided

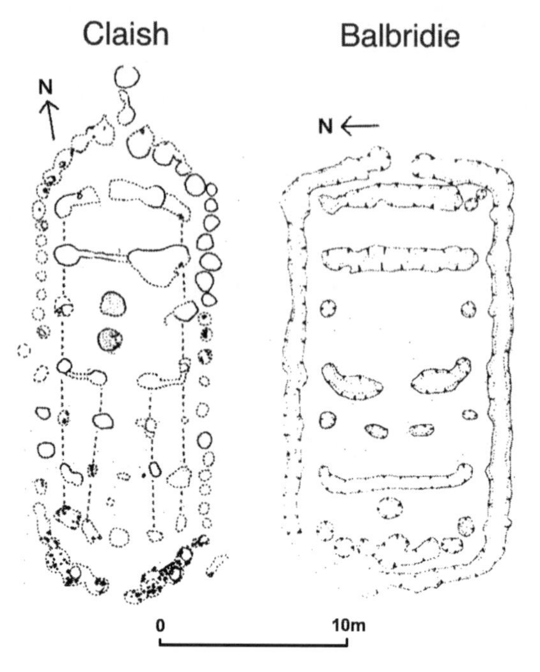

FIGURE 3.5 *The timber halls at Balbridie and Claish (Source: Barclay 2003: figure 8.3)*

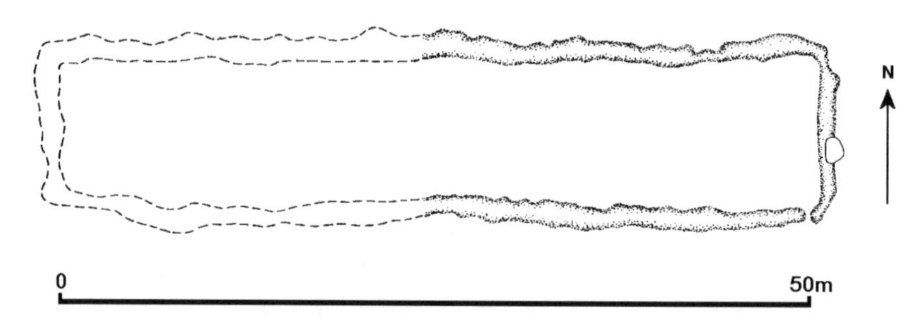

FIGURE 3.6 *The enclosure at Inchtuthil. The interior space was enclosed by a timber fence, set into the surrounding ditch*
(Source: Barclay and Maxwell 1991: figure 7)

into two sections by a transverse line of posts. Many of the perimeter posts, which were made of mature oak, had been burnt *in situ.*

One of the few exceptions to the burning of Earlier Neolithic enclosures is Castle Menzies, near Aberfeldy in Perthshire, where a sub-rectangular enclosure made of many hundreds of timber posts was erected in the Earlier Neolithic (Halliday 2002). There is little evidence that this structure was burnt, however the small amount of charcoal found was of oak, like the structures outlined above. The burning of timber structures became less common in the Later Neolithic – enclosures at Balfarg, Littleour and Carsie Mains, built a number of centuries later were not burnt (Barclay

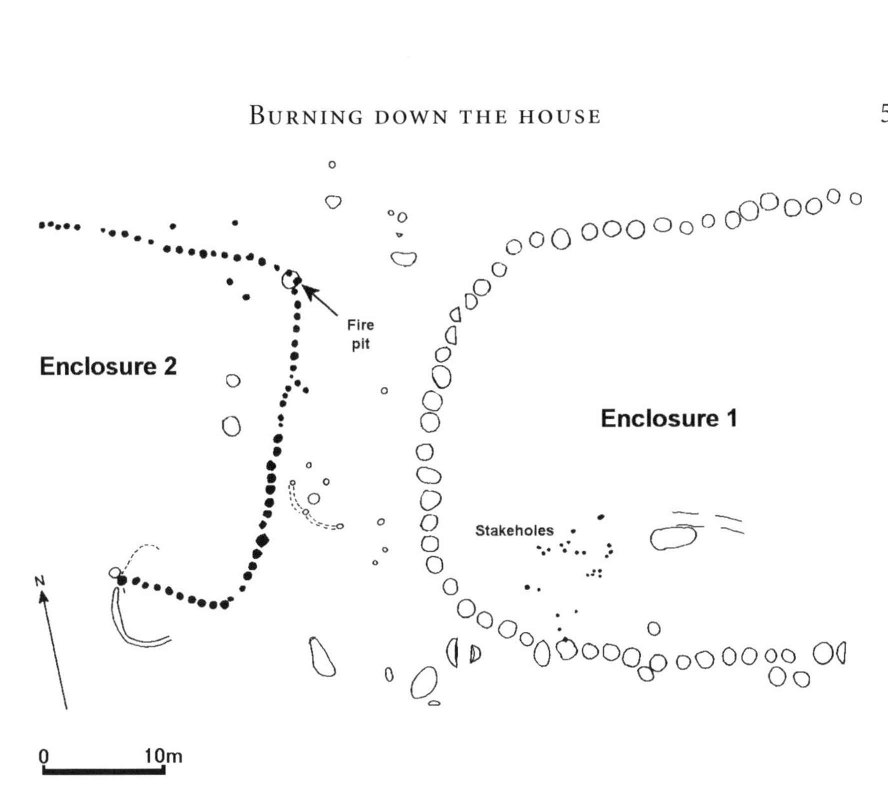

FIGURE 3.7 *The enclosures at Bannockburn. These too were defined by posts and were also burned down. Features outwith the enclosures probably belong to the earlier settlement phase (Source: Rideout 1997: figure 4)*

and Maxwell 1998; Barclay and Russell-White 1993; Barclay and Brophy 2004) (see Chapter 6). It would seem that the practice of burning was particularly prevalent in the first few centuries of the Earlier Neolithic.

BURNING DOWN THE HOUSE IN IRELAND

The practice of burning oak buildings extended outside of Scotland too. Many timber structures, interpreted as Earlier Neolithic dwellings in Ireland, also show evidence for major episodes of burning when excavated (Armit et al. 2003). Like the larger-scale, less obviously domestic structures in Scotland outlined above, these also seem to have been burnt down. At Coolfore, for example, one of two rectangular houses, excavated in advance of motorway construction, had extensive evidence for destruction by fire (O'Drisceoil 2003). The houses were set within a dense area of archaeological features that included a cobbled activity area, three external hearths and twenty-seven pits. One house appears never to have been completed as only fragments of bedding trenches, which were filled with occupation debris, were found. House 2 was rectangular (6 by 5.1 metres), aligned east to west and defined by slot trenches which held timber uprights (Figure 3.9). The slot trenches had held radially split oak planks that had been burnt *in situ*.

At Cloghers in County Kerry another structure, also interpreted as a domestic dwelling, was burnt (Kiely 2003) (Figure 3.10). The rectangular house (13 by 7.8

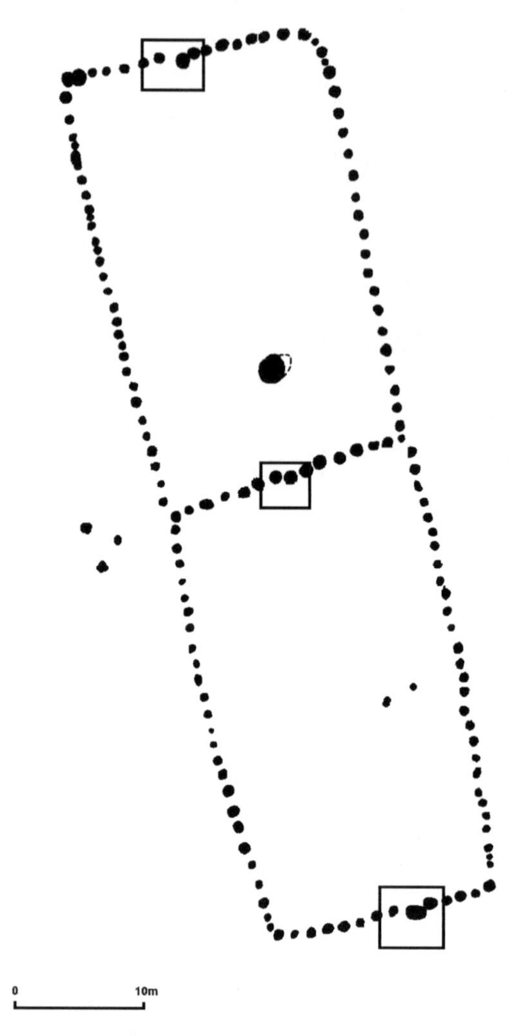

FIGURE 3.8 *Douglasmuir. The possible entranceways are marked by rectangles. The pits outside the lines of the main enclosure are the possible settlement remains (Source: Kendrick 1995: figure 2)*

metres), aligned east to west, was made of oak planks and stakes. The north wall of the structure had been burnt *in situ* and the fire brought settlement at the location to an end. The house and its contents too seem to have been burnt, as a prolific assemblage of artefacts was found inside, including pottery, stone tools and a polished stone axe. Cereal grains and the bones of domesticated cattle and sheep were also recovered. In County Derry a further Neolithic house (6.2 by 4.3 metres), was found to have traces of burning (McSparron 2003) (Figure 3.11). The site was only partially excavated, but circular concentrations of charcoal in the construction slot of the rectangular structure suggests that the oak posts of this building were also burnt down (McSparron 2003: 174).

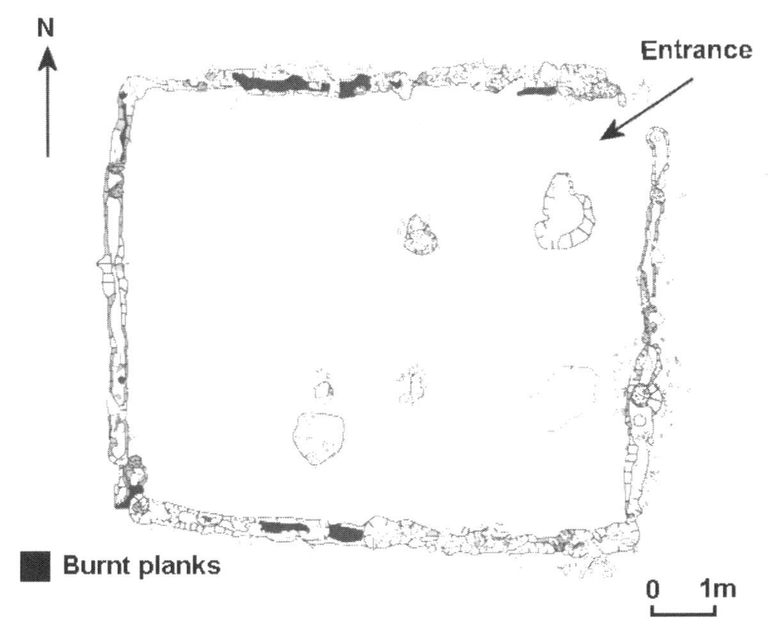

Figure 3.9 *House 2, Coolfore, Co. Louth (Source: O'Drisceoil 2003: figure 21.3)*

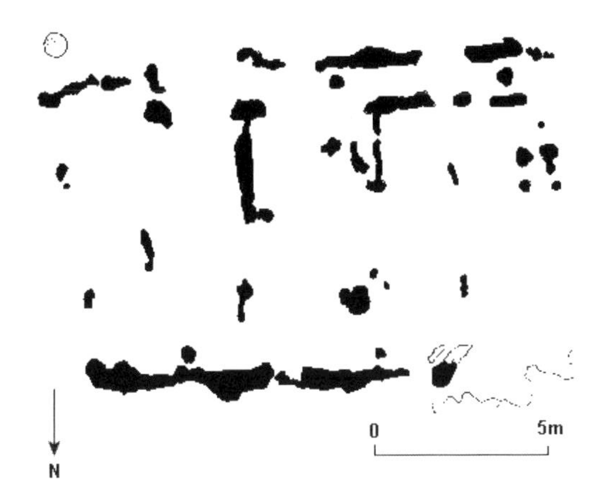

Figure 3.10 *The fragmentary remains at Cloghers, Co. Kerry (Source: Kiely 2003: figure 22.2)*

At Ballyharry, a series of Neolithic buildings found during excavations in advance of a pipeline demonstrate a complex sequence of construction and destruction (Moore 2003) (Figure 3.12). The first structure on the site was a sub-rectangular post-pit structure (13 by 6.5 metres) defined by a number of stone-packed postholes with an internal division. At some stage the posts of this structure were removed and the building was replaced by a smaller slot-trench structure of post and plank construction. The charred posts and planks of this house were clearly visible in the construction trench.

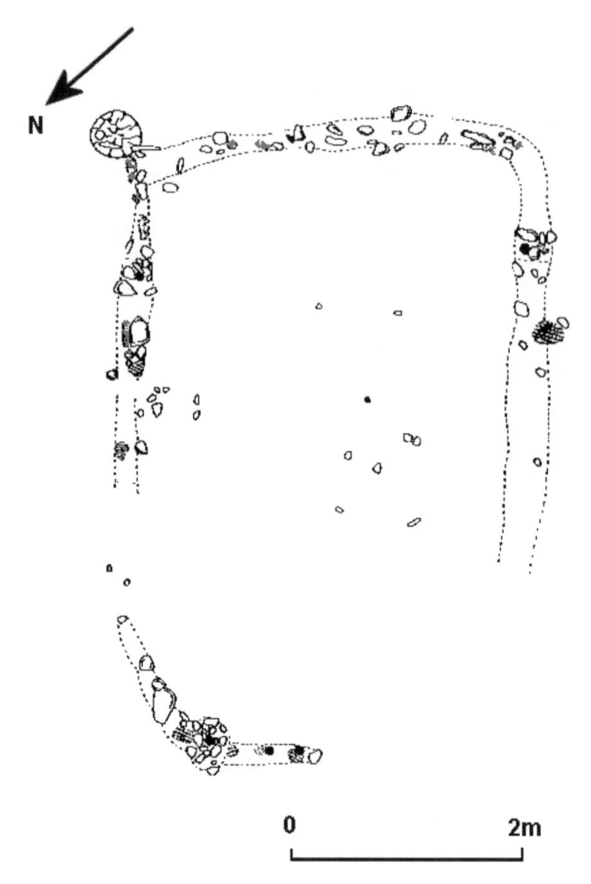

FIGURE 3.11 *The Neolithic house at Enagh Townland, Co. Derry*
(Source: McSparron 2003: figure 20.1)

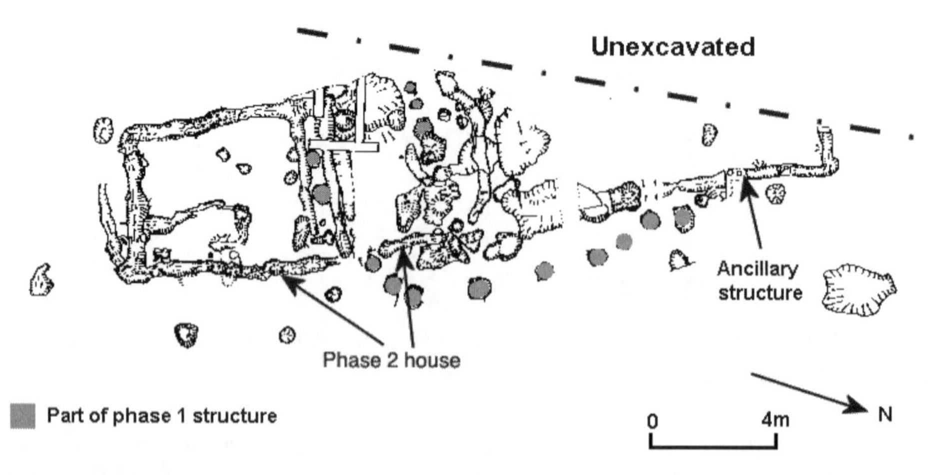

FIGURE 3.12 *The two buildings at Ballyharry, Co. Antrim. Elements of the earlier building are marked in grey*
(Source: Moore 2003: figure 18.2)

The excavator suggested that the house had been burnt as an act of aggression (Moore 2003: 157). However, burning is so common in Irish house-sites it may be that the destruction was more formal (O'Driscеoil 2003). The house was subsequently rebuilt and extended, and at a later date the posts were removed, perhaps to be used in the construction of another house nearby (Moore 2003: 159, 161). The activity at this site was intense and long-term: thousands of sherds of Earlier Neolithic pottery were found along with a large number of stone tools and domesticated resources.

Structures other than houses were also burnt. A rectangular structure found near a court tomb in County Donegal was also destroyed by fire (Dunne 2003) (Figure 3.13). This building was unlikely to have been domestic as it was set on a steep incline; it may instead have been associated with activities carried out at the nearby court tomb as a cremation pyre was found a short distance to the southwest (Dunne 2003: 170). One of the multiple palisades at Thornhill, County Londonderry, surrounding a number of Neolithic buildings was also burnt in the Earlier Neolithic (McSparron 2003; Moore 2003; Logue 2003: 154–5).

These Irish Neolithic houses are amongst the few published in detail, but are representative of a wider phenomenon. Recent contract archaeology has uncovered yet more burnt houses (Richard Bradley pers.comm.). The burning of oak structures also occurred in England. For example, some of the timber structures under the long

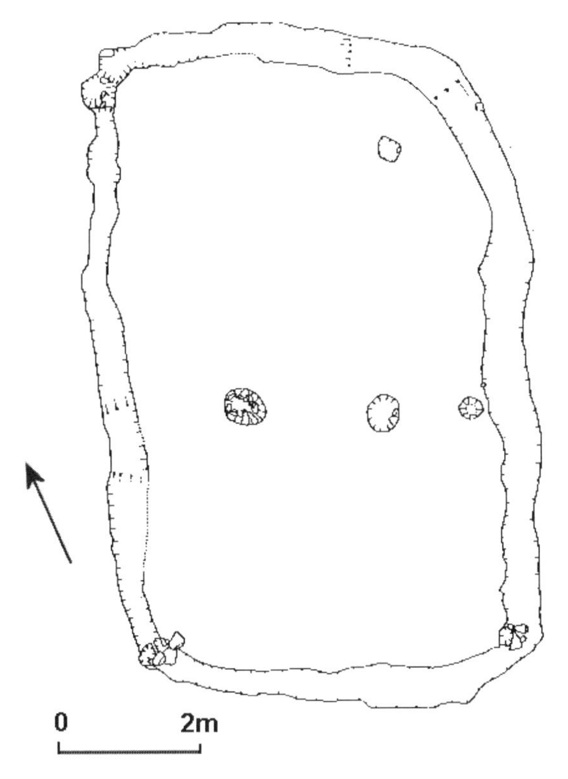

FIGURE 3.13 *The structure at Drummenny Lower, Co. Donegal (Source: Dunne 2003: figure 19.2)*

barrow at Nutbane, Hampshire, were burnt down (Morgan 1959) and at Street House, Cleveland, a mortuary structure defined by massive posts was burnt with at least five human bodies inside, along with an elaborate timber façade (Vyner 1984). Many other pre-mound structures at long barrows in northern England also seem to have been burnt, often as part of the cremation of human bodies (Manby 1970). The burning of timber sites in the Neolithic also extends to much simpler and smaller-scale structures in England; at Hertfordshire, near Saint Albans, a human body was cremated inside the hollowed trunk of an oak tree (Niblett 2001).

What is remarkable about these structures is that they all belong to the first few centuries of the fourth millennium BC, the period generally accepted as marking the beginning of the Neolithic in Britain and Ireland. Yet many of these structures are given different classifications by archaeologists despite the similarities in the treatment of these structures. Some are classified as cursus monuments, such as Holywood North and South, others as mortuary enclosures (Inchtuthil) or houses (the Irish examples), or timber halls (Balbridie and Claish) along with a range of other classifications, yet all share very similar endings and were built within a matter of generations of one another. Was the burning of all these different types of structure deliberate?

THE MECHANICS OF BURNING: ACCIDENTAL OR DELIBERATE?

The difficulty in burning down timber structures should not be underestimated. This matter has been examined in detail on southeast European Neolithic sites where much slighter timber and daub houses were burnt down (Stevanović 1997; Tringham 1991). Stevanović, in a detailed study, found that the burning of the houses was almost certainly deliberate as the temperatures that seem to have been involved indicated that some sort of fuel must have been provided to help the houses burn (Stevanović 1997). Fire always burns upwards and total burning of a timber structure, as seen at many of these sites, is unlikely to occur unless fuel is constantly replenished (Stevanović, 1997: 376; Vyner, 1984: 156). Stevanović cites the example of a substantial experimental long house that was accidentally set on fire by sparks from the hearth. The walls of the long house were not substantially damaged and the burning would not have been detectable archaeologically. In Ireland the roofing and planking material of the houses may have provided some of the fuel for a fire, but in structures such as the massive unroofed timber enclosures in Scotland it is unlikely that accidental lighting would have led to such catastrophic burning. In the long barrow structures in England, brushwood fuel must have been added to help burn the structures. Vyner (1984: 156), for example, proposed that large quantities of brushwood would have been needed to burn the façade of the Streethouse timber structures as these seem to have been free-standing posts with little indication of planking or wattling needed to provide fuel for the fire. Morgan too (1959: 34) highlighted the need for brushwood, especially in light of the fact that many of the posts burnt so well that they continued to burn below ground. This is true of many of the Scottish enclosures, where the reason we know they were burnt at all is due to the fact that the timbers burnt to the very bases of the foundation trenches and stone packing and post bases were substantially affected by heat. At Inchtuthil, the fire was so hot the subsoil around the posts was burnt a bright orange/red. The fact that many buildings and structures were subject to repeated burnings shows the deliberate nature of this practice. At Holm Farm, for example, there were potentially eight different burning incidents (Thomas 2000: 86).

One of the distinctive aspects of the burning of these timber structures is the type of timber used. Every structure outlined above was made of oak. Oak is one of the most resistant species of wood to decay, if not the most resistant (Cartwright and Findlay 1958: 275). Oak trees themselves are one of the longest-living species in British woodlands, potentially lasting in favourable conditions over 400 years (White 1995: 129). Given this, it seems all the more paradoxical that the lives of the Neolithic structures were ended artificially by fire. Again it seems to point to the deliberate nature of these burnings: at least some of the timbers of these structures could have been recycled given their resistance to decay.

Gone in a flash: ritual, drama and memory

Given the need for fuel and the extent to which these structures burnt it is clear that their burning would have needed people in attendance to gather and place fuel and to stoke the fire to ensure the burning continued. In many cases people tended to the fires until almost every last trace of the structure was burnt. At some sites people returned to re-enact the burning episode. Given the deliberate nature of the burnings it is clear that these events would have been spectacular. Especially so if performed at night (Bradley 2005; Svensson 2002). Also, given the size of some of these sites, for example the large Scottish enclosures, it is clear that very large numbers of people may have been involved in the firing episode. These events may have lasted for some time, given the evidence for the extent to which these structures were burnt. An element of danger would also have been involved. At Inchtuthil part of the fenced enclosure fell inwards, and at the Irish houses and the roofed mortuary structures such as Nutbane the potential for accidents involving falling burning timbers must have been great. The element of danger would have added to the drama of the event.

All this points to deliberate and dramatic ritualised motivations for the burning of these enclosures. Ceremonial activity is dependent upon a sense of drama and involves actions as well as words, often using media such as song and dance to provide participants with an *intense experience* (Tambiah 1979: 114). Ritual performances often use stereotyped sequences of events and formality and repetition are common aspects of ritual practice (Bell 1992: 92; George 1991: 17; Tambiah 1979: 115). The deliberate burning of timber structures would certainly form part of an intense experience, perhaps heightened by a sense of danger and augmented by the visceral quality involved in the act of burning. This act was also often repeated.

Stevanović, in southern Europe, and in this country, Thomas, have linked the deliberate burning of structures with the creation of memories. Stevanović has linked the transformative nature of fire with ways of remembering a place, people or events

(Stevanović 1997: 388). In southwest Scotland, Julian Thomas, drawing on work by Küchler, has suggested that the destruction of monuments was a way of inserting a place into tradition (Thomas 2000). The physical structure of the timber enclosures in Scotland would not in themselves prolong memory. Memory is sustained through the actions and performances held at monuments; the physical structures often serve merely as backdrops to ritual (Argenti 1999; Connerton 1989; Forty and Küchler 1999: 7). However, the destruction of these buildings would be a very effective means of remembering, as it could form part of a dramatic performance that would aid the retention of memories associated with both the events surrounding the monument's construction and its subsequent use and destruction (Küchler 1987, 1999: 64). The burning of these enclosures would have been a highly dramatic event, requiring great investment in time and resources. In this way it would have formed an important event in the history of the participating community. The creation of memory may have been aided by a phenomenon known as 'flashbulb memory' where people have particularly clear recollections of the circumstances associated with a dramatic event (Küchler 1987; Williams 2003). Memory can be very unreliable unless particular cues are in place to aid remembrance; memories are never exact replicas of external reality and all memories are subject to significant distortion (Schacter 1995). Flashbulb memories are, in contrast, subject to much less distortion. While not exact copies of the original events, flashbulb memories are associated with a high level of recall *clarity* and *vividness* (Brewer 1995: 49; Groeger 1997: 216; Schacter 1995: 25). Moreover, flashbulb memories are commonly linked with events that allow the identities and memories of individuals to be linked with external historical events that often form part of collective memory (Groeger 1997: 220). Flashbulb memories are often associated with accidental or incidental events beyond the control of the viewer, however in the case of the burning of the timber enclosures, these were highly orchestrated and organised actions that were undoubtedly deliberately designed to be memorable and spectacular.

LOWLAND SCOTLAND AND DOMESTICITY

The immensity of the timber structures built in Scotland can be contrasted with many of the traces of settlement that have been excavated in lowland Scotland. To date, few definite domestic buildings like those found in Ireland have been found in lowland Scotland. Settlement often involved the digging of pits or the erection of timber structures, but these were often much slighter than any of the structures highlighted above. The evidence from lowland Scotland suggests that a large degree of settlement mobility was involved in Neolithic life. As Alexander has recently noted:

> The Neolithic settlement record consists mainly of artefact scatters, post-holes, pits and stake-holes representing camp sites of varying duration which may have been visited repeatedly. It is probable that domestic structures on such sites were of light construction, possibly even tents, and have left almost no trace. (Alexander 2000: 65)

The degree to which settlement in the lowland Neolithic remained mobile is debatable, indeed the timber halls themselves have at times been interpreted as normal domestic structures (Rowley-Conwy 2002). However, as the excavators of Claish noted, 'Balbridies and Claishes are really rather rare' (Barclay et al. 2002: 120). Including unexcavated and undated examples identified in cropmarks, structures of this kind can be counted on one hand. The buildings are much larger than the structures identified in Ireland as houses, in the region of four times as big, and the term 'hall' is likely to be quite appropriate (Barclay et al. 2002: 132). Balbridie and Claish also have much in common with structures interpreted as mortuary or ritual structures, sharing a 'vocabulary of architecture' and similar life histories (Barclay et al. 2002: 124). It seems hard to argue, even if we were to suggest that Balbridie-type structures were purely domestic buildings, that they were the settlement norm in the Neolithic of lowland Scotland. Instead it seems more likely to suggest the scale of these structures indicate they were a building constructed to house large social gatherings of regional significance (Topping 1996).

Much more common settlement traces in Scotland seem to be represented by scatters of pits and ephemeral features. Occasionally some of these sites contain evidence for much smaller-scale, slighter rectangular, oval or circular dwellings, however these were rarely substantial buildings and could not have been maintained over a long period of time (Atkinson 2002: 184; Barclay et al. 2002: 120). The evidence suggests a large degree of mobility remained in the lifestyles of many Neolithic communities in lowland Scotland. For example, at Chapelfield Cowie, Stirling, two kilometres to the south of the Bannockburn enclosures, traces of light circular constructions seem to represent short-lived but repeated occupation in the Neolithic (Atkinson 2002) (Figure 3.14). Oval and circular stake-built structures found in association with pits seem to represent a series of occupations throughout the Neolithic. The structures were defined by stakes enclosing an area of around 3 to 4 by 2 to 3 metres. There were a series of structures at this site, but it is likely that only one or two ever stood at one time as some were overlain by others (Atkinson 2002: 134). Associated with these structures were a number of large pits, one of which contained hearth-like material, others domestic debris (Alldritt 2002). Some of the pits had been recut, but over a very short period of time (Atkinson 2002: 186). The remains at Chapelfield would seem to represent the periodic revisiting of a site for settlement over a period of years with significant gaps (perhaps decades or even centuries) between visits.

Similar stake-defined structures have also been found at Beckton Farm, Lockerbie (Pollard 1997). One structure was associated with a central hearth and the remaining floor deposits contained Earlier Neolithic pottery (Atkinson 1997: 184; Pollard 1997: 77). Nearby were two Later Neolithic structures associated with Grooved Ware. A range of other features including stakeholes, hearths and fire-pits and four-post structures were found in the vicinity of the structures. Like Chapelfield, these structures seem to represent the repeated but short-lived occupation of the area throughout the Neolithic period (Pollard 1997). An even more ephemeral structure has been found at Lamb's Nursery, Midlothian (Cook 2000) (Figure 3.15). This consisted of an arcing slot set around a posthole, which may be the remnants of a circular structure

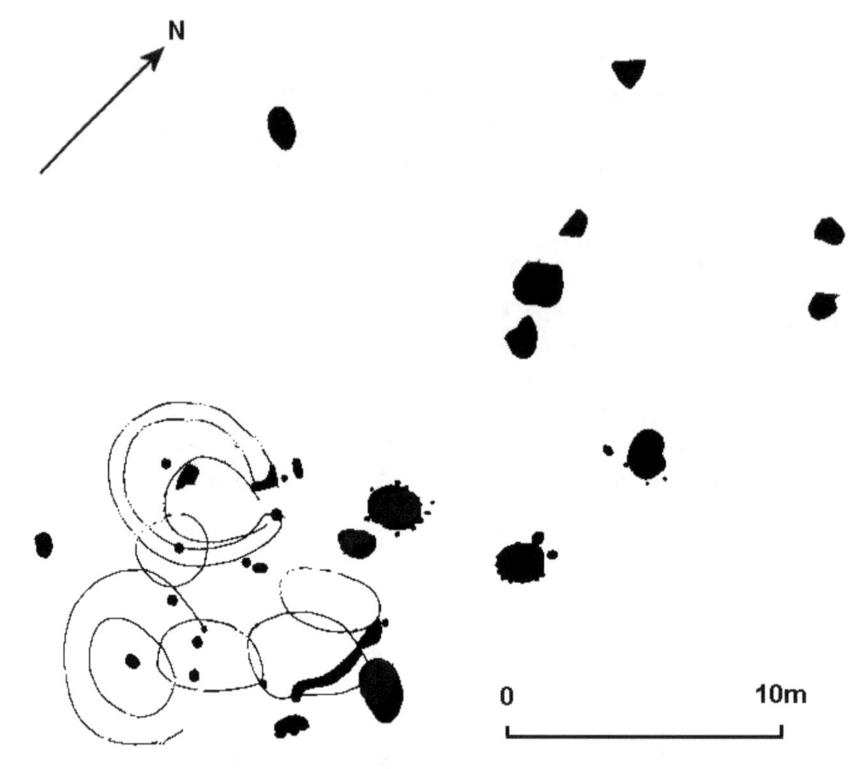

FIGURE 3.14 *Chapelfield Cowie. A series of stake-built structures was constructed amongst a series of pits. The two larger structures with entrances are similar to those at Beckton Farm, Lockerbie (Source: Atkinson 2002: figure 2)*

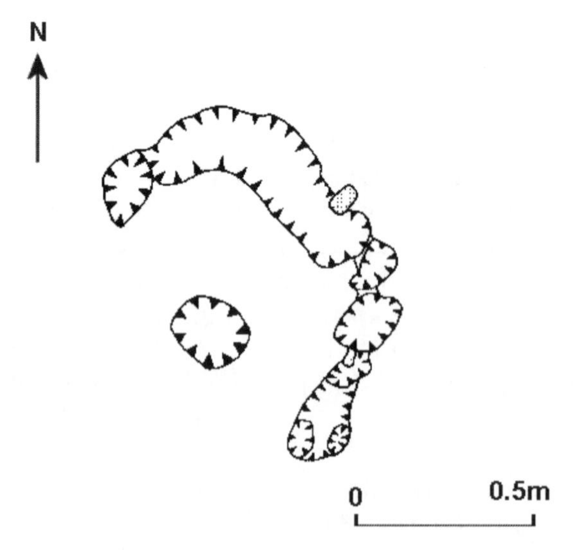

FIGURE 3.15 *Lamb's Nursery Structure A (Source: Cook 2000: figure 3)*

or a windbreak (Cook 2000: 108). This structure was also associated with pits and other dug features.

This is not to suggest that there were no substantial Earlier Neolithic houses in the lowlands. A larger building may have been present at Biggar Common, South Lanarkshire (Johnston 1997). Numerous stakeholes and postholes have been found here, which may have formed a bow-ended structure. However, the suggested walls are represented by a disparate set of features of varying sizes, which may cast doubt on the nature of this structure. Over 1,300 sherds of Earlier Neolithic pottery and a large number of stone tools were found in association with the features, which does suggest some permanency to the occupation here. A series of Earlier Neolithic pits at Deer's Den, Aberdeenshire, could also have formed a larger domestic structure (Alexander 2000). An 'elongated cluster' of pits gives the impression of a structure in plan, but few, if any, of the pits had evidence for having held timber uprights (Figure 3.16). The pits may have simply defined an area of activity. Like the site at Biggar Common, unusually large amounts of Neolithic pottery and lithics were recovered here, but the radiocarbon dates from the site suggest a single phase of activity. At Ratho, near Edinburgh, three pits, containing Earlier Neolithic pottery, were found in association with two rectangular timber structures (Smith 1995). However, these structures are undated and had no internal features suggesting their function. The three pits, probably dated from a single period of activity as at least two of the pits shared pottery sherds from the same vessel.

One of the few reasonably coherent buildings, that could just qualify as being in lowland Scotland, is at Kinbeachie Farm on the Black Isle in Ross-shire (Barclay et al. 2001) (Figure 3.17). A series of plough-truncated features seems to represent a rectangular building around 7 by 4 metres, similar to some of the smaller Irish

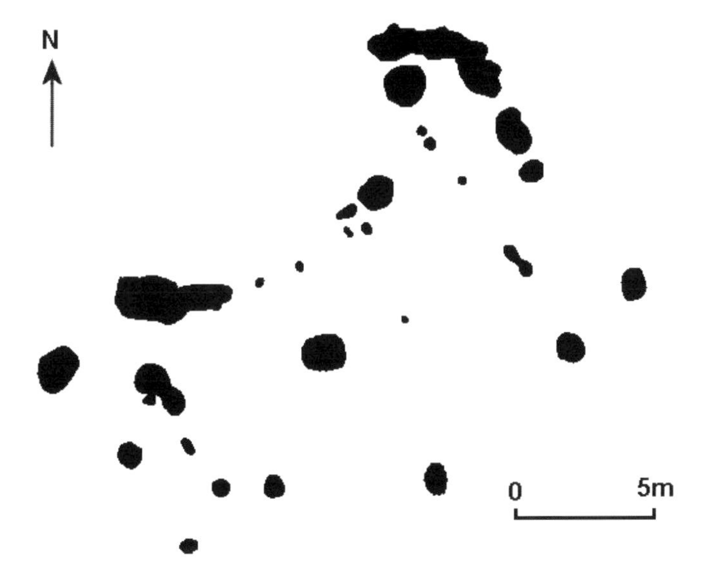

FIGURE 3.16 *Deer's Den, Aberdeenshire (Source: Alexander 2003: figure 5)*

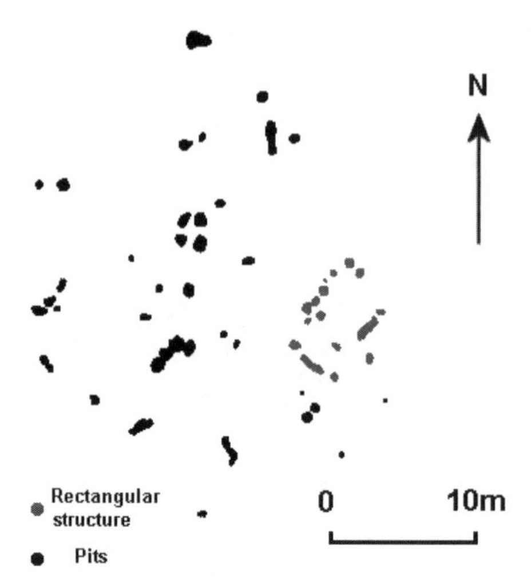

FIGURE 3.17 *Kinbeachie Farm. The rectangular structure is highlighted in grey (Source: Barclay et al. 2001: figure 2)*

domestic structures. However, despite the presence of a substantial building the site was not thought to represent prolonged use. There were few inter-cutting pits and the finds showed little evidence of extended use (Barclay et al. 2001: 74). The structure was associated with a small amount of Impressed Ware pottery, some carbonised cereals and a small number of stone tools. However, finds were generally sparse.

Scatters of pits of varying numbers are more common finds than structural remains on Earlier Neolithic sites. These pit-group sites are regularly excavated and seem to form a consistent element in the Neolithic settlement record of lowland Scotland. For example, at Dubton Farm, Angus, the remains of settlement activity seemed to consist solely of a series of pit groupings (Cameron 2002). Seven groupings of Neolithic pits were found in four different areas across an extensive site. Some of the pits had evidence for *in situ* burning and there was a distinctive group of eight massive pits, some measuring up to 4 metres in diameter, which may have been associated with crop processing (Cameron 2002: 69; Church 2002). The pit groups contained Earlier Neolithic, Impressed Ware and Grooved Ware pottery suggesting intermittent activity over an extended period of time, much like the evidence for settlement at Chapelfield and Beckton. Pits also characterised the activity at Grandtully in Perthshire (Simpson and Coles 1990). Some of the pits shared sherds of pottery from the same Impressed Ware vessels, suggesting that at least some of the features belonged to a single phase of activity. A lack of weathering on the sides of the pits also indicated that they remained open for only a short period of time (Simpson and Coles 1990: 34). A smaller number of pits were found at Blairhall Burn, Dumfriesshire, where three pits or postholes contained Impressed Ware pottery and flakes from Cumbrian polished stone axes (Strachan et al. 1998) (Figure 3.18). Pit groups of varying sizes have also been found at Easterton of Rosisle, Spurryhillock, Brownsbank Farm and Brackmont Mill and many other sites (Alexander 1997; Barclay 2003; Coles

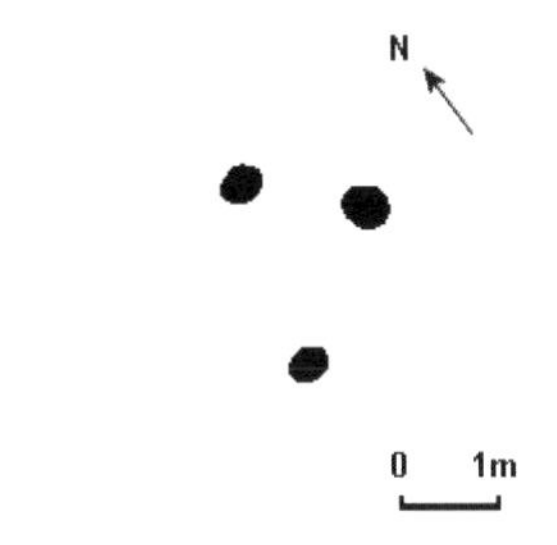

Figure 3.18 *The pits at Blairhall Burn (Source: Strachan et al. 1998: figure 6)*

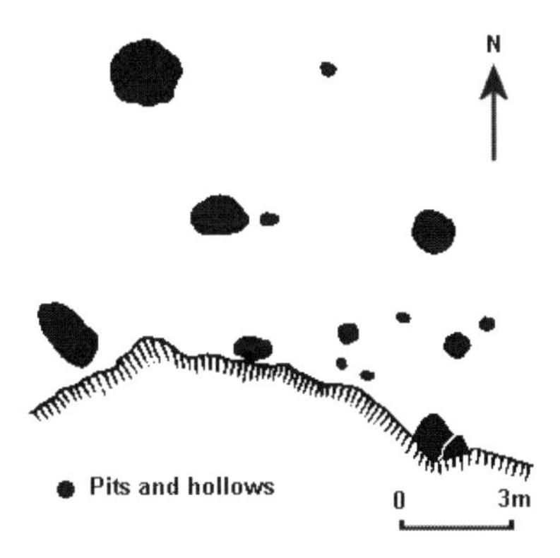

Figure 3.19 *The pits and hollows under Boghead mound (Source: Kinnes 1992b: figure 7.4)*

1966–7; Walker 1968; Ward 2000a). Possible settlement traces in lowland Scotland have also been found in more unusual contexts. For example, under a burial mound at Boghead in Moray, hollows and stakeholes, associated with Earlier Neolithic carinated bowl pottery and flint, have been found and interpreted as earlier settlement activity on a site that was to be later used for burial (Burl 1984) (Figure 3.19). The stakeholes and hollows may represent the remains of windbreaks and working areas of a series of short-lived occupations (Burl 1984). Earlier Neolithic pottery and lithics have also been found under the burial mound at East Finnercy (Lievers et al. 2000).

Despite what has been argued in the past, it is clear that Neolithic settlement in lowland Scotland retained a large degree of mobility (Barclay 1997; Rowley-Conwy 2004). The stake-built structures at Chapelfield cannot have been durable buildings: they can perhaps be compared to historically documented travellers' huts or tents or seasonally-used shielings huts in Scotland that were designed to be easily transportable (Ritchie 1997: 39, figures 4.1–4.4). The stake-built structures would not have lasted a significant length of time before they decayed. Even large-diameter oak stakes will only last a few years if set in the ground (Cartwright and Findlay 1958: 275) and there is little evidence for repair of these structures. Settlement was renewed at Chapelfield, but new huts were laid directly on top of older ones, suggesting that these had decayed sufficiently to allow the imposition of new ones on top. The remains at

Chapelfield would seem to represent the periodic revisiting of a site for settlement over a period of years with significant gaps between visits. The two latest structures on the site are comparable with the Later Neolithic structures at Beckton Farm, suggesting that there may have been a substantial break in occupation, perhaps centuries, between these final structures and the earliest ones (Atkinson 2002: 185). At Beckton the earliest structure was associated with Earlier Neolithic pottery and was even more ephemeral than the Chapelfield structures and the ones associated with Grooved Ware at Beckton. The site at Beckton suggests short-lived settlement in small hut or tent-like structures at widely separated points during the fourth millennium BC. The evidence from Lamb's Nursery also suggests intermittent occupation over a short period of time (Cook 2000: 109). Other sites consist simply of pits and other scattered features. The groups of pits at Dubton might suggest at least seven distinct phases of settlement activity on the site: each of these groups tended to be associated with a distinct assemblage of pottery, some with Earlier Neolithic carinated bowls, others with Impressed Ware (Herne 1988; Thomas 1999a: chapter 4, figures 5.1, 5.10). The larger pits in particular seem to be separated from the other groups by their size and the radiocarbon dates suggest these may be somewhat earlier than the other groups (Figure 3.20). These may have been used for crop processing, but other finds suggest the exploitation of upland and moorland zones some distance from the site location (Church 2002). Assemblages of lithics are generally poor on these sites. The artefact assemblages are much smaller than those associated with sites in the Northern Isles where substantial Neolithic architecture is much easier to identify (Barclay 1996, 2003; Sheridan and Sharples 1992). The small number of finds can also be contrasted with the often huge numbers of finds associated with the Irish house sites (Armit et al. 2003). This phenomenon might suggest, like the architecture itself, that settlement was shifting, transient and ephemeral. Many of the sites were found to contain some quantity of imported lithics indicating 'a familiarity with places (and people) beyond the immediate vicinity', again perhaps suggesting a relatively fluid settlement lifestyle (Cameron 2002: 69). Many of the lithic scatters found in lowland Scotland suggest short-term ephemeral activity as many are found to cover areas with only very slight and insubstantial features (Barclay and Wickham-Jones 2002). The most convincing examples of a more substantial building, other than the timber halls, is Kinbeachie. However, although a rectangular wooden house may have stood on the site, the evidence suggests that the settlement was not used for an extended period of time. Very few artefacts were found at Kinbeachie and the pits and finds suggests a single period of use (Barclay et al. 2001). Overall, the evidence from lowland eastern and southern Scotland suggests that settlement shifted on a regular basis. The excavated evidence is dominated by structures that could not have lasted for any significant period of time, while other sites suggest that settlement was renewed on a site periodically. Settlement shifts might have ranged from at the most generational shifts as at Kinbeachie, but may more commonly have been seasonal or annual shifts as represented by the more ephemeral structures at sites such as Beckton and Chapelfield. Even at Kinbeachie the number of features is small in comparison to Irish house sites and the time span of the settlement is unlikely to have reached the

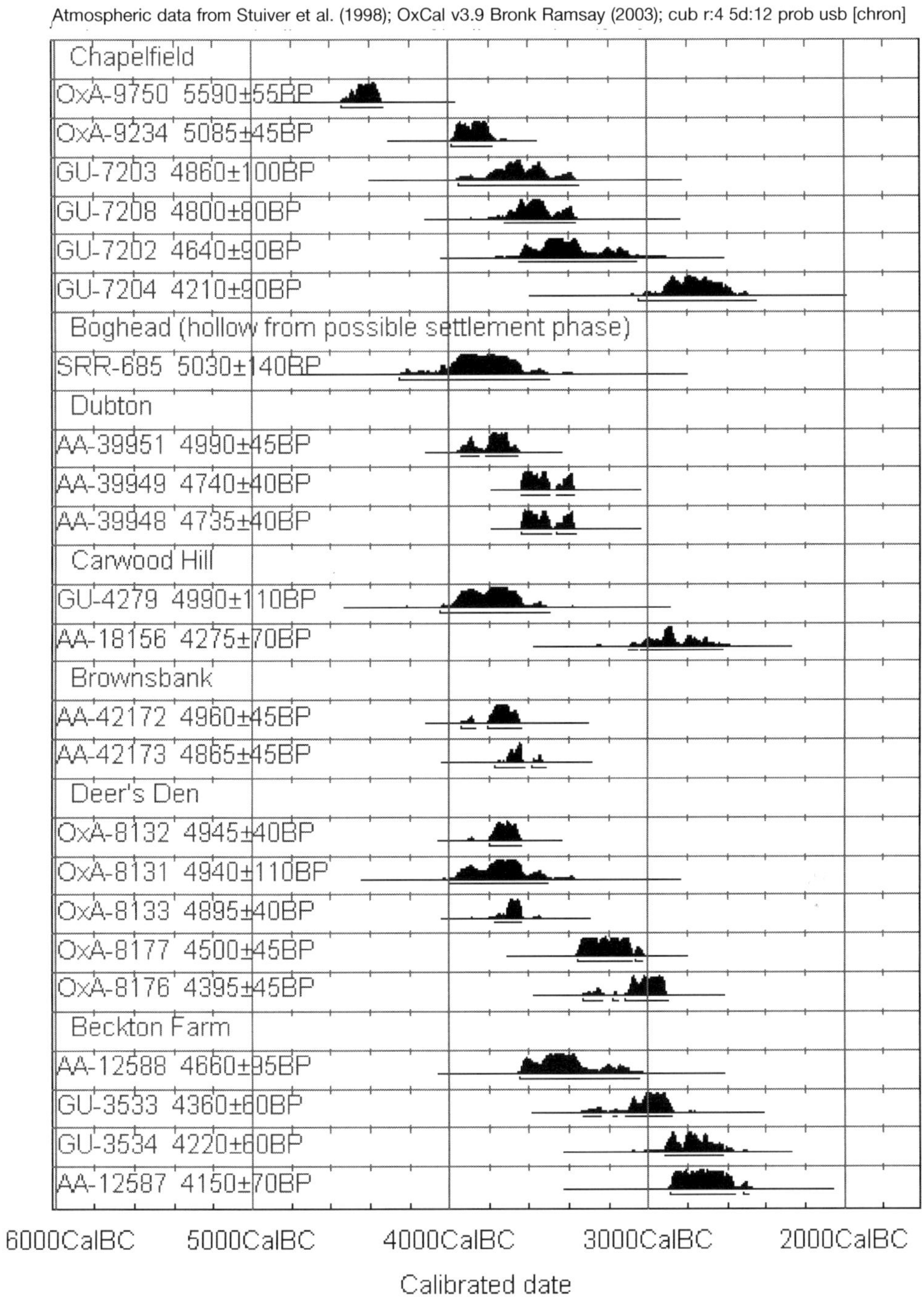

Atmospheric data from Stuiver et al. (1998); OxCal v3.9 Bronk Ramsay (2003); cub r:4 5d:12 prob usb [chron]

Chapelfield
OxA-9750 5590±55BP
OxA-9234 5085±45BP
GU-7203 4860±100BP
GU-7208 4800±80BP
GU-7202 4640±90BP
GU-7204 4210±90BP
Boghead (hollow from possible settlement phase)
SRR-685 5030±140BP
Dubton
AA-39951 4990±45BP
AA-39949 4740±40BP
AA-39948 4735±40BP
Carwood Hill
GU-4279 4990±110BP
AA-18156 4275±70BP
Brownsbank
AA-42172 4960±45BP
AA-42173 4865±45BP
Deer's Den
OxA-8132 4945±40BP
OxA-8131 4940±110BP
OxA-8133 4895±40BP
OxA-8177 4500±45BP
OxA-8176 4395±45BP
Beckton Farm
AA-12588 4660±95BP
GU-3533 4360±60BP
GU-3534 4220±60BP
AA-12587 4150±70BP

6000CalBC 5000CalBC 4000CalBC 3000CalBC 2000CalBC

Calibrated date

FIGURE 3.20 *Radiocarbon dates for Neolithic settlement sites in lowland Scotland*

length of a human generation. This form of settlement seems to characterise the entire duration of the Neolithic in lowland Scotland (see Figure 3.20).

While the differences between the massive oak enclosures and the ephemeral stake-built settlements and pit groups are marked, there is evidence that occasionally these different forms of activity were interrelated. There are examples of the large-scale oak enclosures being built over the former location of episodes of domestic activity. The most convincing example is at the two enclosures at Bannockburn (Rideout 1997). Here, a number of features found in the excavations of the site were not related to the enclosures themselves. These included stakeholes, other small features and larger and shallower pits (see Figure 3.7). Most of these features pre-dated the digging of the enclosure pits. For example, two of the postholes of the second timber enclosure cut what was termed a 'fire pit', which contained most of the pottery found on site (Cowie 1995: 44). As Cowie notes, the range of features that pre-date the enclosure resembles the remains found at other sites interpreted as settlement sites in Scotland and resembles many of the sites outlined above (Cowie 1995: 45). The fire pit may have been used for cooking food and, unlike the enclosure pits, this feature had been used to burn hazel timber and nutshells rather than oak (Cressey 1995: 51). Near to the enclosures an infilled palaeo-channel also contained evidence for occupation with midden-like deposits in the channel itself (Jordan 1995: 43–44). Almost no cultural material can be directly associated with the enclosures, instead it would seem that the enclosures were only built once earlier activity on the site had ceased (Cowie 1995: 45; Rideout 1997: 56). Rideout was cautious in attributing a domestic role to these earlier features, due in part to the later use of the site for the construction of monuments (Rideout 1997). However, we should not assume that there was a clear distinction between ritual and daily life in the Neolithic (Bradley 2003; Richards and Thomas 1984). Elements of domestic life often form the very basis for rituals and it is not unlikely that a former settlement area should be transformed into a monumental one. The pre-enclosure features at Bannockburn would undoubtedly be interpreted as domestic in origin in the absence of the monuments and there is no reason to doubt that the pits, stakeholes and other features derive from an episode of habitation. In this respect the pit and post enclosures at Bannockburn represented the transformation of a relatively ephemeral settlement location into something more substantial.

Excavations at enclosures in southwest Scotland have also shown that these sites were often placed on locations of earlier activity (Thomas 2000). Limited excavations at Holywood North have revealed a number of earlier pits and features bounded by the cursus ditch (Thomas 1999c: 110, 2000: 81) (see Figure 3.8, earlier features circled). One of these pits contained carinated bowl sherds, burnt hazelnut shells, bone charcoal and burnt stones. Another pit contained repeated dumps of burnt material and was located at the apex of the cursus terminal. Other potentially earlier features included a number of postholes, some of which may have formed a small structure, and the alignment of the cursus seems to have been modified in order to incorporate these features (Thomas 1999c: 110). Probable pre-monument pits were also found at Holywood South (Thomas 2000: 81). Some of the pits at Holywood North display a deliberate character in the way in which they were filled, but structured deposition need not rule out a domestic origin for the material deposited (Bradley 2003: 222). The cursus monuments at Holywood were clearly laid out in relation to places that had been previously utilised and the boundaries of the enclosures were modified or aligned to incorporate the remains of the former activity (Thomas 1999c: 110, 2000: 86).

At Douglasmuir, potential settlement remains were also found. To the west of the cursus monument three pits were located (see Figure 3.8) (Kendrick 1995: 35). These were quite different to the ones of the enclosure. These were long and shallow and one contained fragments of Neolithic pottery (pottery was absent within the enclosure itself). Also, around 100 metres to the southeast, further excavation found twenty-three pits and postholes (Kendrick 1995: 35) (Figure 3.21). These consisted of shallow depressions, postholes and larger oval, flat-bottomed pits like the ones near the enclosure. Some of the pits contained Earlier Neolithic pottery and one of the

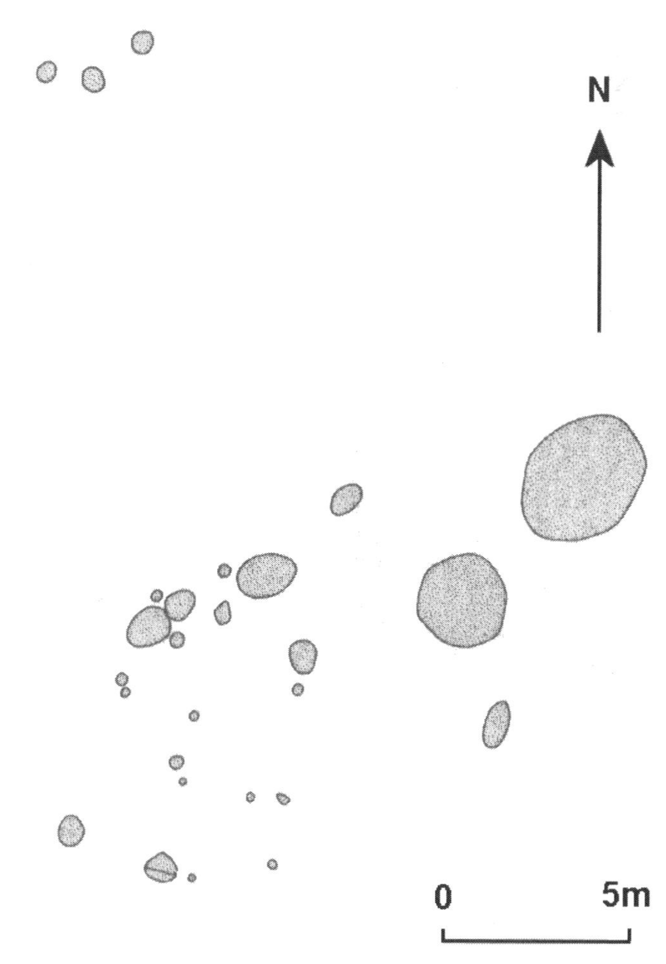

FIGURE 3.21 *The pits to the southeast of Douglasmuir (Source: Kendrick 1995: figure 6)*

flat-bottomed pits contained burnt stones and charcoal-stained soil along with pottery of a similar date to the enclosure (Cowie 1993: 24).

The cremation trenches at Kirkburn were also located in the midst of a number of pit groups that may too represent pre-enclosure settlement (Cormack 1962–3). Six of these pits contained Earlier Neolithic pottery, but many other pits were undated and may belong to the Neolithic phase of activity. These pits contained charcoal, burnt twigs, hazelnut shells, flint flakes, pottery sherds, blackened stones that may have been pot boilers, and greasy black soil deposits that Cormack associated with domestic activity (Cormack 1962–3: 112–13). More ambiguous traces of activity have been located at other sites. Lithic scatters (some that include diagnostic Earlier Neolithic material) and pits have been in close proximity to a number of cursus monuments and timber halls (Brophy 1999b: 284; RCAHMS 1984: no.1; Wordsworth 1991: 41).

Symbolic houses

As well as a number of sites being in close proximity to traces of earlier domestic activity, there are also important parallels between the Scottish post-built enclosures and the form of domestic buildings. A recurring feature of recent reports on excavations of many post-defined enclosures in eastern Scotland has been a section arguing about whether the structure could have been roofed, and if it had been, whether it was a domestic building (for example, Kendrick 1995; Barclay and Russell-White 1993; Barclay and Maxwell 1998). Similar thoughts can be found in an article by Gordon Barclay on Neolithic houses in Scotland, where the ambiguities between actual houses and structures that look like houses, but which probably did not function as such, are outlined (Barclay 1996). These arguments are obviously a product of contemporary concerns: in pre-history it would have been obvious to an observer whether a structure was roofed or not. However, these arguments reveal a broad similarity in the spatial layout of domestic and ceremonial structures, which may have been designed in the past to be deliberately overlapping and deliberately ambiguous.

All of the Scottish enclosures used wooden posts to enclose a space shielded from exterior view. By this act of enclosure the people who built these sites were constructing a form of architecture that ordered space and defined movement (Parker Pearson and Richards 1994). These were buildings that were accessed in particular ways. Like houses, these sites had doorways and internal divisions that had to be encountered in particular ways. For example, at Holywood North, an entranceway was defined by a break in the surrounding ditch (Thomas 1999: 115). Entry to the enclosure involved negotiating a ring ditch and a timber screen, which would have defined access. Likewise, the entranceway at Holywood South was also marked by a ring ditch and the deposits in the ditch terminals were distinct from the ditch deposits elsewhere (Thomas 1999: 110). It is clear that entry was a proscribed activity in the use of the monument (Thomas 1999: 110). At Douglasmuir (Figure 3.8) doorways may have been monumentally closed before the structure was burnt (Kendrick 1995: 32). Points in the transverse divisions can be identified where the lines of posts seem to be interrupted (Figure 3.8). These may have been doorways to the structure that were perhaps shut off through the addition of large posts before the structure was burnt. A burnt cursus monument at Dunragit also had a defined entranceway in one of the terminal ends of the monument (Thomas 2001a). The sides of the enclosure at Dunragit increased in height towards the entrance, highlighting the significance of this access and entry point.

Like Irish houses, all of these monuments were complex architectural spaces that included weighted spaces of varying importance, restrictions on entry and exit, and restrictions on views into the interior (Cooney 2000: chapter 3). Activities carried out in the interior of these enclosures could be cut off from outside participation through the employment of particular architectural devices such as timber screens. The controls over movement and vision are similar to the layout at the timber halls at Balbridie and Claish. Both of these buildings had entrance screens that blocked views into the interior, creating spaces with differing degrees of separation from the outside (Barclay et al. 2002: 104). The screens and posts would have defined set paths of movement through the structure and created spaces of differing significance. Similarly, many of the Irish houses seem to have been carefully divided into sections and the controls on movement seem to have been similar (Cooney 2000: chapter 3). The rectangular form of these houses and the ultimate burning of these structures also suggest links between these buildings and the larger Scottish enclosures. Timber halls were like massively enlarged versions of these smaller domestic buildings (Bradley 2003: 221).

The similarities in the spatial layout of post-built enclosures, timber halls and houses and the 'shared architectural vocabulary' of these structures and the ambiguities inherent in the classification of domestic and monumental sites may have been deliberate (Barclay et al. 2002). Warren De Boer has highlighted the overlap between ceremonial and domestic structures in the New World showing how ceremonial structures were often enlarged versions of domestic buildings or 'big houses' (De Boer 1997). In Britain, Richard Bradley has suggested that some monuments may have been 'big houses' that symbolised the unity of the social groups who built and used them (Bradley 2001: 81). The Earlier Neolithic Irish houses and the large enclosures in Scotland drew on the same principles of order and architecture based on a rectangular conception of space with proscribed entry and exit points and the shielding of important spaces. In this way the large enclosures in Scotland may have been seen as 'big houses' or 'exploded houses' built in a schematic, greatly enlarged way, as an image of an ideal house type.

The location of some of the timber enclosures over settlement remains suggests that at times the construction of these was closely integrated with the settlement pattern of lowland Scotland. Sites such as Bannockburn suggest that at times these 'exploded houses' were built directly over an earlier settlement, while other sites such as Douglasmuir suggest timber structures were situated near to places of settlement. Traces of earlier activity at Holywood North and South were more ephemeral, but perhaps none the less significant. The construction, use, and destruction of these structures may, therefore, have been directly linked with the lifecycles of the communities who constructed them (Gerritsen 1999; Bradley 2002: chapter 2; Carsten and Hugh-Jones 1995), perhaps occurring after a death or other significant event at the settlement locale. The impetus for ritual practice often derives from social disunity, through death or another form of social drama; in these situations ritual acts as a mechanism of redress (Turner 1968). The burning of these structures would have created a memory of a place or an event, allowing the group to move on, to re-establish harmony in the face of disorder (Douglas 1966: 4; Turner 1968: 270, 1982: 112).

CONCLUSION

All of the structures considered in this chapter may have been involved in the creation of memories of people, places and events. The drama of burning would aid the remembering process, creating particularly strong memories. Remembering may have been aided by a phenomenon known as flashbulb memory where memories are recalled with particular clarity and vividness and where people are able to closely relate to the events that constitute collective memory. In Scotland in particular, many of the monuments we classify as different things – timber halls, mortuary enclosures, cursus monuments – seem to be closely related in form and purpose. The architecture of these monuments suggests that all of these structures may have been drawing on the image of the house and the domestic sphere in their construction, albeit in Scotland on a massively expanded scale. Given the ephermerality of everyday settlement, the contrasting massiveness of the timber enclosures and timber halls may seem incongruous, yet these buildings may too have had a short life span, being burnt long before they had decayed. The burning may, however, have been intended to fix the memory of these structures and the events surrounding their construction and use. Sites such as Bannockburn and Kirkburn suggest that at times these structures memorialised places where people had formerly lived or particular events that occurred there. Through the burning, Neolithic communities in lowland Scotland created some notion of permanency and rootedness from a lifestyle which involved moving through the landscape on a regular basis.

The burning of the timber halls, mortuary structures, cursus monuments, Irish houses and the other types of structure outlined above occurred at a distinct phase at the very beginning of the Neolithic. In Scotland at least, Later Neolithic timber structures were allowed to decay naturally, not burnt down (Barclay et al. 2002). It would seem that the practice of burning was particularly prevalent right at the start of the Earlier Neolithic. It may be, with the onset of the Neolithic and the need to rely more closely on previous generations in terms of the labour investment in farming and herding, that memories related to the past were particularly valuable during the Earlier Neolithic. The process of burning may have been the way in which memories of the past and previous generations were celebrated and retained. Through destruction, something more permanent was created.

CHAPTER FOUR

Planting trees, planting people: long and round barrows in eastern Scotland and beyond

> Of an ancient tree that has presided over successive human generations it would seem more appropriate to say that it has played its part in the domestication of humans rather being domesticated by them. (Ingold 2000: 86)

Introduction

In eastern and southern Scotland and extending into southern England the visible remains of the Neolithic consist mainly of earthen barrows (Kinnes 1992a). On the ground today these monuments consist of massive mounds of earth or stone. The most common form is trapezoidal in plan and often orientated to the east. These structures are distributed widely in lowland Scotland, with notable concentrations in Aberdeenshire, Angus, Dumfries and Galloway and the Scottish Borders (Figure 4.1). The long and round barrows and cairns are poorly dated, but suggest activity began around the start of the fourth millennium BC and ended at some sites in the second half of the fourth millennium (Kinnes 1992a: 117–19) (Figure 4.2). Excavation has shown that these mounds cover a range of wooden structures that, in Scotland at least, tend to be remarkably similar in form. Large D-shaped postholes have been found under many. These often occur in pairs and appear to represent a single tree split in two and then placed in the ground. The remains of these wooden structures have traditionally been seen as the supports for a mortuary structure of some kind. However, at many of the barrows and cairns it can be seen that the primary features of the monument were the D-shaped posts, which were allowed to decay *in situ*. It was only after the posts had decayed that human remains in the form of skeletal material or cremated remains were added to the monument. This sequence implies that the split tree in the first phase of the monument had more than a structural function and it is suggested that the tree may have been used in rituals that highlighted processes of human growth and decay. As well as the Scottish examples of long and round barrows, English and Irish sites are discussed in this chapter as these provide close parallels for the Scottish material and interpretation of these monuments has been dominated by considerations of sites from outside Scotland (Kinnes 1992a; Scott 1992). It is important to address some of the misconceptions that now centre on this class of monument as a whole, through re-interpretation of some of the 'classic' examples.

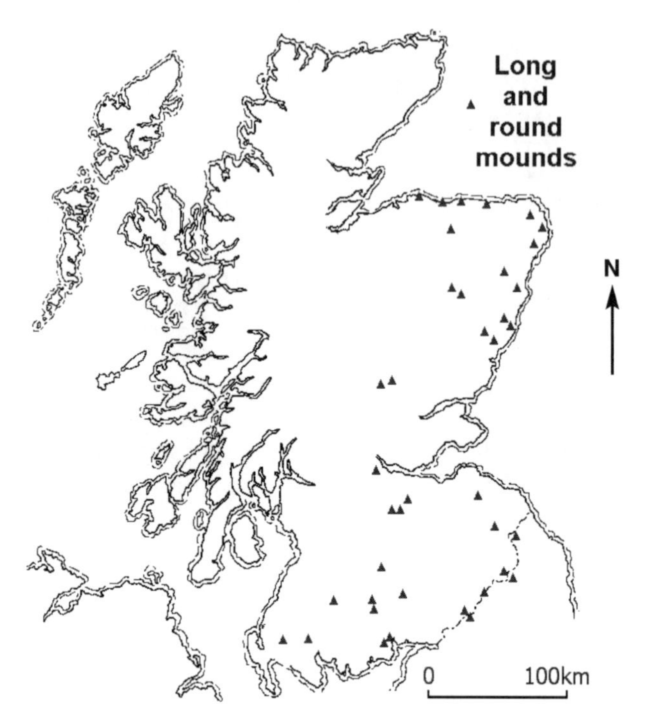

FIGURE 4.1 *The distribution of long and round mounds and cairns in Scotland (Source: Kinnes 1992b: figures 1A.1 and 1A.2)*

EXPOSURE PLATFORMS

One of the most influential articles on the earthen barrows of eastern Britain was written by J. G. Scott (1992). In this article Scott attempted an 'armchair re-excavation' of various long and round barrow structures (1992: 104). He set out with the express aim of finding evidence for raised mortuary platforms for the exposure of the dead. Scott examined a range of structures from England, Scotland and Ireland, beginning with the mortuary enclosure at Aldwincle I, Northamptonshire. Excavated in the 1970s, the site was found to consist of two sets of paired postholes enclosed by intermittent lengths of ditch (Figure 4.3). Scott proposed that the posts were originally part of a raised platform upon which the bodies of the dead had been exposed to the elements. The postholes indicated that the posts had not been removed or burnt, but had instead decayed *in situ.* This led Scott to postulate that the presence of the bodies on the ground indicated that the structure had collapsed through decay and that the bodies had fallen to the ground. At Fussell's Lodge, Wiltshire, Scott proposed a similar sequence and interpretation (Figure 4.4). The primary feature on the site of the barrow was two D-shaped posts set six metres apart, separated by a central posthole. Like Aldwincle I, Scott thought that these posts were part of some form of exposure platform. Between the posts four distinct piles of human bones were found, containing the remains of between at least fifty-three and fifty-seven individuals of all ages.

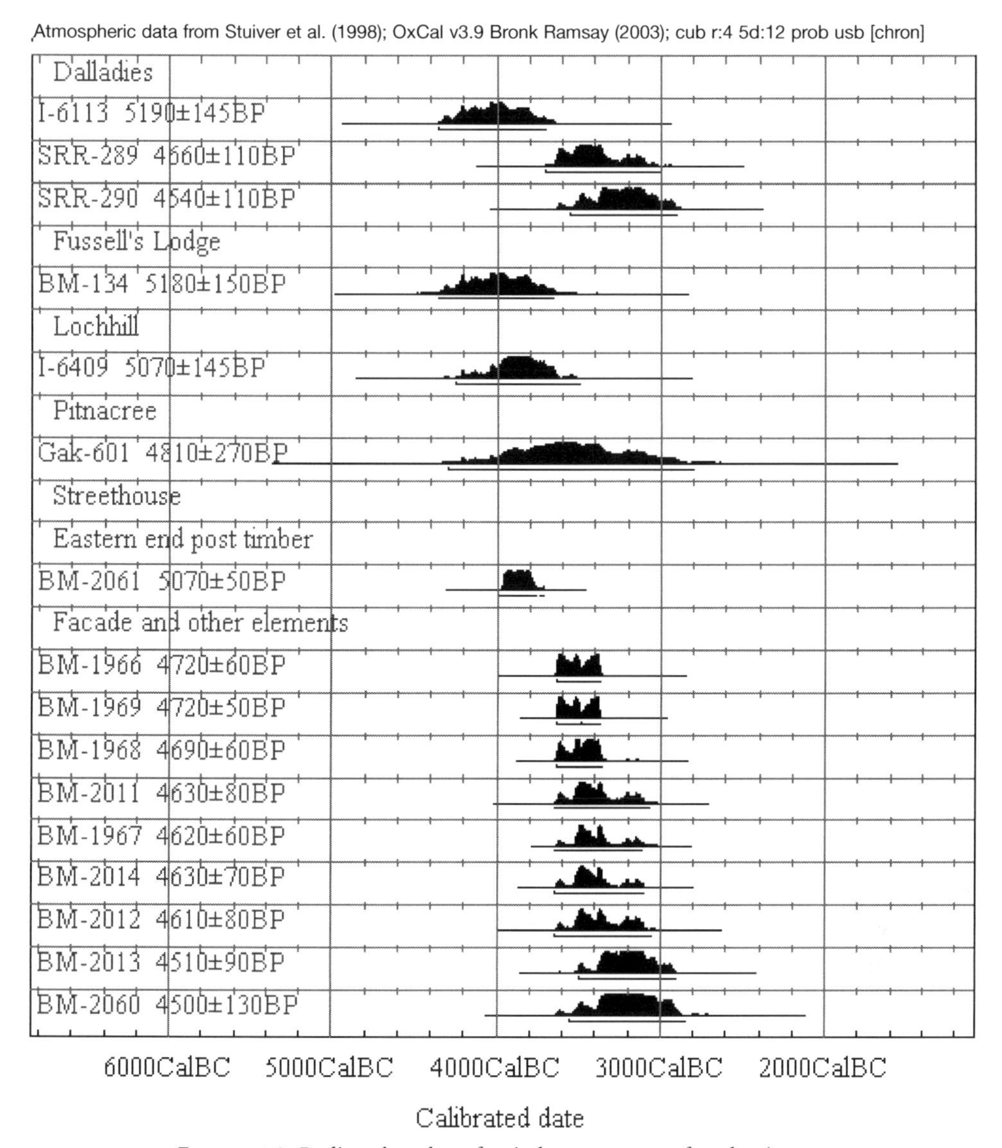

FIGURE 4.2 *Radiocarbon dates for timber structures referred to in text*

The bones were in varying states of decay and preservation. Scott again postulated that the better-preserved bones represented the most recently exposed bodies, while the decayed examples represented the earlier burials, parts of which had fallen from the platform (Scott 1992: 112).

In Scotland, Scott pointed to the presence of paired D-shaped postholes at sites such as Pitnacree, Perthshire and at two closely related sites at Lochhill and Slewcairn, both in Kirkcudbright. Again he thought that these structures represented the supports for exposure platforms. Scott amalgamated the evidence from all of the sites under consideration to suggest a reconstruction of a raised exposure platform,

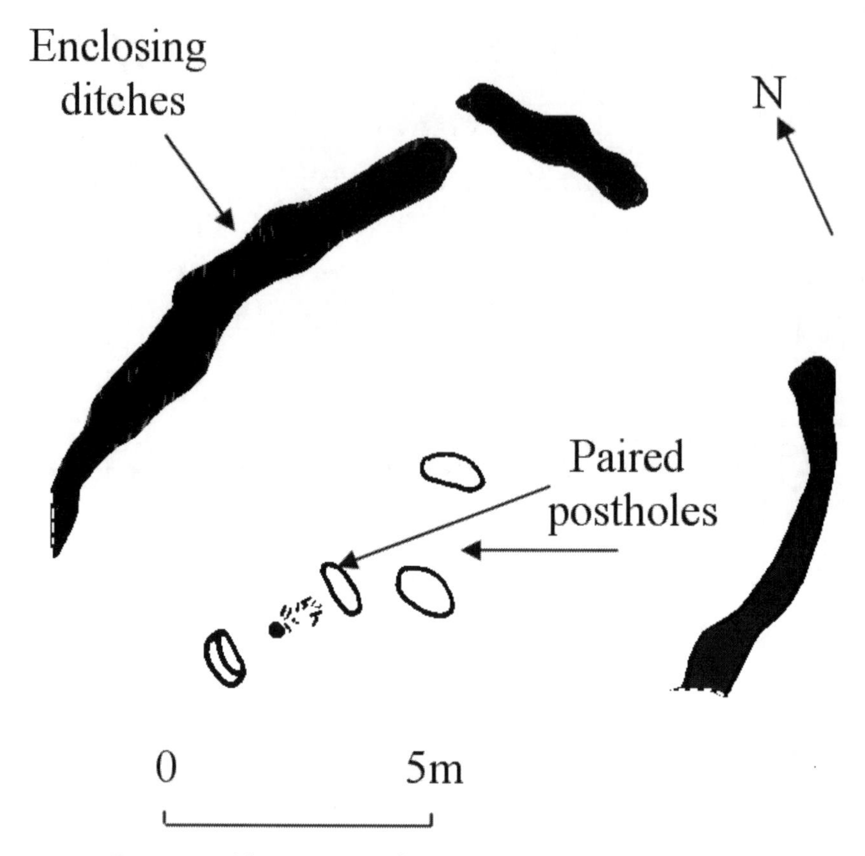

FIGURE 4.3 *The mortuary enclosure at Aldwincle I, Northamptonshire (Source: Scott 1992: figure 8.1)*

showing the various stages in its construction, use and decay (Figure 4.5). Scott's reconstruction is outlined most explicitly in the following extract:

> The dead, exposed aloft, would have been safe from predatory beasts, though not from predatory birds. Inevitably, as bodies decayed and the platform deteriorated, bones would have fallen from the platform to the ground below, and it is reasonable to suppose that the area beneath the platform would have been enclosed by hurdles or some other form of barrier, proof against larger beasts though not against rodents. (Scott 1992: 116)

Scott's reconstruction was a reasonable, if uncritical, interpretation. Scott's interpretation is attractive, as it allows a practical explanation for the widespread appearance of paired postholes underneath long barrows and has since been used for a number of other Neolithic sites, despite the absence of human remains at many of these sites, for example the timber structures at Balfarg (Barclay and Russell-White 1993). However, there are a number of problems with Scott's reading of the evidence.

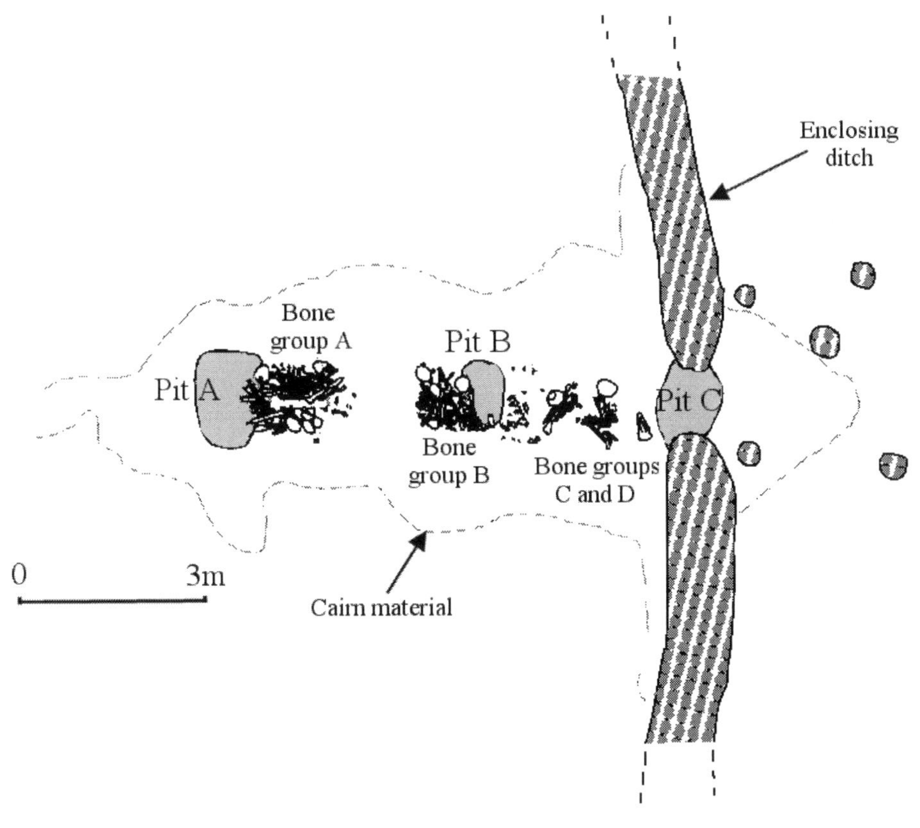

Figure 4.4 *Fussell's Lodge*
(Source: Thomas 1999: figure 6.5)

Decay and absence

At Aldwincle and Fussell's Lodge, Scott highlighted the fragmentary state of the skeletal material and the varying levels of decay within the assemblage of human bone. It seems unlikely, however, that the regular placing of the human remains at these sites resulted from the structural collapse of some form of platform. It would appear that the groups of skeletal material were laid out in a deliberate manner. At Aldwincle I, for example, one of the burials was of a crouched, articulated male, a position that could not have arisen by chance (see Figure 4.3).

Fussell's Lodge, excavated in the 1950s, consisted of a trapezoidal bedding trench that held a number of tree trunks and split trunks surrounding a central area. Within this central area three pits were found and between the two end posts a mass of skeletal material. The middle pit of the three that made up the central setting was covered by skeletal material. Scott believed that the presence of skeletal material both within the upper layers of the central posthole at Fussell's Lodge and overlying this feature indicated the collapse of the mortuary structure over the decayed post and the infill of the upper layers by the falling skeletal remains. It is unlikely, however, that a post was in the process of decay in the central pit, as while skeletal material does indeed overlie

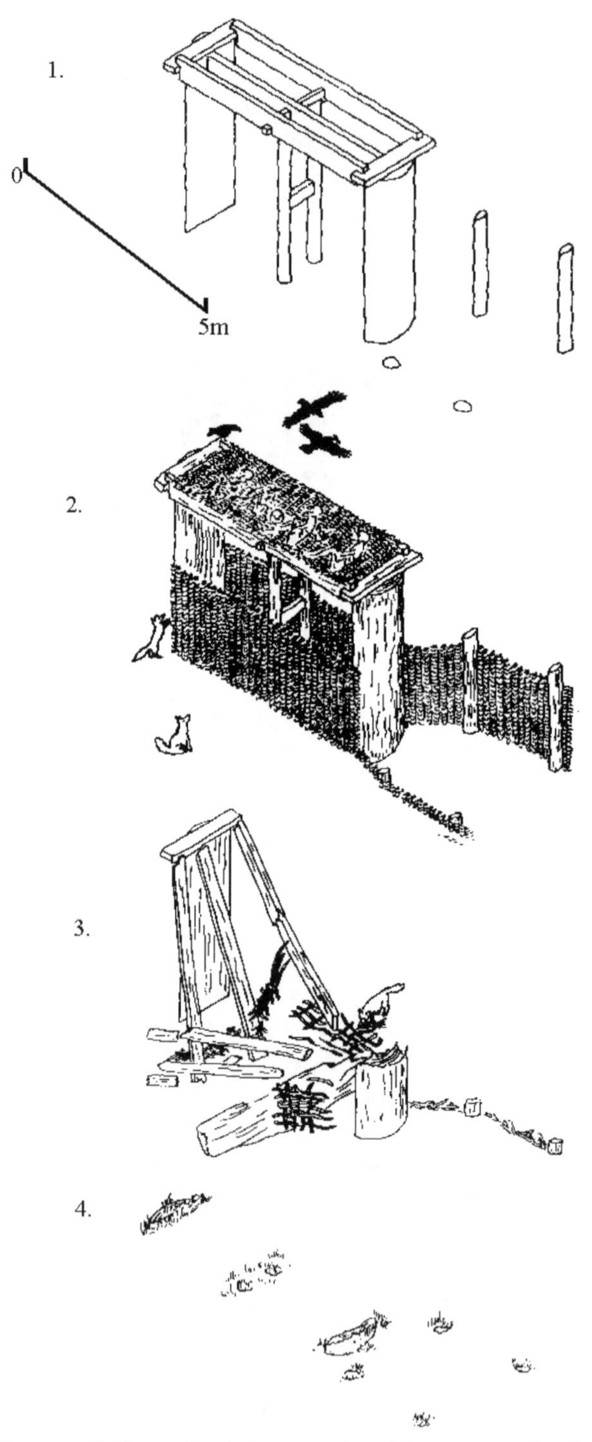

FIGURE 4.5 *Exposure platforms: Scott's interpretation of the structures found underneath many long and round barrows*
(Source: Scott 1992: figure 8.7)

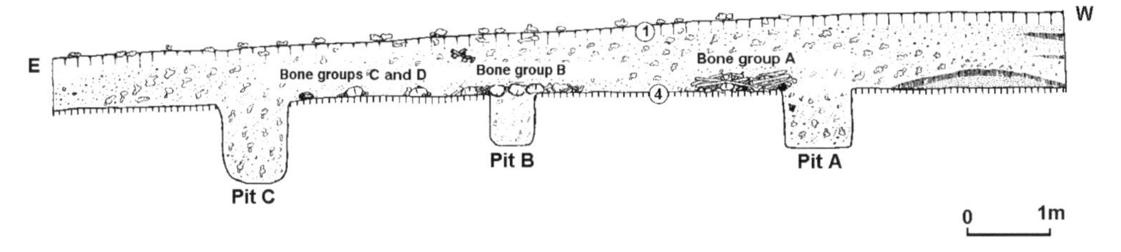

Figure 4.6 *A section through the mound at Fussell's Lodge. Bone group B did not slump into Pit B, suggesting that the pit had been filled prior to the deposition of the skeletal material (Source: Ashbee 1966: plate XI)*

the position of the post, the skeletal remains did not slump into the pit, as can be seen in one of Ashbee's section drawings (Ashbee 1966) (Figure 4.6). Some form of slumping would be expected if the post was present at the time of the deposition of the skeletal material, as the post decay would leave a void into which any material above would slip. Indeed, Morgan notes that there was no clear evidence to suggest the presence of posts in any of the Fussell's Lodge pits (Morgan 1959: 39). It seems more likely that posts had already been removed by the time the skeletal material was deposited. This is supported by the fact that the pits were all partly in-filled with chalk and flint nodules, part of the same material that covered the bodies in a flint cairn. For example, Ashbee notes that the filling of Pit C was 'principally flint nodules, with some earthy chalk, which were at the same time a continuing and integral part of the cairn covering the burials' (Ashbee 1966: 8). The final filling of the pits, therefore, may have been completed at the same time as the burials were deposited. There is evidence to suggest that this filling was carried out carefully and deliberately. In the filling of the central post-hole a deposit of burned and scorched human remains was found, the only location in the large skeletal assemblage where burnt skeletal remains were found. Overlying the pit were seven mandibles, all from young children, almost certainly deliberately placed to mark the position of the former post or posts (Ashbee 1966: 10, 40).

The large number of bodies at Fussell's Lodge were found in four main groups (See Figure 4.4). Although the skeletons were generally incomplete and in varying states of preservation, suggesting different periods of mortuary activity, the bones were not laid out in a haphazard fashion as might be expected from the structural failure of a wooden platform as Scott suggested. Julian Thomas has shown that the bone groups at Fussell's Lodge were laid out according to a quite deliberate selection and composition and highlighted that each group contained varying quantities of particular body parts (Thomas 1999a: 136–7). Ashbee also noted the regularity of the bone deposits: while bone group A was laid out principally in line with the axis of the monument, bone group B was laid diagonally across the axis (Ashbee 1966: 8–10). The most convincing evidence of very deliberate bone placement comes from bone groups C and D. Here, what looked like a complete inhumation during excavation was found, but under later examination it was found that the 'individual' was in fact made up of a number of different bones from various people (Ashbee 1966: 10). This underlines the very deliberate placement of skeletal material at the site: the people who composed these groups reassembled a body from the fragmentary remains of many individuals.

Scott, in support of the exposure platform theory, suggests that the differing condition of the bones at Fussell's Lodge indicated cumulative additions to earlier deposits and that the bones, therefore, corresponded to a number of different episodes of mortuary activity, separated by a significant time span (Scott 1992: 113). Ashbee on the other hand makes it clear that the mortuary assemblage was almost certainly a unitary deposit (Ashbee 1966: 37). While these bones derived from a variety of sources and were of various ages, they were deposited as part of a single phase of activity around the positions of the newly filled pits. Indeed, although the bones were of varying conditions, the pottery associated with the skeletal material was of an unweathered condition, indicating the rapid deposition and sealing of this material (Ashbee 1966: 38). For example, sherds of one pottery vessel were found in amongst the flints covering the bodies and under the bodies, indicating that the bodies and the cairn were laid down rapidly as part of a single phase of activity (Ashbee 1966: 31). By implication this suggests that the partial filling of the pits underneath was carried out as part of this activity. It is also clear that the bodies were not exposed in this location as not a single piece of skeletal material was found in the trapezoidal enclosure outside the central area, an unlikely situation if bones were left exposed to the elements and animals (Ashbee 1966: 9).

All of these observations suggest that the pits at Fussell's Lodge were not part of an exposure platform and do not appear to have been part of any form of structure. The deliberate placement of the skeletal material, in some cases directly over the position of postholes, indicates that any wooden structures present must have decayed by the time skeletal remains were deposited. The pits underneath the flint cairn were not observable until the cairn had been removed, indicating that timber posts did not continue above the cairn or through the mound. The cairn also extended across parts of the trapezoidal enclosure and over two of the four posts found around the entrance. This suggests that all of the timber elements at Fussell's Lodge belonged to a primary phase, distinct from the later mound construction and funerary deposit. The filling of the central three pits with elements of the flint cairn found covering the bodies also suggests that if posts were present in these pits they had decayed by the time the cairn was deposited or were deliberately removed to allow the bodies to be deposited.

SPLIT TREES IN SCOTLAND

The evidence for the erection and decay of split trunks prior to human bone deposition is paralleled at a number of barrow sites in Scotland. The Neolithic round barrow at Pitnacree, excavated in the 1960s, consisted of a mound 30 metres in diameter, under which was found a stone enclosure, within which lay a rectangular stone setting and large, ramped, D-shaped postholes (Coles and Simpson 1965) (Figure 4.7). The rectangular stone setting was found to be associated with a number of cremation deposits. Pre-monument activity may have included an episode of cultivation and land clearance. The initial building phases consisted of the erection of two massive

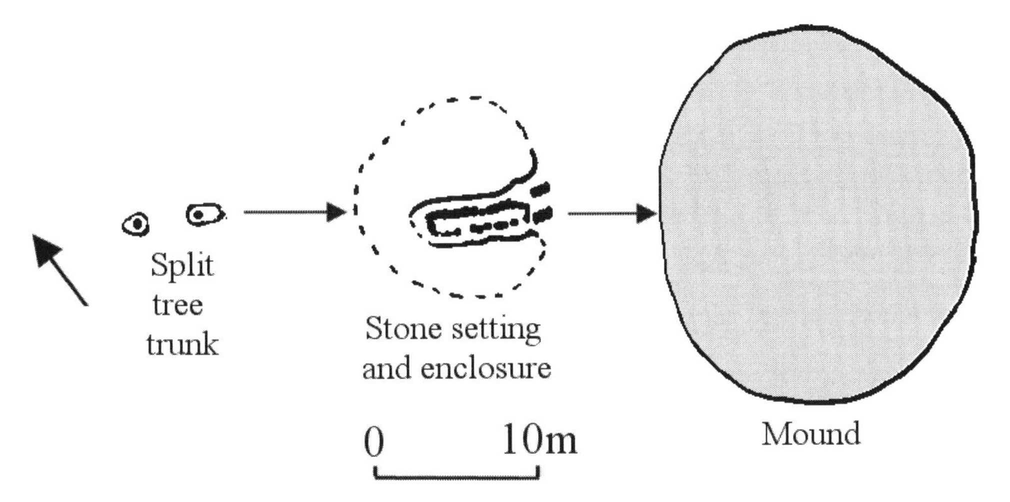

FIGURE 4.7 *The sequence at Pitnacree. The placement of the split trees was one of the primary acts on the site*
(Source: Kinnes 1992b: figure 7.6)

timber posts, over a metre in diameter. These posts were part of a 'single massive tree trunk which had been split in half' (Coles and Simpson 1965: 40). After the split tree trunk was erected there was a large gap in activity as it is clear that the posts had decayed by the time the subsequent parts of the monument were built (Coles and Simpson 1965: 40). Once the posts had decayed, the sequence of construction at the monument seems to have accelerated, with a number of differing features apparently built soon after one another. First, a horseshoe-shaped enclosure, with a roofed entrance, was built around the position of the posts. Within this enclosure and around the former position of the western part of the split trunk, three cremation deposits were placed. These burials were quickly covered by a low rectangular stone setting, which had an entrance to the southwest (Figure 4.8). This stone setting partly overlay the position of the timber posts. Finally, the massive earth and stone barrow was built, made of turf, earth and surrounded by a drystone wall kerb. Mound construction must have been underway during the deposition of the cremations and the construction of the rectangular stone enclosure as one of the cremations lay partly under the stone setting and partly within the makeup of the barrow. A significant period of time between the split tree trunk setting and the later stone features associated with the cremation deposits is suggested by the differing conditions of the pottery recovered. The pottery lying within the pre-monument soil and some of the pottery lying on the surface was of a weathered condition. This is in contrast to a number of sherds that seem to have been deposited immediately prior to the construction of the horseshoe setting that were of an unweathered condition (Coles and Simpson 1965: 41). The difference in the relative conditions of the pottery associated with different parts of the monument suggests a substantial period of time between the initial phases and the closing of the site. The evidence at Pitnacree strongly suggests that the tree trunk set up in the first phase of activity had decayed long before

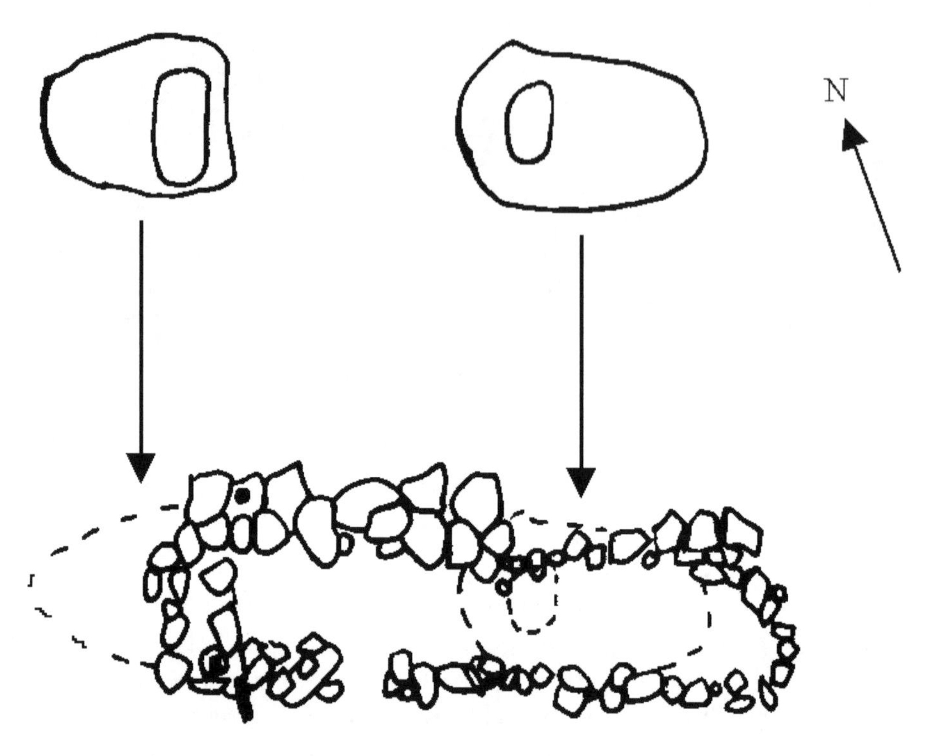

FIGURE 4.8 *Pitnacree: detail of the relationship between decayed posts and stone setting (Source: Coles and Simpson 1965: figure 3)*

the other structures were erected and that the cremation deposits were deposited during the closure of the site as part of the mound construction.

From outward appearances, Slewcairn, in Dumfries and Galloway, must have looked like a very different monument to that at Pitnacree when it was excavated in the 1970s (Masters 1973b: 80). The final monument at Slewcairn was a stone-built cairn with an accessible chamber, similar to the Clyde-style monuments of southwest Scotland, and very different to the closed, mainly turf, mound at Pitnacree. However, the pre-cairn activity revealed at Slewcairn was found to be very similar to that at the Perthshire monument. Three massive pits were found (Figure 4.9). In the two outermost pits the outlines of massive D-shaped posts were found, the remains of two

Phase 1: Split tree trunk and posts

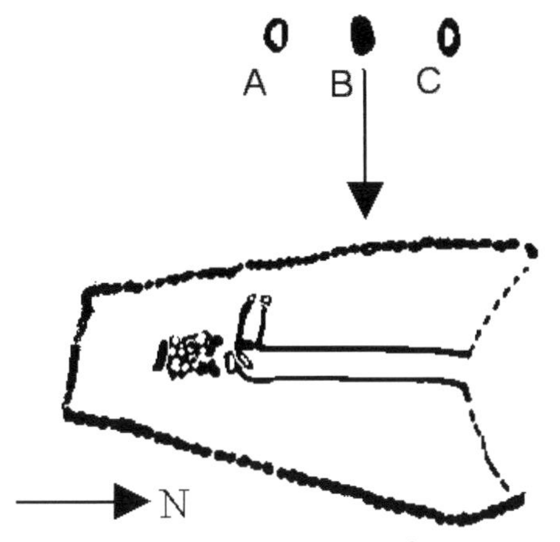

Phase 2: Stone mortuary enclosure and cairn

Figure 4.9 *The sequence at the Slewcairn (Source: Kinnes 1992b: figure 7.3)*

halves of a split tree trunk (Masters 1987: 167). Between the two halves of the split trunk a further pit was found, which may have held two smaller posts. This linear arrangement of posts could be said to be suitable for supporting some sort of platform for the exposure of the dead as interpreted by Scott, however, like Pitnacree, human remains were only introduced to the site *after* the tree trunk and posts had decayed. Cremated bone was found in the upper levels of both of the split trunk pits (Masters 1976: 39, 1977: 20, 1978: 5). The filling of the southern pit was particularly suggestive:

> the southern pit . . . like that at the northern end, was shown to have held a massive D-shaped post in its primary phase. Later, the post appears to have been removed, although the stob was left *in-situ*, and the upper half of the pit used to contain a filling of small granite boulders, black soil and cremated bone. (Masters 1980: 4)

The evidence from the outermost pits shows that the tree trunk had decayed to such an extent that when the posts were removed or fell the bases were left in place. The upper halves of the postholes were then reused to deposit cremated bone, black soil and boulders. This deposit was identical to the filling of a wood and stone structure that overlay the former position of the posts. This structure consisted of a small rectangular setting of stones up to four courses high and the remains of a slight wooden superstructure that had been burnt down. Inside the setting of stones, further cremated remains were recovered. The rectangular setting of stones and timber elements appears to have been constructed and perhaps burnt while the outer cairn was being built (Masters 1980: 4). Like Pitnacree, it would seem that the deposition of human remains occurred at the same time as the construction of the cairn. The main structures of the monument identifiable on the ground today were built only once a split tree trunk had decayed. Human remains were placed on the tops of the decayed bases of the tree trunk and formed part of the filling of a rectangular stone setting similar to the setting within the horseshoe enclosure at Pitnacree.

The major pre-cairn elements at Lochhill, located less than 6 kilometres from Slewcairn, closely mirrored the structure under the cairn at Slewcairn (Masters 1973a; 1973b) (Figure 4.10). Again, three large pits were found. The two outer pits originally held D-shaped posts, deriving from a split tree trunk, and the central pit had held two

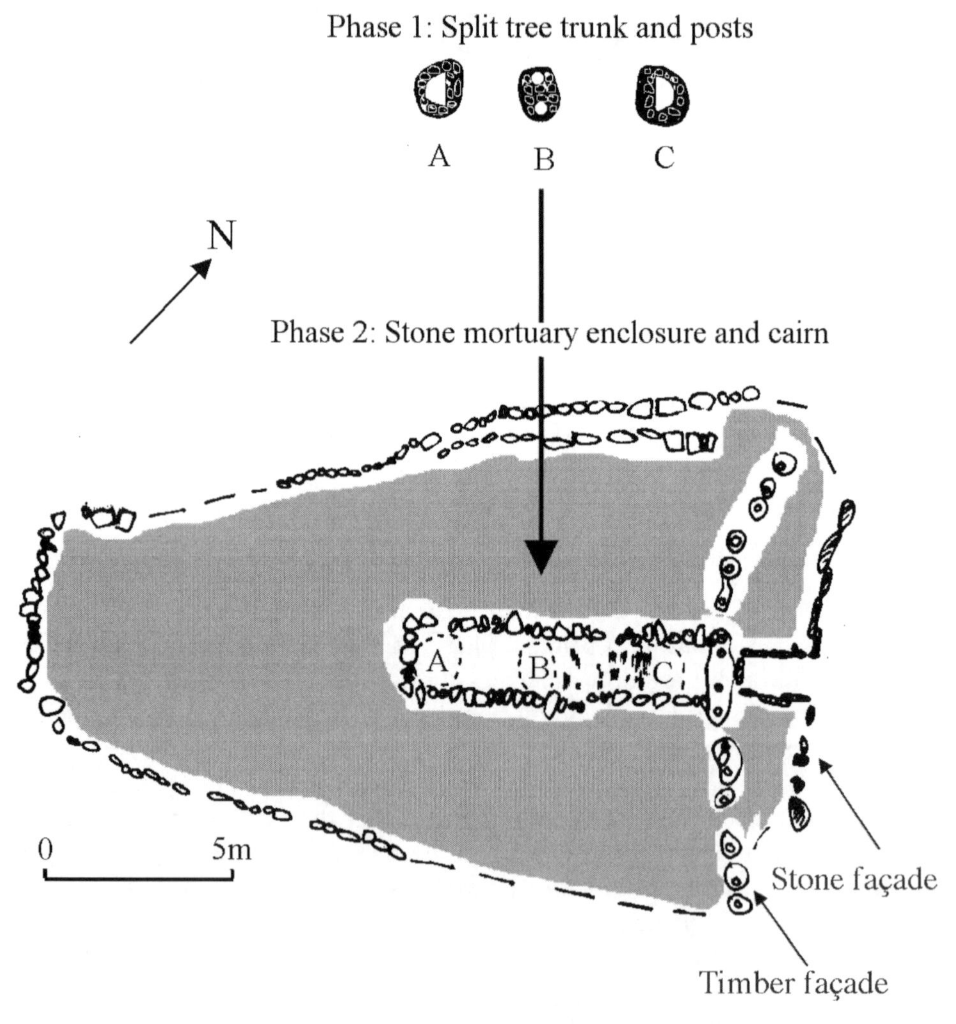

FIGURE 4.10 *The sequence at Lochhill. Both the split trunks and the burnt façade pre-dated the stone cairn*
(Source: Kinnes 1992b: figure 7.1)

smaller posts (Masters 1973a: 97). Around the posts a small rectangular setting of stones, similar to those at Pitnacree and Slewcairn, was found. This stone setting was bonded into the lower courses of the outer cairn, indicating that this was built as part of the main body of the final monument. Between the mid and outer posts there was a burnt oak plank floor. The cremated remains of what probably represented a single individual were found on the floor and partly in amongst stones heaped into the centre of the rectangular stone setting (Masters 1973a: 97). A timber façade stood in front the eastern pit. This had been destroyed by fire. Originally, all of these structural elements were identified as part of an integral whole, but were not thought to be part of a raised mortuary platform (Masters 1973a: 100). Since the later excavations at Slewcairn the sequence has been reinterpreted with the split trunk forming a primary focus. There was no evidence for the posts having continued up through the cairn and no evidence for the deliberate removal of the posts, nor for their destruction by fire (Lionel Masters, pers. comm.). The burnt oak flooring upon which the cremated remains were found occurred only between posts A and B, indicating, at the very least, that the rear D-shaped post was not incorporated into the mortuary structure. Consequently, there may have been at least two distinct periods of construction at Lochhill, with erection of a split tree trunk which was then allowed to decay and the subsequent construction of the other elements of the monument. The tree trunk may have taken a substantial period of time to decay and consequently there must have been a substantial gap in time between the tree trunk and the cremation deposit and burning (Masters, pers. comm.). The evidence suggests that the sequence was very similar to that which occurred at Slewcairn.

Dalladies long barrow in Kincardineshire was excavated by Stuart Piggott in response to its imminent destruction through the expansion of a nearby gravel quarry (Piggott 1971–2) (Figures. 4.11 and 4.12). The report of the excavations is confusing and contradictory in places and the exact nature of the site is open to interpretation. Piggott's original interpretation of the site suggested three main phases to a timber and stone structure found underneath an earthen barrow. Phase 1 involved the digging of three massive pits and two smaller pits (see Figure 4.11). Small timber uprights were then erected in each pit. Piggott suggested that this timber structure represented the supports for a mortuary house, which had decayed *in situ*. This was then replaced with a timber and stone structure, the timber element of which was burnt down. This held a cup marked stone, a flint knife and the unburnt cranial fragment of a child. This structure was then sealed with stone and incorporated into the massive trapezoidal barrow (see Figure 4.12).

While Piggott's sequence is in broad agreement with those at Pitnacree, Slewcairn and Lochhill, there are a number of points which suggest even closer similarity. The Phase 1 structure was said by Piggott to have consisted of three large pits with small timber posts held within. As Piggott observes, these pits 'seem disproportionately large to take the not very massive posts indicated by the replacement soil' (Piggott 1971–2: 30). The size and shape of these pits are strongly reminiscent of those at Lochhill, Slewcairn and Pitnacree. The presence of ramps for two of the pits and the sheer size of the pits perhaps suggest that these pits held massive posts, which judging

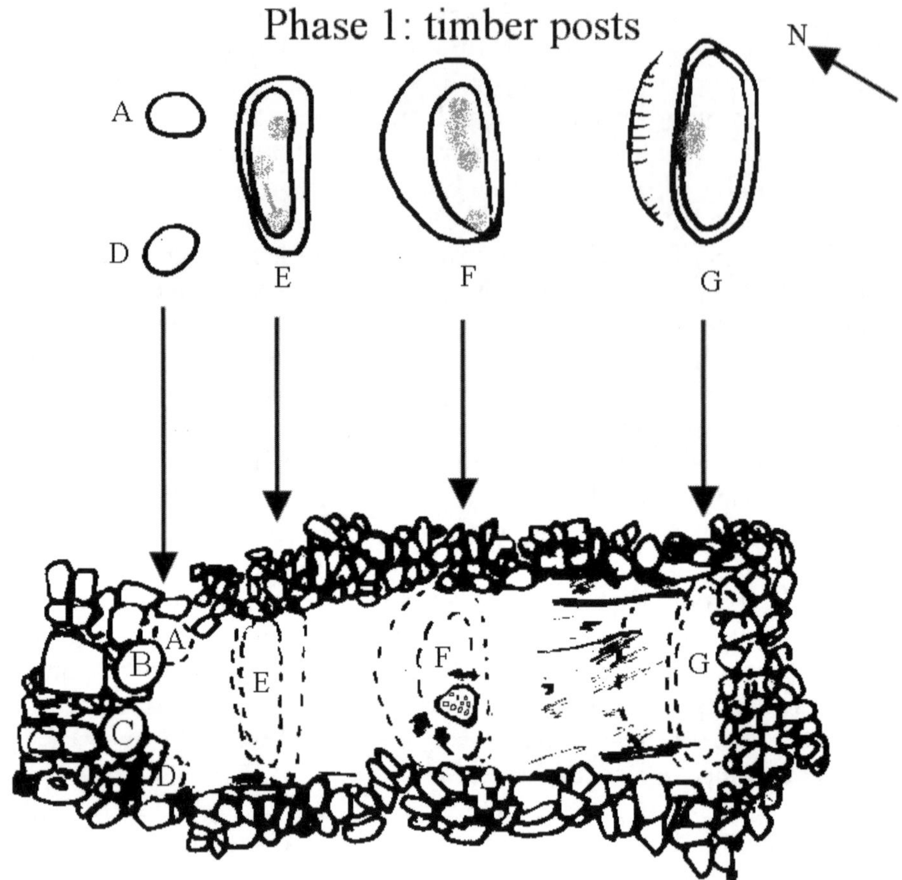

FIGURE 4.11 *The primary phases of Dalladies long barrow. The timber posts and the stone mortuary enclosure*
(Source: Piggott 1971–2: figures 8 and 9)

by their shape may have been sections from split tree trunks. The shallowness of these pits would not securely support small timbers, but would be sufficient to hold the larger base of a split trunk section in place. The smaller posts if present may represent a second construction phase reusing these pits.

Piggott was correct to separate the Phase 1 timber and subsequent stone features at Dalladies. The section through post E indicates the presence of stone and turf above the position of pit E, indicating that any timbers that were held in this pit had decayed before these deposits were incorporated into a rectangular stone setting that formed part of the Phase 2 features (Figure 4.13). Indeed a cup-marked slab found within the stone setting was found to overlie the position of pit F. The smaller pits A and D of

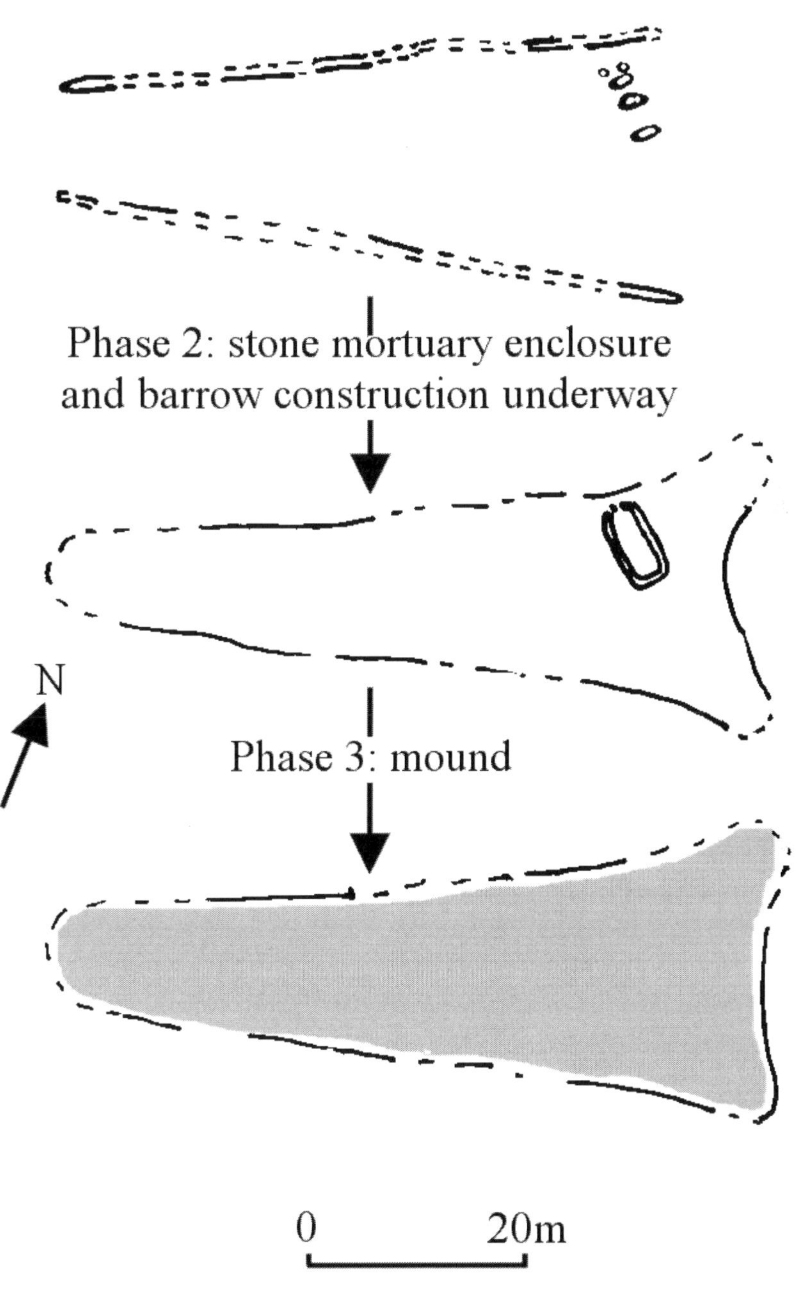

Figure 4.12 *The full sequence at Dalladies (Source: Kinnes 1992b: figure 7.1)*

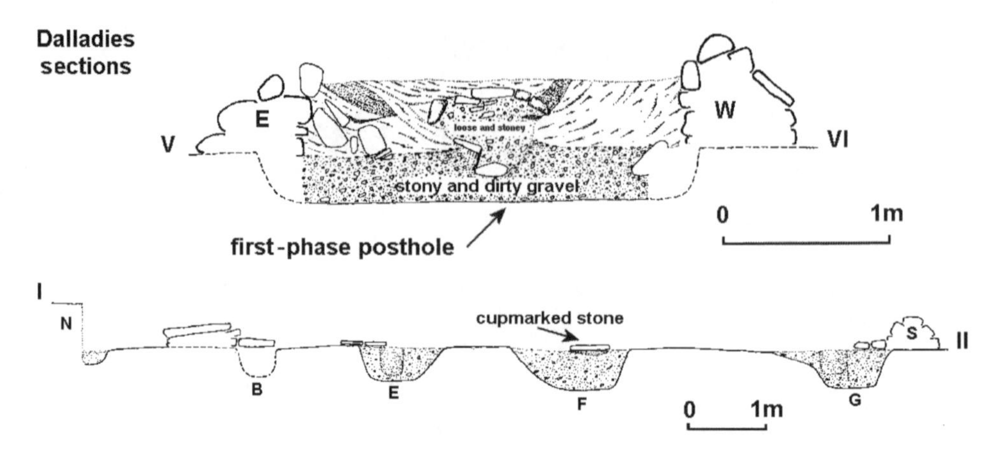

FIGURE 4.13 *Sections through Dalladies long barrow (Source: Piggott 1971–2: figure 7)*

Phase 1 were covered by the walls of the rectangular setting and the two entrance posts to the later rectangular stone structure, posts B and C, cut the former position of these features. The stone structure itself appears to have been part of the closing of the site as its construction was linked to the construction of the revetment to the barrow and was built simultaneously with the lower part of the mound.

The mortuary deposits associated with Dalladies were very limited. The only find of human remains was a single fragment of a child's skull, inside the rectangular stone enclosure. The only other finds were a plano-convex knife made of imported flint, a single pottery sherd and the cup-marked slab. The lack of human remains cannot be explained entirely in terms of acidic soil conditions as the cranial fragment survived despite its relative fragility in comparison to other human bones. The evidence from Dalladies might indicate that human remains were stored within the enclosure and removed for deposition elsewhere before the sealing mound was completed (Piggott 1971–2: 43).

BARROWS WITH SPLIT TREES IN ENGLAND AND IRELAND

Wayland's Smithy, excavated in the 1960s by R. J. C. Atkinson, greatly influenced later interpretations of pre-barrow structures, despite the lack of a full publication until recent years (Atkinson 1965; Whittle 1991) (Figure 4.14). Wayland's Smithy, in the south of England, consisted of an oval cairn, under which Atkinson and co-director Stuart Piggott found two large pits, 'each of which had clearly contained the base of a split tree trunk 4ft in diameter' (Atkinson 1965: 127). The trunks had decayed *in situ*. On a pavement of stones situated between the two pits lay the remains of nine or ten adults, a child of about nine years of age and more fragmentary remains (a minimum of fourteen individuals in total) (Atkinson 1965: 127; Whittle 1991: 70).

Atkinson interpreted the split trunks and timber elements as part of a ridged tent-like mortuary structure that housed the burials. Atkinson argued that the split trunks would have extended up through the cairn and would have formed a landmark visible

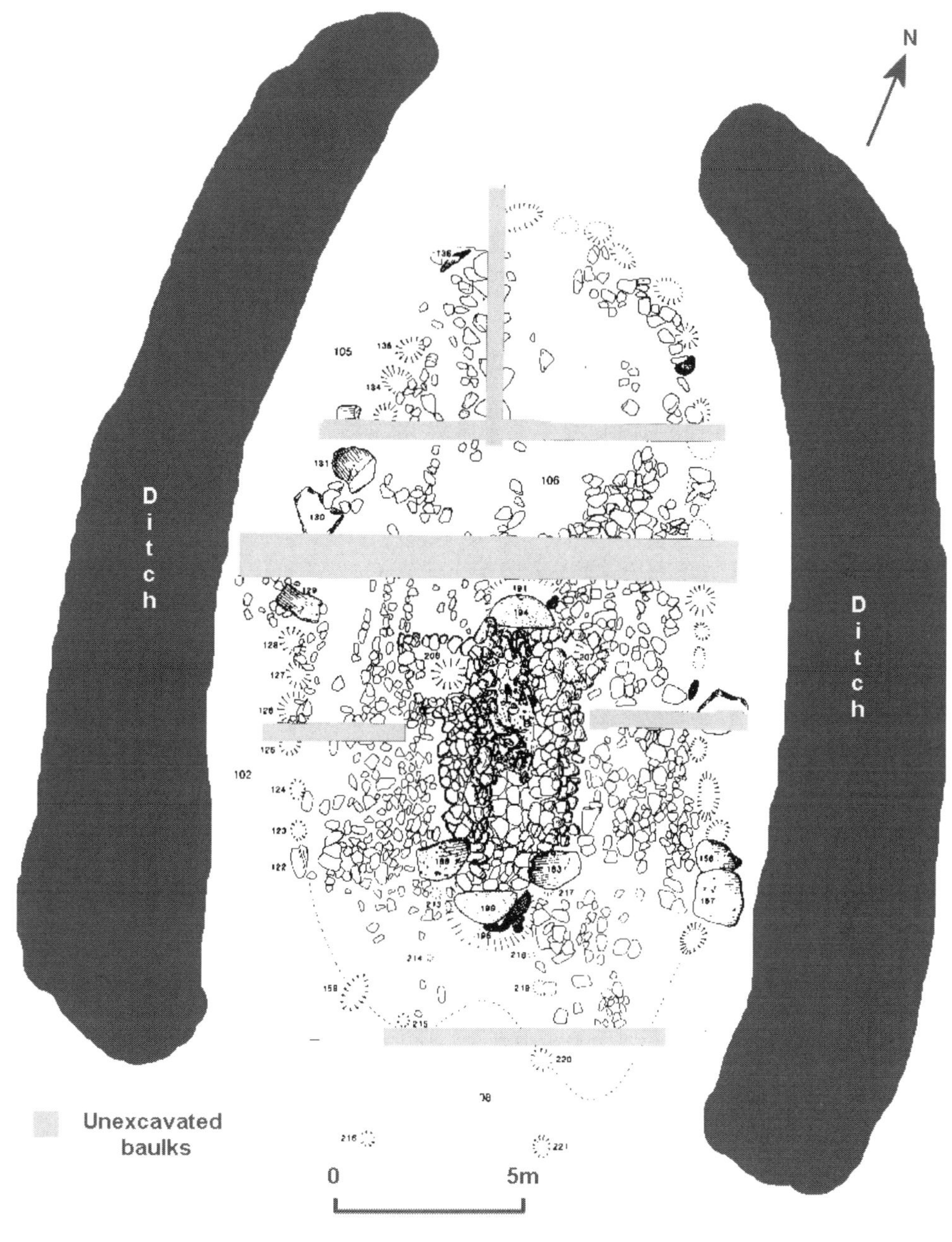

FIGURE 4.14 *Wayland's Smithy*
(Source: Whittle 1991: figure 5)

for miles around. However, there is only contradictory evidence[1] for the split trunks having continued through the mound (Whittle 1991: figure 6, sections 4 and 5). Again, it seems likely that the timber elements had decayed before the stone and burial parts of the monument were in place. Indeed, Atkinson notes that one of the postholes leading from the southern split trunk was covered by a sarsen slab that formed part of the stone paving (Atkinson 1965: 130). This shows that at least some of the wooden parts of the monument had decayed before the mortuary deposit and stone elements were in place. Atkinson suggested the two lines of posts that led from the base of the southern split trunk might have formed part of an exposure platform upon which the bodies had been exposed prior to incorporation in the mortuary structure. However, these posts fan out from the base of the split trunk and make for an unlikely platform base; instead these may be designed to focus attention on the area of the trunks. The author of the full publication (Whittle 1991) did not entirely agree with Atkinson's interpretation and suggested instead that the split trunks may have been part of a much simpler linear box-like chamber, used for successive burials. Alternatively, Whittle cautiously suggests that the split trunks might have been part of an initial phase of freestanding posts. Despite Whittle's caution this seems the more likely scenario. If the split trunks are examined in detail (Figure 4.15), it can be seen that while the faces are parallel, they are substantially offset from one another. The trunk to the north was placed over half a metre to the east of the southern trunk. This would be odd and very awkward if these trunks formed the end posts of a structure. It seems more likely that these trunks, like the fan-shape arrangement of posts to the south, were freestanding posts that decayed before the stone and mortuary elements of the site were added. Preconceived ideas about the form of these timber elements may have affected the excavation and subsequent interpretation of the site, leading to the conflation of separate phases of activity into one main structural phase. Split tree trunks were also used in the partially preserved monument at Haddenham (Hodder and Shand 1988). The constructional sequence at Haddenham seems to mirror that at most of the sites highlighted above. The split tree trunks were the primary feature of the monument and were then replaced by a wooden box-like chamber which held

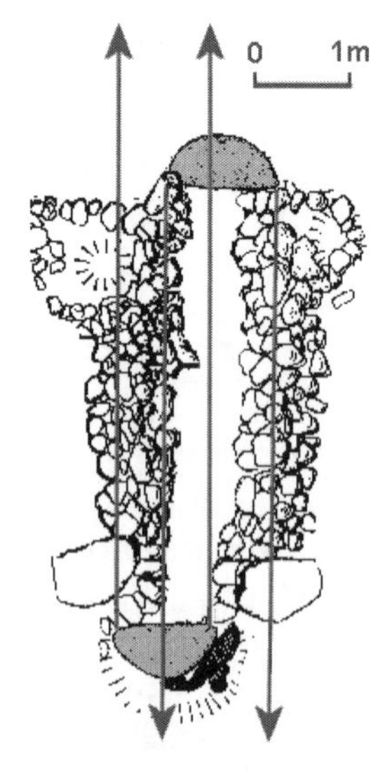

FIGURE 4.15 *Detail of the split trunks at Wayland's Smithy. The trunks are not accurately aligned with one another*

a number of human bodies (Hodder and Shand 1988; Evans et al. 1999: 251; Hodder 1998). The chamber was finally covered by an earthen barrow.

Street House in northern England is a rare example of a pre-cairn or mound setting that may represent a coherent structure (Vyner 1984) (Figure 4.16). In comparison to the monuments above, it seems to have been rapidly built and destroyed. Three pits, enclosed by clay banks, held substantial upright timbers. These were joined by horizontal timbers enclosing a long, thin rectangular space. At least one of the posts was probably a split tree trunk as it was D-shaped in plan (Vyner 1984: 161). A trench incorporating the eastern end pit of the triple setting held many timbers that defined a forecourt opening to the east. The entire wooden structure was set alight, cremating the remains of at least five human bodies within the rectangular setting (Birkett 1984). While Street House appears to be a coherent, single-phase structure, there are some peculiarities about the site. Radiocarbon dates were obtained from various elements of burnt structure. Most of these form a group of dates that span the second half of the fourth millennium (3600–3000 BC) (see Figure 4.2). These were obtained from the façade posts, parts of the horizontal planking and the old land surface. One date stands out from this group and that was obtained from burnt timber that had stood in the large eastern end post: the date for this centres on the period 4000–3800 BC. This was a substantial timber, but the much older date cannot be accounted for solely on grounds of the timber having derived from an older specimen than the others: the post had been cut down at an earlier date than the others, was appreciably older and may have been reused (Vyner 1984: 153). Attention seems to have been focused on this post, as during the destruction of the monument this post was made to burn more than the others, as the pit was marked by a distinct concentration of burnt sandstone rubble (Vyner 1984: 162).

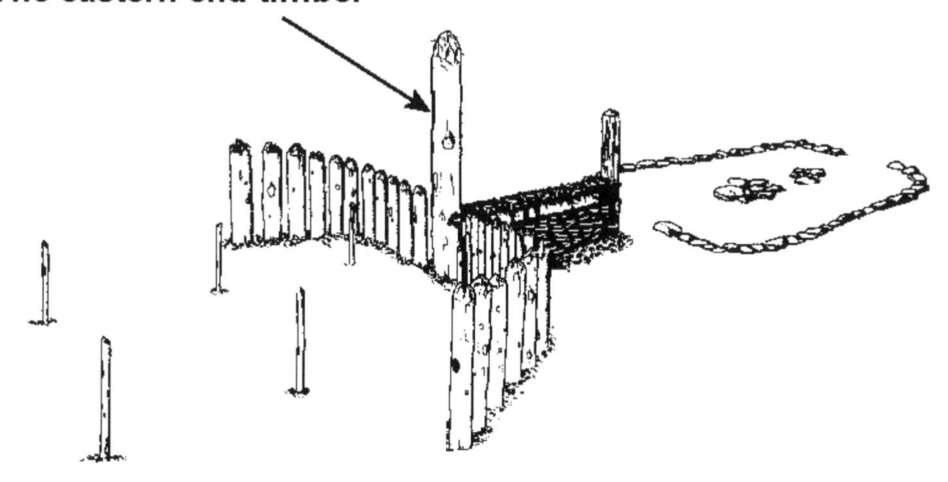

FIGURE 4.16 *Reconstruction drawing of the monument at Street House. The old eastern end timber is highlighted*
(Source: Vyner 1984: figure 9)

Part of the timber structure under the barrow at Nutbane in southern England was also burnt, but timbers associated with human remains were allowed to decay instead of being burnt. The timber structures found under Nutbane represented a number of different phases of activity (Morgan 1959) (Figure 4.17). One of the first constructions was a banked enclosure made by four ditches and banks. Inside the ditches and banks stood two massive postholes at the eastern and western ends. To the east stood a forecourt enclosure defined by four large pits, each of which held a number of posts. Within the banked and ditched enclosure three bodies, two older males and a child, lay between the two massive posts on a layer of light oak brushwood; the bodies were covered in soil. At some point the oak posts in the four pits defining the forecourt to the east were set alight and destroyed by fire. After the destruction, another forecourt was built, this time on a much more massive scale. Oak posts were set in huge bedding trenches. The trenches supported a roofed section defined by uprights and horizontal timbers, flanked by massive freestanding posts which projected westward from the front wall of the roofed section. Around the same time, the banked and ditched enclosure surrounding the bodies was modified and elaborated. The ditches were refilled using the material from the banks and a rectangular fenced enclosure was built around the ditches. One of the massive posts on the western side was removed and in its place another human body, a further male, was placed over its former position. All four burials were then covered by a cairn of chalk after the timbers had fully decayed (Morgan 1959: Figure 5). One of the final acts involved setting the roofed section of the second forecourt structure to the east on fire. This was obviously set alight at the same time as the main body of the long barrow was being built (Morgan 1959: 35).

At Nutbane, we can see that the burials were simply laid on a layer of brushwood between the two large postholes, the bodies were not elevated, nor were they exposed. One of the posts was later removed and a further body was placed on the former position of the post and both posts had decayed by the time the chalk-capping cairn sealed all four burials. The structures associated with the burials were treated in markedly different ways to those that defined the two phases of forecourt buildings. All of the wooden elements associated with the burials in the western area, including the two massive posts, the fenced enclosure that surrounded the filled ditches and the posts within two pits immediately in front of the large eastern post, decayed *in situ*. In contrast, the major elements of both the forecourt buildings to the east were destroyed by fire.

Split trunk monuments were also constructed in Ireland. At Dooey's Cairn in Country Antrim the sequence is difficult to interpret in terms of the usual interpretations of pre-mound or cairn mortuary structures (Collins 1976: 7) (Figure 4.18). A court-type cairn was found to contain a long stone-lined trench within which lay three deep pits. The trench is similar to that at Pitnacree, Lochhill and Slewcairn in Scotland. This seems to have been used for cremating bodies as at Street House, but there was little evidence for actual posts within the pits in the trench and certainly no traces of *in situ* burnt timbers as at Street House. Charcoal and some cremated bone were found over and under a layer of paving in the trench and extended down into two of the three pits. The stone-lined trench had been built as the same time as the

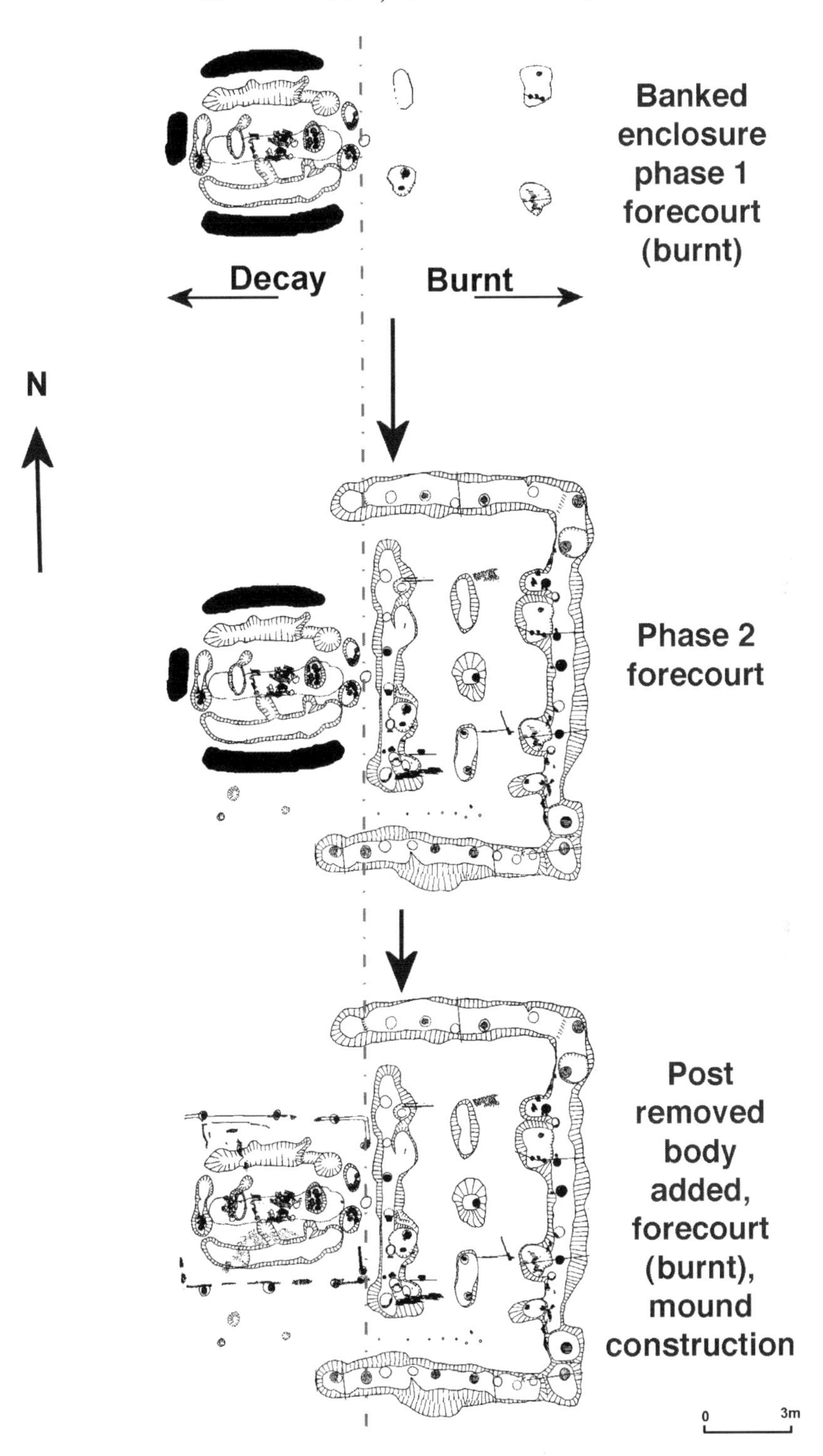

Figure 4.17 *The sequence of construction and destruction at Nutbane*

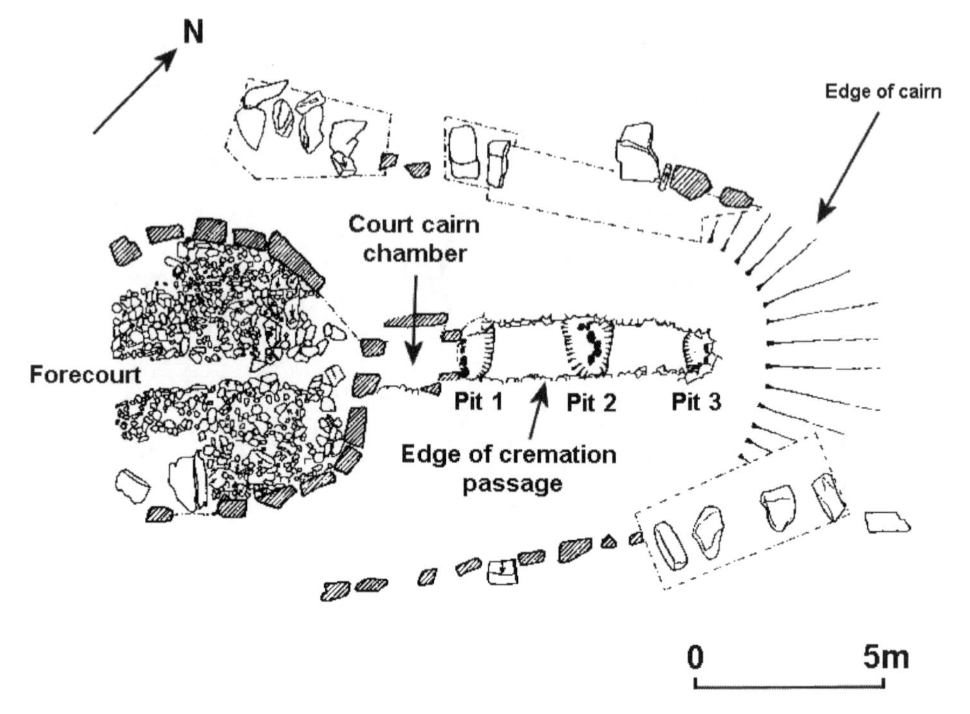

FIGURE 4.18 *The Court cairn, known as Dooey's Cairn, Co. Antrim. Pits 1, 2 and 3 underlie the body of the cairn*
(Source: Collins 1976: figure 1)

cairn, indicating that the cremation and burning was perhaps undertaken at the same time as the construction of the new chamber, which was not used for cremation, nor did the court cairn chamber contain cremated bone (Collins 1976: 6). The burning, therefore, seemed to mark a change in the use of the monument and may have marked the closure of the pre-cairn features. The lack of evidence for posts in the pits and the presence of cremated bone may indicate that posts were removed and the voids partly filled with pyre material, as happened at Slewcairn.

SUMMARY: TREES AS NATURAL SYMBOLS

It can be seen that there are distinct difficulties in interpreting many of these sites as exposure platforms and in many cases the use of the split trunks in any form of mortuary structure is doubtful, as the trunks decayed before human remains were introduced to the site. At Aldwincle I, for example, bodies were carefully laid between two pits and did not fall from an exposure platform and at Fussell's Lodge the deliberate placement of skeletal material and the structured nature of the single-phase burial deposit argues against any form of covering building or raised platform. Furthermore, the cairn that covered the bodies also covered the pits; if present, the posts had clearly decayed or were removed before the human remains were deposited. The human remains may have been deliberately placed over the former position of the posts. A similar interest in the voids of removed posts was found at Nutbane, also in southern England, where a human body was placed over the void of a large wooden post (Morgan 1959). There was a deliberate contrast between the burning of the forecourt structures and the decay of the wooden elements surrounding the bodies at this site. A split tree trunk had been set in two ramped posts at Pitnacree but had decayed long before cremated remains were deposited around a rectangular stone setting. The cremations were deposited at the same time as the mound was built. At Slewcairn and probably at Lochhill too, split tree trunks were removed leaving the bases of the posts in the pits. These pits were then partly filled with cremated and burnt remains deposited inside rectangular stone settings, which were built at the same time as the outer cairns. The sequence at Dalladies is more ambiguous, but the first phase of activity may have involved the erection of a split tree trunk and other timber posts in three large pits and two smaller pits. At some stage, a stone and lighter timber building replaced these. Human remains may have been stored here, but most were probably removed before the main barrow was completed. Street House in northern England may have been a unitary structure in which large split trunks formed a constructional element. However, at least one of the large timbers was much older than the others and may have been reused from an older structure. Unlike the Scottish examples, Street House was used to cremate the human remains found there. In this respect the site can be seen as part of a regional tradition of crematoria (Manby 1970). At Wayland's Smithy, it seems unlikely that the split trunk was part of a structure as they were not placed in a suitable alignment and at least some of the timber elements had decayed before the stone phases of the monument were added.

In summary, it can be shown that the split trunks and timber elements that represented the first phase of activity at many of these sites had decayed long before human remains were introduced. The decay of the trunks may have taken a substantial length of time. As a result, it seems unlikely that these posts formed part of the mortuary ceremonies. Some of these sites may have been subsequently used to process human remains, but this was not necessarily the primary function of these monuments. In Scotland their role in supporting an exposure platform can further be ruled out when it is considered that at three of the four sites discussed in detail above, cremation was the mortuary rite used. The posts were not used to cremate bodies either, as there is no evidence of the posts having been burnt, despite good evidence for the burning of the later stone and timber settings. Furthermore, the bone deposits at all of the sites considered appear to be the result of a single deposit that was part of the closing ceremonies at the sites, often deposited at the same time as the covering mound or cairn was constructed.

Rather than the tree supporting human bodies and being merely part of a functional structure, I suggest that the tree itself was of prime importance and that the dead were offered to the place where the tree had decayed. The confusion over the sequence of events at these sites has arisen due to the fact that the Neolithic groups who built these monuments paid such close attention to the position of the decayed timbers that at some monuments it has been assumed that all of the features of the monument belonged to the same phase of activity. However, it is clear that the erection of the tree formed a distinct and important phase of activity at these sites.

The significance of the tree itself is perhaps emphasised by the size of the timbers used. The size of the timbers are beyond functional necessity (Evans et al. 1999: 251). Many of the split timbers appear to be over a metre in diameter and would have been from very large trees. A platform for holding a human body would not require such massive timbers and it seems odd that such a large tree was used when smaller timbers would have been easier to cut down and erect. Moreover, the act of splitting the tree in half seems overly labour-intensive compared with using smaller timbers. These considerations suggest that the tree played more than a functional role. I suggest that the tree split in half and set up in the pits during the first phase of activity at the sites was of prime importance. This was not necessarily due to its use in a structure, but perhaps due to the symbolism that many different cultures across the world attach to trees. But what would trees have meant to people in the Earlier Neolithic?

TREES AND WOODS IN THE EARLIER NEOLITHIC

It is difficult for most of us today to imagine what it would be like to live in a wooded environment (Figure 4.19). However, as Cummings and Whittle have noted: 'Neolithic existence across much if not most of Europe involved dwelling among trees' (Cummings and Whittle 2004b). After the end of the last Ice Age woodland species spread across the whole of Britain, and by the beginnings of the Neolithic trees dominated the landscape and accounted for much of the vegetation on the British Isles (Tipping 1994; Edwards and Whittington 1997). As a result woodland would have been part of the everyday experience of Neolithic people. This is difficult for us to imagine today with less than 1.5 per cent of the British landscape now covered by trees (Austin 2000: 71). The ubiquity of trees would have created a very distinct environment. Trees compose a landscape and have an affect on the type of flora and fauna that is present, dramatically affecting human perception – reducing visual capabilities, but increasing the use of the other senses (Austin 2000: 69; Jones and Cloke 2002: 88; Rival 1998b). Woodland would have formed the backdrop for many aspects of Neolithic life. Some of the earliest Neolithic activity identified by insect remains is an indication of the grazing of animals in woodland (Robinson 2000). But woodland was more than just a backdrop for Neolithic life. The Earlier Neolithic also marks the period when woodland was first cleared and managed on a large scale. Clearances have been recorded in the preceding Mesolithic, but these appear to be small scale both in temporal and spatial terms (Edwards and Hirons 1984). The Neolithic, on the other hand, represents a period when impacts on the woodland are recorded on an unprecedented scale (Austin 2000: 73; Tipping 1994; Edwards and Whittington 1997). For the first time woodland and trees seem to have became both a resource and a medium for human activity. Timber was used for the first time in large quantities for the construction of massive timber monuments, and for use in shelters and houses.

FIGURE 4.19 *The forest*

The use of trees in ceremonial contexts in Neolithic Britain has been noted before. For example, large assemblages of Earlier Neolithic artefacts have been found in tree throws at a number of sites in southern England (Evans et al. 1999). This has been connected to the likely significance of trees in Neolithic world views. Pollard (2000: 367) has suggested that the dead and woodland may have been intimately connected in the Neolithic and has highlighted general links between timber monuments, trees and woodlands. Trees may have been fundamental to Neolithic world views. Different trees, displaying different natural properties, would have been potent symbols in conceptualising the world around and trees and timber would have been a dominant part of Neolithic life, but how might Neolithic people have related to the woodland?

PEOPLE AND THE NATURAL ENVIRONMENT

> History is the process wherein both people and their environments are continually bringing each other into being. (Ingold 2000: 87)

The beginnings of the Neolithic have traditionally been seen as a revolution in the way people related to the natural world, a time when humans first began to control the growth of plants and animals and when they first *transcended* nature (Childe 1942; Bradley 1993). In this way the farmers who lived and worked amongst the woodland of Neolithic Britain might have seen themselves as controlling and transcending the environment around them. However, as Ingold has shown, traditional farming societies do not tend to see themselves as controlling nature (Ingold 2000: Chapter 5). Instead people see themselves and the plants and animals that surround them as participants in the same world, 'a world that is at once social and natural' (Ingold 2000: 87). For example, although the Dogon of Mali draw contrasts between the 'wild' bush and the village where crops are grown, they do not see themselves as controlling nature. Instead it is nature in the form of the bush that holds ultimate power over human life, and the maintenance of the village depends upon the continual inflow of vital force from the bush (Ingold 2000: 84). As Ingold observes, this is almost the exact inversion of the Western notion of food production as the manifestation of human knowledge and power over nature (Ingold 2000: 84). Trees in the Neolithic allowed fires to be lit and houses and monuments to be built. The clearance of trees allowed food to be grown. In this way woodland might have been seen as allowing human life to continue and to exist in the first place. It might be suggested, then, that trees and woodland may have formed a central and important role in Neolithic life. But what might trees have *meant* to the Neolithic people?

TREES IN BELIEF SYSTEMS ACROSS THE WORLD

> Trees are not simply good to climb, they are good to think. (Davies 1988: 34)

Human cultures derive meaning from the natural world and the natural elements that surround them (Rival 1993: 636, 1998b: 1). Across the world trees have often played central roles in the way people conceptualise the world. Tree symbolism has been used by many different societies in many different contexts. Shared across many different belief systems is the use of trees to make concrete and natural the abstract notion of life: 'all over the world, rituals marking the lifecycle make extensive use of trees'

(Rival 1998b: 7). In the Christian faith, for example, trees are seen as powerful symbols of life and death (Davies 1988: 38).

Being surrounded by woodland, trees would have formed part of Neolithic groups' understanding of the world around them. More specifically, in eastern Scotland, trees may have been used as a means of conceptualising processes of death, decay and renewal. As Austin has pointed out, forests contain trees of the past, present and future and in this way are potent metaphors for thinking about lifecycles. (Austin 2000: 67) (Figure 4.20). Trees are potent symbols of the lifecycle because individual trees display different aspects of birth and death at different times. For example, the seasonal shedding of leaves, leaving the tree bare (bare to the bones) is a yearly demonstration of death and renewal. Trees are also potent symbols of fertility and regeneration due to a number of natural characteristics. For example, trees quickly re-colonise clearings made in forests (Philpot 1897: 88; Rival 1993: 647) and the largest trees of the forest often take a long time to mature in comparison to humans. Moreover, once cut down trees can take a long time to decay or can be reborn, taking on new lives as part of a house, monument or agricultural tool (Austin 2000: 75; Bloch 1998: 42; Bloch and Parry 1992; Davies 1988: 41; Rival 1998b: 12, 22). In many cultures, the cutting down of trees can be analogous to explicit sacrifice. The cutting down of trees is a significant act and must be done in the right way, using the right tools and often requires ritual acts or gift-giving to placate the spirits of the trees (Rival 1998b; Toren 1995: 168; van Beek and Bonga 1992: 70). However, the cutting down of the tree can also be an act of fertility and renewal through its transformation from tree to timber. Many cultures also see objects made of wood as being alive (Rival 1998b: 22). The symbolism and significance of trees and timber may explain why such significance was attached to stone axes in the Neolithic and why such great effort was expended in their procurement, exchange and deposition during this period (Bradley and Edmonds 1993).

Figure 4.20 *Trees of the past and the future*

The links between trees and fertility are often extended to notions of human fertility. For example, the size and permanence of some species of tree can be a symbol of what humans should aspire to with age (Jones and Cloke 2002: 89). Many cultures use mature trees as symbols in lifecycle ceremonies designed to promote bodily growth (Bonnemère 1998: 114; Giambelli 1998: 149; Ingold 2000: 86). Tree and woodland metaphors are also often used in modelling social relations between individuals and groups, as well as having a role in the mediations between the living and the dead (Austin 2000: 66; Daniels 1988: 43; Keen 1990: 101; Platenkamp 1992: 76; Rival 1998b: 8). Connections with ancestors and trees are common, perhaps due to the fact that trees can seem to transcend death in that they often appear to be both alive and dead at the same time (Giambelli 1998: 135; Keen 1990: 101; Rival 1993: 636, 1998b: 23). Perhaps the most direct and important link between trees and humans is the human body.

In many cultures analogies between trees and the human body are often quite explicit (Bloch 1998: 42; Jones and Cloke 2002: 92; Rival 1998b: 8–10). In many cultures, including our own, the separate parts of the tree are connected and often have the same names as parts of the human body. In our own society we connect the trunk of the tree and the torso of the human body with the word 'trunk' and branches are referred to as 'limbs' (Figure 4.21). In many cultures the parallels go further. Wood, particularly the trunk, is often associated with bone, especially the inner heartwood of a tree. The Yolngu of Arnhem Land, Australia, for example, associate tree trunks with bone and leaves with flesh and these are metaphors used by many other cultures (Keen 1990). The connections between humans and trees can extend beyond metaphor and symbolism in some cultures. As Ingold notes, to hunter-gatherers living in forest environments some of the most important persons in the forest are trees (Ingold 2000: 145). Even in our own culture we often imagine forests to consist of living persons:

> In a forest, I have felt many times that it was not I who was looking at the forest. In some days I have felt that it was the trees that were looking at me, that were

FIGURE 4.21 *The trunk*

speaking to me. For myself, I was there . . . listening. (Charbonnier 1959, quoted in Ingold 2000: 276)

The links between trees, fertility, regeneration, lifecycles and the human body are relevant and apt metaphors when considering the barrows and related structures of Scotland. The tree may have originally been cut down (killed) as part of a clearance to create areas for growing crops or for grazing animals. Possible traces of clearance and cultivation have been recorded under a number of the barrows outlined above including Wayland's Smithy, Pitnacree and Dalladies (Coles and Simpson 1965; Piggott 1971–2; Whittle 1991). The death of trees allowed the new ways of life associated with the onset of the Neolithic to take place. The tree was sacrificed but was reborn as two massive timbers to be used at a monument. Once the tree had been felled and removed from the spot that it would have inhabited for generations it was re planted in pits. This planting was not in the traditional sense – the tree had no chance of growing again and instead was allowed to decay. It is uncertain how long the now decaying tree may have lasted, but it would have been a much shorter time than its natural lifespan which far exceeded that of a Neolithic person. The tree's new lifespan would more closely match that of a human. Ritual is often based on a form of substitution where one thing becomes another (Bloch 1998: 39). The tree may have symbolised a human body as trees are good substitutes for humans (Bloch 1998: 40). The body of the tree was rooted to the spot and was allowed to decay. The great size of the tree and the time it would take to decay would have been a potent symbol of permanence and vitality and would have been a powerful tool through which ideas about lifecycles and death could be conceptualised. The trunk may also have been a medium through which Neolithic people could connect to the past. The original tree would have been much older than any of the humans who were involved in replanting it and as such it would have been an object from the past, perhaps connected to the ancestors. The transformation of the mature tree into something closer to resembling a human may have been the exact reverse of the process of a human being becoming an ancestor. Yet central to becoming an ancestor would have been decay: the decay of flesh from the bones, a process that was graphically highlighted in the decay of the split trunk (Figure 4.22).

Analogies between trees, timber and the human body may have continued in the secondary structures at the barrows. The subsequent stone and wooden elements of Pitnacree, Slewcairn and Dalladies used different parts of the tree than were used in the first phases of activity. At these sites the split trunks were replaced with rectangular stone settings roofed by slight timbers and bark (Piggott 1971–2; Masters 1973a, 1973b). At Dalladies the lower timber framework of the second-phase structure was a very slight structure consisting of small (less than 15 centimetres in diameter) timbers or sticks, while higher up freshly stripped birch bark was used as a roofing material (Piggott 1971–2: 35). At Slewcairn the rectangular stone setting was roofed and lined with small timbers and Scots pine bark (Masters 1974: 44, 1975: 28). At Lochhill, pine was also used in the burnt elements of the monument (Masters 1973b: 2). The slender timbers and bark were distinct from the very large-diameter

FIGURE 4.22 *Decay*

trunks used in the split trunk phase. The split trunks were usually around 1 metre in diameter or larger and must have came from a mature, if not elderly, tree. By analogy with traditions of Neolithic monuments elsewhere these were probably from oak trees. Few other native species of such size would be readily available. Oak timber is one of the tree species most resistant to decay with a durable heartwood (Cartwright and Findlay 1958: 275; White 1995: 129–132). In contrast, pine is soft and not particularly durable; the trunks of pine trees rarely reach great diameters (Snow 1903: 130; White 1995: 162). Birch timber is also not particularly resistant to decay; the trees themselves tend to have short lives (White 1995: 33–6). Birch bark separates into many fine paper-thin layers, much like skin (Snow 1903: 68). Cherry wood is strong, but light and easily worked (Snow 1903: 114). There seems to be a deliberate contrast here between the types of wood used in the two phases of activity.

While the massive trunk set up in the first phase of the monuments may have been equated with the body and a symbol of resistance, the bark and the smaller timbers of the softer, less durable trees used in the secondary structures may have been equated with flesh and skin. These soft timbers and bark were burnt, leaving only the stone part of the structure in place. There may be a parallel here with the cremated deposits placed within the majority of the Scottish sites. The deliberate burning of the secondary structures in the Scottish examples may have re-enacted the burning of the body on a pyre. Through the burning of the bark and stone structures the flesh (the bark) was removed leaving only the supporting stone (bone) structure. All of these sites underwent transformations. While sequences vary, each involved the replacement of wooden elements with stone. This may have symbolised the transformation of the living into decaying bodies and finally to ancestors through the associations between different materials and the use of stone in the final structures. Parker Pearson and Ramilisonina have connected the use of timber in Neolithic monuments with the activities of the living, and stone structures with the dead (Parker Pearson and Ramilisonina 1998). It is revealing that at the sites considered here the deposition of human remains was almost always associated with the construction of stone elements that were often quickly sealed by the earth and stone barrows as at Pitnacree or formed part of the newly constructed chambered cairns as at Lochhill and Slewcairn, which were unambiguously for the deposition of dead bodies. In this way, the whole sequence of monument construction and the natural elements used – timber, stone and earth – may have been associated with and symbolised the lifecycles of humans and their transformation to ancestors.

CONCLUSION: THE TREE AS A MODEL FOR HUMAN GROWTH AND DECAY

> People's interaction with their natural environment form the basis of their social practices and understandings of the social. (Rival 1993: 635)

Rather than forming a structural part of the monuments it is possible to view the split tree trunks in the barrows and related structures as a symbol used in rituals that highlighted processes of life and death. The tree was a physical and public manifestation of ideas connected with the fundamental issues that govern human existence. Trees are particularly powerful symbols to use in rituals that highlight human lifecycles, as trees are good substitutes for humans. As a medium through which ideas about the fundamental processes of life and death were played, the tree would have represented a potent symbol of vitality. Trees were fundamental to Neolithic life and may have been seen as what enabled life to continue. The cutting down of the tree and subsequent planting in pits represented the sacrifice of a living thing, an object of great age and maturity. The sacrifice connected a symbol of permanence with the social group perhaps as a means of transferring these attributes to the present and future members of that group. The substantial length of time that such a large tree would take to decay in the ground would form a powerful symbol of continuity and resistance across a number of human generations. In this way it could be shown that life would continue despite death.

NOTE

1. While Section 4 in figure 6 (Whittle 1991) might suggest that the trunks continued through the mound, Section 5 suggests otherwise. Why the sections should indicate different possibilities is difficult to ascertain.

CHAPTER FIVE

Megalithic architecture in Atlantic Scotland

Introduction

Excavations at chambered cairns across Scotland have shown that these monuments are the result of a number of distinct periods of construction. Through detailed analysis of the altering nature of the architecture of these monuments it is possible to link these changes with a transformation in the relationships between the living and the dead in Neolithic society. The secondary phases of many of these cairns involved increasing the capacity of these monuments and adding areas for public display. These changes can be seen as being related to the growing importance of the dead and ancestry in Neolithic society.

There are a number of different traditions of Neolithic megalithic architecture in southern, western and northern Scotland, classified comprehensively in various volumes by Audrey Henshall (Henshall 1963, 1972; Davidson and Henshall 1989, 1991; Henshall and Ritchie 1995, 2001) (Figure 5.1). Early antiquarians such as Petrie, Anderson and Bryce were the first to classify chambered cairns into regional groups and undertook the first detailed excavations of these monuments. Anderson was perhaps the most forward-thinking of these figures and attempted to understand the nature of the burial and structural evidence of the cairns. The early studies of the twentieth century continued to focus on classifying monuments and began to attribute these groups to different cultural groups of people. Figures such as Gordon Childe and Stuart Piggott aimed to identify the origins of these peoples and looked to the Continent for parallels with traditions of Neolithic architecture found there (Childe 1935; Piggott 1954). In the 1960s, radiocarbon dating began to revolutionise interpretations of the Neolithic period and many of Childe's and Piggott's ideas were questioned. In some ways, interpretation became more circumspect and Henshall's first volume aimed to catalogue the many separate cairns, continuing the tradition of classification but with little attempt at interpretation (Henshall 1963). The preface to the 1972 volume outlines some of the uncertainties that Henshall and others were working under at the time (Henshall 1972). What followed in the 1960s and 70s was a reduction in the scale of megalithic studies with focus on the structural sequences of individual cairns and on the development of regional groups (de Valera 1960; Corcoran 1960, 1969b; Scott 1969). Colin Renfrew tried to counter the trend towards

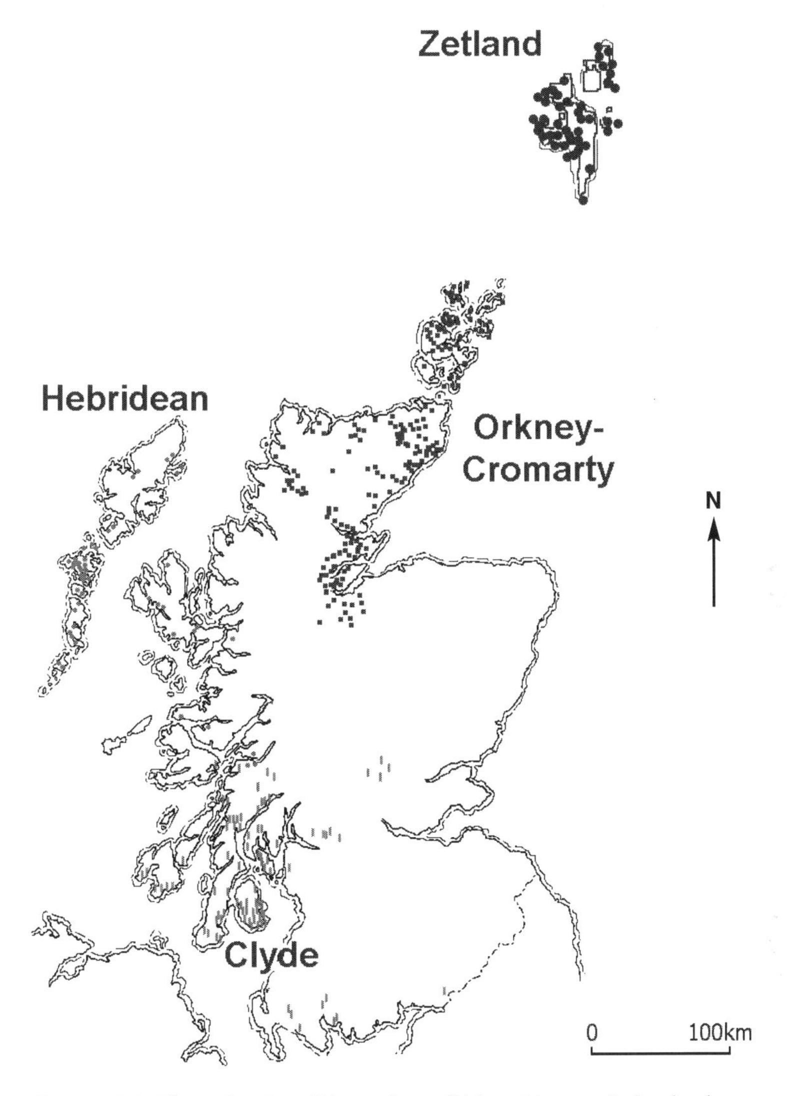

Figure 5.1 *The regional traditions of megalithic architecture in Scotland (Sources: Davidson and Henshall 1989, 1991; Henshall 1963, 1972; Ritchie 1997)*

regionalism by generalising from a number of traditions of megalithic architecture using the distribution of chambered cairns in Rousay and Arran to suggest that these monuments functioned as territorial markers (Renfrew 1976). This interpretation has, however, since been questioned (Hughes 1988). In recent years the social significance of monuments has come to the fore in a wide range of studies (Bradley 1993, 1998; Richards 1988; Sharples 1985; Thomas 1999a). Interest in the structural sequence of individual cairns and typologies of monument traditions has been considered less in recent years, but it seems possible to marry social theory and architectural sequences in order to examine how the significance of monuments may have altered over time. In particular I would like to draw on work pioneered by Corcoran and Scott on the multi-phased nature of many chambered cairns to suggest that the changing form of megalithic architecture in Scotland represented changing attitudes to the dead in Neolithic society. Each tradition of megalithic architecture in Scotland will be examined in order to show that the shifts in attitudes to the dead may have cut across our traditional divisions of chambered cairn architecture.

THE CLYDE CAIRNS OF WESTERN AND SOUTHERN SCOTLAND

Thomas H. Bryce, a celebrated early-twentieth-century anatomist, was the first to take a systematic interest in the group of cairns found mainly in Argyll, Arran and Bute and southwest Scotland. These are now known as the Clyde Cairns due to their original identification around the opening of the Firth of Clyde, but this type of cairn can be found from Perthshire to the Outer Hebrides (Henshall 1963; Scott 1969). Bryce's interest in the cairns arose from an invitation by Dr Ebenezer Duncan of Glasgow to help excavate the Torlin chambered cairn on Arran. Both Dr Duncan and Bryce were interested in the Clyde Cairns primarily as a source of 'ancient crania' (skulls). After work at Torlin, Bryce went on to record a further twenty-three similar cairns and excavated nineteen of them, mostly on the islands of Arran and Bute (Bryce 1901–2, 1902–3, 1908–9).

Clyde Cairns consist of large rectangular or trapezoidal cairns of stone and earth, enclosing a chamber made of large slabs of stone set on end (Figure 5.2). The chamber stones define rectangular areas, often subdivided by septal slabs into smaller compartments. Within the compartments human bone, occasionally of multiple individuals, has been found, along with a range of pottery vessels and stone tools. At the front of the cairn, large standing stones define a forecourt in a semi-circular or v-shaped arrangement. This forecourt area is thought to have been an arena for public display and for rituals associated with the bones of the dead that

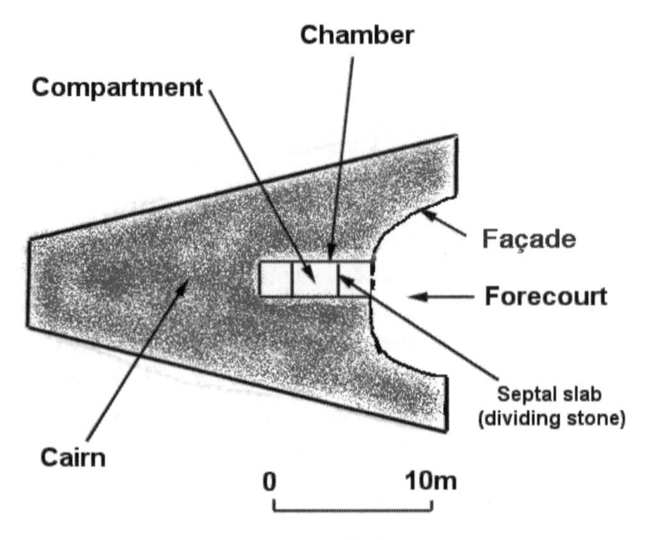

FIGURE 5.2 *An idealised Clyde Cairn*

were deposited within the chambers. The chambers would have formerly been roofed with large flat stones laid across the side slabs of the chamber. There are over 100 Clyde Cairns known today. Most of these are situated around the Clyde itself with notable concentrations on Arran and in Kintyre. Others are found in Dumfries and Galloway and there are a few outliers in the Western Isles and a handful in Perthshire. Few radiocarbon dates are available, but it is clear from those that are available and from the artefacts found within them that the Clyde Cairns represent the earliest Neolithic monumental constructions in this part of Scotland (see Figures 5.3a, b and c).

Increasing contact with the dead: the changing architecture of the Clyde Cairns

Multi-period construction in chambered cairns in Scotland was first noted in detail during the excavation of the Mid Gleniron I and II cairns at Glenluce, Wigtownshire (Corcoran 1969a). Corcoran, a lecturer of Archaeology at Glasgow at the time, excavated the two cairns at Mid Gleniron over four seasons from 1963 to 1966.

The excavations at Mid Gleniron I showed that the primary features of the chambered cairn were two small single-compartment chambers set into two small sub-rectangular cairns without forecourts or portal stones (Figure 5.4). It is unclear whether these two cairns were constructed at the same time or sequentially; however, both were set in a line, their chambers aligned in the same direction. The cairns were only about 5 metres in diameter with single-compartment chambers that would only have allowed limited access due to their small size. The northern chamber was little more than a small 'cist-like' structure, made simply of three large stones set on end, surrounded by a low cairn.

The whole nature of the site changed dramatically at a subsequent phase when the two simple chambers in oval cairns were subsumed in a massive trapezoidal cairn with an elaborate forecourt and an additional third chamber on the western side (Figure 5.5). These additions made a number of important changes to the nature of the monument. The northern 'cist-like' chamber was extended to the north to create a double-compartment chamber. The southern chamber was blocked off and could no longer be directly accessed from the side of the cairn. However, a third larger chamber was added to the west. This chamber was an integral part of the trapezoidal cairn. To the north, an elaborate semicircular façade was added. Within the forecourt, a number of pits containing quartz and evidence for burning and the deposition of smashed pieces of pottery vessels suggest that activities connected to the burial chambers were being carried out there. The façade itself was visually impressive, made of large standing stones and over 8 metres across. It added to the older northern chamber, providing an impressive doorway or portal to the burial deposits within the chamber. A similar sequence can be found at Mid Gleniron II.

The primary phase at Mid Gleniron II also appears to have consisted of two cairns (see Figures 5.6 and 5.7) (Corcoran 1969a, 1969c).[1] One of the original cairns consisted of a chamber made up of two large stones and a drystone inner wall

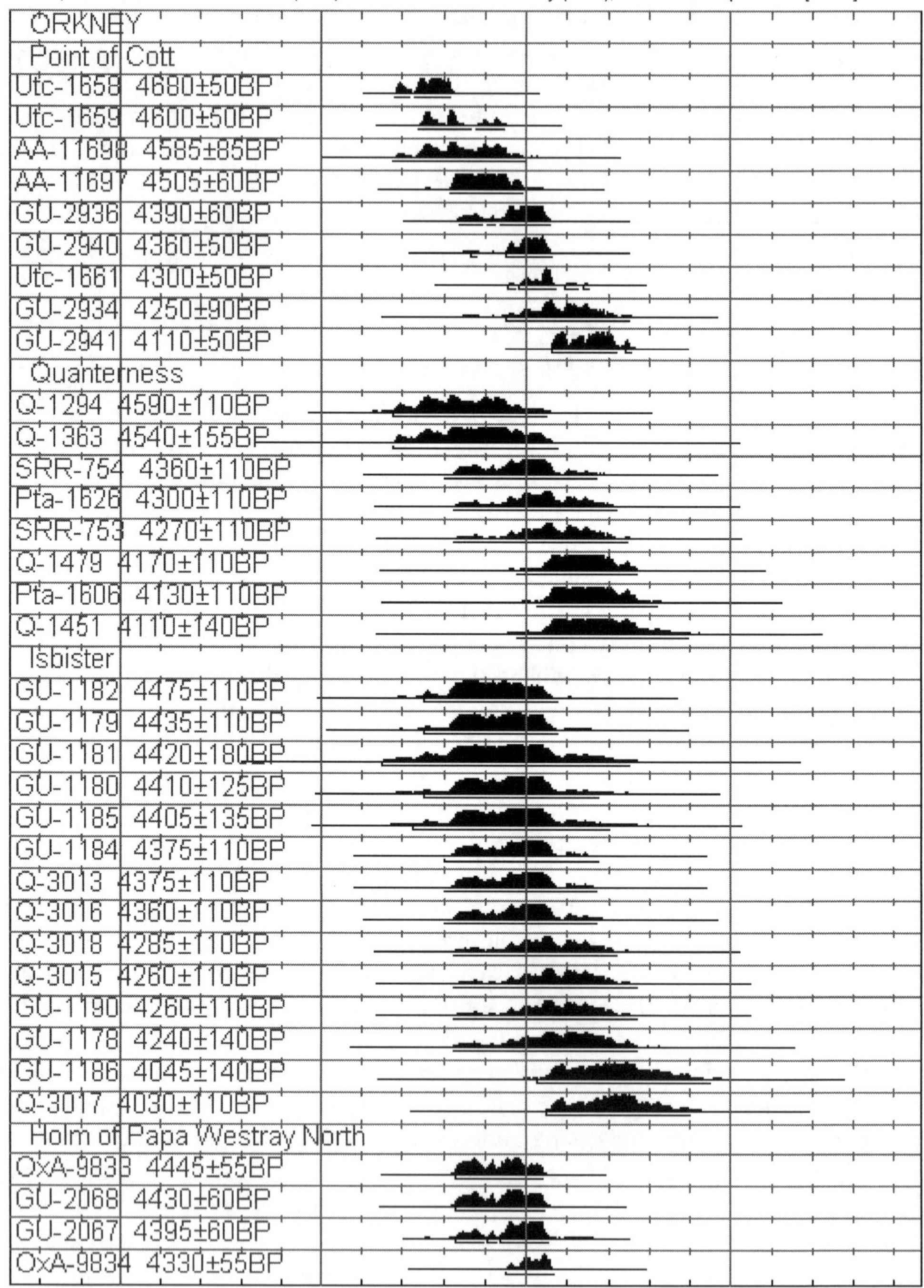

FIGURE 5.3a *Radiocarbon dates for chambered cairns in Scotland*

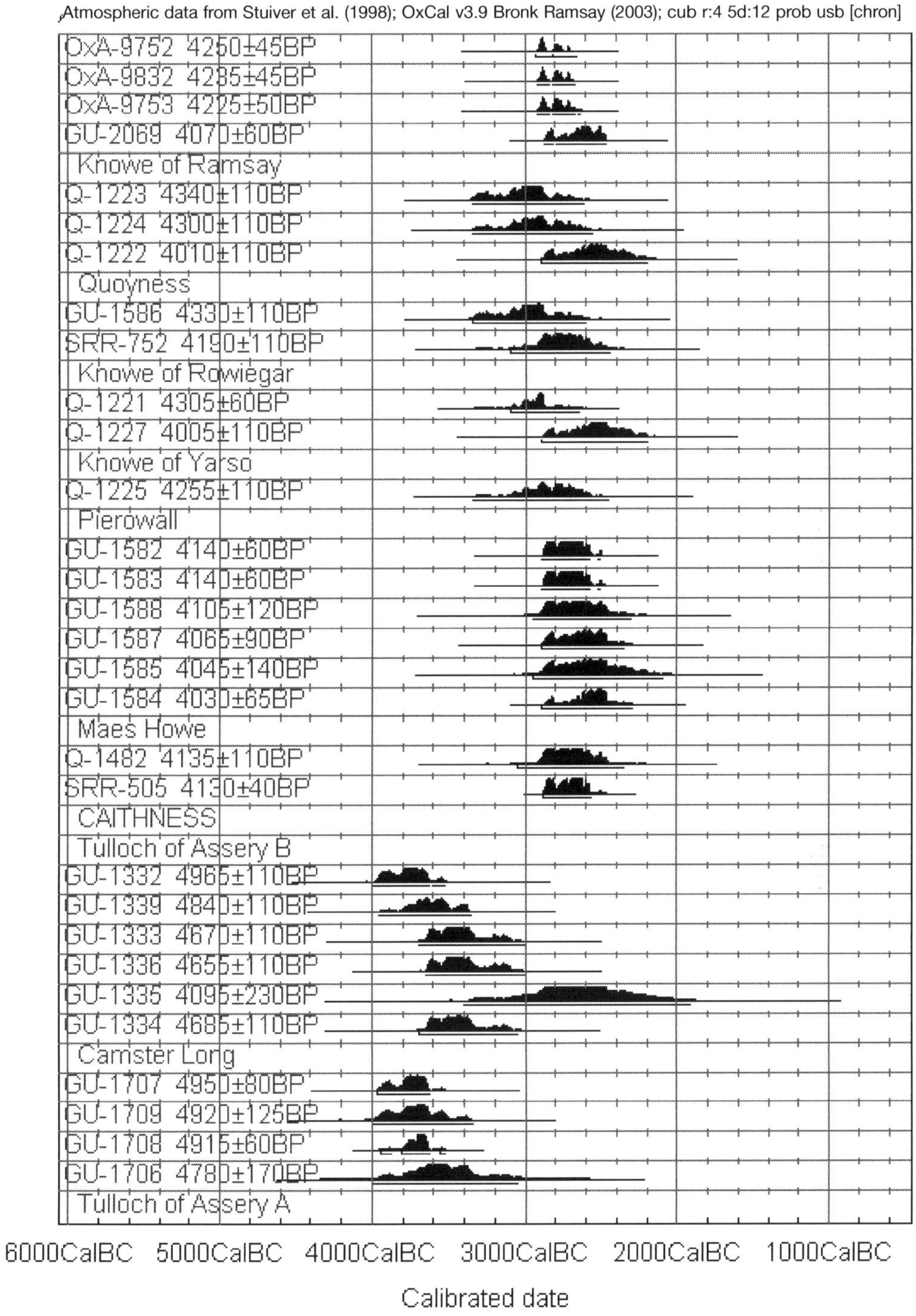

Atmospheric data from Stuiver et al. (1998); OxCal v3.9 Bronk Ramsay (2003); cub r:4 sd:12 prob usp [chron]

OxA-9752 4250±45BP
OxA-9832 4285±45BP
OxA-9753 4225±50BP
GU-2069 4070±60BP
Knowe of Ramsay
Q-1223 4340±110BP
Q-1224 4300±110BP
Q-1222 4010±110BP
Quoyness
GU-1586 4330±110BP
SRR-752 4190±110BP
Knowe of Rowiegar
Q-1221 4305±60BP
Q-1227 4005±110BP
Knowe of Yarso
Q-1225 4255±110BP
Pierowall
GU-1582 4140±60BP
GU-1583 4140±60BP
GU-1588 4105±120BP
GU-1587 4065±90BP
GU-1585 4045±140BP
GU-1584 4030±65BP
Maes Howe
Q-1482 4135±110BP
SRR-505 4130±40BP
CAITHNESS
Tulloch of Assery B
GU-1332 4965±110BP
GU-1339 4840±110BP
GU-1333 4670±110BP
GU-1336 4655±110BP
GU-1335 4095±230BP
GU-1334 4685±110BP
Camster Long
GU-1707 4950±80BP
GU-1709 4920±125BP
GU-1708 4915±60BP
GU-1706 4780±170BP
Tulloch of Assery A

6000CalBC 5000CalBC 4000CalBC 3000CalBC 2000CalBC 1000CalBC

Calibrated date

FIGURE 5.3b *Radiocarbon dates for chambered cairns in Scotland*

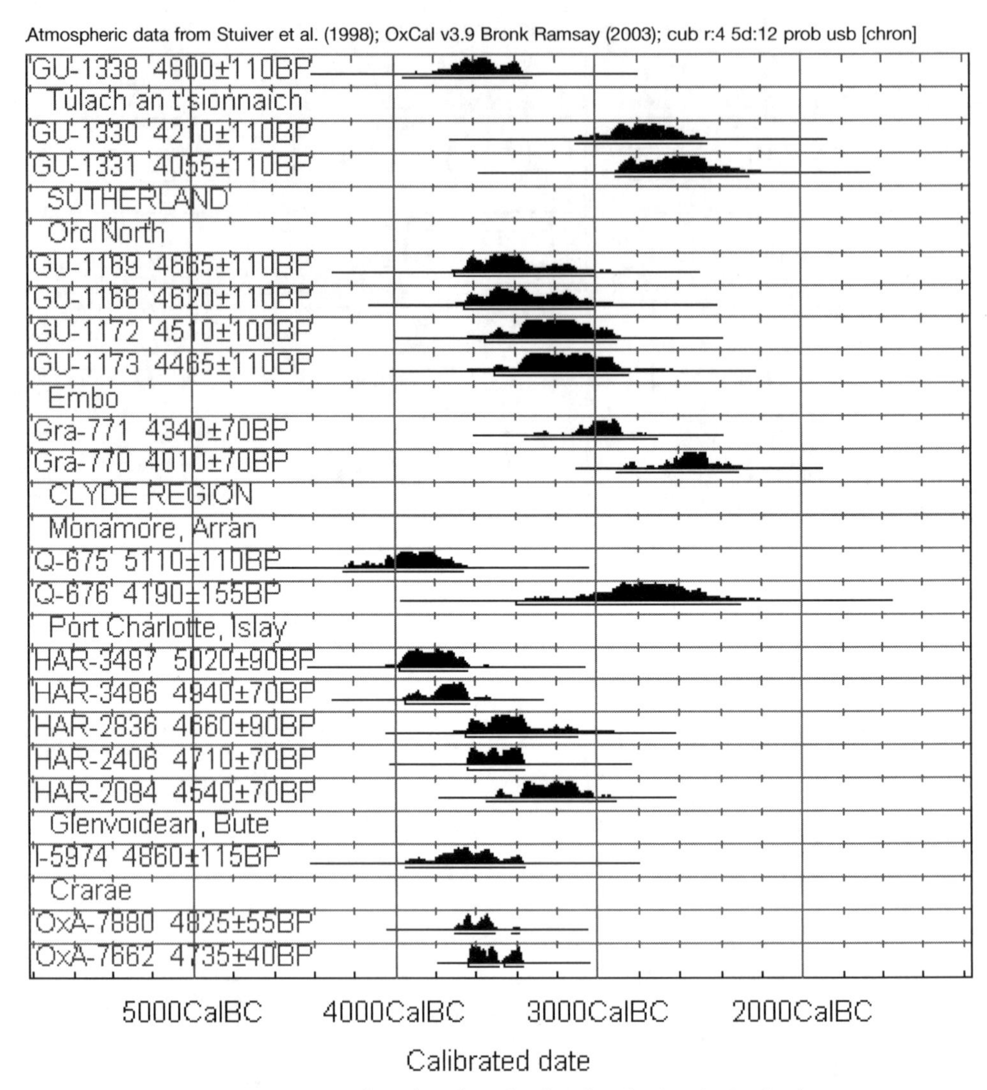

FIGURE 5.3c *Radiocarbon dates for chambered cairns in Scotland*

(Figure 5.6). The cairn was oval with a boulder kerb defining its outer edge. The chamber compartment was very small – the large side stones are less than 1.5 metres in length and the compartment was less than half a metre wide. It is estimated that the compartment would have been roofed at a height of less than 1 metre (Corcoran 1969a: 58). As a result the burial space would have been a very cramped location where access was difficult. Indeed, it seems as if the chamber may not have been intended to be accessible. The boulder kerb of the cairn does not stop at the entrance, but instead continues across the entrance area, effectively sealing the chamber.[2] The other cairn was even less accessible than this (Figure 5.7). Here a closed compartment, made of upright stones, was surrounded by a low circular cairn. As at Mid Gleniron I, subsequent developments at the site radically altered the nature of the monument.

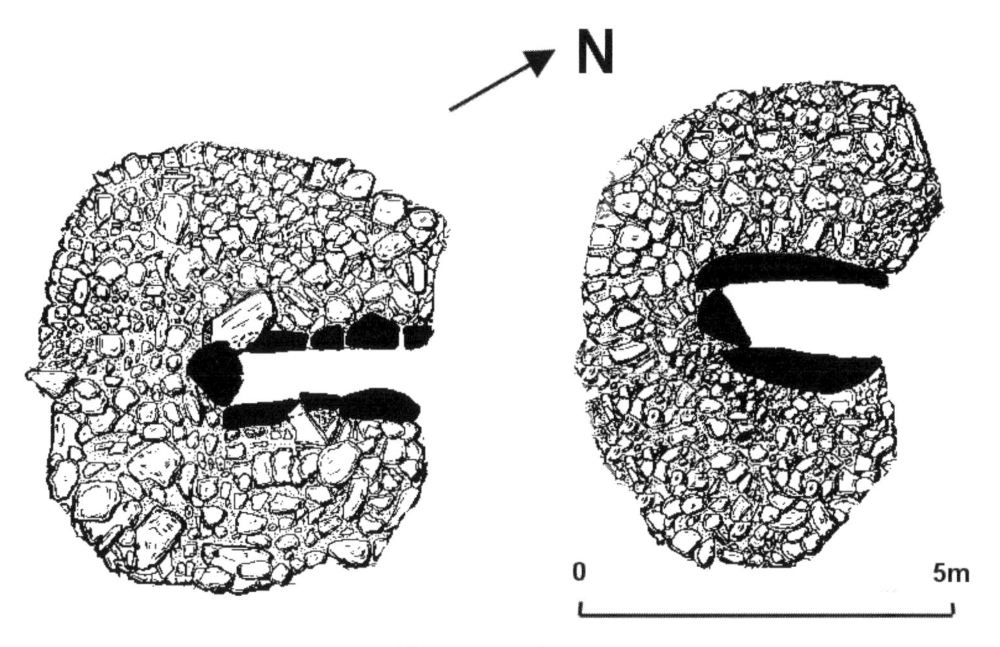

Figure 5.4 *The primary cairns at Mid Gleniron I (Source: Corcoran 1969a: figure 3)*

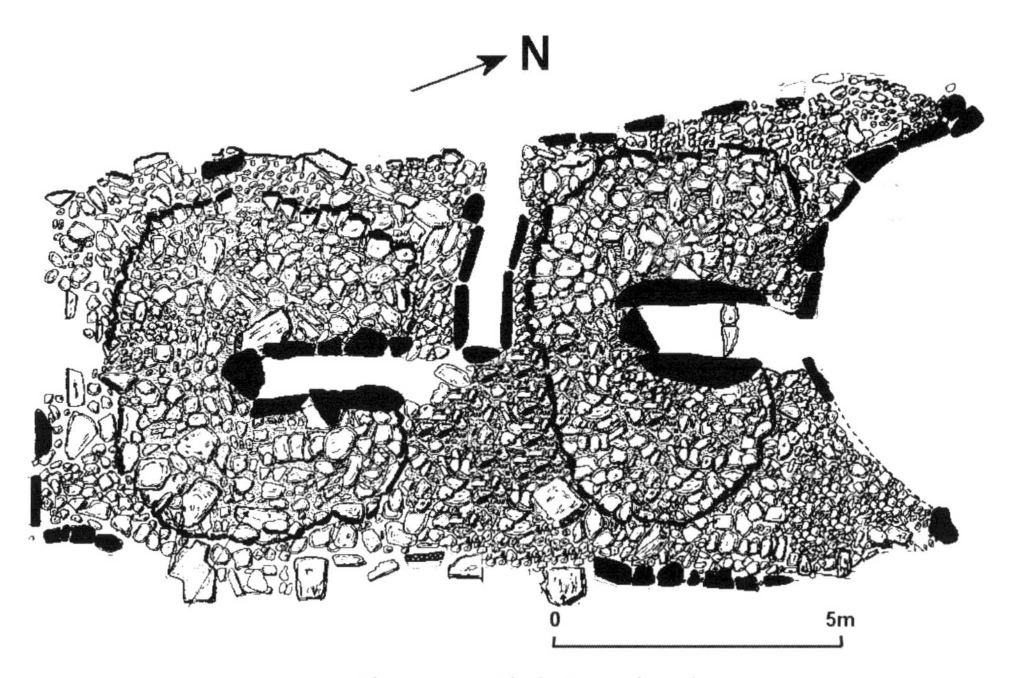

Figure 5.5 *The cairn at Mid Gleniron I after enlargement (Source: Corcoran 1969a: figure 3)*

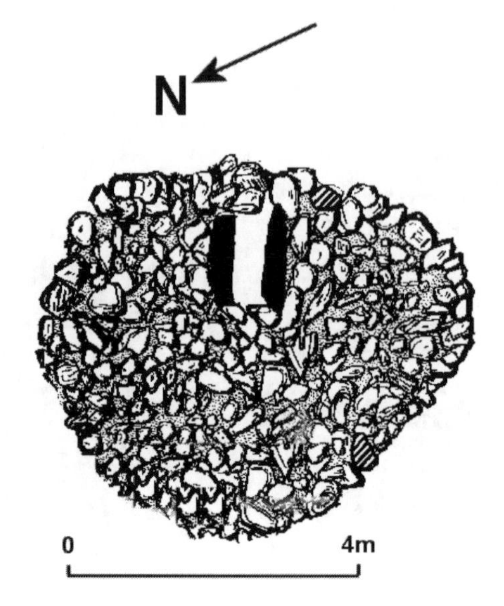

FIGURE 5.6 *Mid Gleniron II primary cairn (Source: Corcoran1969a: figure 9)*

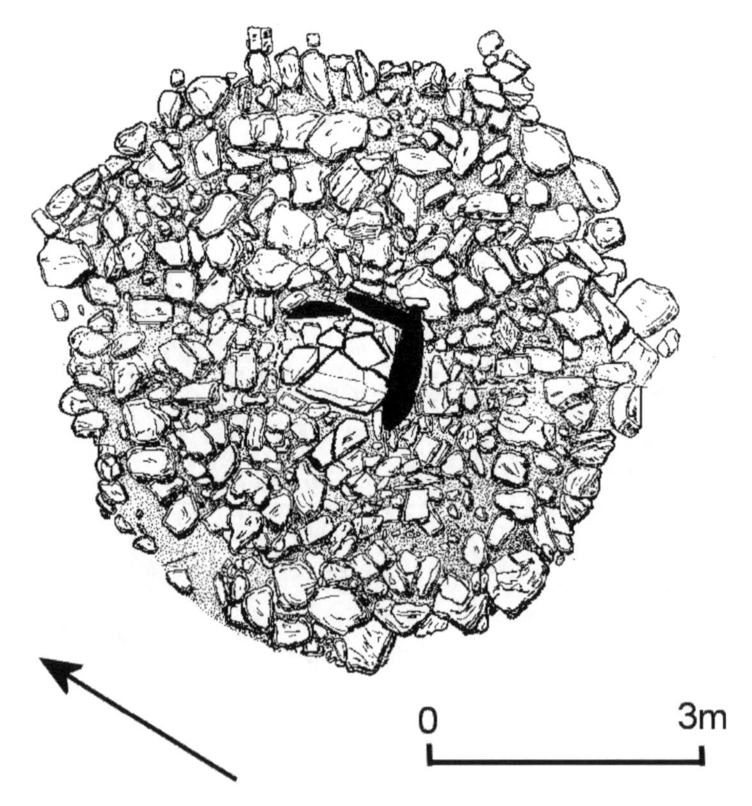

FIGURE 5.7 *Mid Gleniron B (Source: Corcoran 1969c: figure 3)*

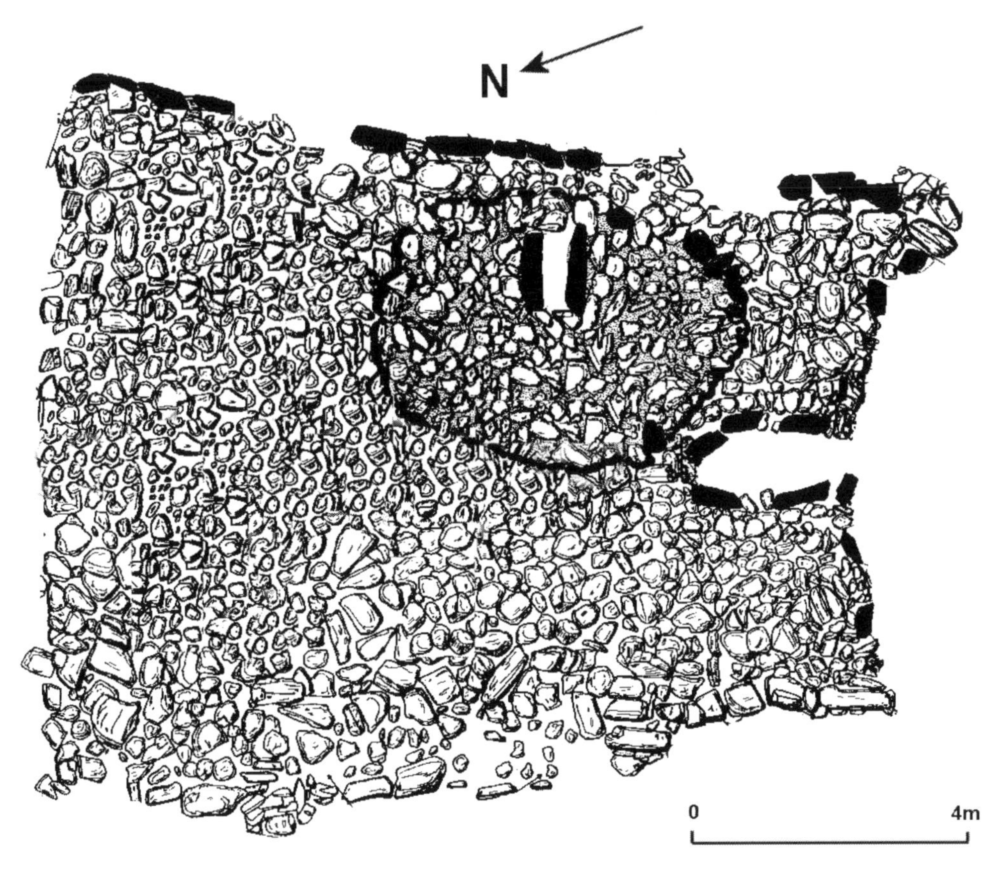

Figure 5.8 *Mid Gleniron II after cairn enlargement (Source: Corcoran1969: figure 9)*

The second phase of construction at Mid Gleniron II involved the construction of a massive trapezoidal cairn around the shell of one of the primary cairns (Figure 5.8). This effectively sealed access to the small cairn. However, the new cairn included a larger chamber in the southern end. This opened directly onto a shallow forecourt area. The new chamber was over twice as long as the original chamber in the oval cairn. Moreover, it was almost twice as wide, allowing easier access to the chamber area and creating a much larger space for depositing the remains of the dead and associated artefacts. It would also seem that the chamber remained open for some time after it was constructed. The chamber was blocked, but not until many centuries later in the Early Bronze Age. The new chamber not only presented a more accessible monument than the original cairn, but was also used over a much longer period of time.

Cairnholy I and II: different monuments, similar sequences?

Stuart Piggott excavated the two Cairnholy chambered cairns in the 1940s (Piggott and Powell 1948–9). Both of the monuments are situated on high ground above the valley of the Kirkdale Burn in Galloway, about 150 metres apart. Piggott excavated the

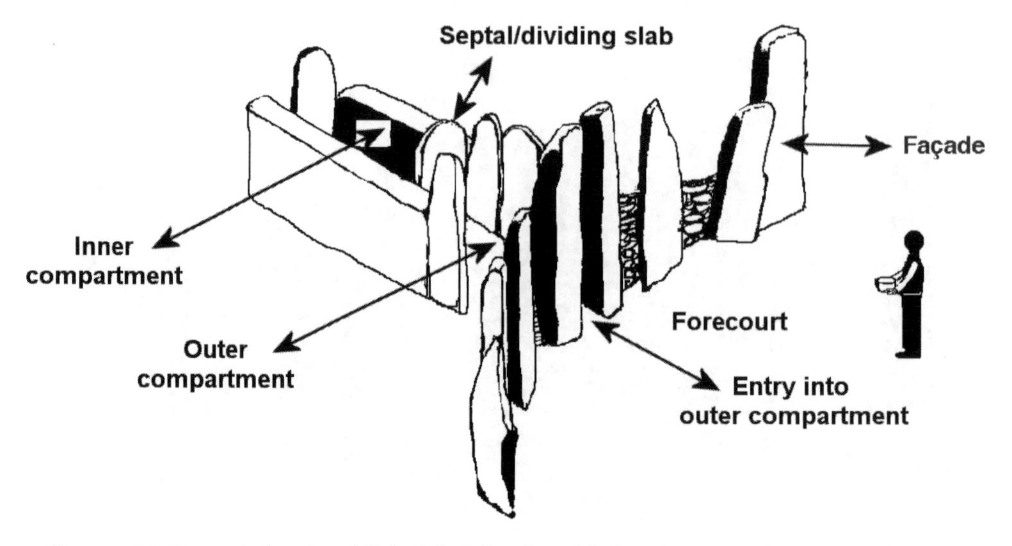

FIGURE 5.9 *Isometric drawing of Cairnholy I chamber with the cairn removed. Entry into the inner compartment is blocked by the septal/dividing slab*

Cairnholy monuments before archaeologists really began to think about multi-phasing in chambered cairns. However, Scott has argued persuasively that the monuments are of more than one period of construction (Scott 1969). At Cairnholy I, the main chamber of the monument does not really make sense as an accessible burial space (Figure 5.9). The façade and portal stones lead into a small compartment, but movement into the inner chamber of the monument is impossible. The dividing stone between the two compartments is huge – almost a metre-and-a-half tall and much taller than the side slabs of the compartment.

Corcoran's excavations at Mid Gleniron I and II uncovered the entire monuments. However, Piggott (unlike Corcoran) did not excavate enough of the cairn material to reveal the areas where evidence of multi-period construction might have been found. Nevertheless, the short section through the cairn that Piggott did excavate at Cairnholy I does seem to show that, like the Mid Gleniron monuments, the outer trapezoidal cairn hides within it suggestions of an earlier cairn structure. Piggott excavated a section running perpendicular to the chamber orientation, through the cairn material to the southern edge of the trapezoidal cairn. In Figure 5.10 the section seems to show an inner cairn that is constructed of a quite different material to the outer part of the cairn. While the inner cairn is made of rounded tightly packed boulders, the outer part of the cairn is made of smaller, more angular, boulders with a greater amount of soil. The two parts of the cairn are further divided by what appears to be a substantial inner kerb made of large flat slabs set sloping against the inner cairn. This inner cairn may represent the primary cairn construction on the site. This closely mirrors other megalithic sites where small round cairns seem to have been expanded through the addition of a less substantial 'skin' of cairn material (for example, Corcoran 1964–6). In this way it would seem that, like at Mid Gleniron I,

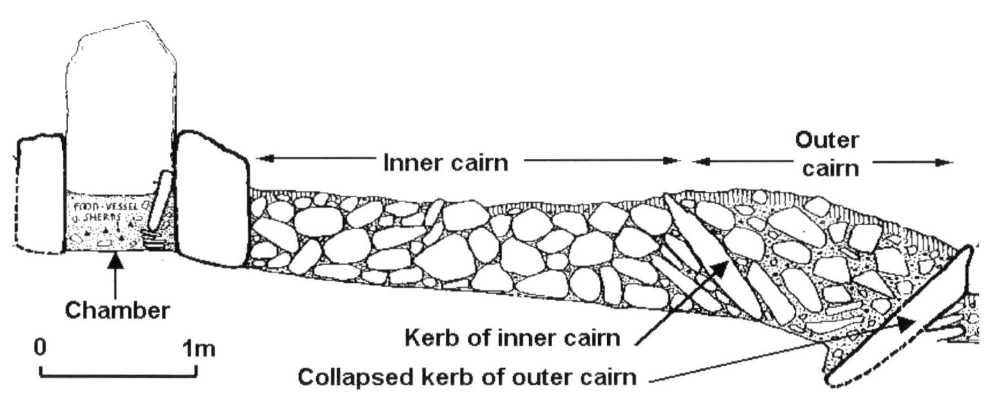

Figure 5.10 *A section through Cairnholy I (Source: Piggott and Powell 1948–9: figure 6)*

the chamber was extended with the construction of the façade, forecourt, trapezoidal cairn and an additional compartment (as suggested by Scott on the form of the chamber alone; see Scott 1969). It seems likely that the original monument would have consisted of a simple single-compartment chamber surrounded by an oval or round cairn. The chamber of the initial monument would not have been easily accessible. The massive stones of the chamber create a closed cist or stone box-like construction. As Piggott noted, access could only have been gained by standing on the cairn and removing the heavy capstone (Piggott and Powell 1948–9: 118).

With the second phase of construction the nature of the monument seems to have altered. The primary chamber was incorporated into a larger chamber despite the difficulty in accessing the original chamber. However, the chamber extension was quite different to the inner compartment. Unlike the original monument, access to the new chamber did not necessitate the removal of a huge closing slab. Instead, repeated access was made possible through the provision of a defined doorway made of two large portal stones. The outer compartment was also paved, perhaps indicating that repeated access to the chamber was needed. Moreover, this outer compartment was directly linked to a forecourt over 6 metres in maximum width. In the forecourt area numerous hearths and spreads of broken pottery and stone tools were found. The extension of the cairn and chamber involved an increase in activity surrounding the chambered cairn. Like at Mid Gleniron I and II, it would seem that the extensions to the monument reflected radical changes in how the monument was used. More specifically, like Mid Gleniron II, it would appear that the monument changed from a small cist-like construction to an imposing monument designed for repeated access and with the space for large public gatherings. Cairnholy II also appears to have been extended. Here a simple single-compartment chamber seems to have been extended to the east through the addition of a second compartment and a pair of portal stones (Scott 1969: 193–4).

On mainland Argyll and southwest Scotland there are two main types of chambered cairn: the Clyde type and the Hebridean passage grave (Henshall 1972). These two types are named after the two areas where the densest distribution of each type is found: the passage grave found mainly in the Western Isles and the Clyde Cairns found mainly in Argyll. Although classified as different types of monument, each seems to have undergone similar structural changes.

At Achnacreebeag, in Argyll, a Hebridean passage grave monument was excavated by Graham Ritchie in the late 1960s (Henshall 1972: ARG 37). The primary form of the monument at Achnacreebeag was a small, round cist-like structure within a round cairn 18 metres in diameter (Figure 5.11). No access to the cist was available from the edge of the cairn: if the chamber had to be used the upper part of the cairn would have had to be dismantled and the capstone removed (Ritchie 1997: 75). The excavator commented that accessibility was probably not a feature of the primary monument: 'perhaps it is most likely that deposits were introduced at the time of building and the tomb was then closed' (Ritchie 1997: 75). The monument was subsequently extended with the addition of a small passage grave and cairn extension to the southeast part of the earlier round cairn (Figure 5.12). The passage grave had an entrance to the southeast and was constructed of boulders and drystone walling. Portal stones marked the entrance. The remains at Greadal Fhinn suggest a similar

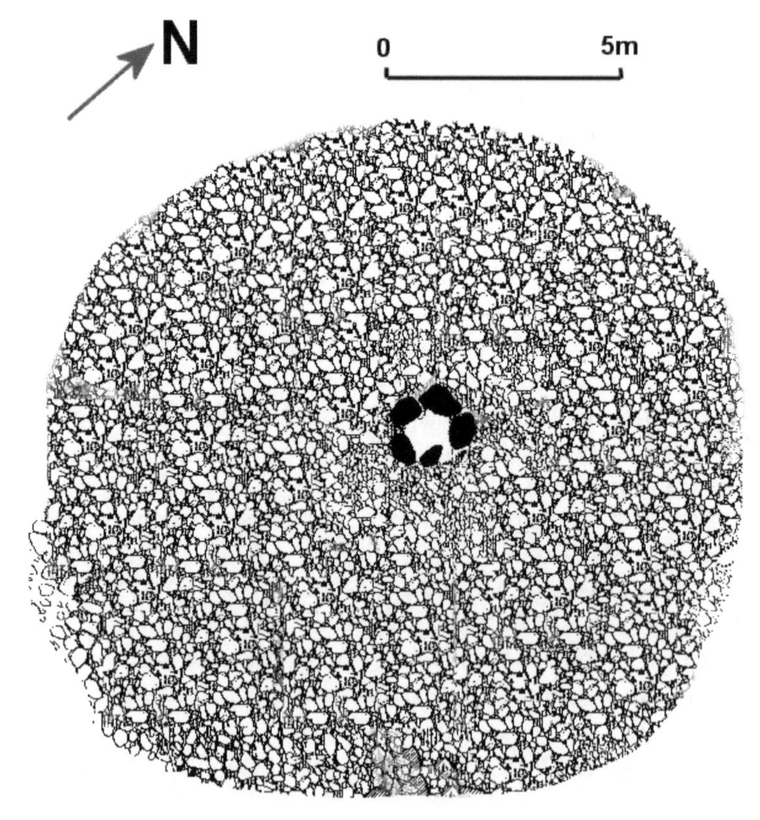

FIGURE 5.11 *Reconstruction of Phase 1 cairn at Achnacreebeag (Source: Ritchie 1969–70: figure 1)*

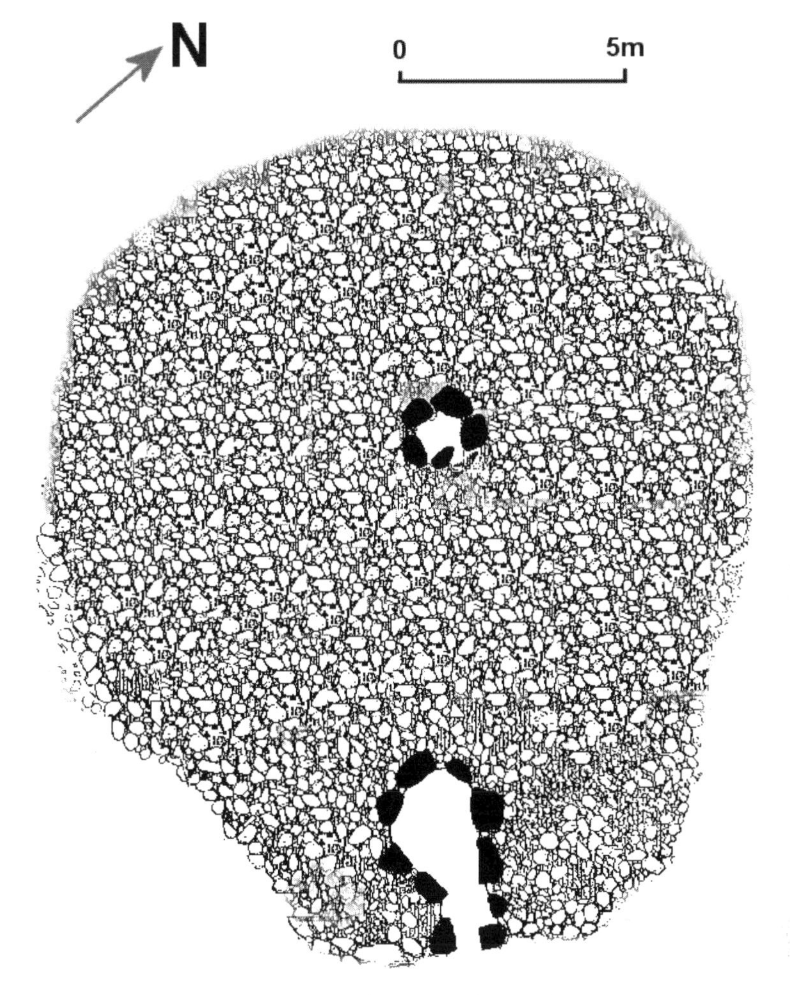

Figure 5.12 *Phase 2 at Achnacreebeag*
(Source: Ritchie 1969–70: figure 1)

sequence and the primary phase of Achnacreebeag finds parallels in the cairns at Rahoy and Clach an t'Sagairt (Henshall 1972: ARG 39, 40 and 48).

The Orkney-Cromarty tradition of northern Scotland

Orkney

The Orkney-Cromarty tradition of chambered cairns (defined in the most detail by Henshall 1963) are passage graves, where the burial chamber is approached by a low passage. The group is found in the northern part of Scotland, in the counties of Inverness-shire and Ross-shire, Sutherland, Caithness and across the Pentland Firth in the Orkney Isles (see Figure 5.1). The chambers in the Orkney-Cromarty tradition are usually defined by upright slabs of stone, often forming 'stalls', dividing the burial space into separate compartments. Richards (1992a) likens these slabs to a series of doorways. The extent to which phasing in cairns can be identified relies on the extent to which these monuments have been studied in the past, as the various counties in which these cairns are found have had varying histories of research.

In Orkney, the chambered cairns were noted and excavated from an early date, due to the activities of a number of early antiquaries, the most outstanding of whom was George Petrie (Davidson and Henshall 1989: 6). There was also an intense period of study in the 1930s and 40s stimulated by the preparation of the Royal Commission volume on the islands' ancient monuments (RCAMS 1946). Some of the most impressive monuments on the islands were excavated at this time by Walter Grant, a landowner on the island of Rousay, and his collaborator J. G. Callander (Callander and Grant 1933–4, 1934–5, 1935–6, 1936–7). A third major period of fieldwork was begun in 1972 by Colin Renfrew who aimed to put the cairns in a chronological framework using the now available radiocarbon dating, and attempted to interpret the social structure of Neolithic society through an examination of the changing form of chambered cairns through time (Renfrew 1976, 1979). More recent work by Colin Richards has questioned some of Renfrew's assumptions on the use of chambered cairns in Orkney, and has interpreted part of the symbolic significance of the monuments (Richards 1988, 1992b). Richards has also aimed at a more comprehensive view of Neolithic society through an active consideration of the use of space in tombs, houses and the wider landscape (Richards 1993b, 1996b, 1998).

The multi-phased nature of chambered cairns on the Orkney Isles has not been examined in as much detail as that of the Clyde Cairns, perhaps due to the fact that the contents of the Orcadian tombs has been better preserved and most interpretation has been focused on the significance of the burial deposits (Renfrew 1979; Richards 1988; Jones 1998) and the taphonomic nature of that deposit (Barber 1988). There are a handful of excavated and unexcavated cairns that suggest that cairns were modified over time. On the small uninhabited island of Calf of Eday, Calder excavated a cairn that almost certainly has two main construction phases (Calder 1936–7) (Figure 5.13). Inside the rectangular cairn Calder found a small double-compartment

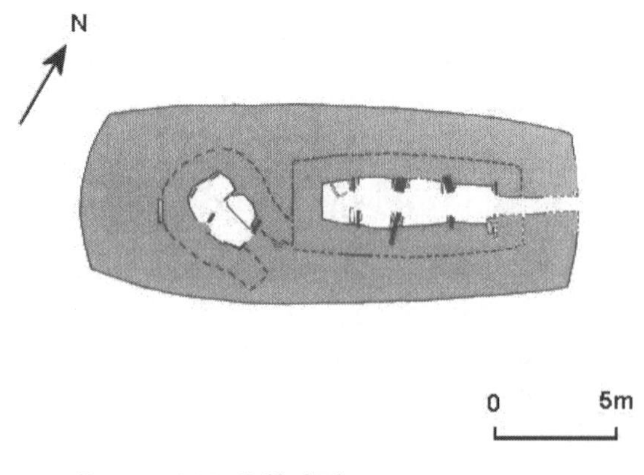

FIGURE 5.13 *Calf of Eday*
(Source: Davidson and Henshall 1989: 108)

chamber and a larger four-compartment stalled chamber. Calder thought that the smaller chamber had been added to the larger, but as Davidson and Henshall and others have pointed out it is more likely that the larger was added to the smaller as the entrance to the smaller appears to have been blocked by the addition of the larger cairn (Davidson and Henshall 1989: 107; Sharples 1985). Indeed the chamber passage was found to be carefully blocked with masonry and there were very few finds in the chamber, perhaps suggesting that the contents had been cleared out before closure. The construction of the new chamber significantly increased the capacity of the monument and the new chamber was roofed at a greater height, increasing the accessibility of the burial deposits (Calder 1936–7).

The recently excavated Papa Westray North cairn is paralleled by the types of primary cairn found in the Clyde-style of monument (Figure 5.14). Here, a small single-compartment chamber surrounded by an oval cairn was later subsumed by a rectangular stalled cairn. The small single-compartment chamber appears to have originally been a free-standing structure as there were distinct differences in the masonry between this and the larger mass of the cairn (Davidson and Henshall 1989: 24). The chronology of the monument cannot be accurately dated however, as the radiocarbon dates for the small chamber seem to relate to its blocking when the stalled cairn was built (Ritchie 1995: 41–4) (see Figure 5.14). The new chamber was much more elaborate than the early cairn and incorporated four large compartments, divided into eight separate burial areas by the central passage. The external appearance of the cairn would have been much more imposing than the earlier monument. Davidson and Henshall (1989: 25) have also suggested that some of the larger stalled cairns may be the result of a series of enlargements. Joints in the masonry walls and the varying heights, spacing and alignments of the dividing slabs at monuments such as the Knowe of Ramsay and Midhowe might indicate cairn enlargement. However, this possibility was not noted in Callander and Grant's extensive excavations on Rousay.

While cairn enlargement and elaboration seems to be less common in the Orcadian monuments, the overall sequence of construction suggests that increases in capacity and the provision of public gathering spaces became an increasing priority through time. The earliest cairns are thought to be the simple bi or tripartite chambers set in

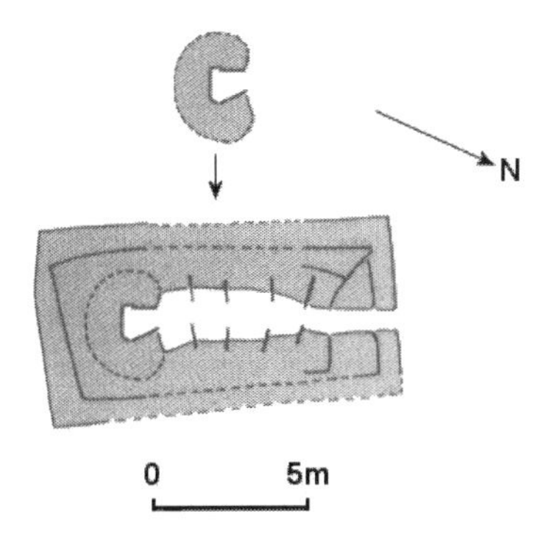

FIGURE 5.14 *The sequence at Papa Westray North (Source: Davidson and Henshall 1989: 121)*

small round cairns (Davidson and Henshall 1989; Renfrew 1979; Sharples 1985). Indeed the finds from a number of this type suggest that this is the case. In a small number of monuments of the tripartite type, pottery resembling styles found on the Scottish mainland has been found (Davidson and Henshall 1989: 77). The Scottish mainland cairns, within which this type of pottery is found, have radiocarbon dates extending back to the first few centuries of the fourth millennium BC (Davidson and Henshall 1991: 83; Sharples 1986) (see Figures 5.3a, b and c). This would be earlier than any currently dated megalith on Orkney (Davidson and Henshall 1989: 95–8). This supports the typological sequence that places the small round cairns on Orkney at the head of a sequence of development, paralleling the evidence from the Clyde region. The design of these early cairns was later elaborated on to form the stalled cairns that consist of four or more compartments usually set within large rectangular cairns, resulting in the massively enlarged versions at Midhowe, Knowe of Rowiegar and Knowe of Ramsay (Sharples 1985: 64). The construction of the final stalled cairns may have overlapped with the latest tradition of chambered cairn construction found on the Orkney Islands, the Maes Howe tradition. These cairns are built to a different conception of space in which the linear nature of the stalled cairns was transformed into the cruciform layout of the Maes Howe-type chambers, approached by massively elongated passages (Richards 1988). While the architecture of the chamber and passage restricted access to the burial deposits creating a private central area at the heart of the tomb (Richards 1988: 54), the outside spaces of these monuments were transformed. Unlike the Clyde Cairns, forecourts are rare in the earlier Orcadian monuments. Instead, focus was directed towards the configuration and elongation of the interior burial space over time. However, some of the cairns of the Maes Howe tradition incorporated elaborate outside spaces for public gatherings. The most impressive example is that of Maes Howe itself, where a large exterior platform, defined by a circular ditch and bank, surrounds the mound. Another example is that at Quoyness (Bradley 1998: chapter 7; Childe 1951–2: chapter 6). The platform at Maes Howe was an integral part of the design (Childe 1954–6). Platforms were also added to some of the older styles of cairn (Davidson and Henshall 1989: 26) and the platforms of these monuments became the focus for extensive activity (Sharples 1985: 69).

Caithness and the southern Highlands

Caithness was the focus for some of the earliest and best excavations of chambered cairns in Scotland. The first records were made by A. H. Rhind, a successful local landowner and antiquarian (Davidson and Henshall 1991: 6). He excavated a number of cairns in the county in the 1850s with the express aim of recovering human skulls for a comparative ethnological study (as Bryce later did at the cairns on Arran and Bute). In the 1860s Joseph Anderson, soon to be the Keeper of the National Museum in Edinburgh, excavated and recorded a number of chambered cairns in Caithness (Anderson 1865–6, 1866–8, 1870–1). Anderson's excavations were of a high standard for the time and he published a number important papers on the results (Davidson and Henshall 1991: 6). Anderson was ahead of his time in many ways, noting the possibility that many chambered cairns were the product of multiple phases of construction almost a century before the issue was revived and became a major point for discussion in the 1960s.

Anderson and the factor of the Thrumster estate near Wick, R. I. Shearer, excavated a number of cairns, including six round cairns and a number of more complex long and horned cairns. Excavations on the horned cairns, such as Camster Long and Ormiegill, led Anderson, in a report for the Society of Antiquaries of Scotland, to suggest: 'It may be perhaps conjectured . . . that both the short and long cairns may have been originally chambered circular cairns, similar to those described in my former paper, the horned structure having been subsequently added to them' (Anderson 1866–8: 493). Anderson was suggesting the sequence of construction outlined almost a century later by Corcoran and Scott for cairns found in the Clyde region and beyond. We can see in Anderson's rather sketchy plans that he and Shearer had detected interior wall faces around the chambers in the long and horned cairns (Figure 5.15).

Later, in the 1960s, Corcoran mounted a rescue excavation of three cairns at Loch Calder in Caithness in advance of the level of the loch being raised (Corcoran 1964–6). This was before his excavations at Mid Gleniron I and II in Dumfries and Galloway. At the time, Corcoran did not comment to any great extent on the possibility that the cairns may have had multiple phases of construction, but later reinterpreted the cairns in the light of his excavations at Mid Gleniron (Corcoran 1972). He argued that Tulloch of Assery A, presented as a unitary structure in the original report, may have began life as a single small round cairn that was later subsumed into a double-horned cairn with an additional chamber (Corcoran 1972: 34). Anderson's excavations at Ormiegill and Garrywhin were also highlighted as possibly paralleling the sequence at Tulloch of Assery A. Tulach an t'sionnaich was also reinterpreted, with Corcoran suggesting that the cairn went through a whole series of enlargements and developments. The cairn may have again begun life as small circular cairn which was then modified through the addition of a heel-shaped façade, creating a distinct forecourt area. This was later modified, again through the further addition of a long tail and further masonry around the heel cairn (Figure 5.16). The cairn at Tulloch of Assery B may have been enlarged, but maintained its original circular form.

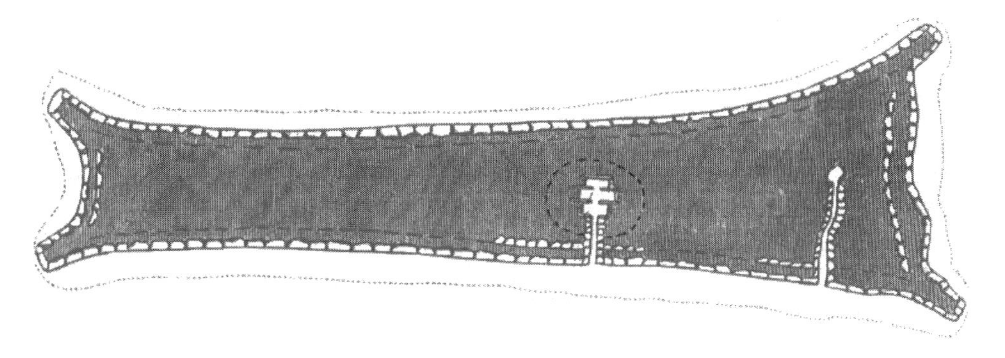

FIGURE 5.15 *Anderson's sketch of Camster Long. Anderson has marked the evidence for a circular cairn around the tripartite-type chamber*
(Source: Anderson 1866–8: plate LXI)

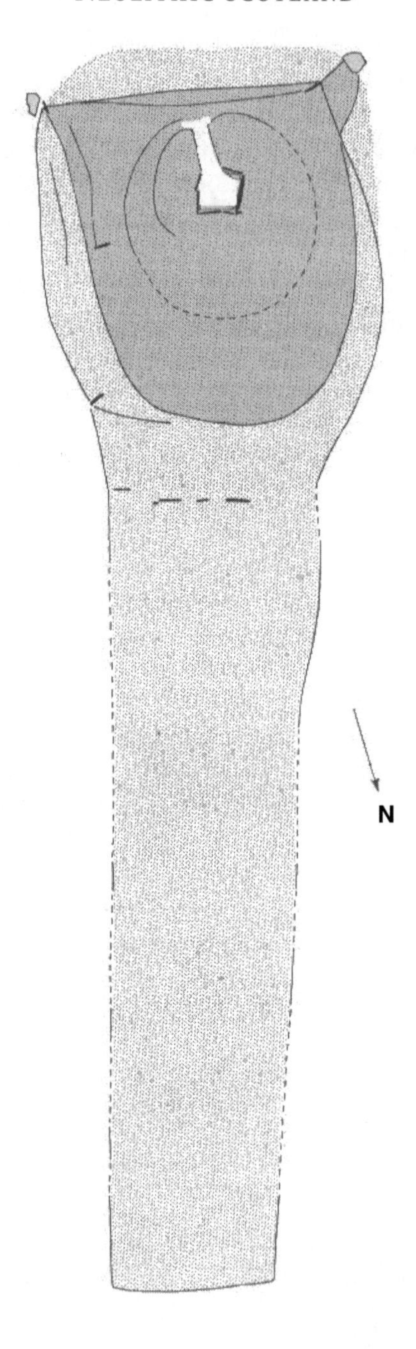

FIGURE 5.16 *The final monument at Tulach an t'Sionnaich (Source: Henshall 1972: 549)*

One of the most impressive cairns excavated by Anderson and Shearer, in the nineteenth century at Camster, was re-excavated by Corcoran and Masters in the 1970s, following the monument being taken into guardianship, by the then Inspectorate of Ancient Monuments (Davidson and Henshall 1991: 10). The excavations at Camster Long, published by Masters (1997), suggested that two small round cairns had later been subsumed into a massive trapezoidal long cairn with elaborate horned forecourts, much like Anderson had proposed in the nineteenth century. Chamber A, an unusual pentagonal chamber, was found to be held within a small round cairn, only 7.5 metres in diameter. The passage changed alignment at the point where the round cairn met the bulk of the long cairn. Chamber B, a more common tripartite type, also had hints of having stood originally in a small circular cairn and there were changes in the roofing of the inner and outer passage and butt joints in the walling of the passage, indicating that the passage was extended when the cairn was subsumed within the long cairn. While the addition of the long cairn did not substantially alter the capacity of the burial space it did add massive and elaborate stage-like forecourts, which defined two large areas that could have been used for public gatherings. In the forecourt areas, the presence of patches of burning, broken pottery vessels and stone tools hint at forecourt ceremonies. In Caithness, many of the other long cairns appear to be of multi-period construction. The plans of monuments such as Brawlbin Long, Cnoc Freiceadain and Na Tri Sithean suggest that long cairns were added to round or heel-shaped monuments (Davidson and Henshall 1991: 55 and CAT 6, 18 and 41). Roger Mercer has argued that the sequence may be the other way round at Warehouse South, where the round cairn is in a better state of preservation than the long cairn (Mercer 1992), but the long cairn remains unexcavated and Davidson and Henshall doubt this alternative sequence (Davidson and Henshall 1991: 58).

The study of the chambered cairns of Sutherland, Ross-shire and Inverness-shire proceeded at a much slower pace than the Caithness and Orcadian monuments (Henshall and Ritchie 1995, 2001). In Ross-shire and Inverness-shire, there were no antiquaries of the calibre of Rhind or Petrie in the north and no Royal Commission survey until the war years to stimulate interest (Henshall and Ritchie 2001: 23–4). The study of the Sutherland cairns began late in comparison to those further north (Henshall and Ritchie 1995: 6). However, excavations at Embo by Audrey Henshall and Wallace in 1960 revealed two chambers set within a round cairn (Figure 5.17). These were of markedly different design and it is likely that one was added to the other, although which chamber was primary is arguable (Henshall and Wallace 1962–3; Henshall and Ritchie 1995: 135–40). The addition of a new chamber would have substantially increased the burial space. The Ord North, the only other comprehensive excavation in Sutherland, indicated that the cairn was of one phase (Sharples 1981). However, an extensive platform was added around the cairn at a late stage in the history of the cairn, reminiscent of developments in Later Neolithic Orkney. An elaborate version of this sequence appears to be present at Fiscary where a platform seems to have been built to join together two earlier cairns (Henshall and Ritchie 1995: 106, SUT 29). These platforms provide large areas for exterior audiences.

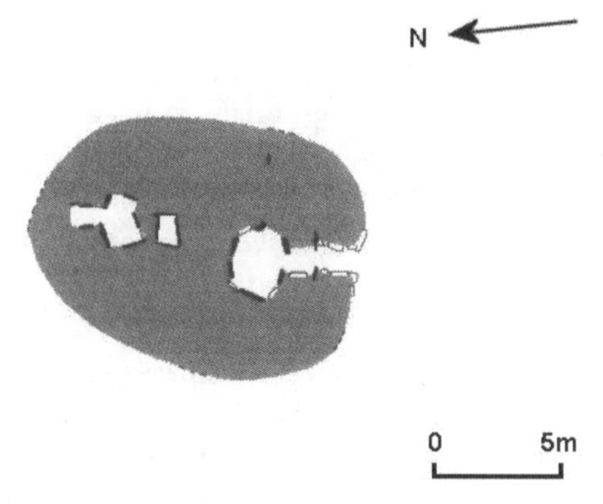

FIGURE 5.17 *The double-chambered cairn at Embo, Sutherland (Source: Henshall and Ritchie 1995: 136)*

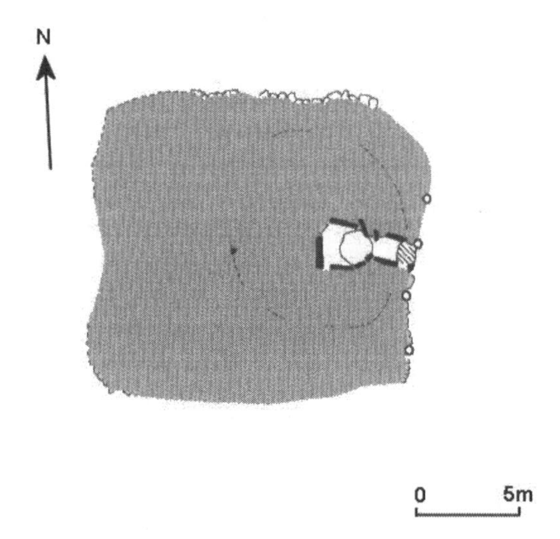

FIGURE 5.18 *Balvraid. Cairn enlargement (Source: Henshall and Ritchie 2001: 231)*

In the Central Highlands, although only a handful of cairns have been excavated, there is much to suggest that many of the cairns found here may also be the product of a number of phases of construction. Henshall and Ritchie (2001: 58–9) list many attributes of excavated and unexcavated cairns in the region that suggest that these were of multi-phase construction. Cairn enlargement is suggested both by excavation at Balvraid (Figure 5.18) and Carn Glas and by surface remains at sites such as Balnaguie, Boath Short and Red Burn (Henshall and Ritchie 2001: INV 51, ROS 12, 6, 11, 36). Chambers of different plans under the same cairn suggest the incorporation of additional chambers in an existing cairn (ROS 22, 61) and the site at King's Head Cairn suggests that a small single-compartment chamber was replaced with a much larger, increased-capacity chamber (ROS 25). The cairns at Kilcoy South (ROS 24) and

Scotsburn Wood East (ROS 47) look like they had small compartment chambers which were extended and enlarged through the addition of extra compartments. The changes at many of these monuments increased the burial space and/or increased the monumentality of the cairns. Both changes suggest the increasing importance of these sites.

The Northern and Western Isles: the Zetland and Hebridean tombs

On the Shetland Isles there is a group of cairns, known as the Zetland group, that is distinct from the Orkney-Cromarty tradition (Henshall 1963: chapter 5). These are small passage graves set, normally, in round or heel-shaped cairns, with simple round or trefoil chambers. Virtually nothing was known of these cairns until work began on the Royal Commission survey of the islands in the 1930s (published in 1946: RCAMS 1946). Before the commission volume appeared, Bryce (the excavator of the Clyde Cairns) wrote an inventory of the heel-shaped cairns on the islands (Bryce 1939–40). Bryce noted that the centre of the heel cairn at Vementry had the appearance of originally being domed and inside the heel cairn a circular wall around the chamber can be identified (Bryce 1939–40: 26–8) (Figure 5.19). This is not bonded into the wall of the heel cairn and the heel cairn partly blocks the entrance, therefore it looks as if the heel cairn was added to a small round cairn during a second phase of construction at the site (the passage may have been accessed through a drop-down entrance). The addition of the heel cairn makes the monument much more imposing and more markedly defines the entrance and a forecourt area. There are also traces of earlier circular cairn elements in other examples (Henshall 1963: 141–3).

Like the Shetland monuments the Hebridean group appeared late in the archaeological records, although there was an earlier Royal Commission volume, published in 1928 (Henshall 1972: 111; RCAMS 1928). Previous to this there were two nineteenth-century excavations of atypical tombs and Beveridge, an antiquarian, also excavated three chambers, with little success, in the early twentieth century (Beveridge 1911). The Hebridean tombs, the distribution of which is concentrated on the Western Isles, are a

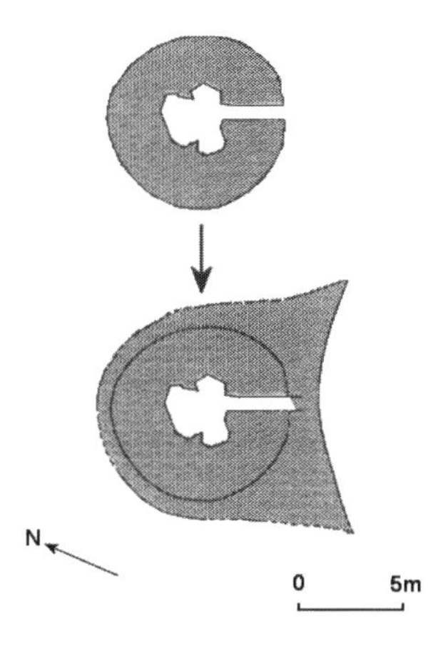

FIGURE 5.19 *The sequence at Vementry, Shetland (Source: Henshall 1972: figure 17.1)*

form of passage grave, generally larger than the Shetland examples, often in round cairns and occasionally with pronounced funnel-shaped forecourts. In addition to the Hebridean form there are also a handful of Clyde-style cairns on the west side of North Uist. The mix of traditions in the Western Isles was noted almost 'despairingly' by archaeologists such as Childe, Powell and Daniel in general works on British prehistory due to their desire to classify regional groups of tombs as belonging to separate cultures of people (Henshall 1972: 112). However, as Armit notes, the architecture of these separate traditions is attuned to the same basic forms of ritual organisation and the changes in form may have fulfilled the same purposes (Armit 1996: 76).

Most of the Hebridean cairns are round but there are a small number of long cairns, most of which give the impression of having originally been round cairns to which long tails have been added (Henshall 1972: 130). Craonaval on North Uist may offer a close parallel to Achnacreebeag in Argyll as the cairn has a closed square cist-like chamber in the centre with a larger accessible chamber possibly added to the eastern side of the cairn (Figure 5.20). Many of the Hebridean cairns also appear to have been enlarged at some point in their history, for example the cairn at Oban nam Fiadh has an inner kerb that relates to the opening of the passage but not to the exterior edge of the cairn (Figure 5.21). Funnel-shaped forecourts themselves may have derived from cairn enlargements, enabling access once the cairn has been extended without having to enlarge the passage of the chamber (Henshall 1972: 141) (Figure 5.22). Platforms were also added to some of the cairns (Henshall 1972: 131).

OUTWITH SCOTLAND

Many of the regional traditions of architecture in England, Wales and Ireland also demonstrate the trend towards increasing monumentality and capacity and the

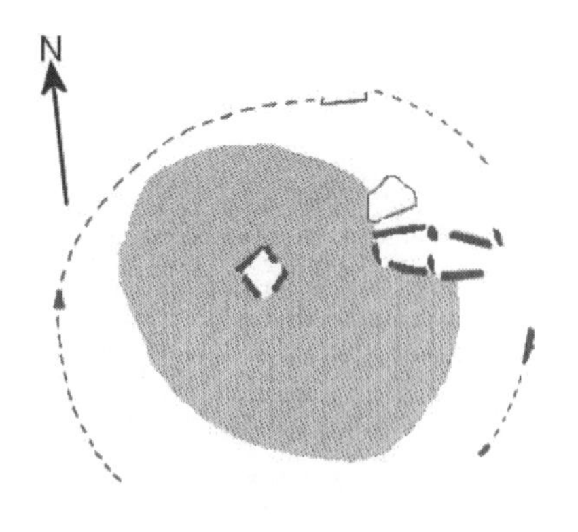

FIGURE 5.20 *Craonaval*
(Source: Henshall 1972: 513)

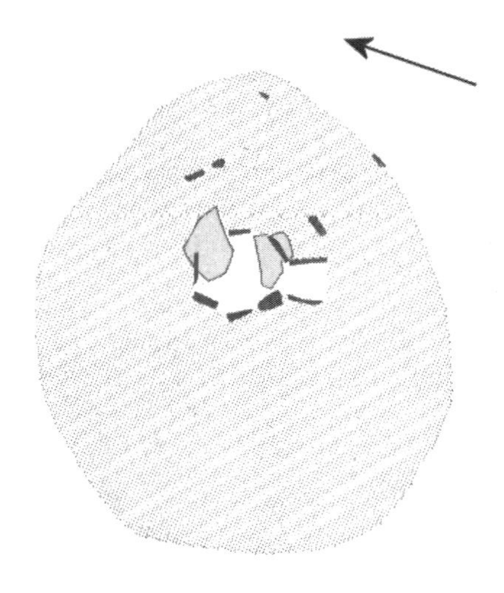

FIGURE 5.21 *Oban nam Fiadh*
(Source: Henshall 1972: 525)

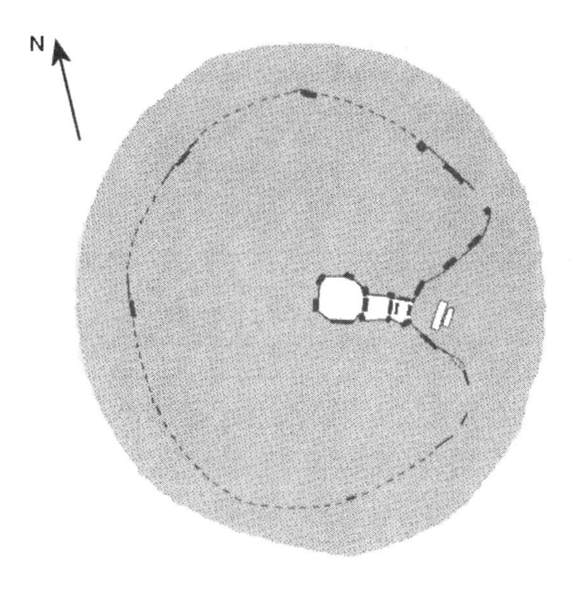

FIGURE 5.22 *A funnel-shaped forecourt at Rudh' an Dunain*
(Source: Henshall 1972: 485)

addition of public gathering areas. In the Cotswold-Severn group of megalithic monuments, found in Wales and western England, small circular cairns also appear to be the earliest form of cairn (Corcoran 1969b: 80). These forms were later elaborated through the addition of long cairns, façades and additional chambers. At Notgrove, for example, a small closed polygonal chamber in a circular cairn was later superseded by a massive trapezoidal cairn with an elaborate megalithic chamber (Figure 5.23). At

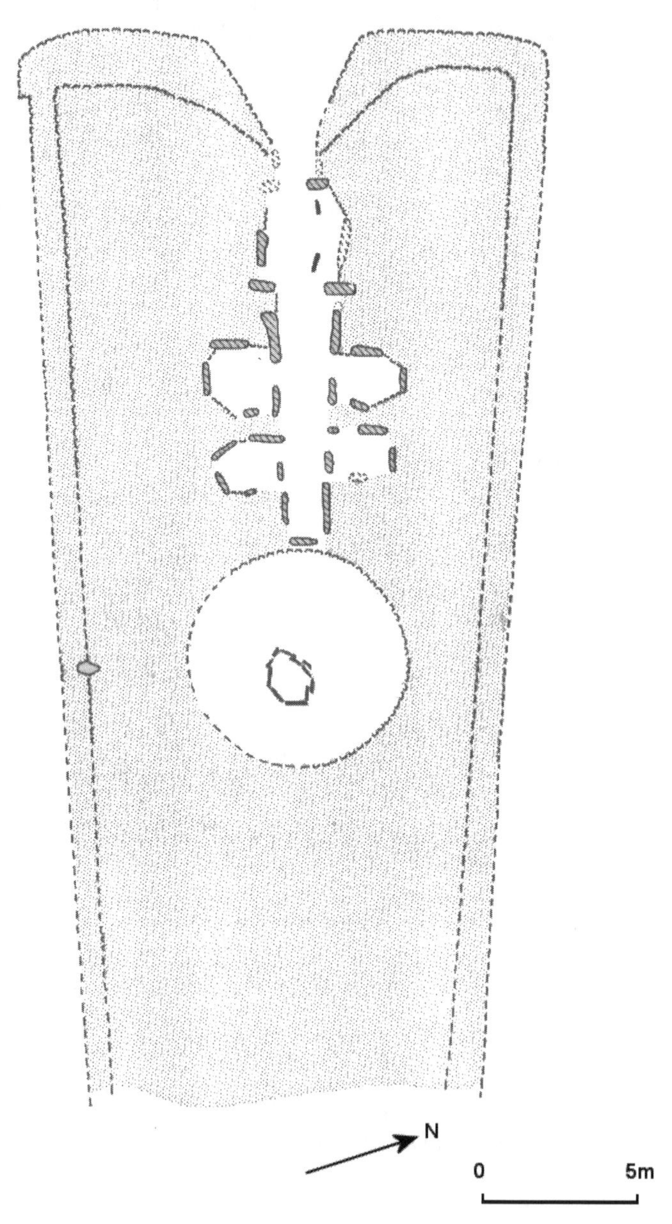

FIGURE 5.23 *Notgrove (the western end of the cairn is not shown) (Source: Corcoran 1969a: figure 12)*

both Pipton and Ty Isaf, round cairns were later incorporated within trapezoidal cairns, despite the difficulties in incorporating the earlier structures, resulting in chambered cairns with rather irregular designs (Figures 5.24 and 5.25). In Wales, Dyffryn Ardudwy (Figure 5.26) would traditionally be classified as a portal dolmen, but the primary phase of the monument shares many similarities with the beginnings of megalithic architecture elsewhere (Powell 1973). The first monument constructed consisted of a closed chamber defined by six uprights arranged in a rectangular manner, closed by a large capstone. The chamber was set in a small oval cairn. This monument would have closely resembled the simple primary monuments at Cairnholy II, Achnacreebeag and Mid Gleniron. The cairn at Tregnifath, Anglesey, was found to have at least three phases of construction (Smith and Lynch 1987). The first phase was also a small single-compartment chamber set within a small round cairn (Figure 5.27). The earliest monument forms in nearly every tradition of megalithic architecture across the British Isles may have been of closely comparable form (Figure 5.28). These consisted of small, sometimes closed, compartments set within

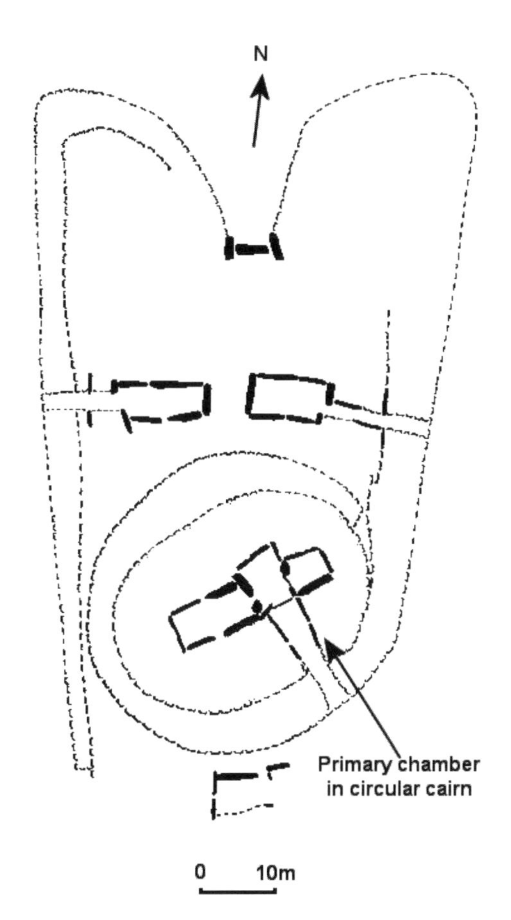

Figure 5.24 *Ty Isaf*
(Source: Corcoran 1969a: figure 22)

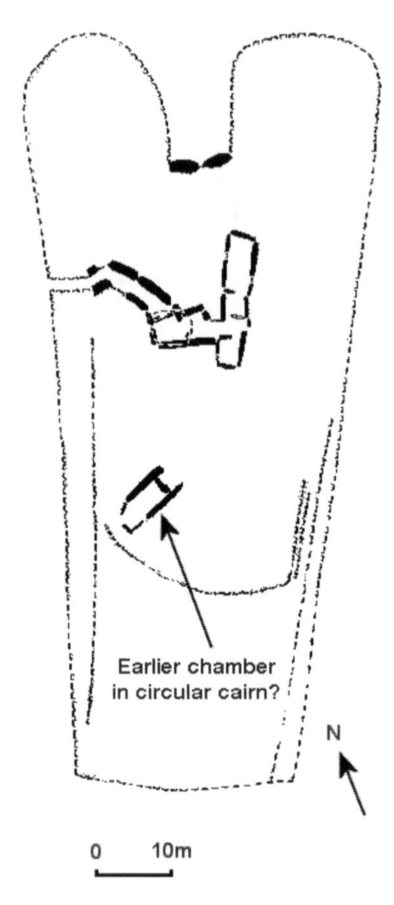

FIGURE 5.25 *Pipton*
(Source: Corcoran 1969a: figure 23)

round or oval cairns. In every tradition it would appear that these early monuments were rapidly modified and subsumed within more elaborate monuments.

THE DEVELOPMENT OF MEGALITHIC ARCHITECTURE

In the Clyde Cairn tradition it can be seen that the cairns developed from simple, occasionally closed chambers, to larger, more accessible chambers set within cairns that incorporated areas for public ceremonies and gathering. The addition of forecourts was accompanied by increased evidence for the use of areas outside the cairn for activities associated with burning, the consumption of food and the breaking of pottery vessels. In the Orkney-Cromarty tradition similar developments can be identified. In Orkney, while individual monuments were less often extended, the sequence of monument construction over a substantial period of time suggests that monuments increased in capacity. Here there seems to have been a particular focus on the internal areas of the monuments rather than forecourts. The internal areas

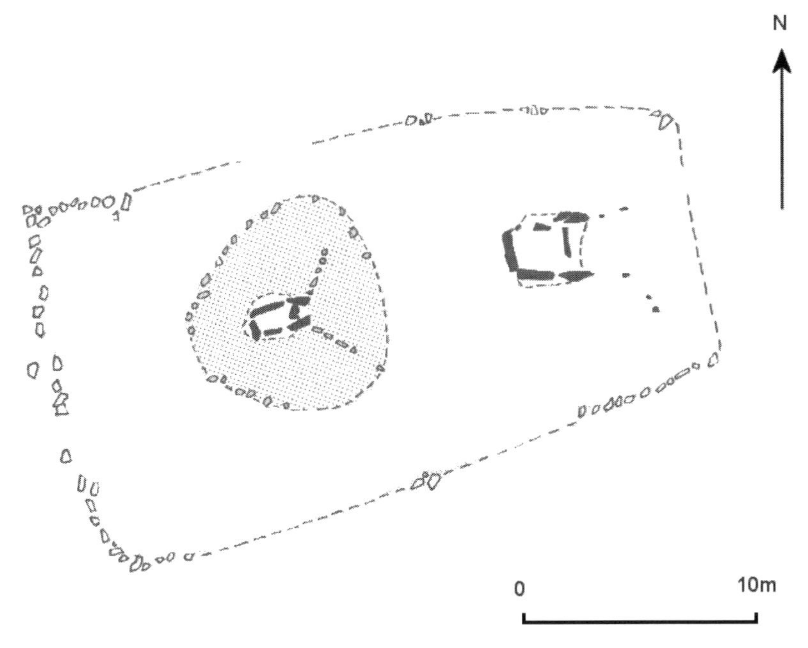

FIGURE 5.26 *Dyffryn Ardudwy*
(Source: Lynch 1969: figure 45)

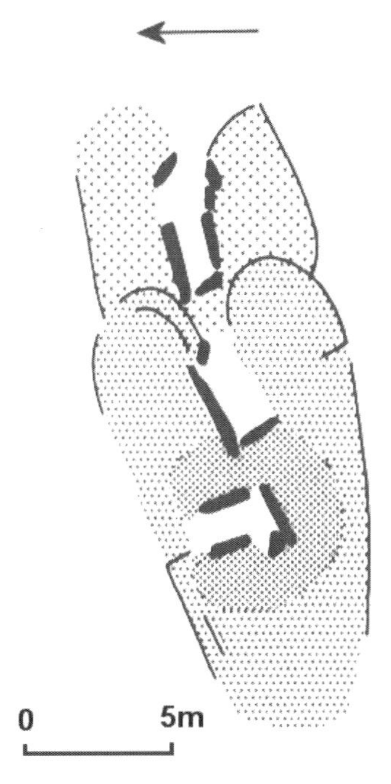

FIGURE 5.27 *Trefignath*
(Source: Smith and Lynch 1987: figure 21.1)

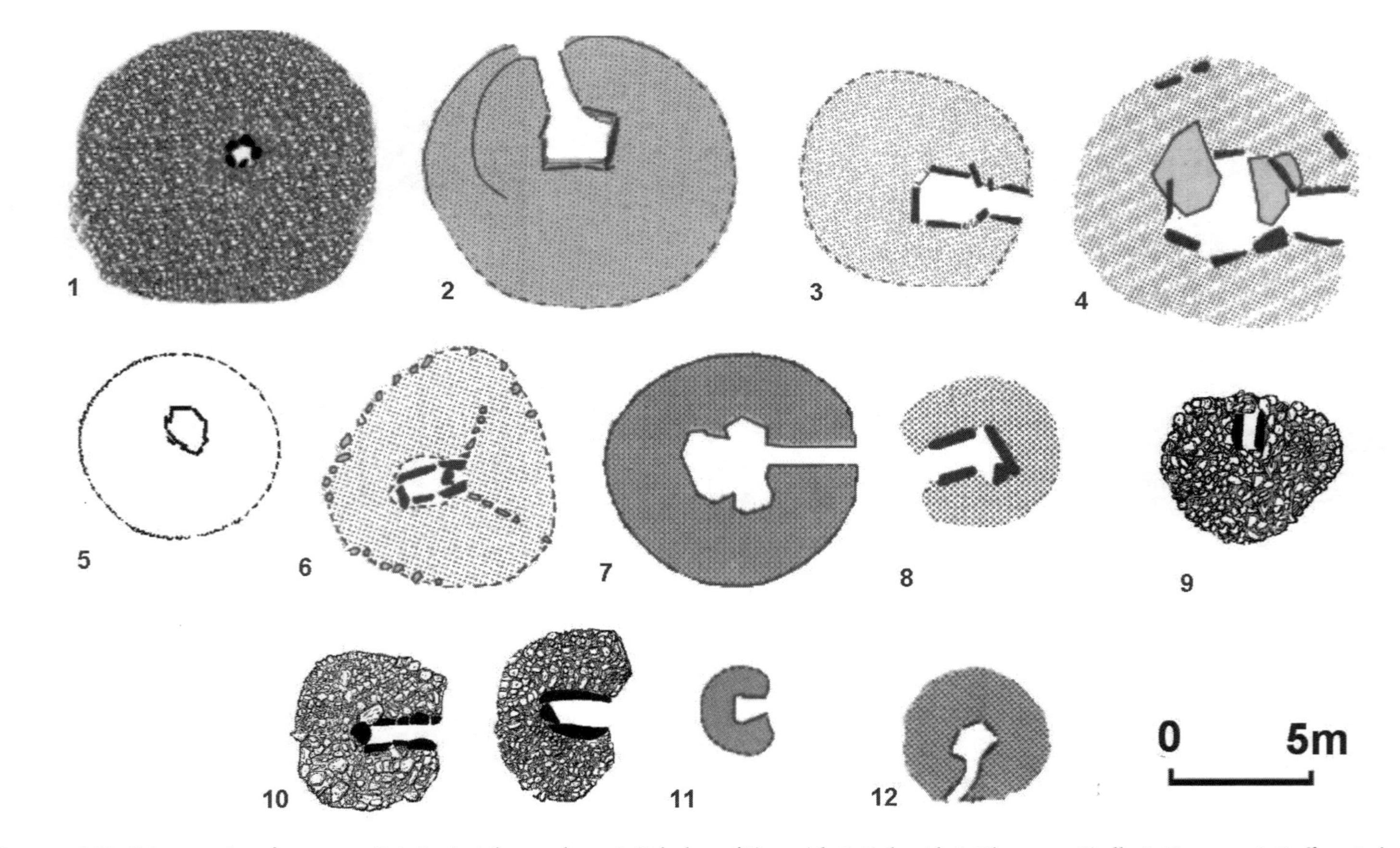

FIGURE 5.28 *Primary cairns from across Britain. 1. Achnacreebeag, 2. Tulach an t'Sionnaich, 3. Balvraid, 4. Oban nam Fiadh, 5. Notgrove, 6. Dyffryn Ardudwy, 7. Vementry, 8. Tregnifath, 9. Mid Gleniron II, 10. Mid Gleniron I, 11. Holm of Papa Westray North, 12. Camster Long*

increased in size and more space was provided for bodies to be placed and increasing numbers of participants could be accommodated inside the monuments. In the final tradition of passage-grave architecture on Orkney, the Maes Howe type of cairn, the sequence of increasing accessibility and capacity is reversed, but areas for public gathering outside the monuments become more common. Passage lengths became increasingly long and the views into the tombs became more restricted and fewer people could be accommodated inside. At the same time platforms were incorporated into the new traditions and platforms were added to some of the older monuments suggesting that the gatherings at these monuments were becoming larger in scale, while those allowed access to the deposits inside became fewer in number (Bradley 1998: chapter 7; Richards 1988). In Caithness, tombs like Camster Long display a similar sequence to many of the Clyde-style monuments, where small round cairns were subsumed within long cairns that actively incorporated areas for gathering within their architecture. At Camster these forecourts were of massive proportions and assumed the appearance of stages (Figure 5.29). Further south, sequences rely mainly on surface inspection alone due to the lesser history of research in these areas. However, many of the monuments in Sutherland and the Central Highlands indicate that monuments were increased in capacity and monumentality over time. Likewise, the Hebridean tombs were also elaborated on through the addition of funnel-shaped forecourts, extra chambers and platforms. All of these changes would have directly impacted on the visual senses and bodily actions of the gathering participants at these monuments, providing increasingly formalised stages and architectural pointers to attention and action. Performance is central to ritual in that ritual involves actions as well as words, and architecture can be used to control and frame performances (Bell 1992; Tambiah 1979: 114). Performance is also central to remembering (Connerton 1989). The addition of forecourts and the increased activity in the forecourts of the chambered cairns suggest that the activities surrounding death and the disposal of

FIGURE 5.29 *Camster Long forecourt*

bodies in the cairns were becomingly increasingly ritualised and the need to remember the dead was growing in importance. The increasing accessibility of these monuments suggests that the relationship between the living and the dead was changing and becoming more intimately connected.

CHAMBERED CAIRNS AND ANCESTOR RITUALS: CONNECTING WITH THE PAST

The changing architecture of the chambered cairns of Scotland has a number of parallels in a range of monumental architecture across Europe. Richard Bradley has observed a similar development from small, often closed monuments to larger accessible tombs in the Carnac region of Brittany. Bradley has linked these developments with a change from one way of treating the dead to another. This change, Bradley argues, would have marked a major transition in the way people related to the world around them (Bradley 1998: chapter 4). John Barrett has stressed the differences between funerary rituals and ancestral rituals in human belief systems (Barrett 1988). Funerary rituals are primarily concerned with the disposal of a human body. In contemporary society this can take the form of burying a person in a grave or cremating their remains and scattering the ashes or storing them in a sealed burial urn. Each individual is remembered in their own particular way and usually the person's identity remains intact even after death through the erection of gravestones or some other form of memorial. The most important aspect of funerary rituals is that, once buried or cremated, people do not normally have access to the material remains of that individual, indeed the main emphasis in funeral ceremonies is severing our links with the deceased; moving on after death and refocusing on the living.

Ancestral rites are very different. Ancestral rituals are a means of establishing the presence of the dead amongst the affairs of the living. Both funerary rites and ancestral rites involve the use of human remains, but the ways in which these are manipulated are very different. Ancestral rituals normally entail the ability to have repeated access to the dead. In ancestor rituals: 'among the places and symbols used may be funerary architecture and the bones of the dead' (Barrett 1988: 31). Both funerary rites and ancestry rites may include construction of places for the dead. However, the form of the architecture associated with each form of belief system tends to be very different. Funerary rites will tend to involve structures that separate the dead from the living; in other words, the dead are no longer accessible. Architecture associated with ancestor worship, on the other hand, will normally involve structures where the dead can be visited and where the material remains of the dead can be venerated, manipulated and perhaps even removed. This is done in order to invoke the dead in the affairs of the living. Ancestry rites, therefore, involve a very intimate relationship with the dead and their material remains. With the development of the increasingly accessible chambered cairns, continuities between the dead and the living could be easily expressed (Bradley 1998: 59). In this way the changing architecture may have reflected a fundamental change in the relationships between the living and the dead.

Changing relationships

The fundamental differences between funerary and ancestry rituals may help us understand the developments in the architecture of the various traditions of megalithic architecture in Scotland. While the changes in architecture were not always from a closed monument to an accessible monument, as in Brittany, the changes do suggest that the importance of ancestry and the prominence of the dead in Neolithic society was growing. In the Clyde region, the changing form of the architecture seems to emphasise increasing accessibility. At Cairnholy I, for example, access to the mortuary area in the primary monument would have necessitated the removal of a heavy covering slab and would require walking over the cairn to get to the mortuary area. Similarly, at Mid Gleniron II the primary cairns were sealed soon after construction, or required at the very least the dismantlement of a stone kerb in order to gain entry. This may indicate that the relationships with the dead at these monuments during the early stages of the Neolithic were tentative. These were more like funerary structures than tombs designed for ancestor worship. The architecture of the early monuments did not allow easy access to the remains of the dead. With the development of the larger chambers the dead became more accessible. This could be connected to the increasing importance of ancestry and increasing utilisation of the remains of the dead in rituals designed to invoke the ancestors in the affairs of the living.

However, the change from closed to accessible monuments was not the most significant change. A more common trend in the Clyde Cairns and the traditions further to the north and west was a change in capacity and the secondary addition of areas for public gathering. The enlargement of existing chambers and the addition of new chambers would have marked a significant increase in the capacity of these monuments. More dead bodies could be deposited and the increased chamber area and height would allow the sorting and manipulating of human remains. The addition of arenas for public display would perhaps indicate that the rituals were also becoming the focus for a larger group of people. Both of these changes might indicate that rituals associated with the dead were becoming a progressively more important part of Neolithic life. Access to the dead became increasingly ritualised and ever more a part of the ceremonies of the living, ceremonies perhaps tied to notions of kinship and inheritance.

The growing emphasis on access to the dead seems to cut across the traditional typological groups of chambered cairns in Britain. The final form of the chamber at sites such as Achnacreebeag and Cairnholy and others were different, but the changes in architecture achieved the same purpose. With the secondary extension to the monuments clearer continuity between the exterior and interior area of the monuments was expressed. Direct access to the remains of the dead was made easier. With the development of the rectangular and trapezoidal cairns these monuments began to more closely resemble the shape and form of Earlier Neolithic domestic structures (Hodder 1990, 1994). In this way, the dead were domesticated and the worlds of the living and the dead became more closely integrated. The traditional focus on defining different forms of tomb, although important, has partly masked the fact that the use of space in each type of chambered cairn seems to have evolved in similar ways.

THE KNEE BONE IS CONNECTED TO THE THIGH BONE, THE THIGH BONE . . .

If the development of the cairns marked the increasing importance of ancestry in Neolithic society it is perhaps important to examine the forms that this took. In all of these traditions connections with the past seem to have been made primarily through the manipulation, removal and addition of human remains within the chamber area.

In the Clyde region, the highly acidic soils do not make for ideal preservation of bone material. However, there are a handful of tombs where the bones deposited in the chamber do survive. Inhumation appears to have been the primary rite in the monuments (Henshall 1972: 82). Two of the tombs where the bone evidence was best preserved also happen to be amongst the first Clyde Cairns excavated by Bryce in the 1900s, at Torlin and Clachaig on Arran (Bryce 1901–2). At Torlin, Bryce found the skeletal remains of at least six adults and two children. However, they were not neatly laid out in individual deposits. In contrast, the bones were found in a jumbled mass. The bones of one individual, for example, were found all over the chamber: 'The long bones lay chiefly along the walls of the cist [compartment] in great confusion. The skull was placed face down, and tilted somewhat on its right side . . . an ulna lay on one side, a humerus on the other' (Bryce 1901–2: 83). Bryce's description gives a vivid picture of the way in which the bones were found. However, the bones were not placed in a completely random manner, for at both Torlin and Clachaig, skulls lay invariably in the corners of the compartments and the long bones along the walls of the chamber. Andy Jones has suggested that the placement of the human bones within the chambers, with the skulls at the end and the long bones along the sides, was part of an attempt to lay out the mass of bones in the form of a human being (Jones 1999: 347). Individual identities of the dead may have been amalgamated, producing a human body made up of all the different parts of a range of dead ancestors. In this way, older remains and newer remains could be mixed, blurring the boundaries between the past and the present.

It would also appear that, in some instances, bones were removed from the chambers. For example, at Clachaig Bryce noted that 'in no instance could all the bones of the skeleton be accounted for' (Bryce 1901–2: 83; Henshall 1972: 81). At Clachaig and Torlin a minimum of twenty-two individuals were represented by the skeletal remains, but only nine collarbones were identified and although eighteen upper-arm bones were recovered and twenty-one femurs, none of these could be paired. Fifteen adult jawbones and two jawbones from children were found, indicating that at least five were missing. It could be argued that preservation levels account for missing bones, but some of the largest parts of the human body and those most resistant to decay were grossly under-represented (Henshall 1972: 81).

FIGURE 5.30 *Midhowe, Orkney*

In Orkney, human bone has been better preserved and there are superior records of the contents of the tombs when excavated. Colin Richards has highlighted some of the evidence for bone sorting and removal in these chambers (Richards 1988). At Midhowe on Rousay, burials were deposited whole on stone benches and once the flesh had decayed bones were pushed to the back of the shelves or placed in piles underneath (Figure 5.30). While whole skeletons were present, the piles of bones representing older internments always had certain bones missing, indicating that some had been removed. At Knowe of Yarso there was a distinct bias towards skulls in the bone assemblage. The skulls were of varying conditions and none retained their mandibles, suggesting that these had perhaps been amalgamated from a variety of different mortuary contexts. Human remains may even have circulated in the domestic context: a fragment of skull was found in the Earlier Neolithic house at the Knap of Howar (Richards 1988: 49). Richards also accounts for the discrepancy and incoherence of the radiocarbon dates for the cairns of Orkney (see Figures 5.3a, b and c), which often do not match the expected date ranges for particular styles of monuments, due to the removal and redeposition of bones both within and between sites. For example, the large numbers of individuals in the latest tombs may indicate the incorporation of older remains, cleared from older monuments, in the chambers of newly built cairns (Richards 1988: 50). There is a virtual absence of human remains in the earliest tripartite style of cairns (Richards 1988: figure 4.2). In this way, the actual physical remains of people may have been used to make connections to the past. This may be paralleled in the Clyde region. Evidence for burials within the primary phases of Clyde Cairns is disappointingly lacking. Indeed, upon excavation the primary chambers have normally been found to be entirely empty, containing not even a single sherd of pottery in some cases (Ritchie 1969–70; Marshall and Taylor 1976–7; Piggott and Powell 1948–9). It seems possible that the reason for them being devoid of any material residue and skeletal remains may be that they were removed and incorporated into the cairn extensions and placed in the new, accessible, parts of the monument to create clear links between the relics of the past and the present users of the monument. The removal of human bone from older monuments and its incorporation in more recent chambered cairns may have been one of the ways in which Neolithic groups created a history of the community and a sense of continuity with previous generations. These ways of remembering were played out on a very physical level: the cairn extensions physically altered the monuments of the past and the incorporation of older skeletal material within the new monuments would have meant that the physical remains of ancestors could now be part of the public displays in front of monuments that often incorporated 'staged' areas that framed these displays.

The burial evidence from other areas of Scotland tends to be frustratingly meagre. In Sutherland, only one of the chambered cairns, Embo, has detailed records of burials. A small number of individuals were represented by the skeletal material recovered, but only a small part of each of the skeletons was present – a situation that could not be accounted for by preservation factors alone (Henshall and Ritchie 1995: 51). In Caithness, the process of turning bodies to bone seems to have been accelerated through the charring of bodies. In the seven chambers examined by Anderson thick dark deposits of ash were found, mixed with 'bone ash' and charred and broken bones (Davidson and Henshall 1991: 60). Actual cremated bones seem to have been rare; instead the large amounts of charcoal and common references to charred or scorched bone would seem to indicate that bodies were burnt in order to remove the flesh. Anderson found great quantities of bone in chambers such as Ormiegill, Garrywhin and Kenny's Cairn and thought that the ash layers found in the cairns had accumulated over a considerable length of time (Anderson 1865–6, 1866–8: 501, 1870–1: 294). In contrast, Corcoran found only a small number of burials in the three cairns around Loch Calder, but only one of these (possibly of a later date) was articulated (Corcoran 1964–6). The bodies in the Loch Calder cairns were deposited already de-fleshed and most bodies were represented by only a few fragments of bone. Some of the bones had been scorched, like Anderson reported, and cut marks on a skull and scoring on other bones indicated that flesh had also been cut from the bodies. The evidence seems to concur with the Orcadian evidence where bones were transferred between different contexts and also removed from bodies that had been deposited whole at certain cairns. In Caithness, there seems to have been added emphasis on transforming bodies to bone, by the means of fire or by cutting the flesh from the bone. Decaying flesh is often connected with pollution and the idea that people can only become ancestors once they are transformed to bone is a widespread belief (Barrett 1988; Richards 1988; Parker Pearson and Ramilisonina 1998). In the Hebrides, similar practices have been identified. At Unival, whole bodies were placed in a small cist in the chamber and burnt and scorched to aid the removal of the flesh. Bones were then removed and placed against the walls of the chamber and some of them were removed altogether (Scott 1947–8). At Clettraval, the burning or scorching was obviously taken to its extreme as fragments of cremated bone were found there (Scott 1934–5). In all of these traditions of monuments it would appear that bone sorting, removal and the transferral between contexts characterised the use of these monuments.

CONCLUSIONS

Through the analysis of the architecture of these cairns it has been possible to draw out a number of interpretations relating to the changing significance of these monuments, changes that cut across different styles of architecture. In the first part of this chapter we saw that the final form of these cairns hide, in many cases, the varied and changing history of these sites. The original form of many of these monuments, particularly in the Clyde region, seems to have been single-compartment chambers set within small cairns. It was only at a later date that these monuments were enlarged and began to resemble what we see today. These enlargements made the monument more accessible and included arenas for public display. In other traditions, cairns and chambers were enlarged and forecourts were added, transforming the appearance of the cairns and making them appear much more monumental and imposing. Increasingly, Neolithic people used dead bodies and bones as a way of remembering the past and as part of a means of structuring the present and the future. The development of new styles of monument and cairns indicates a growing reliance on notions of ancestry and inheritance in Neolithic life. The manipulation of human bone within the chambers involved a deliberate blurring of the past and the present through the amalgamation of the bones of many different individuals, perhaps as a means of suggesting continuity between past and present human generations and the land that they worked.

The enlargement of older monuments indicates a long-term commitment to a place. This desire to connect with the past could be linked to a changing sense of time and place in locations where farming was practised for the first time. The anthropologist Meillassoux has noted important distinctions in the conception of time of hunter-gatherers and farmers (Meillassoux 1972). Hunter-gatherers tend not to invest large amounts of time in acquiring their food – hunter-gatherers did not need to plant crops and wait for them to mature. Farmers, in contrast, often rely on previous generations for their success – cereal-growing often requires the long-term investment in a particular area of land and requires long-term maintenance of the soils and growing conditions. Meillassoux linked these important differences to the stronger sense of genealogy often found amongst farmers in comparison to hunter-gatherers and associated this sense of genealogy with the importance of ancestry amongst many farming communities. Earlier Neolithic Scotland was a place and time of transition where new lifestyles associated with the new technologies of farming were being adopted. The changes at this time may have been relatively rapid (Schulting and Richards 2002). The past may therefore have quickly became a resource through which social relations could be formulated and structured. Chambered cairns may have been one of the most significant places where Neolithic society was renewed and reconfirmed. The changing nature of megalithic architecture may give us a window on the transformations in society that occurred at this time, when the living and the dead became better acquainted.

NOTES

1. The cairn in figure 7 is not securely dated, however the similarities with the other primary cairns at Mid Gleniron suggest that this cairn belongs to this period (Corcoran 1969a: 96–100, 1969c, 1972: 36).
2. It is possible that the kerb could have been dismantled to allow access to the chamber as in a number of side-entered Severn-Cotswold tombs. However, the architecture does imply a lesser degree of accessibility than the later chamber form.

CHAPTER SIX

The emergence of monument complexes

The Later Neolithic period in Britain and Ireland has traditionally been seen as a major period of change. Many of the more regional monument traditions and pottery styles were, to a degree, replaced with styles of monument and material culture that drew on traditions found across the length and breadth of the British Isles (Ashmore 1996: chapter 4; Burl 1976; Barrett 1994; Bradley 1984: chapter 3; Bradley and Chapman 1986; Malone 2001: chapter 6; Megaw and Simpson 1979: chapter 4; Thomas 1999a). Some of these developments appear to have occurred as a gradual process of change in social practices in areas to the north (Bradley 1998: chapter 7). However, in other areas such as the south of England, change appears to have come about more abruptly with the adoption of practices and material culture more common in distant areas (Barclay 2000: 282; Thomas 1999a). However, the changes that occurred in the Later Neolithic have perhaps been overstated: in many ways and in many regions the structure of Neolithic society remained the same. This is particularly evident in the continuing significance of monumental landscapes. Many of the large enclosures constructed in the Later Neolithic were built in places that were already significant in the economic, social and ritual cycles of the Earlier Neolithic.

As we have seen in the earlier chapters, the monuments of the Earlier Neolithic can be viewed as a number of overlapping regional trends. This is highlighted by the number of past archaeological works that have classified these traditions into groups that are still largely recognised today. Thus Audrey Henshall was able to write two volumes outlining a number of regional styles of Earlier Neolithic chambered cairns (Henshall 1963, 1972) and these groups are still studied as such today (for example, Phillips' 2002 study of the Orkney-Cromarty cairns). Henshall herself drew on work by much earlier archaeologists who at an early stage in the development of Scottish archaeology were able to identify much the same groups (Bryce 1901–2, 1902–3, 1908–9). Other Earlier Neolithic traditions have wider distributions, for example cursus monuments are found across much of eastern Britain (Barclay and Harding 1999), but there are discrete groupings of these monuments. For example, Brophy (1999a and b) has commented on the distinctive nature of the Scottish cursus monuments and the pit-defined cursus monument remains a peculiarly Scottish phenomenon. Also, the burning of the Scottish cursus monuments (see Chapter 3) is not a feature found commonly in England. The sharing of architectural styles across the British Isles during the Earlier Neolithic may be as much part of the process of Neolithicisation as actual evidence of subsequent contact between these separate regions (see Chapter 2).

Attempts have also been made to group the monuments of the British Later Neolithic into regional traditions (for example, Burl 1969; Barnatt 1989). However, this has been much less successful than the identification of distinct Earlier Neolithic traditions. Burl's attempt (1969) identified a number of regional groups of henges, but it is important to note that many of the definitions are based on features of the monuments that can now be seen as part of the Early Bronze Age use of these sites (Bradley 1998: chapter 9). Likewise, it is interesting to note that two of the most distinctive groups identified in Barnatt's 1989 survey of stone circles: – the recumbent stone circles and Clava cairns of Scotland – have now been shown to be Early Bronze Age rather than Later Neolithic sites (Bradley 2000a, 2000b, 2005).

One of the most significant aspects of the Later Neolithic was the construction of large-scale monumental enclosures, epitomised by sites in the popular consciousness such as Stonehenge and Avebury in southern England. Often these constructions were on a much larger scale than the earlier traditions of monuments (Bradley and Chapman 1986; Renfrew 1973). Monuments not only increased in size in the Later Neolithic, but also began to be grouped more closely together, creating what archaeologists have termed 'ceremonial complexes' (Barnatt 1989: chapter 3; Bradley 1993: 108–9). Ceremonial complexes or monument complexes are loosely defined as the places where a wide range of structures, often of more than one period, have been found in the same location. The largest monument complexes are often associated with concentrations of objects made from non-local materials (principally stone axes) and the monuments themselves may reference traditions more commonly found elsewhere in the British Isles (Bradley 1993: 110). The presence of non-local references and influences may indicate increasing contacts between regions in the Later Neolithic. This may relate to one of the most compelling aspects of monument complexes: their location within the geography of Scotland. There is an important association between monument complexes and natural routeways across the landscape. From the Earlier Neolithic and possibly earlier, landscapes situated at the heart or junction of these routes were utilised and monumentalised and became the places through which Neolithic society was maintained. These routes may have formed the main means of communication in prehistoric Britain and this was undoubtedly one of the contributing factors to their increasing significance through time.

The Later Neolithic has often been seen as a distinct chronological phase of the Neolithic: many authors have postulated a break or a restructuring of Neolithic society at this time. In the following two chapters a different approach has been adopted that emphasises the continuities of traditions of building and use of the landscape in the Earlier and Later Neolithic. For example, monumental complexes cannot be seen merely as a phenomenon of the Later Neolithic; the use of these landscapes often stretched back to the Earlier Neolithic and beyond. The most compelling aspects of these complexes are the time-depth of the activities that occurred in these landscapes, activities that included monument building but not to the exclusion of other social and economic practices. It is impossible to consider Later Neolithic Scotland without reference to the earlier trajectories of social development.

As a way of further introducing the main forms of Later Neolithic monumentality, the places that have been identified as monumental complexes in Scotland will be outlined. This is an important undertaking as these complexes have not been considered in detail previously and their histories and structural components have not been compared and contrasted. Not every potential monumental complex has been considered here; however, a wide range of places including previously little-publicised locations will be considered as a means of examining the nature of what we might define as a monument complex and as a means of examining the ways in which the archaeological record of the Later Neolithic compares with the Earlier Neolithic patterns and traditions. The first complex is the monument complex at Balfarg, Fife, which represents one of the largest known concentrations of Neolithic monuments in Scotland (Barclay and Russell-White 1993; Mercer 1977–8; Ritchie 1974). This complex included a series of large-scale Later Neolithic enclosures, but like all of the complexes highlighted in this chapter it will be seen that the history of these places stretches back much further. The long-term histories of these landscapes should be examined to assess the ways in which they developed over time and this must include their environmental and economic histories if we are to produce fuller understandings of these places. These aspects are ones to which I shall return later. First, it is time to take a tour of some of the major archaeological landscapes of Scotland.

THE CEREMONIAL COMPLEXES OF NEOLITHIC SCOTLAND

The Neolithic archaeology of Balfarg, Fife, has been extensively excavated and provides much detail on the development of monumental landscapes (Barclay and Russell-White 1993; Mercer 1977–8; Ritchie 1974). A whole series of monuments was excavated at Balfarg during the 1970s and 80s in advance of development (Figure 6.1) (Mercer 1977–8; Ritchie 1974). The earliest structural remains found on the site consist of a number of pits at Balfarg Riding School, indicating activity in the area prior to the main phase of monument construction (Barclay and Russell-White 1993). Large numbers of Earlier Neolithic pits were found in two different areas, each of which had pottery assemblages dominated by differing styles of pottery. The differences in pottery and the spread of radiocarbon dates (Figure 6.2) might indicate two major phases of settlement or a series of repeated occupations of the area over an extended period of time. Large stones deposited in the upper layers of some of the pits may have marked previous occupations for future visits, as has been found elsewhere (for example, Case 1973; Stone 1949: 289). Impressed Ware pottery was also found at Balfarg Riding School under two ring cairns and this may represent further phases of activity in the area after the main phases of Earlier Neolithic pit-digging (Barclay and Russell-White 1993: 117).

The most significant aspect of the excavations at Balfarg was the identification of a series of Later Neolithic monuments of varying forms. Two timber buildings were

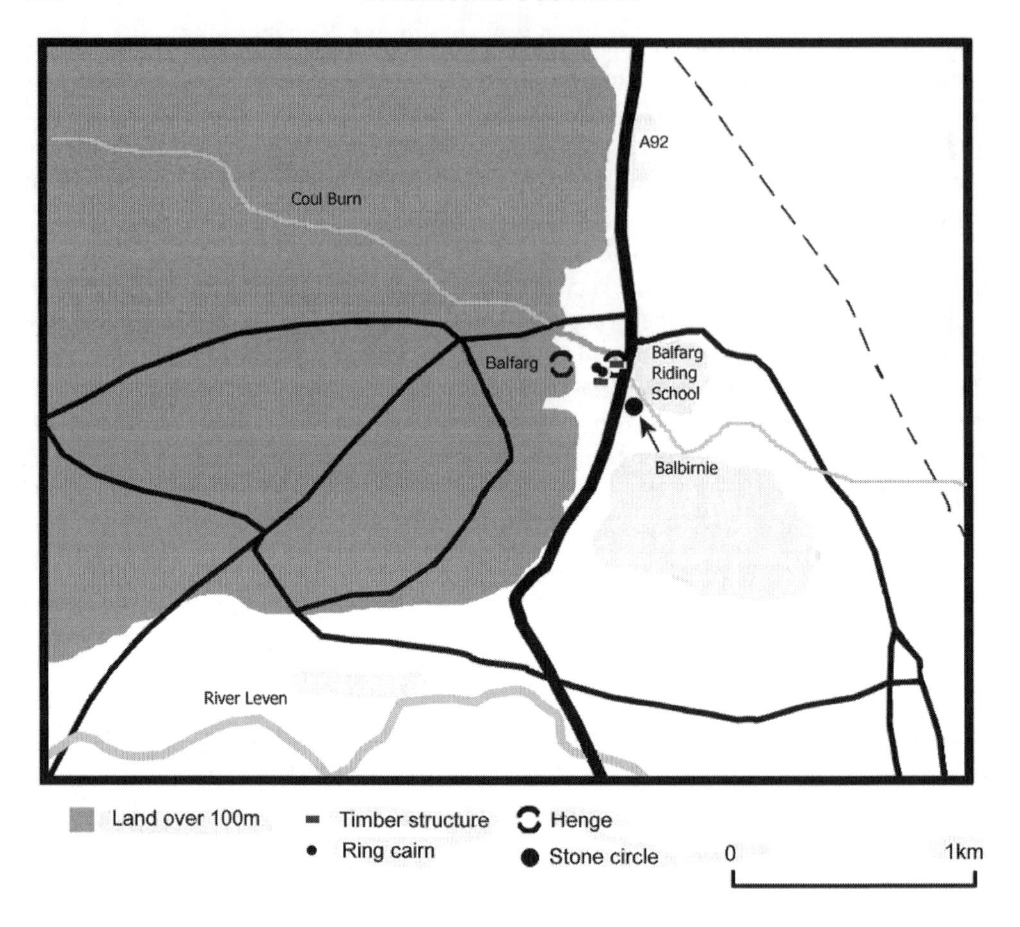

FIGURE 6.1 *The monument complex at Balfarg. The site is located between two watercourses*

located in the vicinity of the Earlier Neolithic pits. These structures closely resemble Earlier Neolithic buildings excavated at Balbridie, Aberdeenshire, and Claish Farm, Tayside, but in this case they were closely associated with the use of Later Neolithic Grooved Ware pottery and neither of the buildings were roofed or burnt down (Barclay et al. 2002: 110, 124; Ralston 1982) (see Chapter 2). Structure 1 was rectangular, around 20 by 10 metres, and aligned north-south (Figure 6.3). The outer postholes of the structure were substantial, regular and appeared to be of one phase. In contrast, in the interior there was substantial evidence for post replacement and the layout of the posts was more haphazard, suggesting the structure was not a roofed building. Structure 2 was of similar form and dimensions and also appears to have been unroofed. Structure 2 was surrounded by a circular ditched enclosure and was covered by an earthen barrow or mound, which also contained Grooved Ware pottery. The ditch of the circular ditched enclosure contained Grooved Ware, Beaker pottery and cereals and wild plant remains along with charcoal and stone tools (Figure 6.3). The radiocarbon dates suggest that this enclosure was dug at the same time as the timber structure inside was in use (Figure 6.2). Further contemporary

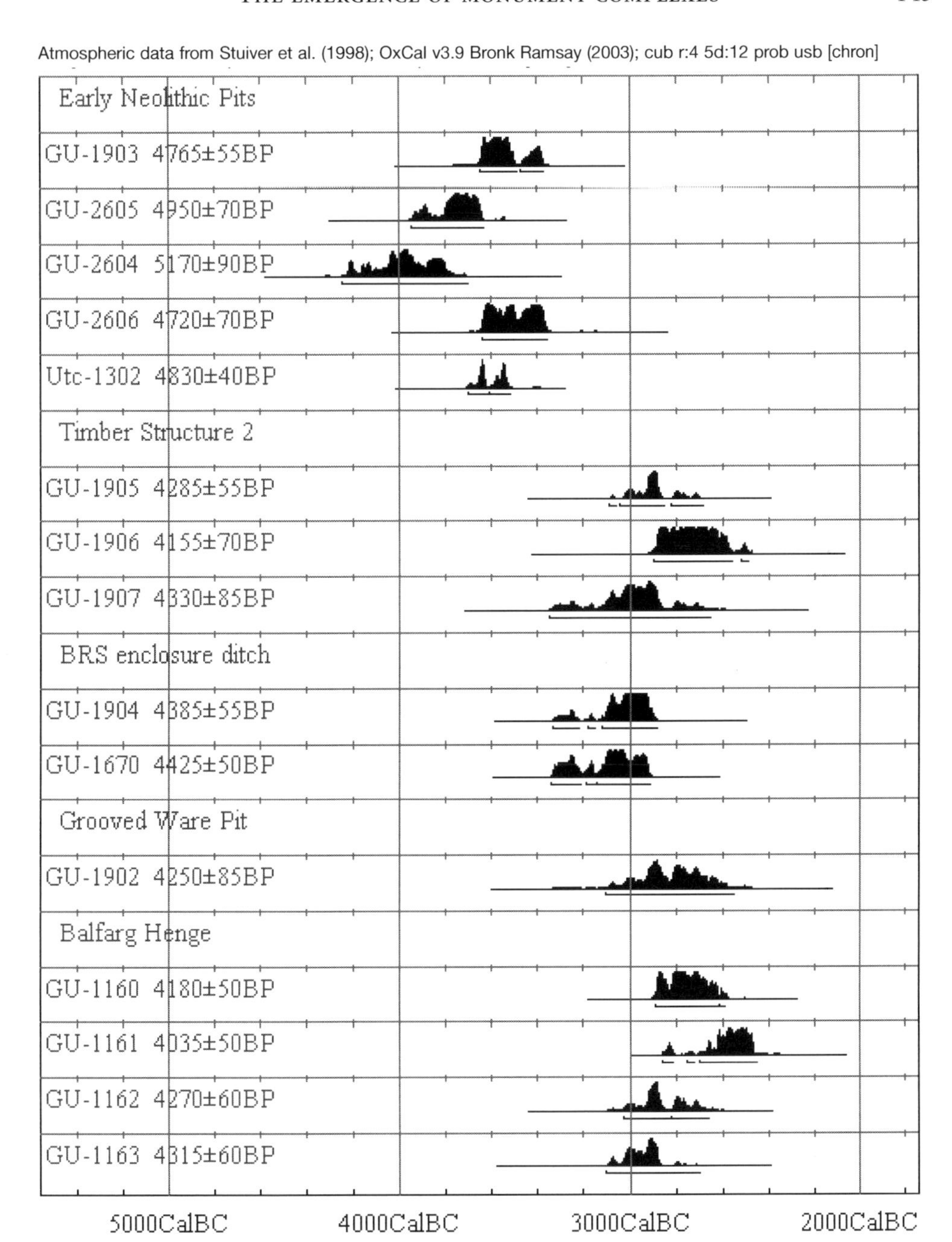

FIGURE 6.2 *Radiocarbon dates for Balfarg and Balfarg Riding School*

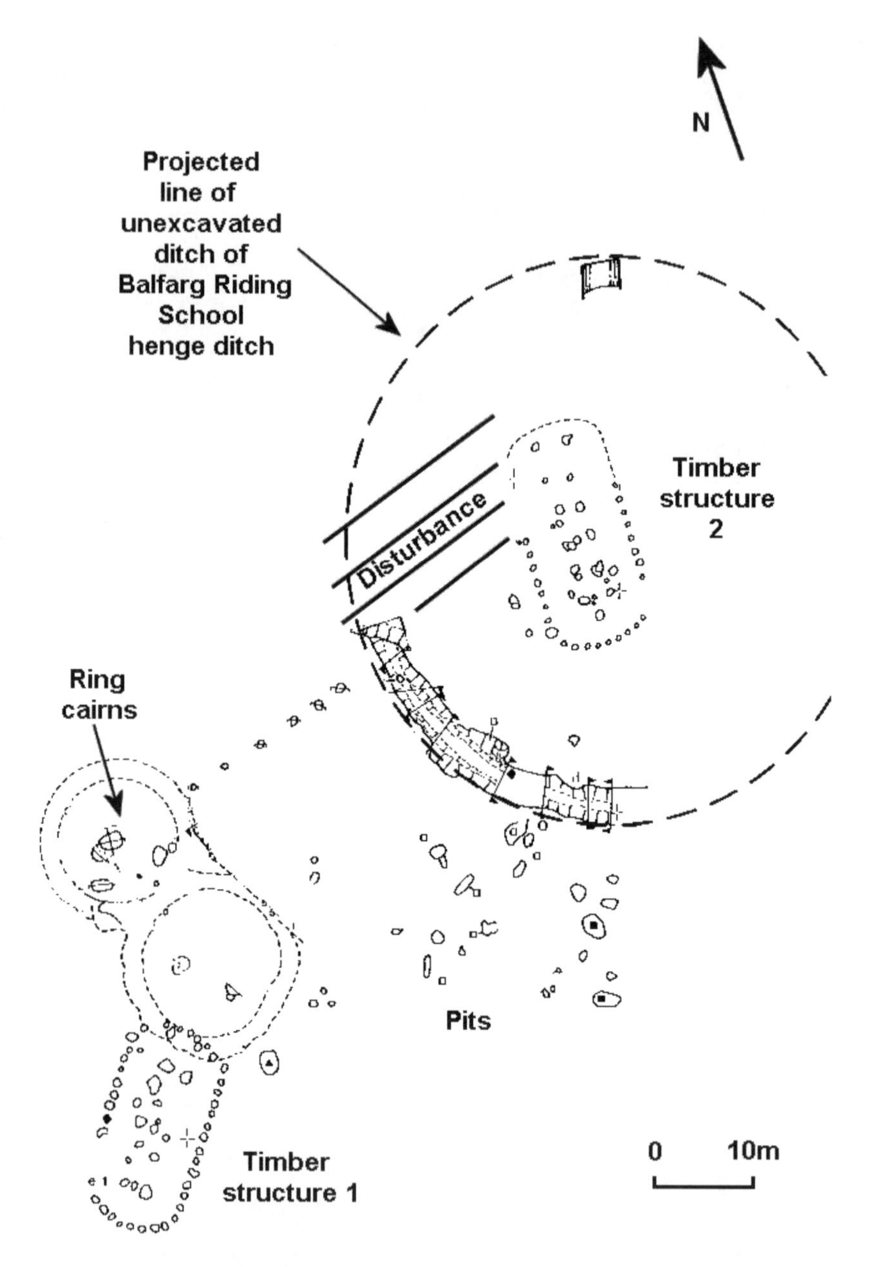

FIGURE 6.3 *Balfarg Riding School. The henge, timber structures and Area C pits (Source: Barclay and Russell-White 1993: figure 6)*

activity around the enclosure is indicated by five Grooved Ware pits that contained charcoal and burnt bone and lithics (Figure 6.3).

The largest monumental structure at Balfarg was undoubtedly the henge monument, excavated by Roger Mercer in the late 1970s, located less than 200 metres to the west of the timber structures (Mercer 1977–8; Mercer et al. 1988) (Figure 6.4). At the

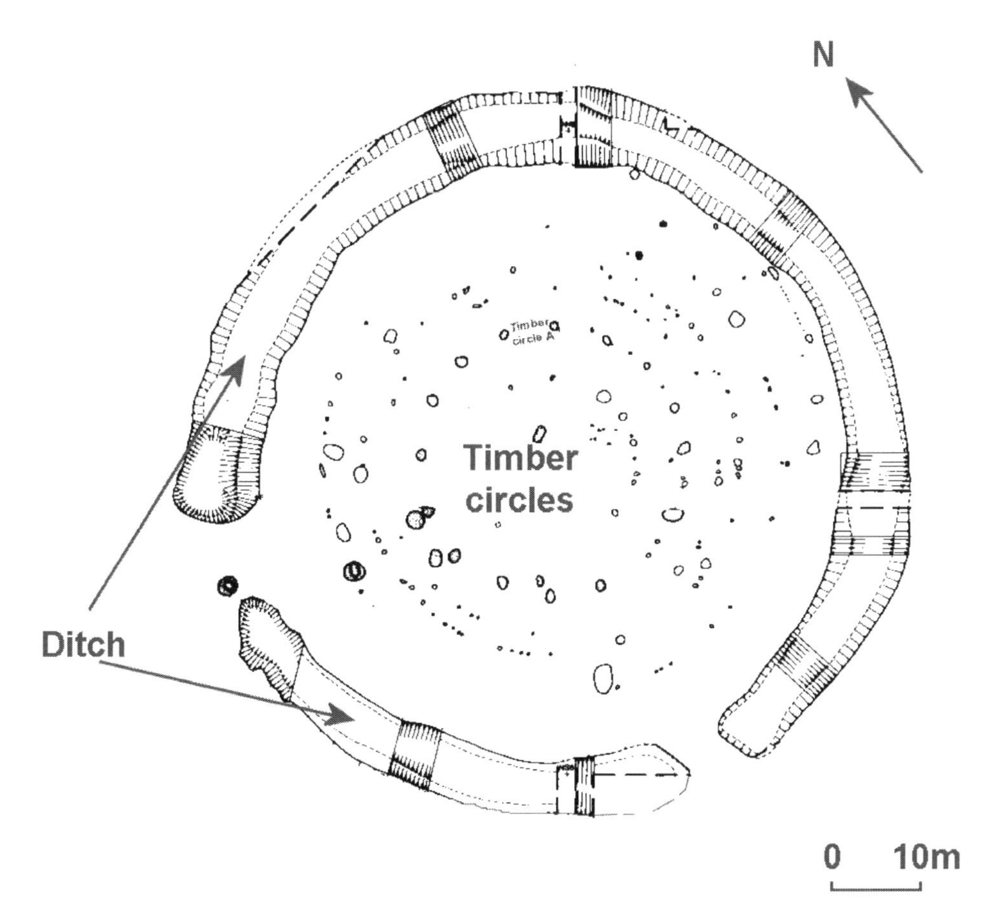

Figure 6.4 *Balfarg henge. A series of timber circles were enclosed by a ditch and bank (Source: Mercer et al. 1988: figure 3)*

henge, the first phases of activity on the site involved the deposition of large amounts of deliberately smashed Grooved Ware pottery in the western area of what was to become the interior of the henge. The deposition activity was associated with the burning of wood and bone and some of the pottery sherds themselves were scorched.

Soon after the pottery deposition, as many as six concentric settings of timber posts were erected on the site. The largest circle consisted of a ring of seventeen timber posts with a porch-like arrangement on the western arc. Pottery and lithic finds were concentrated around this porch, suggesting it functioned as an entrance (Mercer 1977–8: 84). Inside the circle itself, burnt material, cremated or burnt bone and a number of sherds of Grooved Ware were found, some of which was from the same assemblage deposited in the initial activity at the site. At least five further concentric settings of posts were erected in relation to this circle, each of a different circumference and post size. The timber circles were at some later date enclosed by a massive ditch and bank, which would have substantially restricted physical and visual access to the site (Mercer 1977–8; Mercer et al. 1988). The ditch enclosed a substantial area almost 65 metres in diameter, somewhat larger than the earlier ditched enclosure around timber structure 2. Inside the henge, two stone settings were erected some time after the timber circles themselves had decayed. A further stone setting was also constructed around 100 metres to the south of the rectangular timber structures at Balbirnie (Ritchie 1974) (Figure 6.5). The Balbirnie stone circle was around 15 metres in diameter with ten standing stones graded in height to the south. In the centre a rectangular 'hearth-like' setting of stones was found (Ritchie 1975–6). It is clear that the landscape at Balfarg represented a major focus of Neolithic activity, only some of which is still visible today.

Another significant (and excavated) henge complex is at North Mains in Perthshire (Barclay 1983) (Figures 6.6 and 6.7). Like Balfarg, the earliest features identified at North Mains were scattered Earlier Neolithic pits and similarly in the Later Neolithic, two timber settings were erected, before a henge ditch and bank enclosed the site. The Later Neolithic timber settings consisted of a circular setting of large oak posts (Figure 6.8). The ditch enclosed an area almost 30 metres in diameter, but the bank and the ditch may not have been constructed until some time later in the Early Bronze Age (DES 2003b). In contrast to Balfarg and Balfarg Riding School, very little pottery, if any, was associated with the henge and timber circle phases of the site.

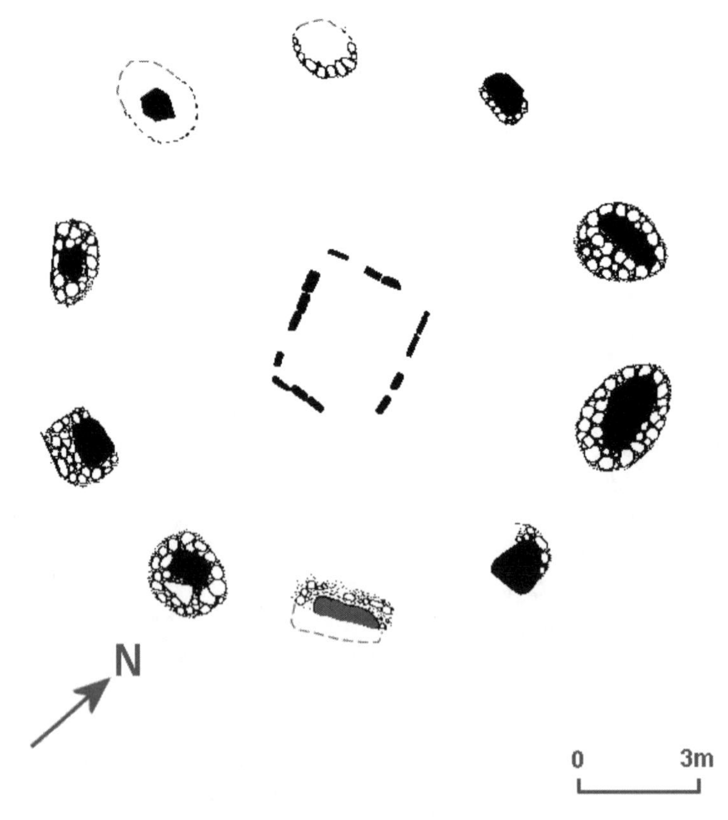

FIGURE 6.5 *Balbirnie stone circle. Placed centrally was a large rectangular setting of stones (Source: Ritchie 1974: figure 2)*

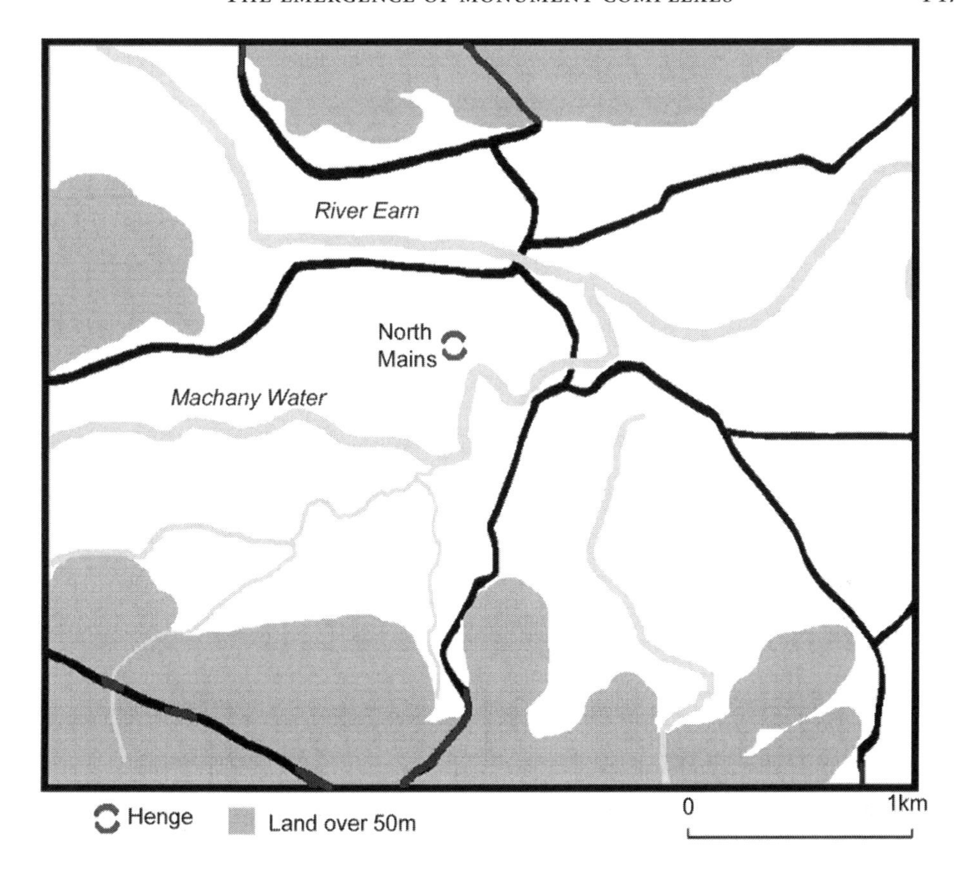

Figure 6.6 *The location of North Mains henge. The site is criss-crossed by a number of roads and waterways*

The sequence at Cairnpapple Hill in West Lothian followed a very similar trajectory to that at North Mains and Balfarg (Figure 6.9). Cairnpapple Hill was the first henge monument in Scotland excavated, by Stuart Piggott in the 1940s, to modern standards (Piggott 1947–8; Barclay 1999) (Figure 6.10). Recognisable activity on the site began in the Earlier Neolithic, like North Mains and Balfarg, with the deposition of pottery. The pottery found in the excavations consisted mainly of unstratified finds which had been incorporated into later features (Piggott 1947–8: 79). Two stone axes were found in similar circumstances, one was a Group VI (Langdale, Cumbria) type, while the other was a Group VII axe from Graig Lwyd, North Wales. The deposition of Earlier Neolithic pottery and stone axes may have been associated with less ephemeral remains. Six hearths have been found at the site, which may be associated with the early activity as one was found under the bank of the henge (Barclay 1999: 32).

In the Later Neolithic, the sequence of development closely followed that at Balfarg and North Mains with the erection of a setting of timber posts which was then enclosed by a ditch and bank with two entrances (Barclay 1999). In the centre of the timber setting a rectangular area of pits and a three-sided cove-setting were constructed. Piggott compared this last feature with Later Neolithic cove-settings found

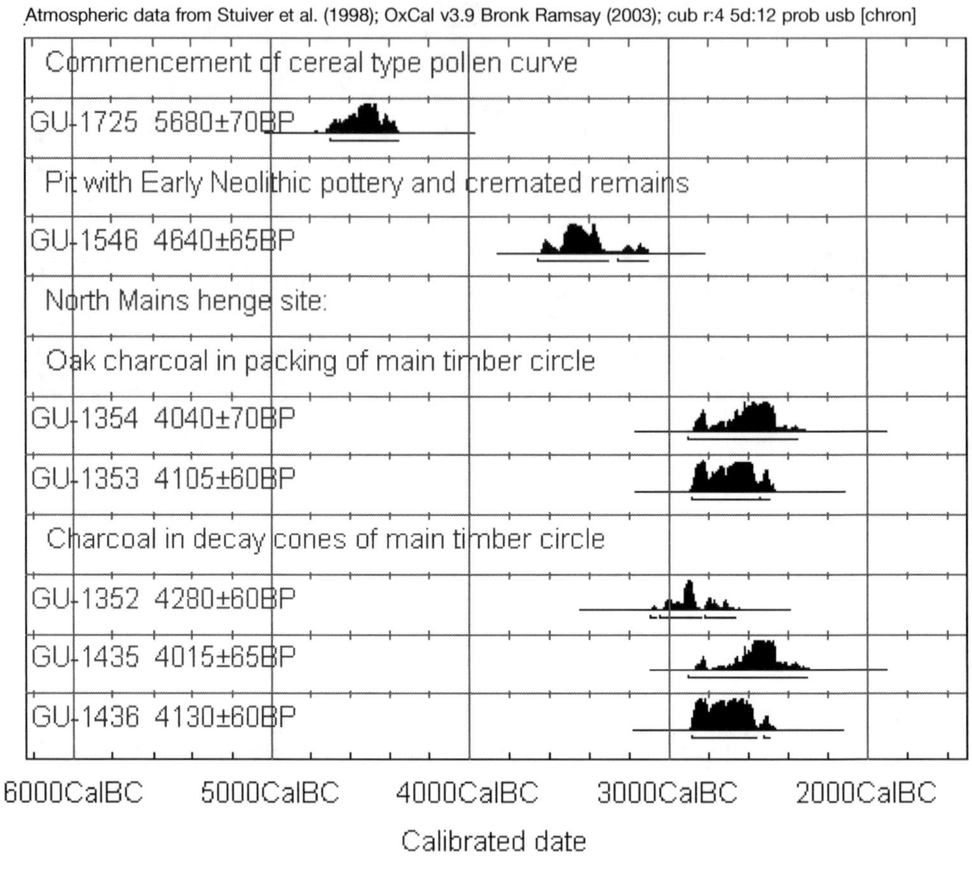

FIGURE 6.7 *Radiocarbon dates for North Mains henge and pollen core dates*

at sites such as Avebury and Arbor Low in England (Piggott 1947–8: 113). The feature also shares similarities with the rectangular hearth-like settings found at the Stones of Stenness and at Balbirnie stone circle, and with similar features at Site IV, Mount Pleasant, Dorset, and Stanton Drew, Somerset (David et al. 2004; Ritchie 1974, 1975–6; Wainwright 1979: figure 16).

The Upper Clyde valley represents perhaps one of the densest concentrations of Neolithic monuments and settlement known in Scotland and contains a more diverse range of monumental structures than the sites outlined above, albeit spread over a larger area (Figure 6.11). The archaeological record of the Earlier Neolithic period in this landscape is different to that at the sites described above as it may include a large enclosed site at West Lindsaylands. Monumental building achieved an altogether much larger scale in the Later Neolithic, with the construction of a series of henge monuments and other enclosures in the valley and the routes leading to it. The most spectacular monument constructed was in an upland basin at Blackshouse Burn where two parallel rings of oak posts with a stone bank in between was constructed, enclosing an area almost 300 metres in diameter. The size of this enclosure compares

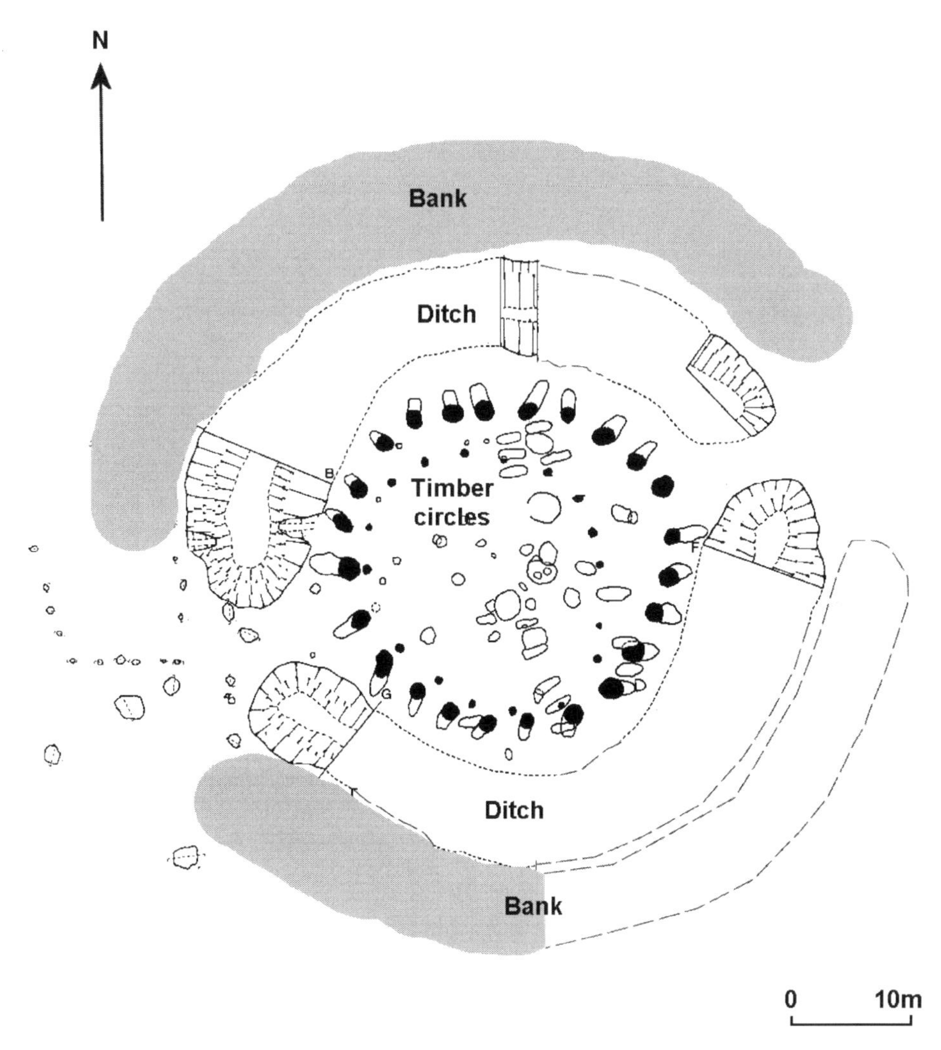

FIGURE 6.8 *North Mains henge and timber circle (Source: Barclay 1983: figure 3)*

with the great henge monuments of Durrington Walls and Avebury in southern England (Wainwright 1989). No other monument of comparable size is known in the region (RCAHMS 1978: no. 171). On the ridges around the enclosure there are numerous cairns and extensive evidence for prehistoric settlement (Lelong and Pollard 1998; RCAHMS 1978).

Earlier Neolithic activity in the Upper Clyde Valley may have included the building at West Lindsaylands, one of the few possible causewayed enclosures identified in Scotland – a distinctive type of large-scale Earlier Neolithic enclosed monument (Oswald 2001). These enclosures were used for a variety of purposes in the Earlier Neolithic including feasting, deposition and for the exposure of the dead. They are usually identified by their distinctive boundaries that include a number of breaks or

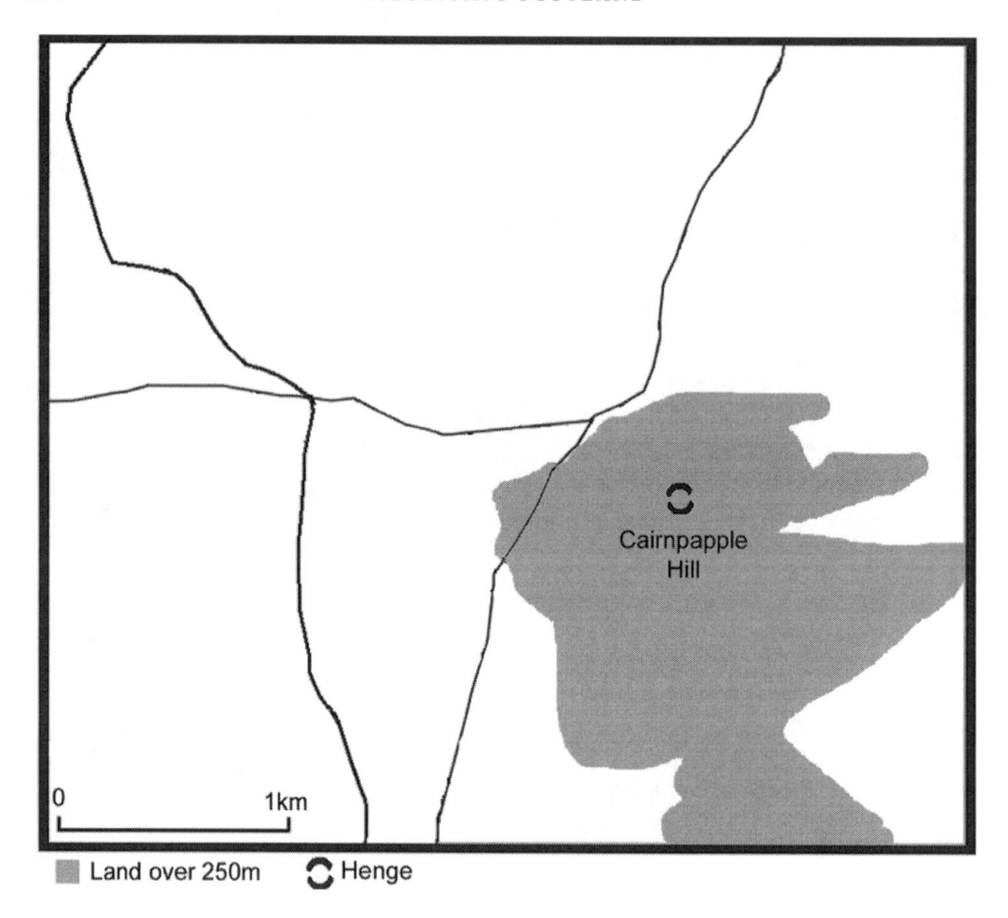

FIGURE 6.9 *The location of Cairnpapple Hill henge. The site is situated on a hilltop*

causeways. Cropmarks and a recent resistivity survey at West Lindsaylands indicate a D-shaped enclosure, set onto the River Clyde, defined by two curving ditches each with a number of breaks (Nelson 2003; RCAHMS 1978: no. 323). Its form suggests that this may be a causewayed enclosure. To the east lies a possible pit-defined cursus monument (Figure 6.11) (Nelson 2003).

In the Later Neolithic the labour invested in monument construction massively increased with the unparalleled construction of a series of enclosures in the valley. The valley contains a dense concentration of Later Neolithic monuments that includes all of the henge monuments identified in the region, six in total (Figure 6.11). Normangill henge lies in a small valley in the south leading to the Upper Clyde Valley, while a few kilometres to the north is Hillend, a possible henge, which has been partly eroded by the River Clyde (Armit et al. 1994; RCAHMS 1978: nos 169 and 303). Further up the Clyde another possible henge is situated at Westside about 7 kilometres to the north and on the opposite bank of the Clyde lies Craigie Burn (RCAHMS 1978: nos 291 and 324; Sharpe and Hamer 1999). The henge at Weston lies outside the main valley to the northeast but is on a routeway that leads towards the valley (RCAHMS 1978: no. 170).

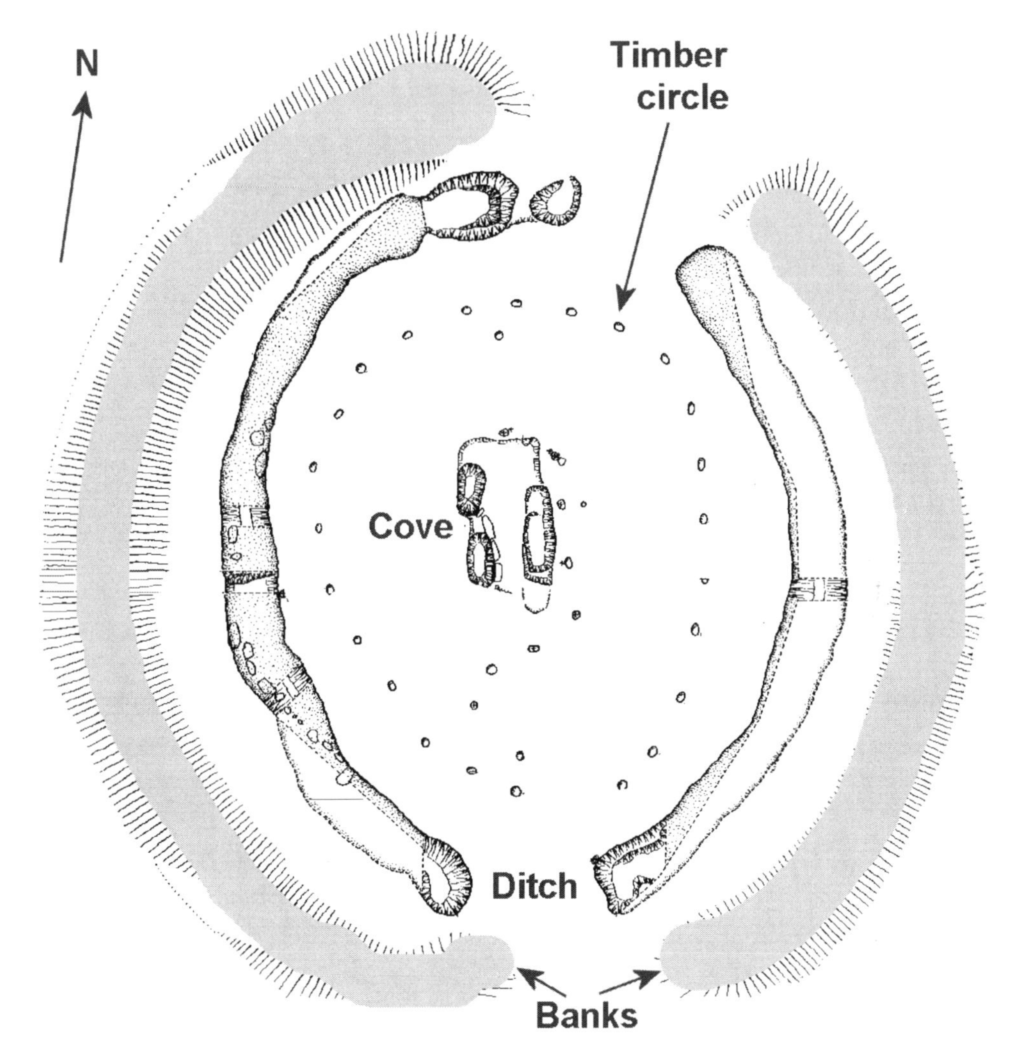

Figure 6.10 *Cairnpapple Hill henge*
(Source: Piggott 1947–8: figure 3)

Just above the town of Biggar in the valley lies the sixth possible henge site, at Balwaiste, defined by a ditch with entrances on the northeast and southwest (RCAHMS 1997: no. 116).

The enclosure at Blackshouse Burn is unusual in that it is located away from the valley henges in an upland basin amongst the Pettinain Hill range (Figure 6.12). The enclosure was originally defined by two parallel rows of oak posts set just over 8 metres apart that may have been joined by planking, which would have formed a significant barrier to movement and vision (Lelong and Pollard 1998). The enclosure is almost 300 metres in diameter with a circumference almost a kilometre long, so large that at times it is difficult to see the opposite side when standing near the edge of the enclosure (Lelong and Pollard 1998: 44). After the posts were erected, a bank of

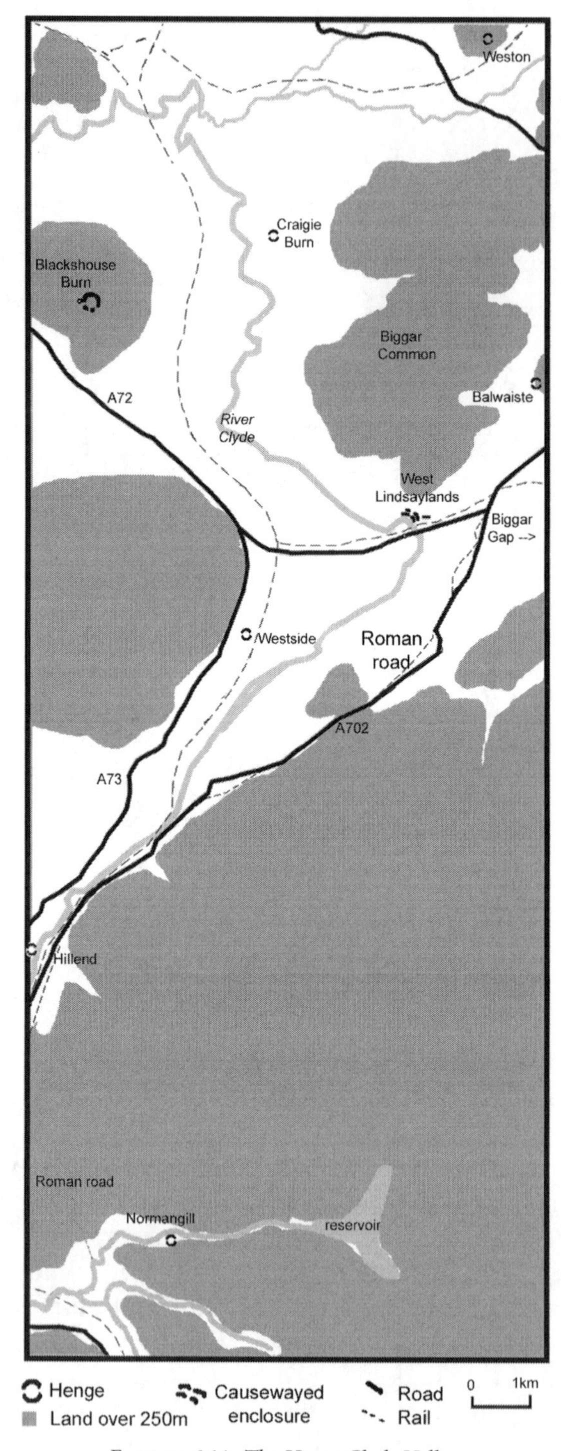

FIGURE 6.11 *The Upper Clyde Valley*

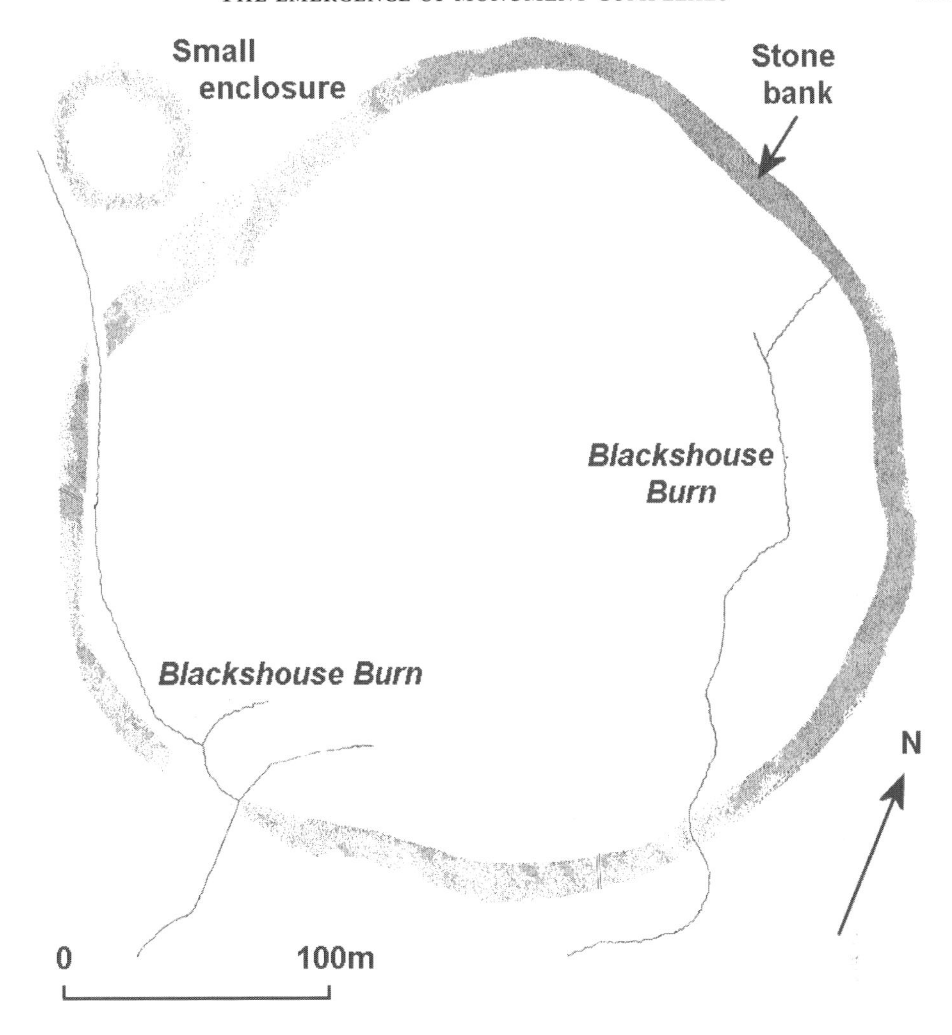

FIGURE 6.12 *Blackshouse Burn. The monument encloses both heads of the Blackshouse Burn (Source: RCHAMS 1978: no. 171)*

stones was laid between, creating an irregular bank, and after the posts had decayed a final stone capping layer was added (Lelong and Pollard 1998: 45).

The initial phases of Blackshouse Burn would have resembled the timber enclosure, which was constructed around the same time at Meldon Bridge in the Borders. Like so many of the sites already mentioned the earliest dated structural evidence found at Meldon Bridge included the digging of pits. The pits at Meldon Bridge, which were possibly dug and filled over a prolonged period of time, mainly contained Impressed Ware pottery (Figure 6.15). However, the sharing of vessels between pits in particular locations suggests that some were elements of contemporary activity (Speak and Burgess 1999).

In the Later Neolithic, in the early third millennium BC, a spectacular wooden barrier was erected to enclose an area of land at the confluence of the Lyne Water and

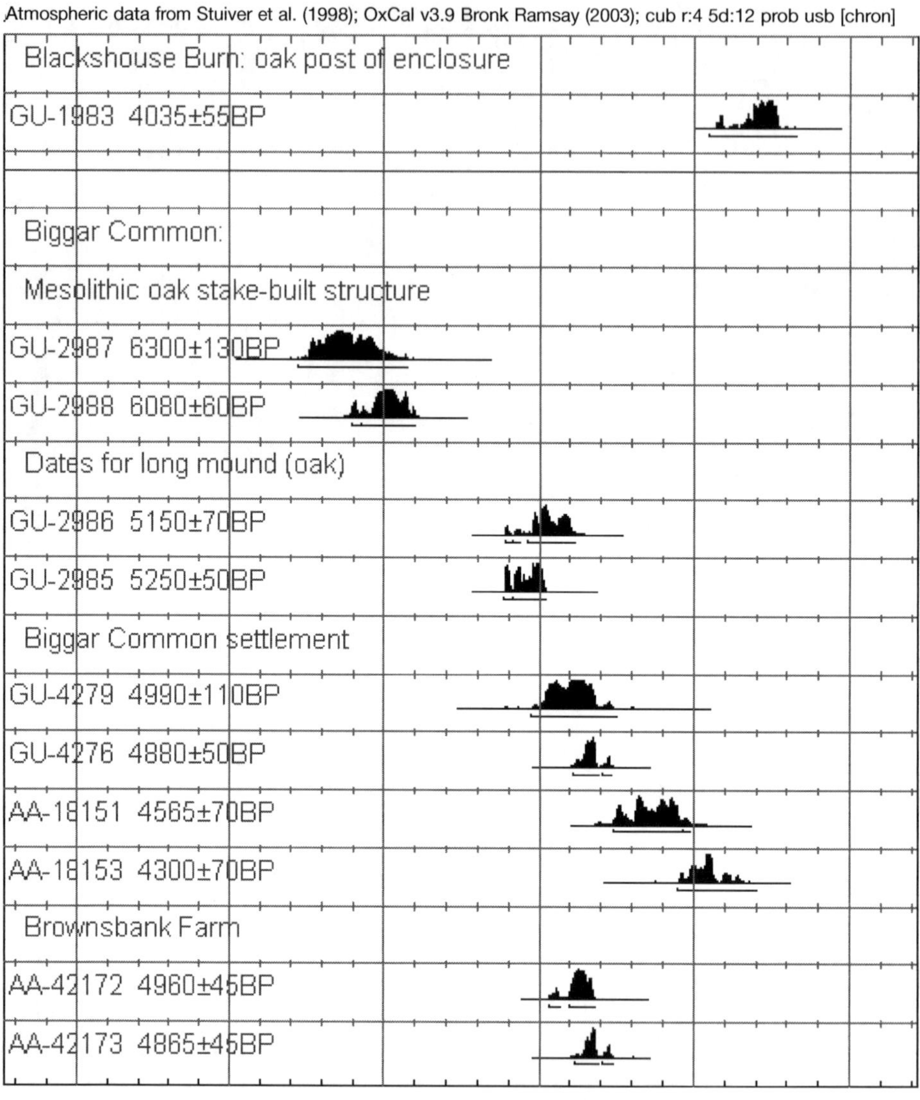

FIGURE 6.13 *Radiocarbon dates for Blackshouse Burn, Biggar Common and Brownsbank Farm*

the Meldon Burn (Speak and Burgess 1999) (Figures 6.14 and 6.15). The posts of the barrier may have stood up to 4 metres high and extended for almost 600 metres; the larger posts would have weighed two tonnes or more and were joined by planking. None of the posts appear to have been replaced, and the barrier appears to have stood and decayed within the space of a century. Three sockets were found inside the enclosure; one contained the truncated remains of a monolith. This may indicate that, like Balfarg and Machrie Moor, timber monuments were augmented by stone additions.

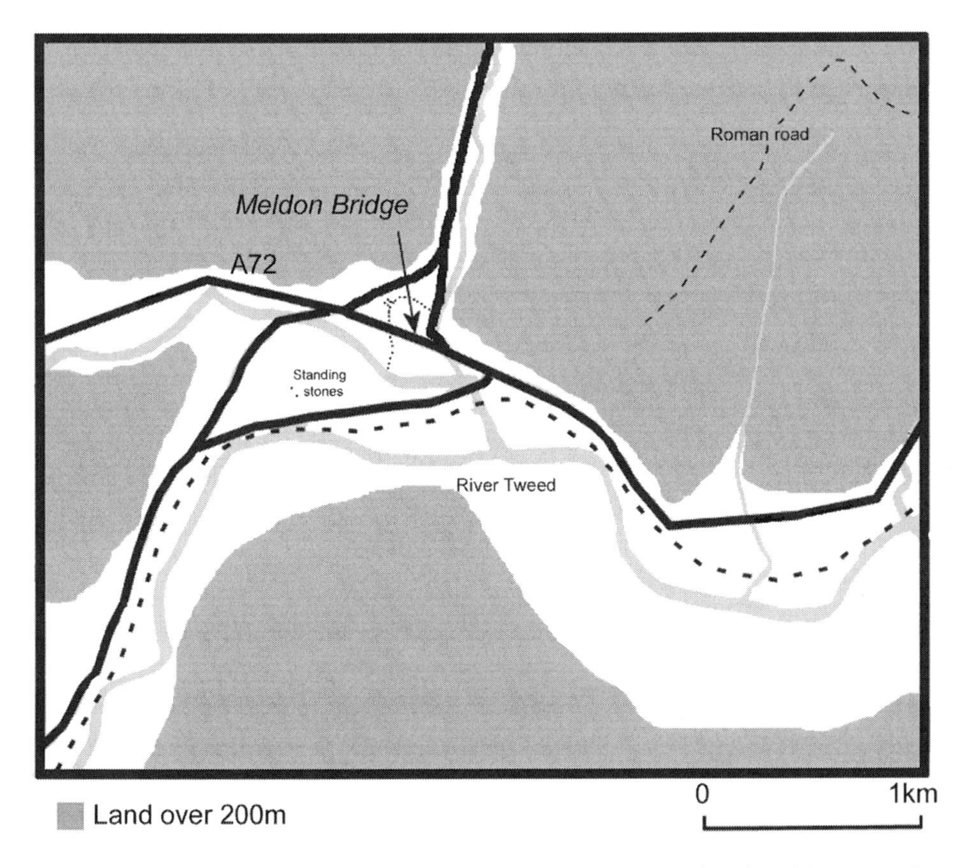

FIGURE 6.14 *Meldon Bridge. The site is located at the centre of a number of road (ancient and modern), rail and water routes*

A series of enclosures incorporating similar architectural elements to those at Meldon Bridge and Blackshouse Burn were also constructed at Dunragit in the middle of the third millennium BC (Figures 6.16 and 6.17). Unlike Meldon or Blackshouse, more than one timber monument was constructed (Thomas 1999b, 2001a, 2001b, 2002). The site is on a flat expanse of gravel outwash, near to the extensive dune system of Luce Sands where widespread evidence of Neolithic and Bronze Age activity has been uncovered over many years (Idle and Martin 1975; Cowie 1996; Wilson 1875–6, 1880–1, 1898–9) (Figure 6.16). Earlier Neolithic activity on the site also involved the construction of a timber monument, in this case one of the largest examples of a post-defined cursus monument (Thomas 2001a). This was over 200 metres long, aligned southwest to northeast, with sides between 2 and 3 metres high, increasing to probably 4 or 5 metres high at the northeast end where an entrance was located in the northeast terminal. The cursus monument had been burnt down like the monuments described in Chapter 3.

In the Later Neolithic the most spectacular features in the Dunragit landscape were three rings of timber posts (Thomas 2001b) (Figure 6.17). The inner ring was a free-standing timber circle, around 120 metres in diameter, which had been replaced on at

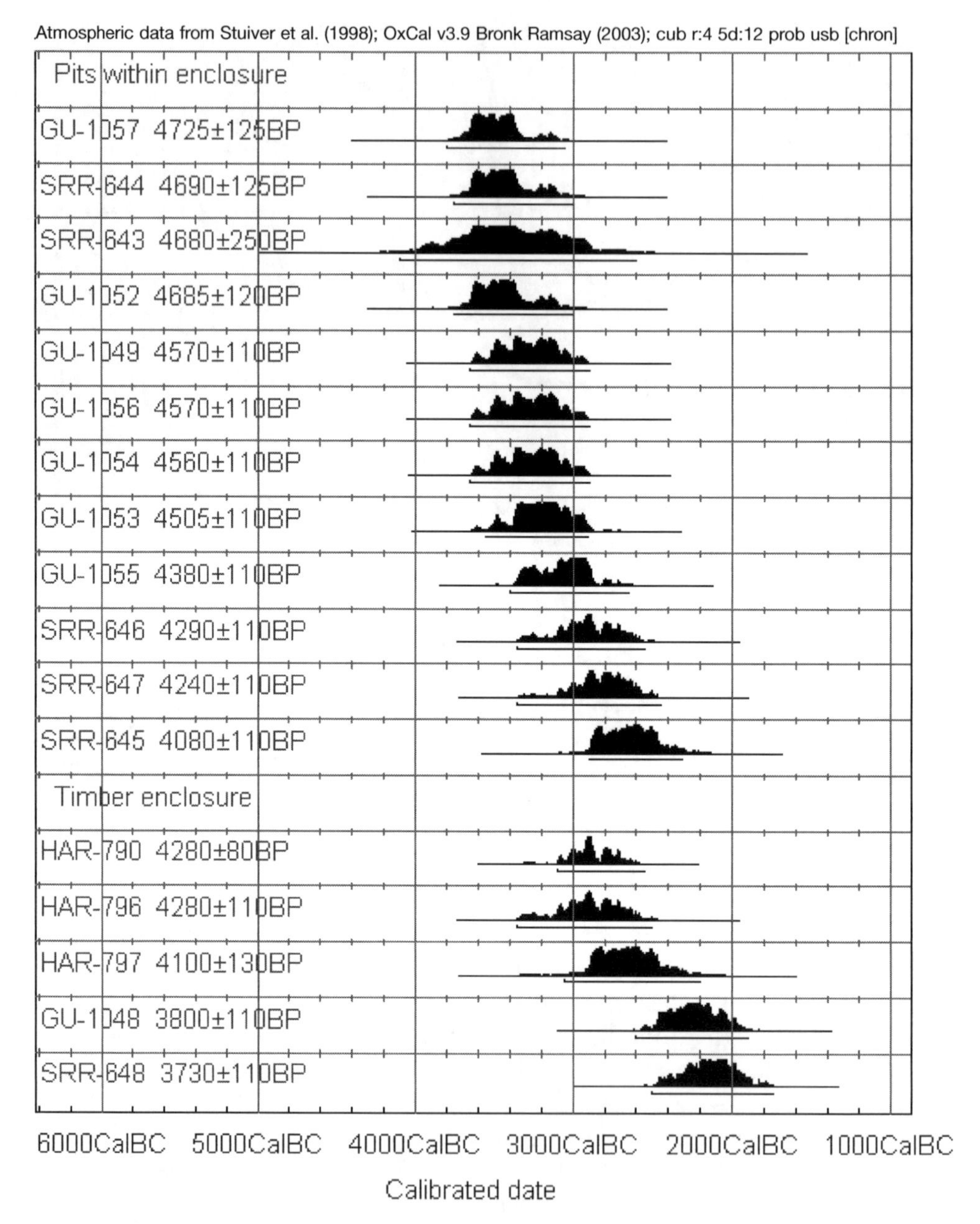

FIGURE 6.15 *Radiocarbon dates for Meldon Bridge*

least one occasion. In contrast, the two outer rings were continuous barriers enclosed with planking or fencing. The middle ring had a long entrance avenue of posts, very similar to the avenue at Meldon Bridge (Figure 6.17). The outer circle was almost 300 metres wide, like the enclosure at Blackshouse Burn. Not all of these enclosures may have stood at the same time as the entrances to the middle and outer rings do not align and the inner ring had at least two phases of construction. The radiocarbon

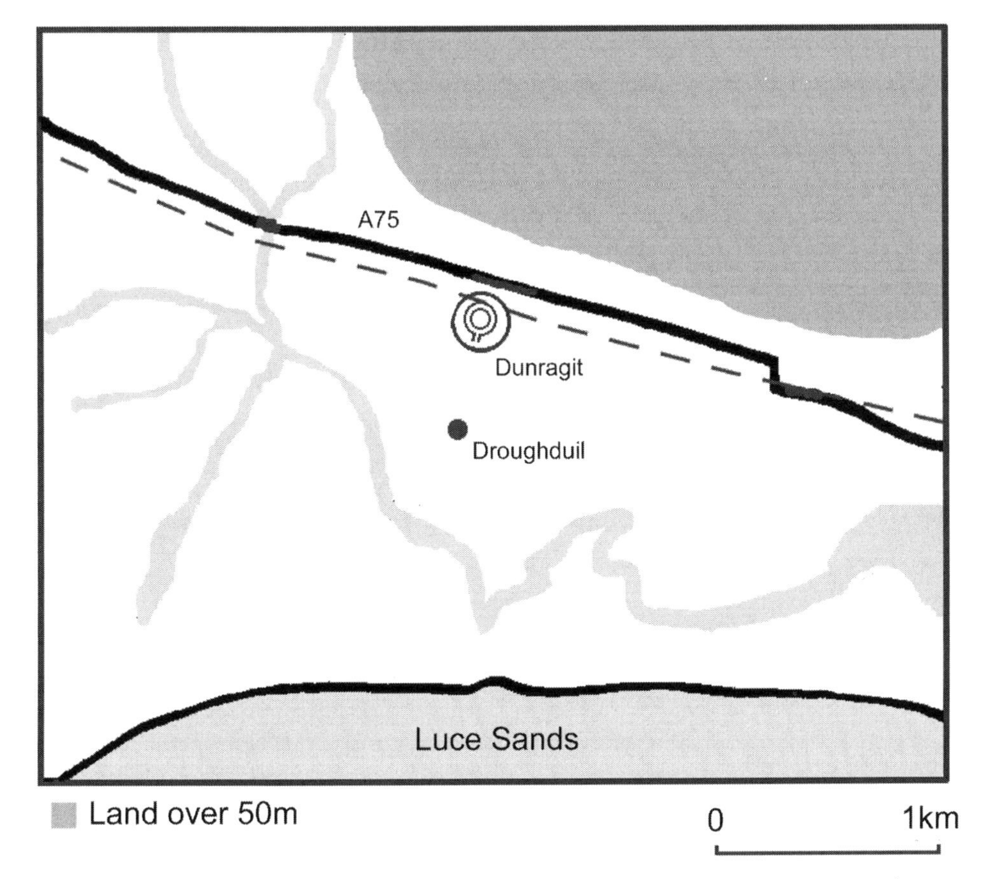

FIGURE 6.16 *Dunragit. The site is located next to the extensive dune system at Luce Sands, providing easy access to the sea*

dates, however, represent a reasonably defined period of activity centred on the centuries 2800 to 2500 BC, roughly contemporary with the construction of timber enclosures at North Mains, Blackshouse Burn and Meldon Bridge (Figure 6.18). Between the timber enclosures and the Luce Sands, to the south-southwest, lay a large mound (Thomas 2002) (Figure 6.19). The entrance avenue of the middle timber palisade at Dunragit was aligned on the mound, which was almost 10 metres high. This mound may have formed a viewing platform enabling views into the timber enclosures (Thomas 2002). It is clear that the Dunragit area was an intensively used landscape in the Neolithic. The sheer numbers and scale of monuments in this area are not easily paralleled and further smaller enclosures and monuments have been recorded in the vicinity and a short distance to the west at Drumflower (Cowley and Brophy 2001; RCAHMS 1987: no. 161).

A similar sequence of monument construction has been identified to the east near Dumfries, at Holywood, where Earlier Neolithic cursus monuments were augmented in the Later Neolithic by the construction of a large circular enclosure, albeit constructed of stone rather than timber (Thomas 1999c, 2000). Like Meldon Bridge the

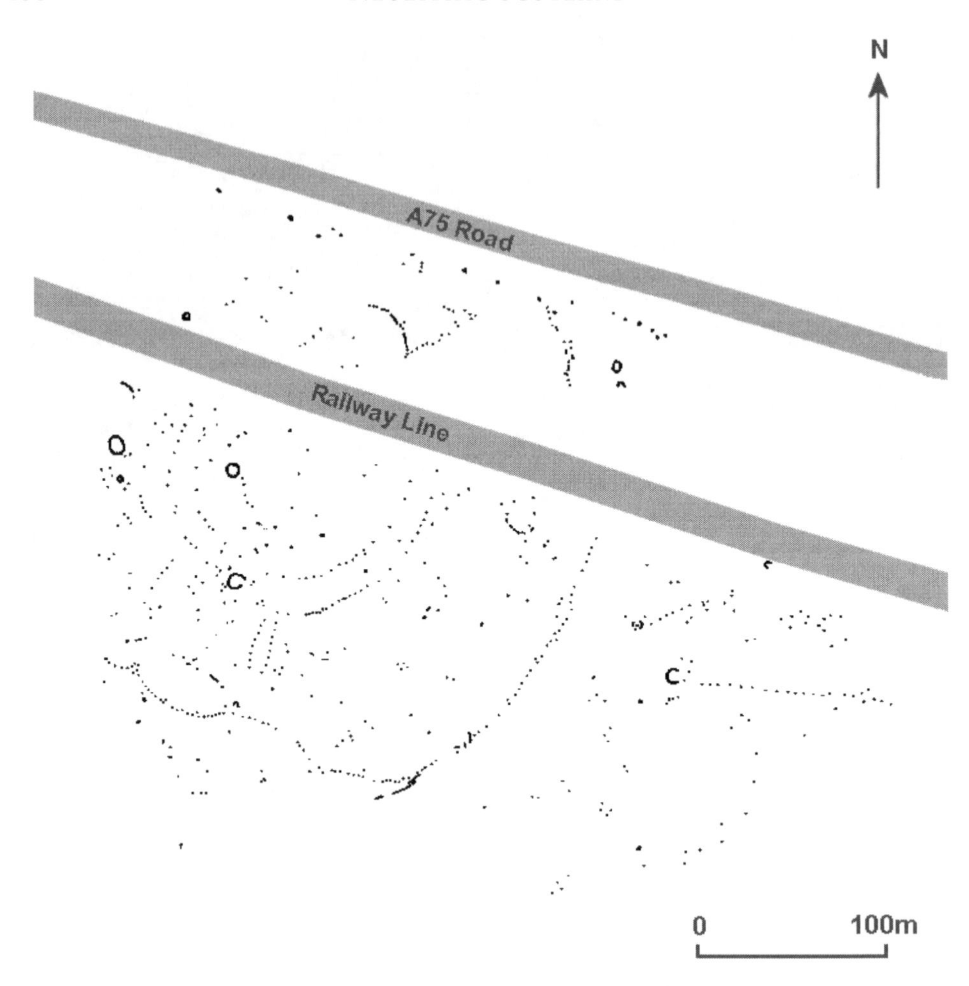

FIGURE 6.17 *Dunragit. The timber enclosures are bisected by the railway line and the A75. Droughduil mound in located a short distance to the southeast (Source: Thomas 2002: figure 1)*

site is located between two watercourses, the River Nith and one of its tributaries (Figure 6.20). The cursus monuments at Holywood (considered in Chapter 3) were amongst some of the larger Scottish examples and combined earthwork and timber elements in their construction (Brophy 1999a) (Figure 6.21). Holywood North was the larger of the two, around 400 metres long by 30 metres wide, aligned north-northeast to south-southwest; Holywood South was more rectangular with squared terminals and slightly shorter at 285 metres long. Both monuments were defined by ditches with internal banks, with lines of interior posts. Like the cursus at Dunragit, both of these cursus monuments were destroyed by fire (Thomas 1999c, 2000). Nearby a series of post alignments, which had also been destroyed by fire, was excavated at Holm Farm (Chapter 3) (Thomas 2000: 86) (Figure 6.20). These were aligned along the course of the nearby watercourse. In the Later Neolithic, monument construction utilised different media. A short distance to the southwest of the Holywood

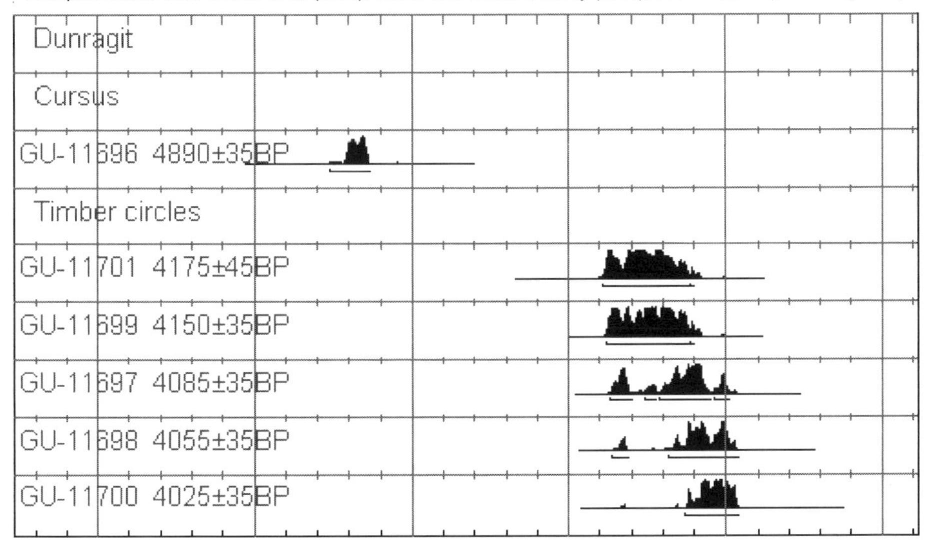

FIGURE 6.18 *Radiocarbon dates for Dunragit*

FIGURE 6.19 *Droughduil mound*

monuments a large stone circle was built. The Twelve Apostles stone circle would have been one of the largest stone circles in Britain, but now consists of only eleven stones, of which only five are still standing (Figure 6.21). There may have originally been eighteen stones defining an interior area of over 5,000 square metres (Burl 1995: 124). Only four are local; the others appear to have been brought from Irongrey Hill almost 3 kilometres away (Burl 1995: 124).

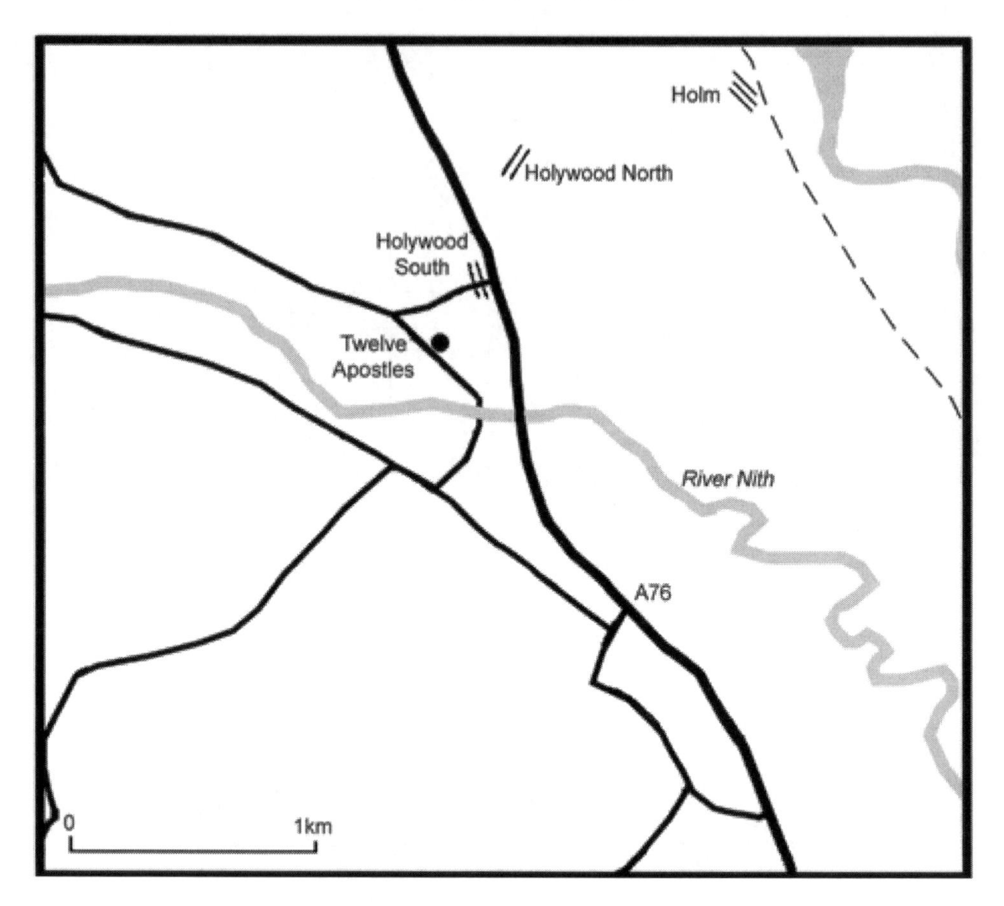

FIGURE 6.20 *Twelve Apostles, Holywood North and South and Holm*

The monument complex at Machrie Moor on the west coast of the island of Arran was quite different to those outlined above. Rather than a small number of larger enclosures the most obvious remains at Machrie consist of a series of smaller stone circles (Figure 6.22). Arran contains one of the densest concentrations of prehistoric archaeology in Scotland, including almost half of the known Clyde-type chambered cairns and many stone circles (Henshall 1972; Barnatt 1989: figures 52 and 53). Earlier Neolithic activity in the Machrie landscape included the construction and use of at least four Clyde-style chambered cairns (Bryce 1901–2; Pierpoint et al. 1980). Sherds of Grooved Ware in one of these chambers suggests these monuments may have seen continued use in the Later Neolithic period. A number of Earlier Neolithic pits have also been found in the area during the excavation of two of the stone circles on the moor (Haggarty 1991) (Figures 6.23 and 6.24). Some of these contained Earlier Neolithic carinated-bowl sherds, pitchstone, flint and hazelnut shells. Postholes, gullies and other shallow features were also located. Earlier Neolithic activity at Machrie may have also included the construction of a large enclosure. A large ditch terminal cut by a number of Earlier Neolithic pits was located where two

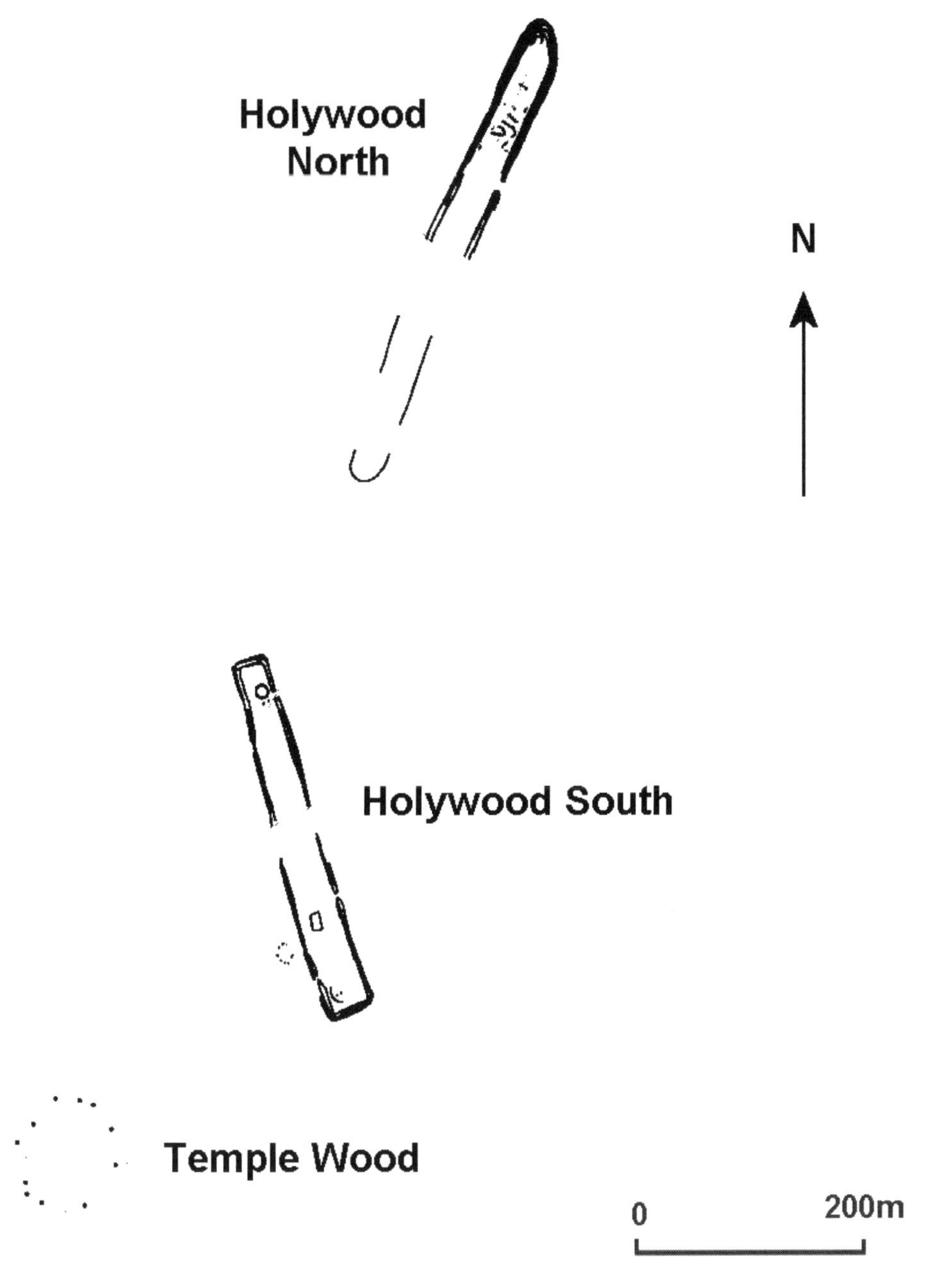

FIGURE 6.21 *The relationship between the Holywood cursus monuments and Twelve Apostles stone circle (Source: Brophy 2000: figure 4.5)*

of the later stone circles were to be constructed (Figure 6.23) (Haggarty 1991). The top of the ditch was capped with stones, amongst which carinated-bowl sherds were found. This feature may have been part of a monument, perhaps a causewayed enclosure, like that at West Lindsaylands, or, less probably, part of an Earlier

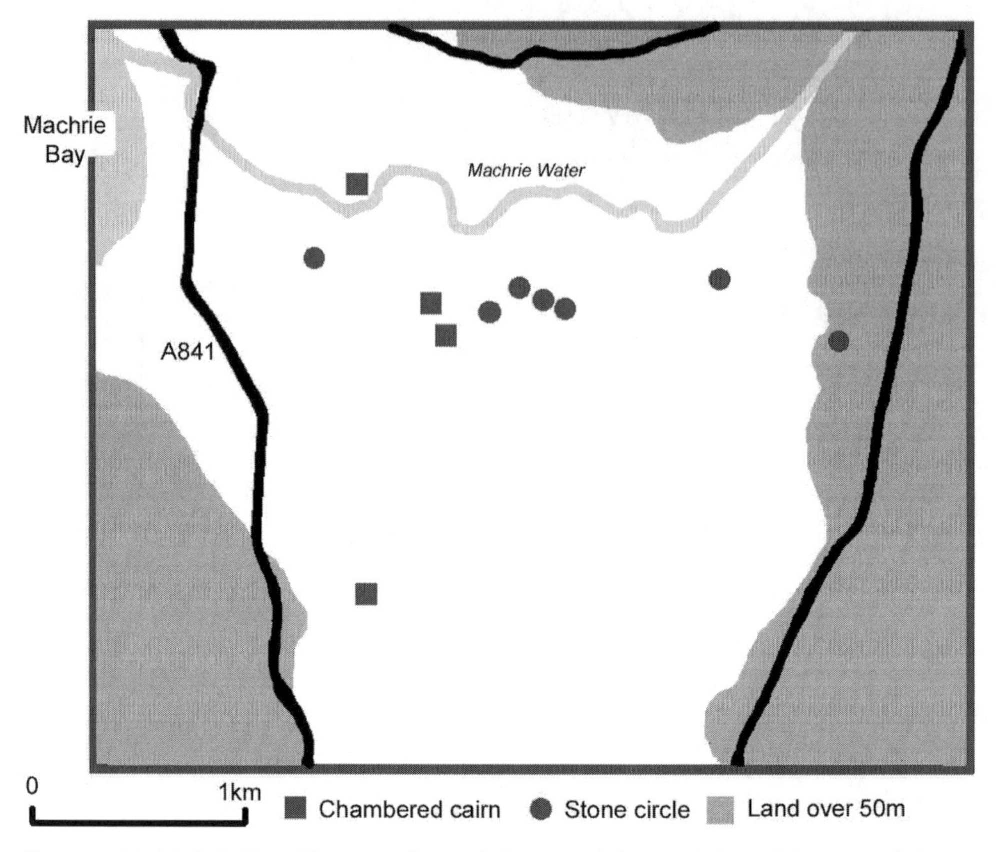

FIGURE 6.22 *Machrie Moor. The group of stone circles on Machrie Moor is located close to Machrie Bay*

Neolithic field system as found elsewhere on Arran (Barber 1997; Donnelly et al. 2000) (see Chapter 2).

The Later Neolithic monuments on the moor consisted of a series of circular monuments, the most obvious of which are the abundant stone circles, a major feature of the landscape even today. Under two of the stone circles timber phases have also been identified (Haggarty 1991) (Figure 6.25). The more elaborate timber monuments included a five-post horseshoe setting and an inner and outer ring of posts (Figure 6.25). After some time, both timber settings were replaced by stone settings (Figure 6.26). Numerous other stone circles were also constructed in the vicinity, including circles made of tall sandstone monoliths, a four-post circle and circles surrounding cairns (Bryce 1862; Burl 1980; Fairhurst 1977; MacArthur 1861: 51–2; Name Book 1864).

The dense distribution of smaller-scale monuments found at Machrie Moor is perhaps paralleled by those situated in Kilmartin Glen, Argyll, another distinct concentration of prehistoric monuments in Scotland (RCAHMS 1999: 12) (Figure 6.27). Like Machrie Moor, Earlier Neolithic activity included the construction of a number of chambered cairns around the edges of the valley. Two cursus monuments were also built at the northern and southern entry points to the Glen. Kilmartin contains a

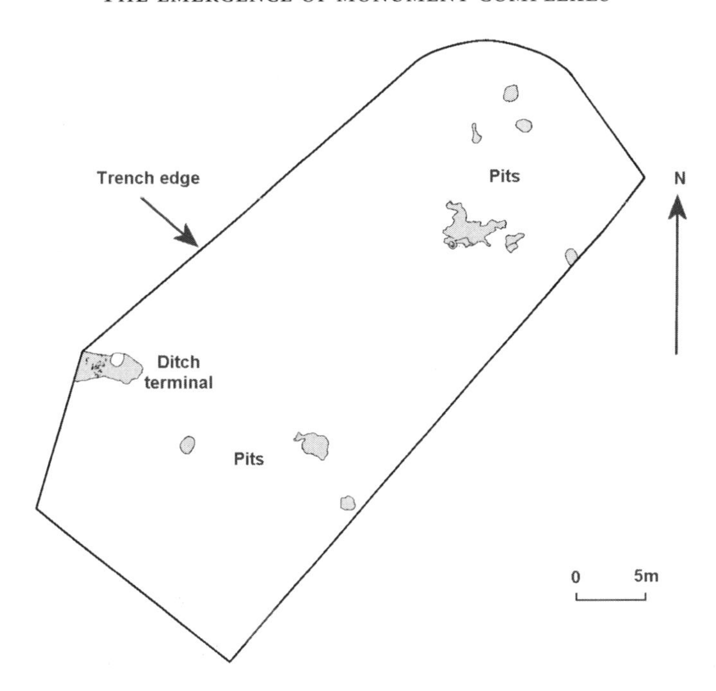

Figure 6.23 *The Earlier Neolithic features at Machrie Moor included a large ditch terminal and a number of pits*
(Source: Haggarty 1991: figure 2)

curious mix of monumental building styles and in the Later Neolithic numerous stone, timber and earth-built monuments were constructed at a number of locations in the valley, including stone and timber circles, henge monuments and stone alignments. The edges of the valley were also marked with rock carvings on natural rock outcrops.

The most enduring traces of Earlier Neolithic activity are the five chambered cairns that survive in the vicinity of the Kilmartin valley (RCAHMS 1999). Most of these are located on the upland margins of the area, with only one, Nether Largie South, within the valley itself (Greenwell 1864–6). Nether Largie South is one of the largest cairns of its type, but was probably only a single element in a denser concentration of Earlier Neolithic monuments in the valley, which included types of unusual form for the region. Two cursus monuments were located in the glen at Upper Largie near the northern entrance to the valley and at Dunadd, near the southern entry. These two monuments represent the only identified cursus monuments in Argyll. The cursus at Upper Largie, excavated in advance of gravel extraction, lay amongst a complex series of features located on a gravel terrace overlooking the valley (Figure 6.28). The earliest feature was a pit-defined cursus monument, which was overlain by a Later Neolithic timber circle (Denison 1997; Ellis 2000; Terry 1997). The cursus or long mortuary enclosure at Dunadd, has been identified from the air and appears to consist of two straight sub-parallel ditches 150 metres long which taper towards a curved terminal at the southeast end (Campbell 1996). The monument lies near the River Add, across the narrowest entry point to the valley.

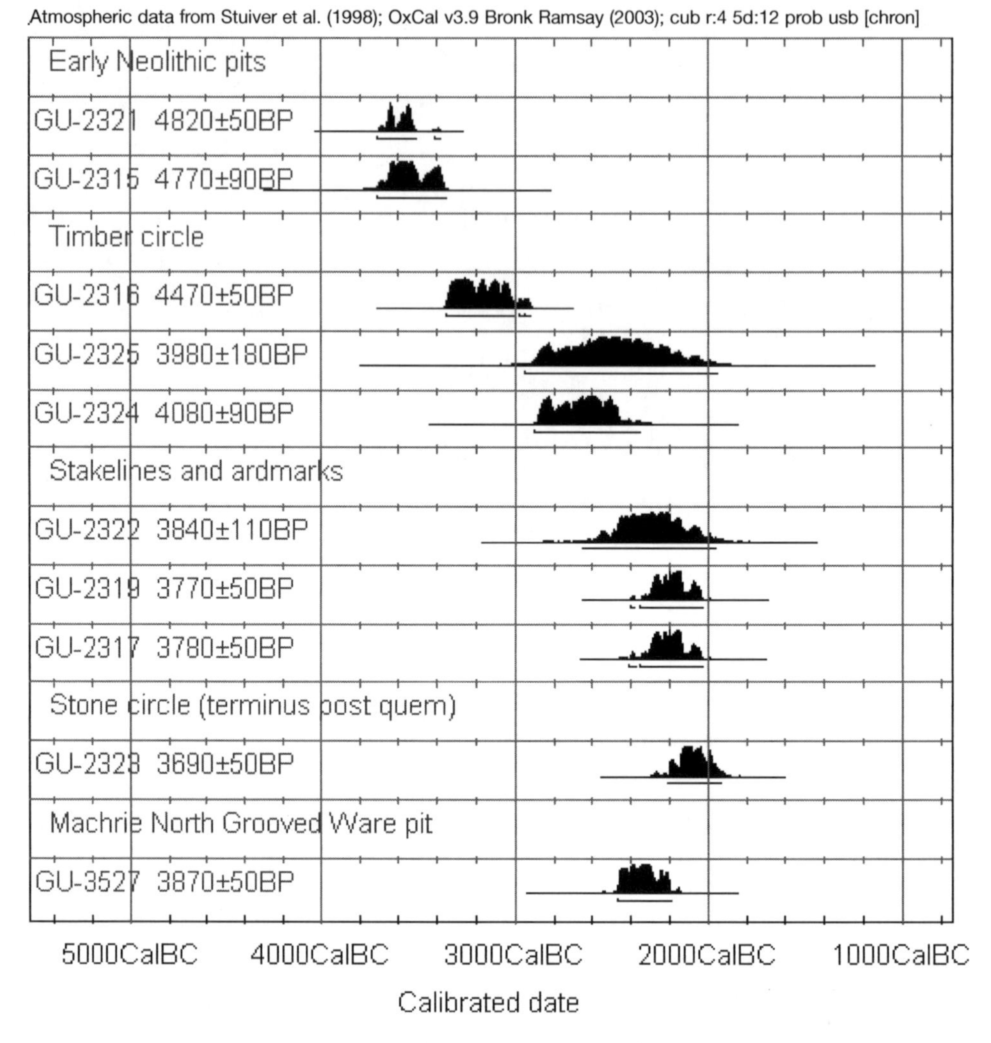

FIGURE 6.24 *Radiocarbon dates for Machrie Moor*

In the Later Neolithic the location of the earlier monuments was augmented by a further series of stone and timber settings. At Temple Wood a series of stone and timber circles was constructed (Scott 1988–9) (Figures 6.29 and 6.30). Two sites were used; the one to the north began as a timber circle, but was subsequently replaced by a circle of free-standing stone monoliths. The site to the south did not have a preceding timber phase; instead a larger circle of stones was constructed, originally consisting of twenty-two uprights, two of which were carved: one with concentric circle, the other with a double spiral carved across two faces of the stone. Further stone circles may have stood in the valley in the Later Neolithic. To the north, under the southwest section of the Early Bronze Age Glebe cairn, Greenwell found a double ring of boulders in the 1860s (Bradley 1993: 92–3; Greenwell 1864–6). Similarly, under the Early

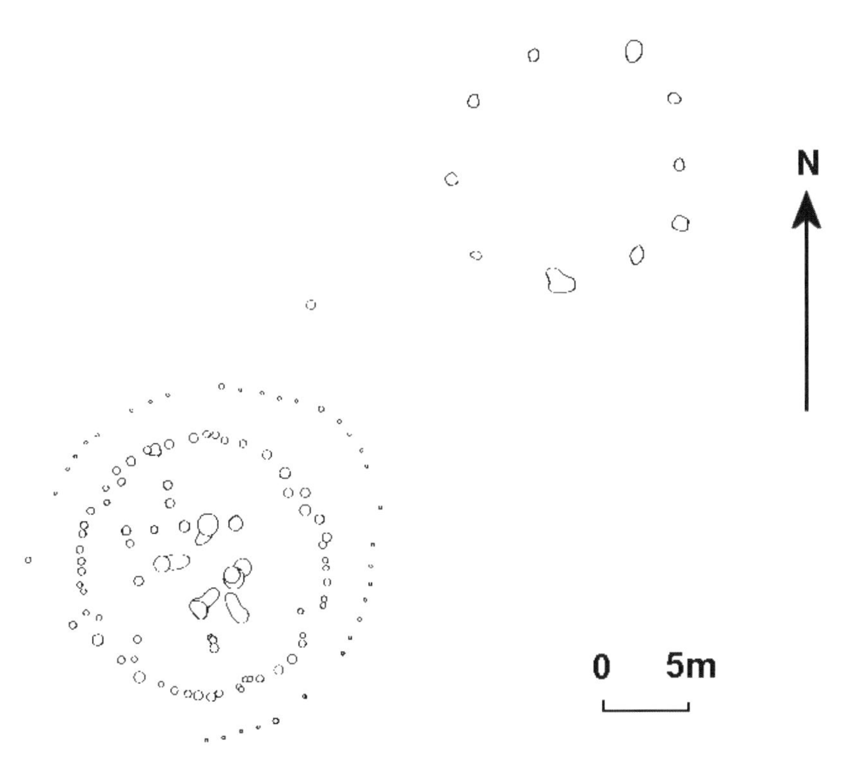

FIGURE 6.25 *Machrie Moor timber circles (Source: Haggarty 1991: figure 5)*

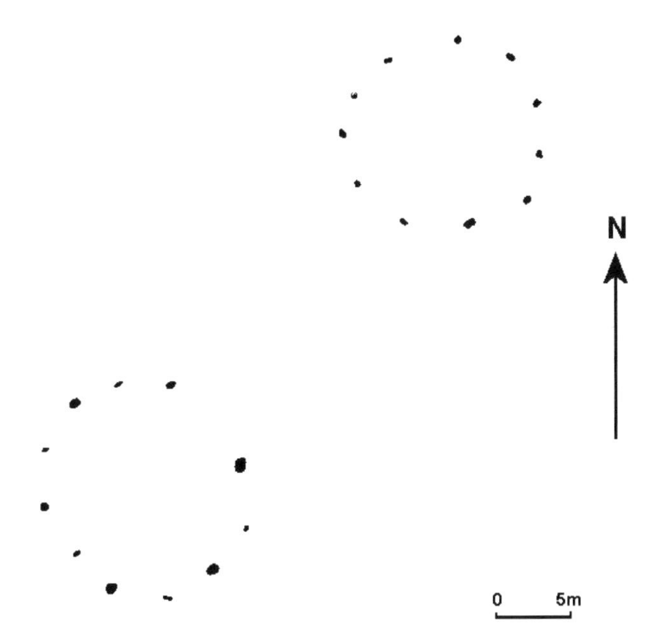

FIGURE 6.26 *Machrie Moor stone circles 1 and 11 (Source: Haggarty 1991: figure 13)*

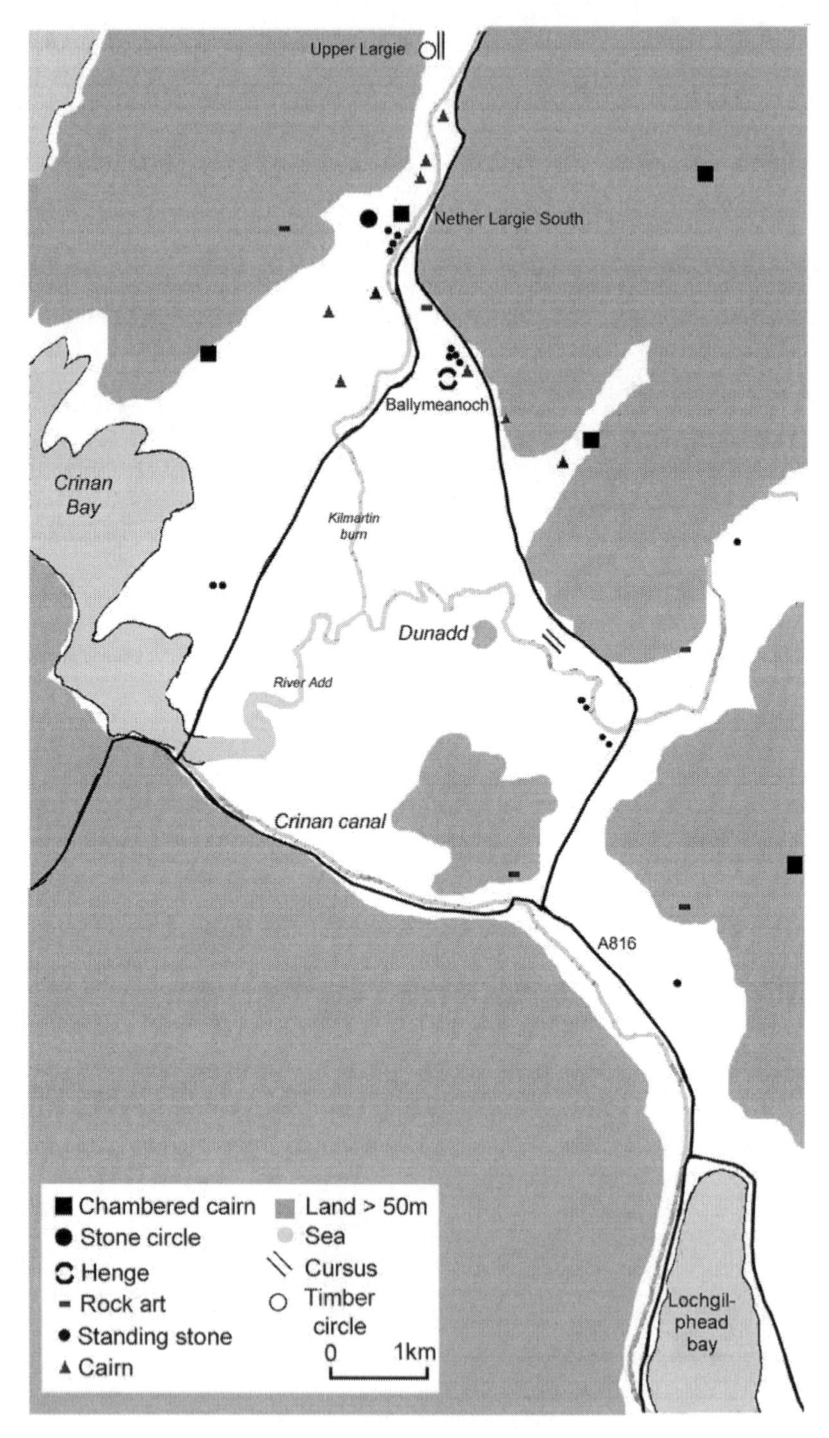

FIGURE 6.27 *Kilmartin Glen*

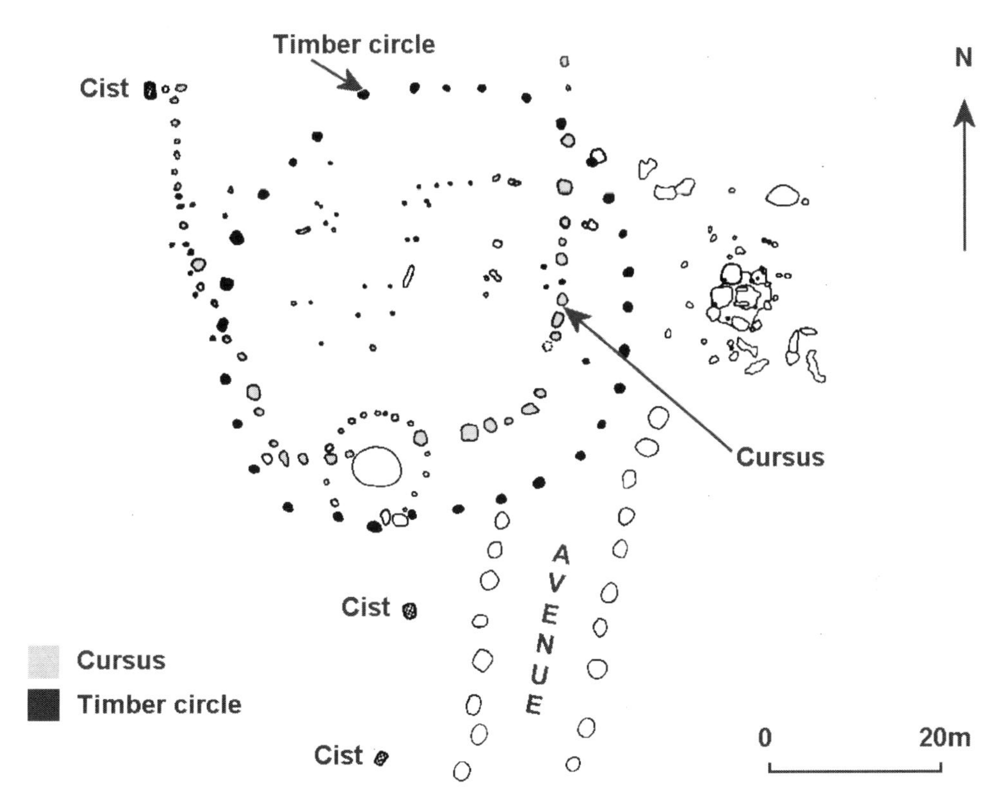

FIGURE 6.28 *Upper Largie. A whole series of different monuments was excavated here, representing a number of different phases of use*

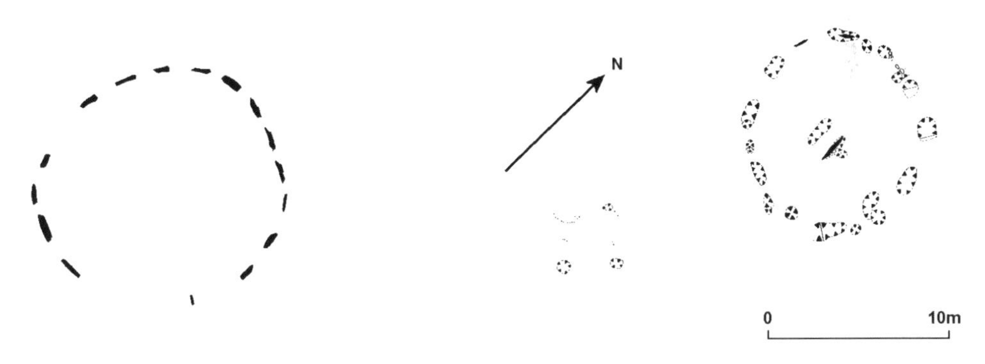

FIGURE 6.29 *Temple Wood stone and timber circles (Source: Scott 1989: figure 3)*

Bronze Age cairn at Nether Largie North, a stone setting, including a stone decorated with pecked circles, may suggest another reused stone circle site (Craw 1930–1).

There are also two major sets of stone alignments in the valley. One of these is at Nether Largie about 250 metres southeast of Temple Wood. The setting is a complex arrangement of over ten individual stones (RCAHMS 1999: no. 222). The other major

FIGURE 6.30 *Temple Wood as it survives today*

alignment is at Ballymeanoch where six stones are arranged in two parallel lines, also aligned northwest-southeast (RCAHMS 1999: no. 199). An outlier to the west of this alignment was excavated in 1977, when three separate cremation deposits were found in the socket. The stone was decorated with cupmarks and had an hourglass perforation through its centre (Barber 1977–8). Nearby Ballymeanoch henge comprises an outer bank with an inner ditch, enclosing an area around 20 metres, with two entrances at the north and south (RCAHMS 1999: no. 22). The timber circle at Upper Largie, found next to the earlier cursus monument, was around 46 metres in diameter, defined by posts set 3 to 5 metres apart, which may have been graded in height towards the southwest (Radley 1993; Terry 1997; Denison 1997).

The Kilmartin Valley was further augmented in the Neolithic through the carving of rock-art designs on natural outcrops situated mainly on the outer edge of the valley basin (RCAHMS 1999) (Figure 6.31). The Kilmartin area contains some of the densest concentrations and the most elaborate rock art in Scotland. The only datable motifs are similar to those found in Later Neolithic passage tombs in Orkney and Ireland and on Grooved Ware pottery (Andy Jones, pers. comm.; Morris 1970–1; RCAHMS 1999: 51; Twohig 1981: chapter 4).

The monumental landscape at Callanish, Lewis, was dominated in the Later Neolithic by a series of stone circles, much like the series found at Machrie Moor on

FIGURE 6.31 *Carvings at Achnabreck*

Arran (Figure 6.32). The most startling site is undoubtedly Callanish I, a large stone circle approached by a number of stone avenues or rows, with a chambered cairn situated in the centre. The southern avenue of the circle is focused on a natural outcrop known as Cnoc an Tursa, around which significant activity was focused. Around Callanish I further smaller circles, stone settings and single standing stones were erected in the Neolithic and Early Bronze Age.

Some of the earliest identified features in the Callanish area were found under the main stone circle at Callanish I itself. These included a small circular ditched enclosure, which had an entrance to the northwest, but no trace of any internal structures (Ashmore 1995). This circular enclosure overlay long parallel cultivation rigs, which had been used to grow cereals. The site fell out of use for some time after this, but around 3000 to 2900 BC a light timber structure was built in the eastern part of the area which was to become the centre of the stone circle (Ashmore 1995) (Figure 6.33). The stone circle consists of standing stones of Lewis gneiss, the tallest of which stands at the centre of the setting and is over 4.5 metres tall.

After the stone circle was completed a further light timber structure was built in the eastern area, between the central tallest stone and the outer ring stones. Soon after, a small chambered cairn was added to the circle. Standing stone avenues, or rows, lead to and from the central circle to the north, east, south and west (Figure 6.33). The

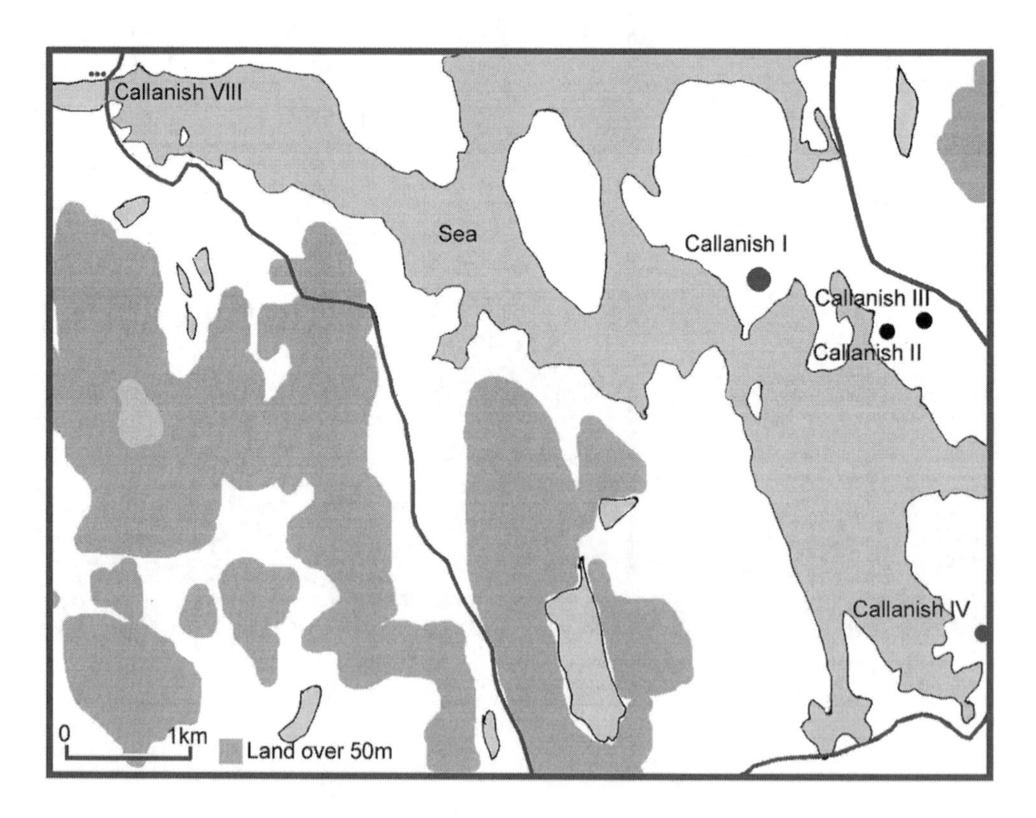

FIGURE 6.32 *Callanish, located amongst a series of sea lochs*

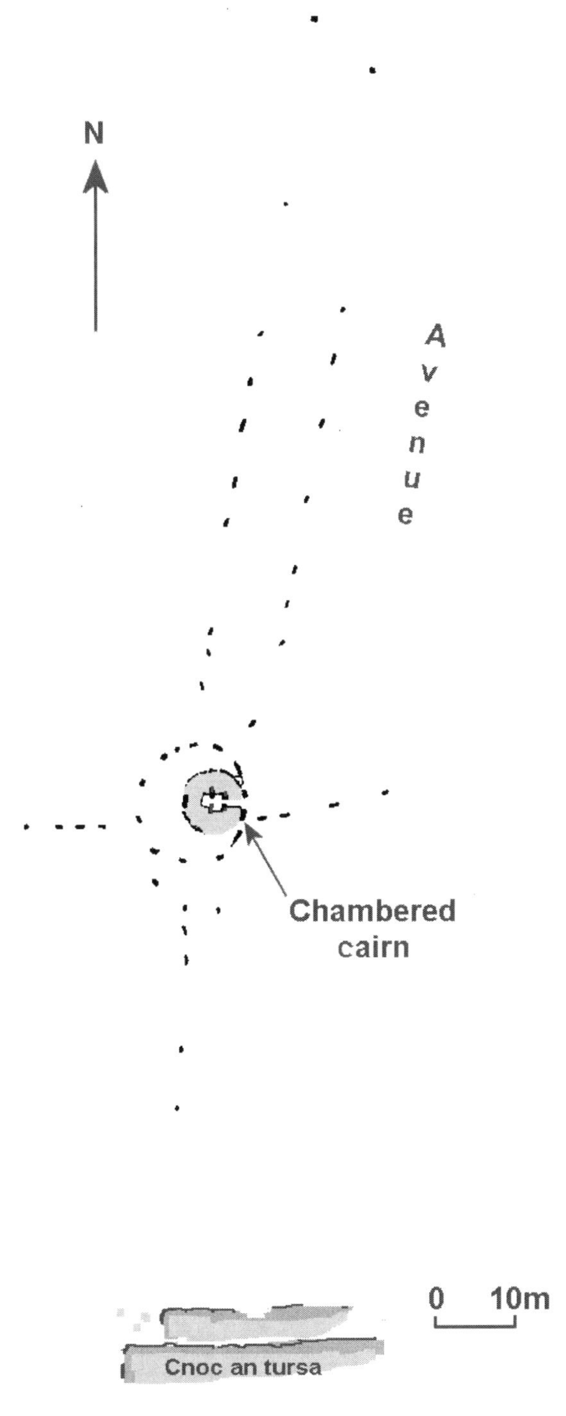

FIGURE 6.33 *Callanish I. The southern avenue is aligned on the natural rock outcrop Cnoc an tursa (Source: Burl 1976: figure 24)*

northern and largest avenue consists of a double line of stones, which narrow slightly towards the circle. The southern row leads from the stone circle towards the rock outcrop known as Cnoc an Tursa (Hill of Sorrow). Cnoc an Tursa may be the source of the stones in the main circle and many of the other settings around Callanish (Richards 2004). Excavations around the outcrop have uncovered a number of features directly in front of Cnoc an Tursa (Coles 1993; Coles and Rees 1994). Activity seems to have been focused on a natural vertical fissure in the rock face. The southern avenue points directly towards this fissure. Charcoal-rich deposits were found in the fissure and these extended beyond the fissure to overlie a large pit immediately in front of the rock face. The edges and fill of this pit had been repeatedly cut by a series of pits and shallow scoops containing worked flint and pottery fragments. Shallow linear features also marked the western and eastern edges of the outcrop. These appear to be composed of multiple and intercutting settings of sockets or postholes and shallow scoops, partly enclosing the site and perhaps forming some sort of horned façade to the outcrop (John Raven, pers. comm.). Activity at Callanish, which included the deposition of Grooved Ware, centred on the centuries following the start of the third millennium BC (Figure 6.34).

Numerous stone settings and standing stones have been located in the vicinity of the main setting at Callanish. At Druim Nan Eum, eleven large pillar stones were recorded by the RCAHMS in 1928, lying near the outcrop (RCAHMS 1928: no. 92). Recent excavations here have shown that these once formed part of a stone circle (Richards 2004). Nearby is Callanish II (Cnoc Ceann a'Gharraidh), a circle defining

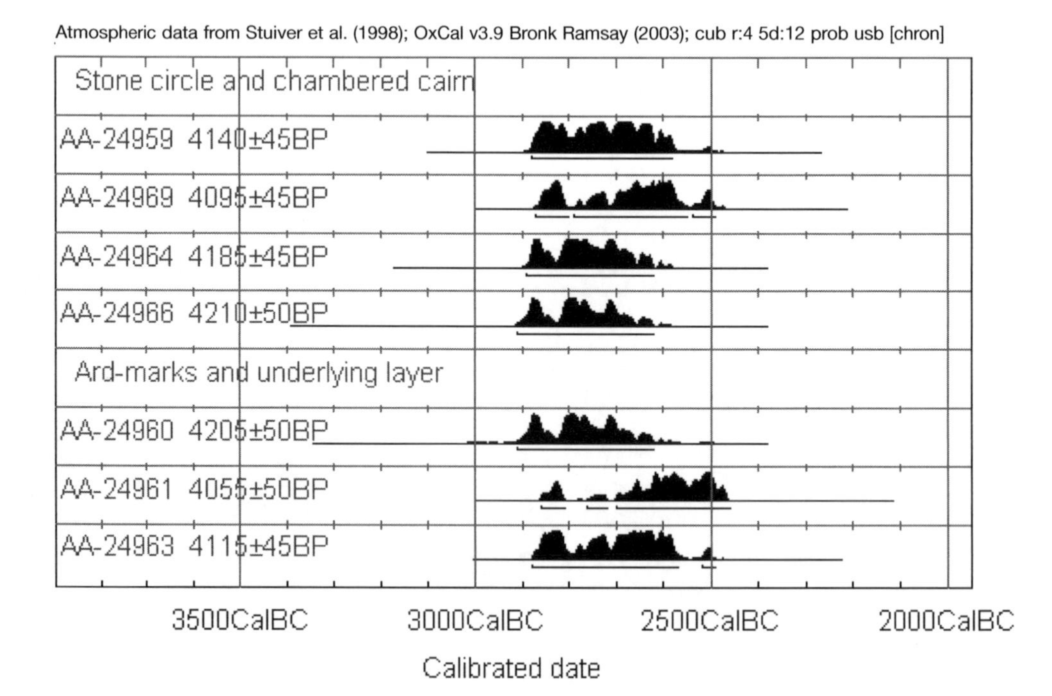

FIGURE 6.34 *Radiocarbon dates for Callanish*

an area around 20 metres in diameter now enclosed by five tall, thin standing stones and three fallen stones surrounding a central cairn (RCAHMS 1928: no. 90). Sockets, possibly for timber uprights, were found when the stone circle was cleared of peat in 1858 (Ashmore 1995: 13, 16). Callanish III (Cnoc Fillibhir Bheag) is a few hundred metres to the east. The circle may have originally consisted of two concentric rings of stones; eight stones now survive on the outer arc, four in the inner (RCAHMS 1928: no. 91). Callanish IV (Ceann Thulabhaig), located near the sea about 3 kilometres to the south of Callanish, consists of a stone ring about 10 metres in diameter with five remaining standing stones (RCAHMS 1928: no. 93). In the centre lies a small cairn. Callanish VIII (Bernera Bridge) is located on the island of Great Bernera. Here, standing stones overlook the narrowest point in the sea-channel that leads from the open sea to the Callanish area (Ashmore 1995: 13).

The Stenness-Brodgar complex is located in the central bowl of West Mainland in the Orkney Isles (Figure 6.35). The complex is one of the best-known monumental landscapes in the British Isles and has been the focus of sustained archaeological investigation. A dense concentration of Neolithic monuments and settlement evidence is found on the Stenness and Brodgar peninsulas, which meet between the lochs of Harray and Stenness. The sites include one of the finest passage graves in western Europe, two stone circles surrounded by henges, burial mounds and stone alignments. In the heart of this complex lies the Later Neolithic village of Barnhouse and further possible Neolithic settlement sites. In this respect, the Stenness-Brodgar area allows an unusual perspective on how monument building related to more everyday practices in the Neolithic.

The earliest activity in the Stenness-Brodgar area may stretch back to the Mesolithic. The Mesolithic period in the Orkney Isles is very poorly understood; however, some of the few Mesolithic finds that have been made have come from the Stenness area (Saville 2000). The finds include lithic material recovered from the area in the earlier part of the twentieth century (Lacaille 1934–5; Wickham-Jones 1990b) and material found more recently on the western shore of the Loch of Stenness (Richards 1993a: 35, figure 3:6).

The earliest structural evidence present in the area is two Earlier Neolithic chambered cairns located around the lochs of Stenness and Harray. One at Unstan is well known, as it is the site-type for a form of decorated Earlier Neolithic pottery (Clouston 1884–5; Henshall 1963: ORK 51). The other is at Staney Hill, a long cairn with a horned forecourt (Davidson and Henshall 1982). The cairn is one of the largest in the islands and may have contained a stalled chamber. The most abundant remains around the two lochs are, however, Later Neolithic in date. These monuments were built on a larger scale than the earlier ones and are much more numerous.

The Stones of Stenness is the most extensively excavated Later Neolithic monument within the Stenness-Brodgar complex (Ritchie 1975–6) (Figures 6.36 and 6.37). A rock-cut ditch defines the Stones of Stenness, over 50 metres in diameter and originally augmented by an external bank or wall. The internal stone circle probably originally consisted of twelve uprights, but has been seriously damaged in recent centuries. The circle has an internal hearth-like setting of stones, approached by an area of paving and

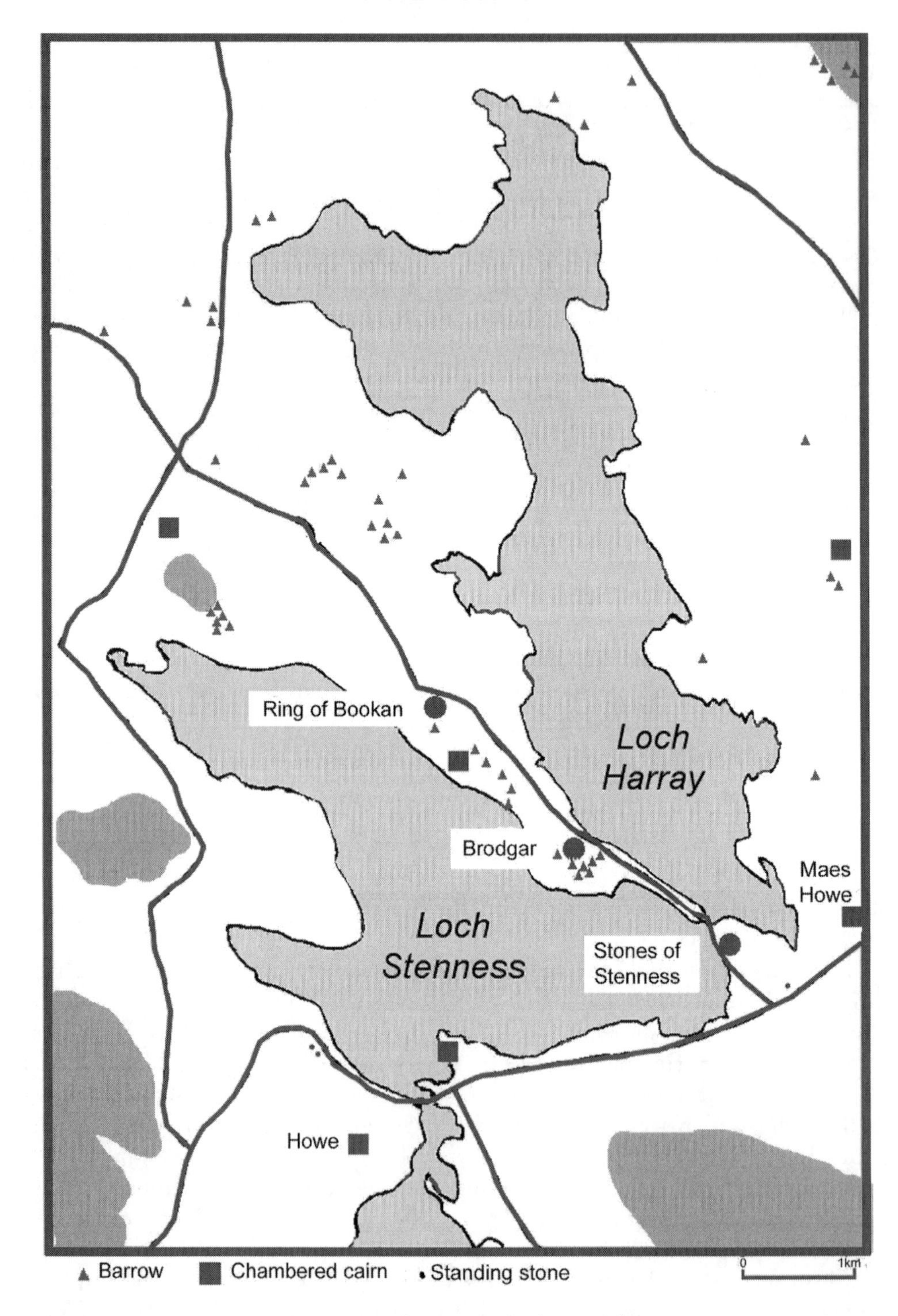

FIGURE 6.35 *The Stenness-Brodgar complex*

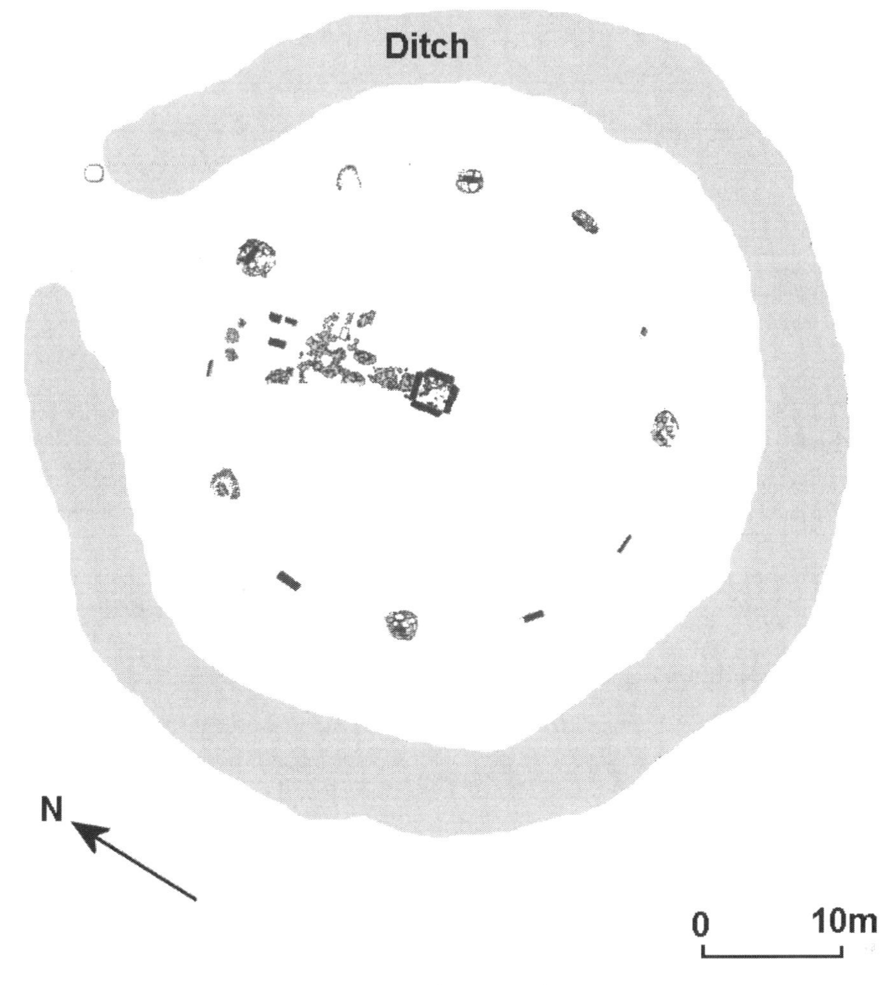

FIGURE 6.36 *The Stones of Stenness (Source: Ritchie 1975–6: figure 2)*

a setting of stones leading from the northern entrance. Human and animal bones were found in the excavated segments of the ditches along with Grooved Ware pottery, some of which resembled vessels similar to ones found at the nearby passage grave of Quanterness and the Later Neolithic village of Barnhouse (Ritchie 1985: 124; Richards 1993a: 190).

To the east of the Stones of Stenness lies one of the most magnificent passage graves in western Europe (Figure 6.38). Maeshowe was first excavated to modern standards by Gordon Childe in the 1950s (Childe 1954–6). Childe found that the tomb was situated on top of a natural knoll, which had been levelled and covered with clay to form a platform. Around the platform a wide ditch was cut. The ditch was encircled by a substantial wall or stone bank, substantially restricting visual and physical access to the interior space (Richards 1992b). The ditch itself, like that at the Stones of

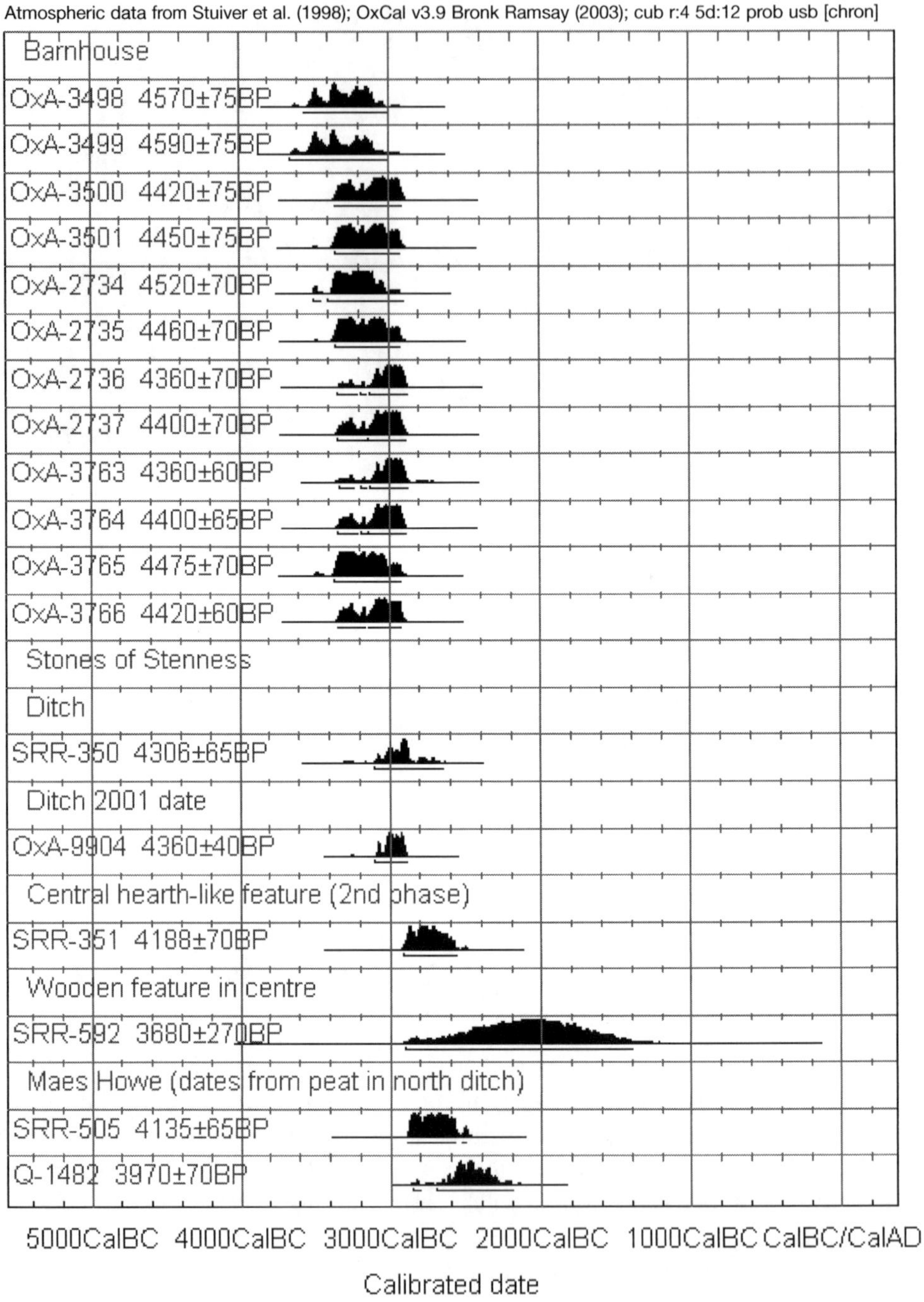

Atmospheric data from Stuiver et al. (1998); OxCal v3.9 Bronk Ramsay (2003); cub r:4 5d:12 prob usb [chron]

Barnhouse
OxA-3498 4570±75BP
OxA-3499 4590±75BP
OxA-3500 4420±75BP
OxA-3501 4450±75BP
OxA-2734 4520±70BP
OxA-2735 4460±70BP
OxA-2736 4360±70BP
OxA-2737 4400±70BP
OxA-3763 4360±60BP
OxA-3764 4400±65BP
OxA-3765 4475±70BP
OxA-3766 4420±60BP
Stones of Stenness
Ditch
SRR-350 4306±65BP
Ditch 2001 date
OxA-9904 4360±40BP
Central hearth-like feature (2nd phase)
SRR-351 4188±70BP
Wooden feature in centre
SRR-592 3680±270BP
Maes Howe (dates from peat in north ditch)
SRR-505 4135±65BP
Q-1482 3970±70BP

5000CalBC 4000CalBC 3000CalBC 2000CalBC 1000CalBC CalBC/CalAD

Calibrated date

FIGURE 6.37 *Radiocarbon dates for the Stenness-Brodgar complex*

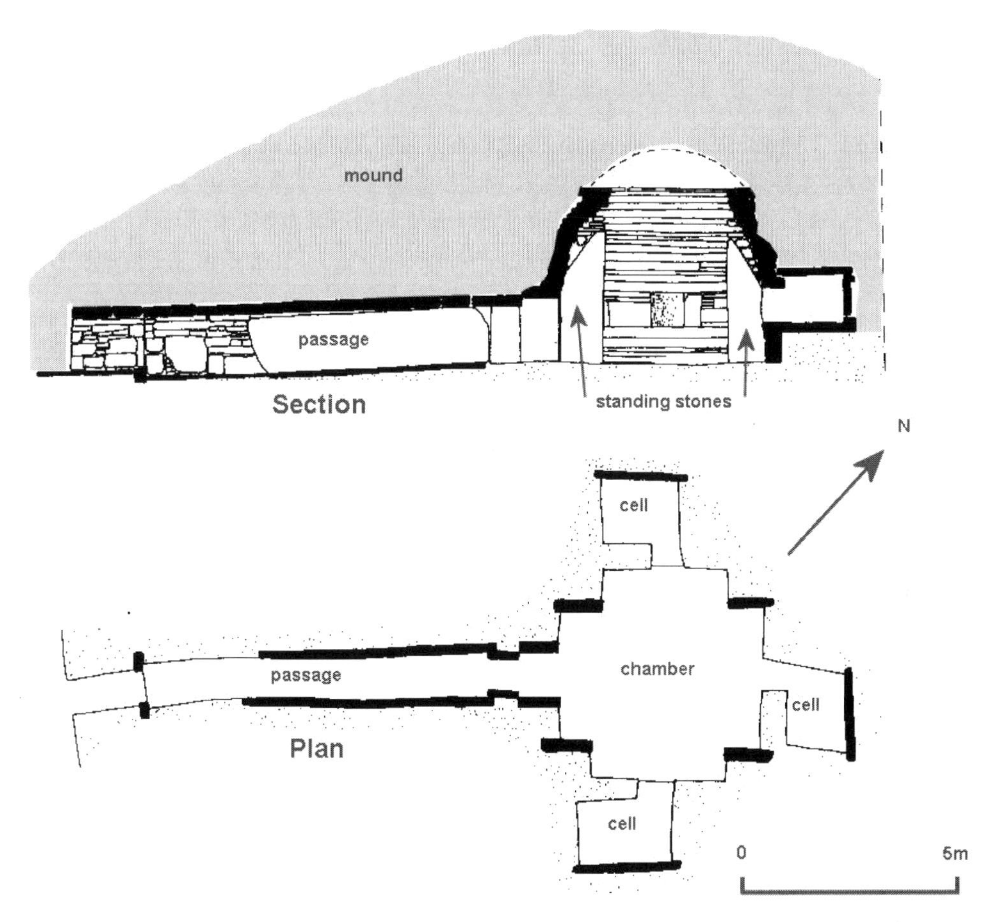

FIGURE 6.38 *Maeshowe. Plan and section (Source: Richards 1996b: figure 4)*

Stenness, may have held open water, further restricting access to the central area (Childe 1954–6: 171; Renfrew 1979: 32). The mound was made of clay and stone and covers a central chamber, approached by an elongated passage. Three side cells radiate from the central chamber. Colin Richards describes the chamber at Maeshowe as the 'highest enclosed space ever experienced by Neolithic Orcadians' (Richards 1993b: 155). The significance of this monument is perhaps highlighted by its orientation: the passage is aligned on the midwinter sunset, which illuminates the central chamber for a few days every year in December.

The passage grave that remains today may have been the final phase of an extensive building programme that involved the erection of a number of different monumental forms. At the rear of Maeshowe recent excavations uncovered a stone socket that was large enough to hold a very substantial standing stone; this may have been part of a stone circle that originally surrounded the passage grave (Richards 1992b: 448, 2005: 243). The missing stones may have been reused to build the passage grave itself. The central chamber incorporates four standing stones in its construction (see Figure 6.38). These do not perform any major structural function. Instead they seem to deliberately mirror the architecture of the nearby stone circles of Stenness and Brodgar and may be reused from a similar monument that was originally situated on the platform (Stuart 1862–4; Richards 1996b: 196).

The remains of a further Maeshowe-type passage grave were found to the southwest of the Stones of Stenness during the excavation of an Iron Age broch site in the 1970s and 80s (Ballin Smith 1994) (Figure 6.39). The Howe was located on a hillside that sloped gently to the Bay of Ireland to the east. The tomb appears to have been built over the remains of two domestic buildings. Under the passage grave two subrectangular buildings were found. One of these was a stalled building with a central hearth that resembles the Earlier Neolithic house at Knap of Howar (Ritchie 1983; Richards 2005: 247). The passage grave itself consisted of a long passageway that entered a small chamber from which cells radiated, similar in form to the larger monument of Maeshowe. In a similar manner, the tomb was encircled by a platform of stone almost one metre high, which in turn was enclosed by a henge-like ditch. Furthermore, a socket for a standing stone was found on the platform and, like Maeshowe, the passage grave may have originally been encircled by a stone setting (Ballin Smith 1994: 21). Some of the stones reused in the later structures on the site bear passage-grave-style pecked designs, which probably originally belonged to the passage grave and may have decorated the chamber (Ballin Smith 1994: 210). To the north, on the Brodgar peninsula, there is a further chambered cairn. Bookan is a circular mound that originally contained a rectangular or cruciform chamber divided into compartments by upright slabs (Henshall 1963: ORK 4). A large flint object, pottery and human remains were found inside when the chamber was excavated in the nineteenth century. The pots may have been Later Neolithic Grooved Ware vessels (Ritchie 1985: 126).

The Ring of Brodgar is the larger of the two stone circles situated on the Brodgar and Stenness peninsulas (Figure 6.40). Small-scale excavations were carried out here by Colin Renfrew in the 1970s (Renfrew 1979). Renfrew found that the ditch at the Ring of Brodgar was rock-cut like that at the Stones of Stenness, and this filled with water soon after excavation (Renfrew 1979: 40). No major internal features were identified at the circle during a magnetometry survey. The outer bank of the circle could have originally been up to 3 metres high, further augmenting the physical and visual barriers to the central space. Another henge-type monument lies to the northwest of the Ring of Brodgar. The Ring of Bookan consists of a wide ditch, partly rock-cut, enclosing an area that is similar in size to that at the Stones of Stenness (Ritchie 1985: 126). There is no sign of an entrance across the ditch; however, the monument has been extensively damaged by ploughing. Within the centre of the monument is an irregular mound or cairn that may be the remains of a central passage grave (Henshall 1963: ORK 45).

There are a number of standing stones situated between the henge monuments of Stenness and Brodgar. These include the Comet Stone, a prominent standing stone near the Ring of Brodgar (RCAHMS 1946: no. 877). The Comet Stone is set on a

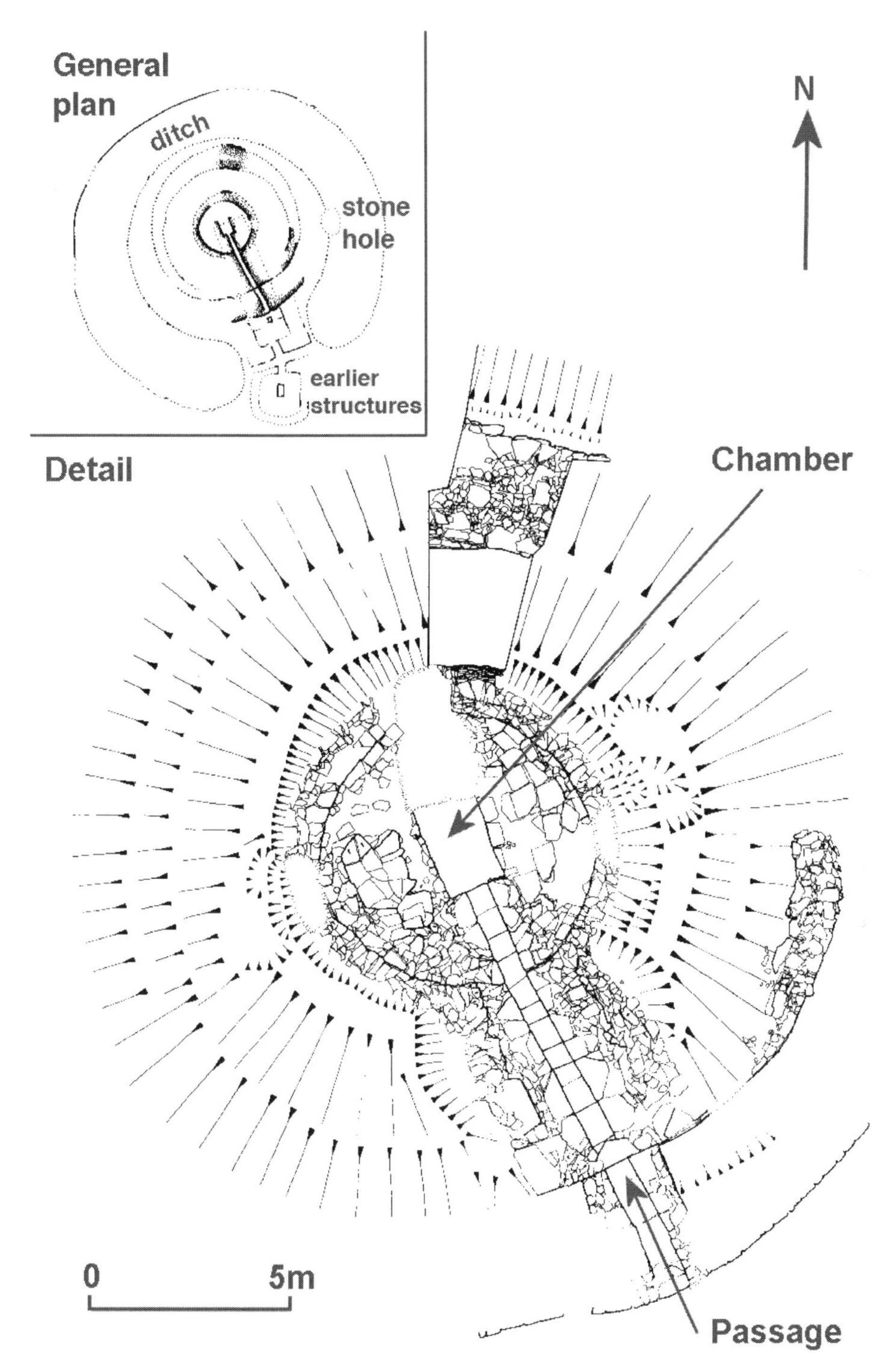

Figure 6.39 *The excavated remains of the chambered cairn at Howe (Source: Ballin Smith 1994: figure 6)*

FIGURE 6.40 *The Ring of Brodgar*

circular mound or platform and appears to have been part of a group as the stumps of two further stones are located there. Further standing stones are found to the south at Brodgar Farm (RCAHMS 1946: no. 878) and at the southern point of the Brodgar peninsula where the Watch Stone stands close to the water (RCAHMS 1946: no. 879). These stones may form part of an avenue or may be a set of portals, settings that formalised access to the area of the large henge monuments (Richards 2005). One of the most interesting standing stones in the vicinity of the circles was a stone known as the Stone of Odin that originally stood to the north of the Stones of Stenness near the tip of the Stenness promontory (Richards 2005: 211–5). The stone was destroyed by a local tenant farmer, Captain Mackay, in 1814, but we have some records of what it looked like (Marwick 1975–6: 30). The stone is thought to have been almost 2.5 metres high and was pierced by a hole near the top of the stone (RCAHMS 1946: no. 909).

MONUMENT COMPLEXES AND THE RELATIONSHIP BETWEEN EARLIER AND LATER NEOLITHIC SCOTLAND

While the complexes outlined above contain a diverse range of monumental structures, there are many similar patterns to their development and form. Each is a distinct regional concentration of monuments that often contains monuments that are unusual in the region. For example, Kilmartin contains the only known cursus monuments in Argyll and the henge monument at Ballymeanoch is one of the very few known in western Scotland and again the only example in Argyll. Similarly, in the Upper Clyde Valley the six henge monuments are the only known examples in the region (Lelong and Pollard 1998). All of these complexes had a range of large-scale monuments that were constructed throughout the Neolithic, with evidence of use stretching back into the Earlier Neolithic and in some cases even earlier. This highlights that monument complexes did not just suddenly appear in the Later Neolithic, but were the result of centuries if not millennia of human action. Many of the monumental landscapes outlined above developed over a long period of time and the Later Neolithic monuments were constructed in places that were already associated with monument building (Barnatt 1989: 151). One of the most important features of the landscapes is the great time depth to the monuments and activity in these places. This can be seen at sites such as Dunragit where a large cursus monument was replaced or augmented in the Later Neolithic by timber circles, or in the Upper Clyde Valley where a whole series of henges and other enclosures was built in a landscape that already had a causewayed enclosure and cursus monument. In other ceremonial complexes the earlier activity was more ephemeral, but nonetheless significant. The rare cultivation traces at Callanish or the pits at North Mains would have been part of an acknowledgement of that landscape as somewhere significant. The continuity of monument building in many of these ceremonial landscapes can be seen at other places, too. At Leadketty in Perthshire, another rare causewayed enclosure site in Scotland is located only 100 metres from a Later Neolithic Meldon Bridge-style pit-defined enclosure (Gibson 2002: 19; Barclay 2001b: 149) (Figure 6.41).

The overlap between traditions of Earlier and Later Neolithic monumentality is not merely in terms of location. At Balfarg, for example, the form of the timber structures are strongly reminiscent of Earlier Neolithic timber halls such as Balbridie, Aberdeenshire and Claish Farm, Tayside (Ralston 1982; Barclay et al. 2002: chapter 3). These timber structures continued to be built in the Later Neolithic elsewhere, too. At Carsie Mains, Perthshire, a rectilinear oak structure of very similar form and dimensions to those at Balfarg was recently excavated (Barclay and Brophy 2004). The structure was about 18 metres by 8 metres, aligned west-northwest to east-southeast, and like those at Balfarg was probably unroofed. Like the Balfarg structures most of the posts had rotted *in situ* and were not removed or burnt. The structure was dated to around 3350 to 2900 BC. These are similar to the dates from Balfarg timber structure 2 and the enclosing henge. At Dreghorn in Ayrshire another rectangular structure closely associated with Later Neolithic Grooved Ware pottery has also recently been excavated (Pitts 2004). A further unburnt timber structure found at Littleour, near to Carsie Mains, has been dated to 3600 to 3100 BC, providing an unbroken sequence for these timber structures throughout the fourth millennium BC (Barclay et al. 2002; Barclay and Maxwell 1998). These timber structures show that some of the developments in Later Neolithic lowland Scotland were created with reference to earlier traditions of monumentality (Barclay et al. 2002: 124). While there was no emphasis on the deliberate destruction of these Later Neolithic timber structures (see Chapter 2), the shape and dimensions of these buildings are strongly reminiscent of these earlier traditions (Figure 6.42). At Carsie Mains, the rectangular structure was located close to a timber circle, which has almost identical radiocarbon dates (Barclay and Brophy 2004). Both of these structures appear to have drawn on the symbolism of trees, a phenomenon already present in the Earlier Neolithic in this part of Scotland (see Chapter 4). The Carsie

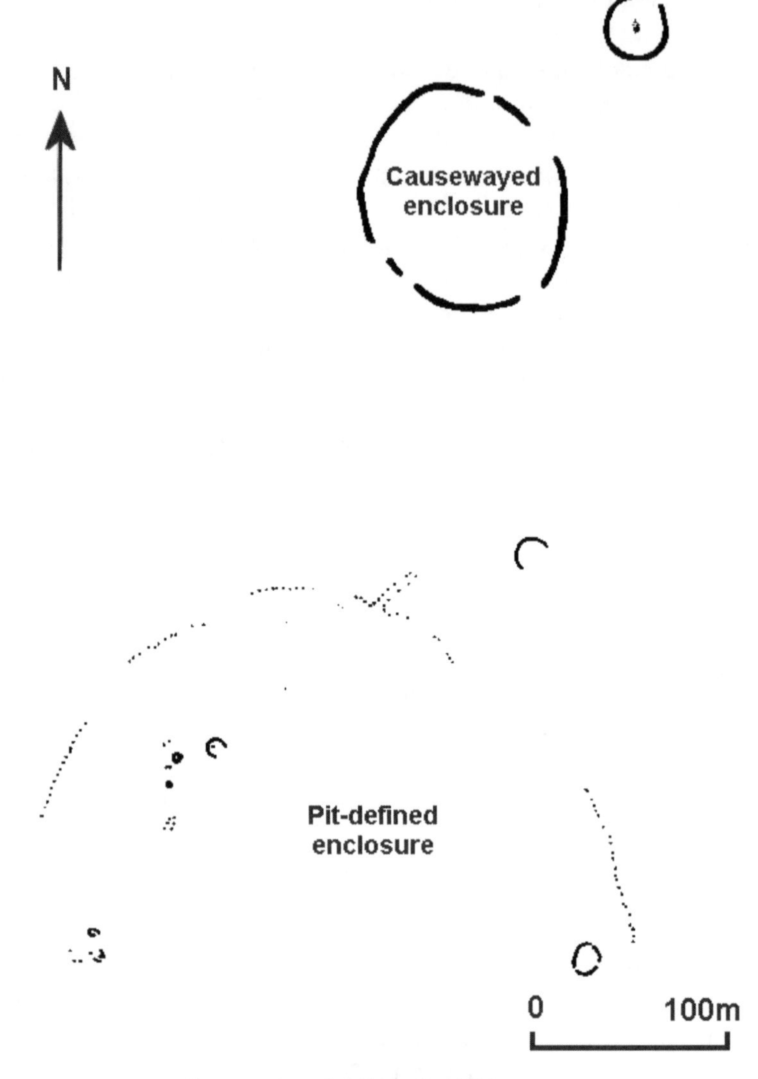

FIGURE 6.41 *Leadketty, Perthshire (Source: Barclay 2001b: figure 4)*

Mains rectangular structure was found to surround a tree-hole and may have enclosed a living tree or at least the former position of a tree and was built during a complex period of woodland clearance and regeneration (Barclay and Brophy 2004). The structures at Carsie Mains were built and used in an area where trees were both deliberately removed and allowed to regenerate (Barclay and Brophy 2004). The relationship between the structures at Carsie, trees and areas of forest harks back to the use of tree symbolism in Earlier Neolithic barrows (see Chapter 4). It may be that people in Later Neolithic Scotland drew on the past as a means of legitimising and enabling the changes in the present.

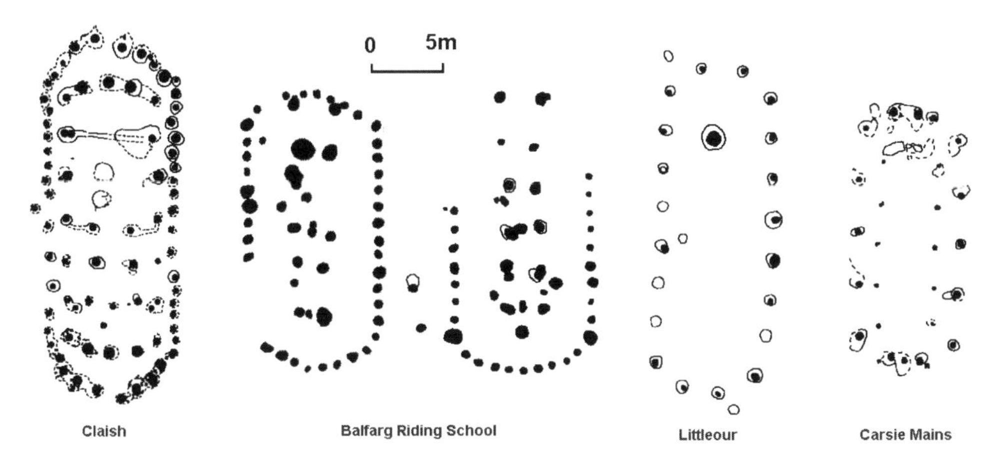

FIGURE 6.42 *Rectangular timber structures from the fourth millennium BC (Source: Barclay and Brophy 2004: figure 13)*

Monument complexes and routeways

While some of the Later Neolithic styles of monument drew on earlier traditions, this was not always the case. New forms of enclosure and ceremony were undoubtedly created. Perhaps one of the most significant unifying aspects of all of the monumental complexes highlighted above is their location on routeways. This has been noted in a general manner previously and for individual sites but without any real synthesis of this theme (for example, Burl's note on the Upper Clyde Valley 1969: 18–19; Atkinson 1956: 174–5; Bradley 1993: 108–12; Harding 2000). As early as 1951 Atkinson, Piggott and Sanders noted that the small number of henges identified at that time were nearly all located in low-lying easily accessible areas in riverine or waterside locations (Atkinson et al. 1951). Atkinson also later highlighted the possibility that Carn Meini, in the Prescelly mountain range in southwest Wales and the source of the bluestones of Stonehenge and a significant monument complex in its own right, was on an important trade route linking Ireland and Wessex (Atkinson 1956: 174–5, 183–6). Atkinson proposed that the importance of Carn Meini was partly due to it being a source for stone axes and due to its use as an important landmark in sea journeys between Britain and Ireland: 'to the trader returning across the sea from Ireland, shielding his eyes from the spray as he peered across the bows of his laden boat, the same summit [Carn Meini] would be the first welcome sign of land ahead' (Atkinson 1956: 175).

In 1976 Aubrey Burl also wrote on the accessible locations of stone circles in the British Isles (Burl 1976: 6). He noted that the largest and seemingly earliest circles were nearly always located next to rivers and in valleys, being situated: 'along the seaways of the western coast of England or Scotland or in north Wiltshire by the Ridgeway and the Oxfordshire prehistoric track connecting the eastern Cotswolds with Wessex' (1976: 36). Burl underlined the ease of movement by water in prehistory and associated the sites of large stone circles with land and riverine routes, with many circles (and henges) being located at the confluences of rivers (1976: 55). Drawing on earlier observations, Burl also noted that the stone circles in Cumbria were located on the trackways that were seemingly used to exchange stone axes with distant communities. Manby and Plint in the 1960s had plotted the locations of flakes and rough-outs of stone axes in the Cumbrian area, and Burl correlated these locations with the major routeways through Cumbria and beyond, along which the main Neolithic monuments were distributed (Plint 1962; Manby 1965; Burl 1976: 65, figure 12).

More recently, Sherratt has noted how the Wessex area, location of the great monument complexes of Stonehenge and Avebury, is at the centre of a trans-isthmian route, situated at the head of three rivers, all of which are called the Avon (Sherratt 1996a: 214). 'Trans-peninsular' or 'trans-isthmian' routes allow dangerous seas to be avoided through the use of inland river routes and/or by carrying boats across short stretches of land (Davies 1946; Scott 1951; Sherratt 1996a, 1996b). Sherratt has suggested that these rivers have the same name as they originally, conceptually, formed part of the same route. The three Avons allowed the notorious seas around Land's End to be avoided and Sherratt argues that the importance of Wessex was partly due to its position at the centre of the routes that linked a number of different regions. In this way the significance of Wessex extended beyond the local area (Sherratt 1996a: 225). The three Avons of Wessex are now followed by three major motorways, the M5, M6 and M4, highlighting the continuity of these routeways (Sherratt 1996b: 6).

Other ceremonial complexes have also been noted for their positions at the centre of a number of land, river and sea routeways. In Ireland, Cooney notes that Bru' na Bóine, the location of the great passage graves of Newgrange and Knowth, is at the centre of important river routeways into and out of Ireland (Cooney 2000b). Jan Harding has highlighted the location of three henge monuments at Thornborough in North Yorkshire on the route of the most accessible passage across the central Pennines, a major barrier to east-west movement in this part of northern England (Harding 2000: 42–3). This is the same route along which Group VI stone axes from Cumbria were distributed into eastern England. In total six almost identical henge monuments are distributed along this route, which follows the flow of the River Ure.

Regarding Scotland specifically, Davies in 1946 wrote of the relationship between monument distributions and sea-routes in the Irish Sea area (Davies 1946). Davies outlined the importance of tidal streams in early sea journeying and noted a correlation between densities of monuments and location in relation to the major sea routes of the Irish Sea. She noted that monuments were clustered on islands, on peninsulas and isthmuses and at inland locations that are particularly visible from the sea (for example, Cumbria) and also highlighted the importance of trans-isthmian routes. Scott also underlined the importance of trans-isthmian routes and outlined some of the major examples in Scotland (Scott 1951). Two of the major routes in prehistory are likely to have been the Luce Bay to Loch Ryan and the Loch Fyne to Loch Crinan routes, avoiding the notoriously dangerous seas around the Mulls of Galloway and

Kintyre respectively. Scott also outlined a small number of routes that cut across mainland Scotland. By far the most important of these is likely to have been the Clyde and Tweed route, by which a boat could travel from the Atlantic seas to the north seas (the west to east coasts) utilising only a small porterage from the head of the Clyde to the head of the Tweed through the Biggar Gap (Scott 1951: 36).

Many of the routes that Scott and Davies outlined are the focus of the densest concentrations of Neolithic monuments and in Scotland one of the important aspects of the location of monument complexes is undoubtedly their position at the centre of natural routeways. For example, as Thomas notes, Dunragit lies: 'at the confluence of a series of natural routeways: northward up the valley of the Water of Luce, east and west along the Galloway coast, and northwest to Loch Ryan' (Thomas 2001a). Indeed, the continuing importance of this location in terms of routeways across Dumfries and Galloway is suggested by the relationship of the site to later routes. The site is bisected both by a railway line and by the A75, the main land routes through Dumfries and Galloway. These routes extend from Gretna in the east, near the English border, through Dumfries and along the coast to Dunragit and Stranraer in the west. The continuity of this route is demonstrated by aerial photographs, which show that the route of the A75 follows that of a Roman road, the construction pits of which can be seen in aerial photographs near Dunragit (NMRS No: NX15NE 70.01). This route was also the major drove route in the region (Haldane 1997). Animals were brought by sea from Ireland to Portpatrick in the Rhinns before being driven through Glenluce towards Dumfries and ultimately to England. The importance of the Dunragit area does not lie merely in relation to land travel. The lowland area in which Dunragit sits, between the Rhinns of Galloway to the west and upland areas to the east, forms a natural routeway between the beach and dunes of Loch Ryan and Luce Sands, one of the major trans-peninsular routes highlighted by Davies and Scott. The trans-peninsular route allows the treacherous seas around the Rhinns to be avoided (Scott 1951: 31). Thus, not only does Dunragit lie at the centre of natural land routes, it also lies in relation to one of the major sea-routes of Scotland.

Kilmartin, like the Dunragit area, also lies on one of the major trans-isthmian routes noted by Scott and represents a dense concentration of monuments and artefacts: 'the geographical position of the area, controlling an important porterage from Loch Fyne and the western mainland of Scotland to Loch Crinan and the Atlantic coast, is one possible explanation of this localised wealth' (RCAHMS 1999: 12).

Undoubtedly the most important routeway at Kilmartin is the one that later became the Crinan Canal. The Crinan-Cairnbaan route makes possible a 16- rather than a 150-kilometre journey between the west coast and the sheltered waters of Loch Fyne and on to Bute and Arran (RCAHMS 1999: 4). In prehistory the route could have been even shorter as smaller boats could exit at the bay of Lochgilphead rather than at Ardrishaig (as the canal does today) and small boats could have travelled further inland from the Crinan end by travelling up the River Add or simply across the flats at high tide. A prospectus published in 1792 attests to the importance of the Crinan route (Directors of the Chamber of Commerce and Manufacture in Glasgow 1792). In this document the directors outlined the difficulties in sailing around the bottom of Kintyre, through the Sound of Sana. Vessels travelling from the Firth of Clyde had to wait for a favourable wind to carry them northwards up the west coast, and if there was not a suitable wind, they had to head for Ireland and anchor there to wait for the north winds. This apparently happened on average on three out of four occasions and the use of this route often resulted in the loss of life. Neolithic boats may not have been sail driven, but the notoriously dangerous currents and tidal pools around the Mull of Kintyre would not have been undertaken easily or lightly (Davies 1946: figure 2). The landmass of Kintyre itself poses many problems to sailors. There is a distinct lack of natural bays and harbours on the west coast of Kintyre and there are tremendous rocks and currents that frequently claimed ships and their crews along this coast (Directors of the Chamber of Commerce and Manufacture in Glasgow 1792: 3). There are further possible trans-isthmian routes in Kintyre, but none provide as quick or as safe a porterage between west Scotland and the Firth of Clyde area. Major land routes also pass through Kilmartin. The modern A816 travels northwards allowing access to the Great Glen and then on to Inverness and northeast Scotland. To the south, the route is the main one through Kintyre towards Campbeltown. Haldane (1997) also demonstrates that one of the major drove routes in this part of Scotland passed through Kilmartin Glassary, close to the main concentration of monuments in the valley. To the south the drove route followed much the same way as the modern road does, with a major gathering place near Machrihanish Bay in the southern part of Kintyre. Kilmartin continued to be an instrumental area in the political geography of Scotland in later periods, as the seat of the early Scottish kings at Dunadd (Lane and Campbell 2000).

As highlighted in Chapter 2, Arran is situated in a nodal location in relation to the major tidal routes of the Irish Sea. On a more local scale, Machrie Moor is located at the end of the String Road, the only major east-west route across the island and next to Machrie Bay, the largest bay on the west coast and an important landing place for small boats. Callanish is also located near to the sea in an important harbouring area. The name Callanish itself originates from a Norse word for a headland or a promontory from which one calls a ferry across a sound (Ponting and Ponting 1977: 10). This link with boats and sea crossings is strengthened by Sharples' observation that the stone circles in this area are distributed around a complex of sea lochs with sheltered anchorages (Sharples 1992: 327). As Burl notes, Callanish is a rare and sheltered bay area on the western coast of Lewis. Sea levels in the Western Isles would have been slightly lower in prehistory (Ponting and Ponting 1977: 3; Ashmore 1995: 6), hence in the Callanish area bays would have been even larger than today with greater inter-tidal areas, ideal for landing and harbouring boats. In the Neolithic, sea levels would have been such that the northern avenue would have begun at the head of a small bay (Geraint Coles pers. comm.). The stone circle is also visible from the sea from a great distance (Burl 1976: 148–9). The Stenness-Brodgar complex is also located in relation to important anchorages. The Loch of Stenness allows direct access to the sea through a small inlet, which exits into the Bay of Ireland. The easy access to sheltered anchorages in these locations may have meant that these places were crucial to the movement between islands. In lowland, inland Scotland, river and land routes were as important as the seaways. As Speak and Burgess note, Meldon Bridge lies at the centre of numerous land and riverine routes:

> To the north the Meldon Burn valley provides access to the Eddleston Water and thence to Edinburgh and the Forth; westwards the tributaries of the Lyne lead to the Upper Clyde, and thence to Glasgow; southwards the Tweed leads upriver into south-west Scotland, and eastwards to the lower Tweed and the North Sea. The present A72 road, which runs through the site from Galashiels and Peebles to Biggar and Glasgow, is only the latest of a series of roads to pass this way, as excavation revealed. (Speak and Burgess 1999: 2)

Meldon Bridge is located on a gravel terrace within the confluence of the Lyne Water and its tributary the Meldon Burn. The Lyne Water flows into the River Tweed a short distance to the southeast. The Tweed is the main communication corridor in this part of Scotland; the many tributaries of the Tweed form an extensive system of waterways over southeast Scotland. The importance of this location, like that of Dunragit, is suggested by the continuity of the routes and, like Kilmartin, by the subsequent use of the area. The area of Meldon Bridge appears to have been a 'nodal point' in the Roman period with forts at Lyne and East Happrew and a marching camp was excavated within the Meldon Bridge enclosure itself (Speak and Burgess 1999: 8). The area also appears to have been an important location in the Iron Age: the area of Sheriff Muir, just across the Lyne Water, may have been a *loca* (tribal meeting place) in the Iron Age (Speak and Burgess 1999: 8).

A Roman road cuts through the enclosure itself, running eastwards from under the A72 towards Meldon burn and the site of a possible Roman bridge (Speak and Burgess 1999; NMRS: NT24SW 91.01). Over the Roman road the remains of an eighteenth-century turnpike road were found and finally on top of all of these earlier routes lies the A72, the major modern land route through the area. Meldon Bridge also lies between two drove routes (Haldane 1997). All of these routes suggest that this is the 'best choice for a lateral route along the Tweed valley' (Speak and Burgess 1999: 53).

The Balfarg complex is also situated between a number of watercourses embedded in the catchments of the rivers Leven and Eden. Barclay (1983: 199) notes that the site is located at the southeast end of the Lomond Hills, which channel access to and from the fertile land of the Howe of Fife to the east and west of the massif. The site is also adjacent to the main modern rail and road routes in the region. North Mains is again located near the confluence of two watercourses, in this case the River Earn and its tributary the Machany Water. The Earn originates in Loch Earn in the western uplands and exits into Loch Tay about 20 kilometres to the east. The North Mains area was also part of the north-south drove route between Crieff and Gleneagles and about 1.5 kilometres to the north lies the Camelon-Cargill Roman road, with many marching camps and signal stations positioned along the route (Haldane 1997). The predominance of watery locations such as Balfarg, North Mains and Meldon Bridge is also evident at the Holywood complex, situated between the River Nith and its tributary the Cluden Water. Both of these watercourses exit into a wide bay to the south, allowing access to the sea. The sites are also bisected by the A76 and close to the major rail route through Dumfries and Galloway, two of the few major land routes across the Southern Uplands. One of the few drove roads in Dumfries and Galloway also passed through the area from a major gathering area to the north along the River Nith, heading towards Dumfries and on towards northern England (Haldane 1997).

At first glance Cairnpapple can seem an exception to these accessible locations and markedly isolated today, situated on the top of a hill, an unusual location for a monument of this type. There are no major waterways or modern land routes near to the site. However, the site does lie between two major drove routes: the alternative routes joining Falkirk and Romano Bridge (Haldane 1997). One of the defining factors in the location of Cairnpapple Hill, however, may have been the remarkable views possible from the summit. To the north and east, the Firth of Forth is clearly visible; North Berwick Law and the Bass Rock mark the entrance to the Firth. To the west Piggott notes that 'in exceptionally clear circumstances Goat Fell in the Isle of Arran can be sighted' (Piggott 1947–8: 71). In this respect, Cairnpapple links many important landmarks in the geography of Scotland, but is not a particularly central location in itself.

In contrast, the Upper Clyde Valley is situated in one of the most accessible locations in inland, lowland Scotland. The Upper Clyde Valley is located on a major trans-isthmian route, at the sources of three major rivers (Scott 1951: 36). The River Clyde to the west links the area to the major water route of the Firth of Clyde and the western seaways. To the east, the River Tweed connects the valley to the North Sea. To the south, a few miles from the origin of the Clyde, lies the River Nith, which passes through Dumfries on its way to the Solway Firth, and then to the Isle of Man, northern England and Ireland (Davies 1946: figure 2). The three rivers that radiate from the Upper Clyde Valley allow journeys by boat from western to eastern Scotland and from Central Scotland to the south. Major land routes also converge at the Upper Clyde Valley and these modern routes were laid on the same routes as a series of Roman roads, again highlighting the apparent continuity of these routeways. The Clyde has formed a broad, open corridor in the valley, forming a natural routeway across southern Scotland, extending from its origin in the Lowther Hills on the South Lanarkshire/Dumfries and Galloway border to its sea exit in the Firth of Clyde (Lelong and Pollard 1998: 13). The flood plain known as the Biggar Gap joins the Clyde and the Tweed to the east and allows passage between these two major river valleys. The routes into the valley seem to have been marked in the Neolithic; as noted earlier, all of the six henge monuments are on the main routeways into and out of the valley. The enclosure at Blackshouse Burn itself is located in an upland area, but inside the enclosure are the twin heads of Blackshouse burn spring, flowing southwards into the River Clyde 3.5 kilometres on.

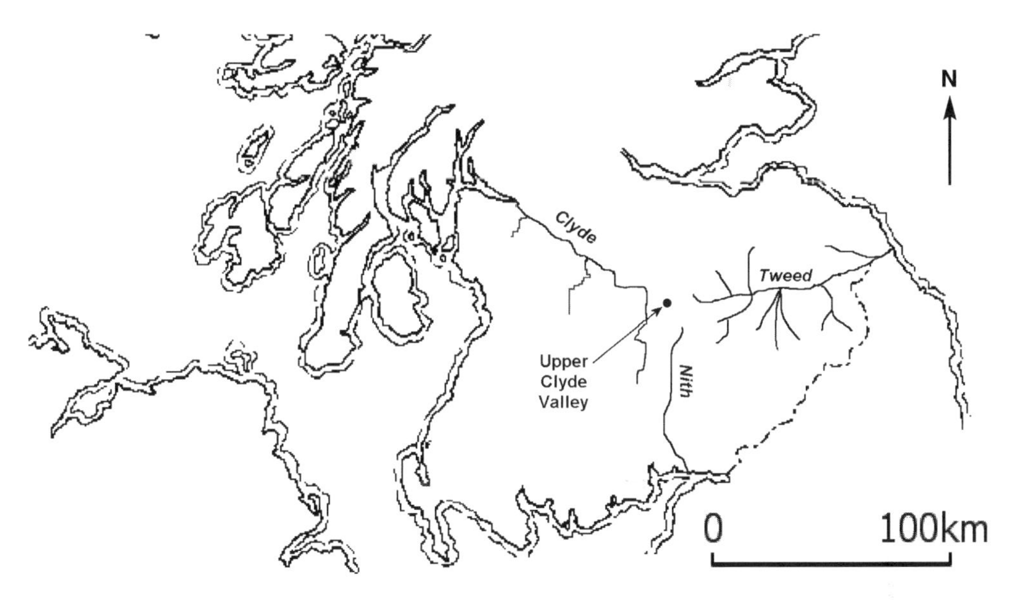

FIGURE 6.43 *The location of the Upper Clyde Valley at the heart of lowland Scotland*

ROUTES LAID UPON ROUTES

The location of the three Scottish monument complexes outlined above is similar to many other monument complexes located across Britain and Ireland. Colin Richards has commented on how the stone circles and burial monuments around the Stenness-Brodgar peninsulas may have seemed conceptually and physically at the centre of the world in the Later Neolithic Orkney archipelago (Richards 1996: 190). In a similar manner, the Upper Clyde Valley may have been seen as the centre of prehistoric, lowland 'Scotland' (Figure 6.43). Here, the heads of three rivers define the outer edges of the valley, creating connections with three different bodies of water. Consequently, the monuments in the Clyde valley are at a critical transitional point between regions, in a similar location to Wessex at the centre of the three Avons (Sherratt 1996a and b).

Reconstructing prehistoric routeways is difficult; we have no preserved Neolithic routeways in Scotland. However, the proximity of monumental complexes to later routes is suggestive. Taylor in 1979 underlined the continuity of routes and tracks: trackways are often laid on earlier paths maintaining routes that were defined in more ephemeral ways millennia previously (Taylor 1979: 153). Taylor suggests that the very first routeways were animal tracks created by migratory animals following the 'best' routes and crossing rivers and waterways at the most easily forded locations; people would use these tracks to follow herds of animals (Taylor 1979: 1–4). In this way, routes would have formed over time through the interaction between animals, people and the natural topography.

The continuity of routeways is suggested by the preserved routes at many of the Scottish monumental complexes. For example, cutting through Meldon Bridge are several roads and tracks of various dates lying on top of one another, suggesting that this line was the best route through this region (Speak and Burgess 1999: 9). Similarly, at Dunragit it is remarkable how the modern A75, the railway line, the medieval drove route and a Roman road all pass through the site of the monumental complex. Each of these routes channelled movement from east to west across southwest Scotland over millennia. The location of both of these sites in relation to Roman sites is noteworthy and is a more widespread phenomenon. Most of the lowland complexes are located in relation to Roman sites: Dunragit, Meldon Bridge, North Mains and the Upper Clyde Valley, while another major monument grouping, albeit unexcavated, at Forteviot has a number of Roman camps adjacent to large-scale, probably Later Neolithic in date, monuments (Gibson 2002). This is a common phenomenon outside Scotland, too (for example, the Hindwell and Walton enclosures; Gibson 2002: 12). In this respect, it is significant that Hanson and Maxwell have noted that the Roman networks of forts and camps were themselves built to dominate routeways in Scotland: 'The intention seems to have been not so much to coincide with concentrations of native population, but rather to control movement and thus localise any disaffection' (1983: 37).

The occurrence of earlier monumental complexes and Roman routes and forts suggests that the locations of these phenomena shared similar objectives. One of the major centres of Roman activity in Scotland was in the Upper Clyde Valley where many Roman routes converged and where a concentration of camps and forts can be found (Hanson and Maxwell 1983: figures 2.3, 2.5 and 4.1). Many of these Roman roads are now followed or overlain by modern motorways, highlighting the continuity of these routes. Indeed, Taylor suggests that many prehistoric routeways are now modern roads (Taylor 1979: 12). This may explain why the distribution of the largest Later Neolithic henge monuments follows the same general routes of the major motorways of Scotland (Figure 6.44). The major henges are located where river and land routes converge.

MONUMENT COMPLEXES AND THE SOCIAL GEOGRAPHY OF NEOLITHIC SCOTLAND

The location of these monument complexes on routeways in places that were easily accessible from a number of different regions suggests that these complexes were not simply built by and for a local community (Burl 1976: 24). It has been suggested in the past that monument complexes evolved due to a resident population intensifying agricultural production (Renfrew 1973, 1976, 1979; Sharples 1992; Telford 2002). This seems unlikely; instead, complexes are more likely to have been created through the evolving and growing interaction between regional communities in the Neolithic. As Bradley and Burl have noted, monument complexes were not necessarily located at the heart of the settlement pattern, but in locations that were easily accessible, in places that could draw on a wide catchment of people (Bradley 1993: 108–10; Burl 1976: 102). Recent fieldwalking at Thornborough, North Yorkshire, seems to corroborate this observation. Fieldwalking around this complex has found that the raw

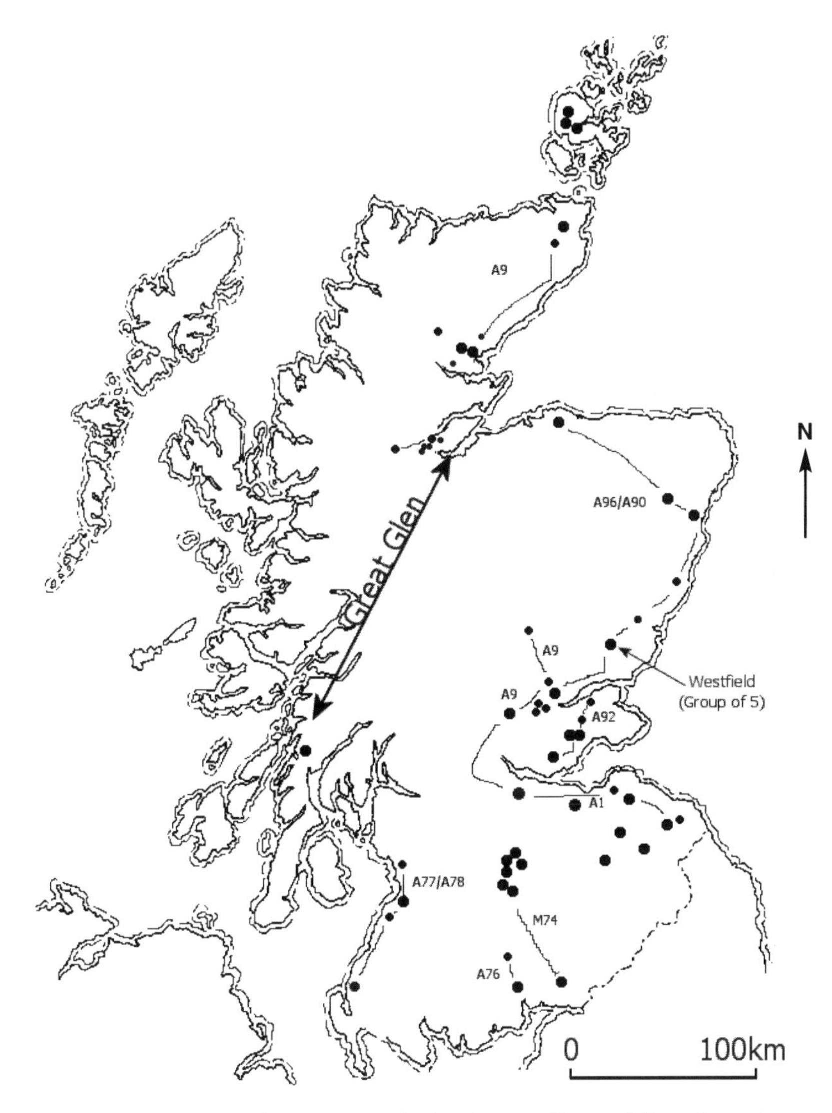

FIGURE 6.44 *Henges and motorways. The distribution of henges follows the main routes across modern Scotland*

materials used in this area included an extensive range of lithic types (Harding 2000: 43). Harding argues that this is not an indication of exchange, as the material includes materials inferior to the native gravel stone tool source, but instead represents the actual movement of people, an 'influx of distant peoples' to the Thornborough area; a position strengthened by the fact that the lithics seem to indicate short-term transient settlement (Harding 2000: 43). In this way the monuments at Thornborough were not the focus of an individual social group but the product of group interaction and social links, focused on a place that is on one of the most accessible routeways across the considerable barrier of the Central Pennines (Harding 2000: 42). A similar phenomenon is suggested by the number of imported stone types present in the lithic scatters and excavated features at Scottish monument complexes in areas that often had good-quality local stone sources. Monument complexes seem to have been places where artefacts and people moved through on a regular basis (Burl 1976; Bradley 1993: 110; Harding 2000). This is the scenario Thomas imagines for the Dunragit area: 'If we were to argue that the monuments represented a gathering point for dispersed and potentially mobile communities, Dunragit would provide an ideal position' (Thomas 2001a). However, these were not just gathering points, but also places where contacts between communities were conducted. In this way, the great scale of the monuments found in these locations can be seen as a symbol, and product, of the interactions between dispersed groups of people. Monuments in this respect were a means of negotiation: a way of symbolising, facilitating and physicalising social relationships. The great monuments of the Neolithic are unlikely to have been simply symbols of personal power or the representations of powerful chiefdoms as has been suggested in the past (Renfrew 1973, 1976, 1979), more likely part of the interaction and communication between separate and dispersed small-scale groups of people. As Mark Edmonds has noted, small-scale societies often 'recognise themselves as elements within extensive networks, webs of relations that they continually acknowledge and renew' (Edmonds 1999: 81). In this respect, monuments were part of this acknowledgment and renewal: symbols of the webs of relations that led to their creation.

CONCLUSION

Neolithic monument complexes are found in recurring landscape locations. These seem to have been positioned at or near the centre of a number of land and sea-routes. For example, the Stenness-Brodgar complex was located between two great lochs, one of which gave access to the sea. The Dunragit and Kilmartin complexes were located next to two of the principal trans-peninsular routes in Scotland. These routes allowed safe passage across western Scotland, allowing some of the most dangerous seas in the British Isles to be avoided. These routes became the focus of some of the most elaborate and long-lived episodes of monument building ever witnessed. Blackshouse Burn and the Upper Clyde Valley may have been seen as the centre of lowland Scotland in the Neolithic due to their position at the centre of three major river routes. All of the other complexes, with the possible exception of Cairnpapple Hill, were similarly located at places where land, river and sea-routes converged. The location of monument complexes on routeways may suggest that these places were not simply built by and for a resident community, but by extensive networks of dispersed communities who perhaps gathered periodically to affirm and renew social connections and relationships. In the Later Neolithic some of the largest monuments ever built in the Scottish landscape were created at a time when communications between groups of people across Britain and Ireland were reaching new heights and at a time when the identities of these island peoples were focused on insular relations. Monument complexes were located in the areas where communications between regions could be best facilitated. These complexes were not a new phenomenon in the Later Neolithic. While many of the later monuments tend to be the largest in scale, complexes were built in places that had already witnessed episodes of monument construction. Once monument building began, subsequent monuments were built, in relation to and acknowledging previous constructions.

CHAPTER SEVEN

The architecture of monumental landscapes

In the previous chapter it was suggested that monument complexes were associated with the gatherings of separate and dispersed small-scale groups of people. In this chapter I will to examine the relationship between the architecture of the monuments and the gatherings held within. References to distant places and dispersed social groupings were often incorporated into the way monuments were constructed, through particular architectural forms and materials. It would seem that the actual act of construction symbolised the nature of the gatherings in these landscapes. It was also suggested that monument complexes in the Later Neolithic augmented landscapes that were already significant in the Earlier Neolithic and perhaps earlier. The extended histories of these landscapes were highlighted and this is a theme that will be continued in this chapter. The environmental evidence from these locations also suggests that the activities undertaken were remarkable and long-lived. This again may be partly related to the location of these complexes on natural routeways and due to the use of these landscapes by dispersed communities of people.

The architecture of the masses

The relationship between monumental complexes and dispersed groups of people is undoubtedly reflected in the size of these constructions. The scale is beyond the ability of the individual small farming groups that seem to have comprised Neolithic society (Thomas 1999a; Speak and Burgess 1999: 109). Large conglomerations of people are not suggested by the settlement traces found during excavation of Neolithic sites (Barclay 1996: chapter 3). The ways in which groups of people converged to build monuments appears to have been materially expressed in the construction methods of the monuments themselves. For instance, the plan and differing construction methods of various sections of Blackshouse Burn suggests it was constructed by different groups of people (Lelong and Pollard 1998: 43). The enclosure was built with great attention to detail, despite the massive scale of the monument. Between the oak posts flagstones had been set on end creating bays and each bay was filled with different kinds of stone and in different ways suggesting that different groups of people built each section, gathering stones from different places around the enclosure (Lelong and Pollard 1998: 44). The different filling of the bays was not to achieve an architectural effect, as, once filled, all the bays were capped with a unifying layer of stone masking the individual bays, 'suggesting that the process of construction was important to the builders, as well as the product' (Lelong and Pollard 1998: 47). The oak posts of Blackshouse were also cut down in different places as the preserved tree rings indicated they had grown in different microclimates (Lelong and Pollard 1998: 45).

If monuments were constructed through the assembly of people from different parts of Scotland in a particular location then it may be that materials from these locations may also have been brought with them. The construction of many other complexes involved bringing materials from distant places to the site of construction. The stones inside Balfarg henge, for example, were of doleritic rock found on the slopes of East Lomond 5 kilometres away and Twelve Apostles is made of stones found on Irongrey Hill around 3 kilometres away. A more extreme example of this is the Later Neolithic passage grave at Newgrange in Ireland which is made of materials from a variety of locations, some brought from as far away as 75 kilometres (Mitchell 1992). At Stonehenge, the bluestones that make up part of the circle were probably brought from southwest Wales (Cleal et al. 1995). In this way, the materiality of monuments themselves may directly reflect the processes of group participation and conglomeration that led to their construction.

The architectural form of many Later Neolithic monuments may have been designed to frame the activities of dispersed groups when they converged at a complex. The enclosure-like form of many of the Later Neolithic monuments is ideal for formal gatherings of varying sizes (Barnatt 1989: 162). The scale of enclosures such as Blackshouse Burn, where it is difficult to see from one side to the other, indicates the potentially massive audiences that could gather at such sites. The circular form, too, is one that is suitable for creating arenas in which space is not readily 'weighted'. That is to say, circular enclosures do not readily create divisions in the gatherings by the creation of spaces cut off from others. In this way these monuments may have emphasised the gathering community as a whole rather than creating and reinforcing divides in that group (Barnatt 1989: 164). In this respect, group identities may have been cemented through ceremonial mechanisms (Barnatt 1989: 213). However, this is not to say that architectural devices were not at times employed as a means of classifying or ranking the audiences that gathered at these sites. Thomas (2002: 1) has compared the Droughduil mound at Dunragit to the massive mound at Silbury Hill, near Avebury. At Silbury Hill, John Barrett (1994: 31) has suggested that the mound represented an elevated platform, which could raise a small number of people above the surrounding landscape, silhouetting them against the sky from within the henge. The Droughduil mound directly overlooks the position of the timber circles and the avenue of the central timber palisade is directly aligned on the mound (Droughduil would actually be a more effective viewing platform than Silbury). The small space that the mound provides would have allowed a small group of people to observe the activities within, and as Barrett has suggested for Silbury, those viewers would have been sky-lined, perhaps symbolically marking the status of the group (Barrett 1994: 31).

At Meldon Bridge, Speak and Burgess think that the elaboration of the structure at the northwest corner indicated that some form of gatehouse or guard structure was constructed here. This formed part of their interpretation of the site as a defensive enclosure built to close off the Meldon promontory (Speak and Burgess 1999: 24, 15). However, the site is overlooked by higher ground on most sides and there is no evidence for the river-side of the enclosure having been closed off, making the defensive role of this monument arguable. Instead, Meldon Bridge can be seen as another form of Later Neolithic monument which was designed to enclose a gathering of people and whose form created a 'place apart' in which ceremonies and gatherings could take place (Gibson 2002: 9; Wainwright 1989: 15). Like the viewing mound at Dunragit, the elaboration of the northwest corner of the timber enclosure might indicate that this enclosure also incorporated some form of viewing platform or 'stage' upon which the more important members of gathering communities could stand. Fleming (1972: 59) has argued that the flattening of some circular enclosures in particular arcs would also have allowed those controlling the activities within these places to adopt visually focal positions. While many of the circular monuments outlined above are not true circles there seems little emphasis on any particular parts of the enclosures apart from the entrance to the timber circles at Balfarg henge and on entrances generally. The avenue entrances at Dunragit and Meldon Bridge, for example, elongate the entry to the enclosures and restrict views into the internal areas (Gibson 2002: 9). This may have been a way of drawing attention to the importance of these monuments and marking a distinction between the interior spaces and the wider landscape. This certainly seems to have been the case at Blackshouse Burn where the interior oak posts were more closely set, implying that the biggest impact on viewers would have been on the spectators inside (Lelong and Pollard 1998: 26).

Space may also have been graded in terms of access at Dunragit where there were three different barriers around a central space (Thomas 2001b). However, the many phases of construction at Dunragit (Gibson 2002: 9) indicate that any hierarchies are likely to have been constantly reworked or necessitated constant renewal. Only the central timber circle appears to have been the focus for the deposition of artefacts, while the middle and outer rings were fenced enclosures blocking views to the inner ring. Access to the central circle may have been closely controlled with only certain members of the gatherings allowed to enter. At the same time, the Droughduil mound may have allowed others to view the ceremonies inside though they were separated from the actual physical practices. The importance of the inner ring is suggested by its replacement on at least one occasion. Moreover, once the second structure had decayed, offerings were placed in the decay cones of the posts.

The most elaborate timber circle found at Machrie Moor appears to have been a very similar construction to the Dunragit enclosures, but built on a much smaller scale (Haggarty 1991). Like Dunragit, the site consisted of free-standing timbers (arranged in a horseshoe setting at Machrie) surrounded by two rings of more closely set timbers, which may have held timber planking, blocking views to the interior. Most of the finds from the site were from the central settings, very much like the situation at

Dunragit. Sherds of Grooved Ware pottery vessels were found in the horseshoe setting and the middle ring of posts, along with stone tools and burnt bone. Like the Dunragit structures, no finds were associated with the outer circle of posts. It would appear that the form and use of the Machrie monument was very similar to that at Dunragit, except that the largest Dunragit enclosure was almost 300 metres in diameter, while that at Machrie Moor was only 20 metres. This perhaps draws attention to monumental complexes where the landscape was dominated by one large monument and those that contained many small sites.

At Callanish, Machrie Moor and Kilmartin the monuments tend to be fairly small in scale, but there are many of them. These have been termed 'equal component' complexes by John Barnatt as no single monument is larger in scale than the others (Barnatt 1989: 133). In contrast, at Dunragit and Meldon Bridge, attention was focused on one much larger monument. As Bradley points out, though, often these monuments are merely large-scale versions of smaller monuments found elsewhere (Bradley 1993: 108). This seems to be the case at Machrie Moor and Dunragit where the monuments are very similar in construction and use, but built on wildly contrasting scales. It would seem, then, that the form of many of these Later Neolithic monuments was based on shared ideas of what a structure should look like and how it was used, but the scale on which it was built was not as important. At Machrie Moor, group labour was focused on the building of multiple structures. These may have all been used at the same time, or each may have been built as a re-enactment of the earlier structure, replaced on repeated occasions, perhaps as part of generational activity. Bradley (1993: 103) compares this sequence to a 'series of Chinese boxes', where structures multiplied over time. In contrast, at many other complexes labour was focused on the construction of a single large-scale enclosure. In these cases, the dynamics of group participation may have been different to those at the complexes dominated by a series of smaller constructions.

The sky, the sun and the incorporation of natural elements

The architecture of the monuments incorporated elements that not only referenced the gathered audiences, but also the wider world. At Balfarg henge the main timber circle and one of the stone settings seem to have been graded in height towards the west (Mercer 1977–8: 80). This may have drawn notions of the cardinal directions and the movements of the sun (in this case the setting sun) into the architecture of the monument. Many of the largest Neolithic monuments incorporate solar and lunar alignments (Ruggles 1999). At Meldon Bridge the avenue appears to have been aligned on the summer solstice sunset (Speak and Burgess 1999: 24), while in Orkney solar alignments are found in many of the Later Neolithic monuments (Richards 1993b, 1996b). Other monuments incorporate, or are aligned on, terrestrial features. For example, the Blackshouse Burn monument encloses the twin heads of the burn of the same name. Lelong and Pollard have highlighted the symbolism of this, connecting the Blackshouse enclosure with notions of fertility in the Neolithic (Lelong and Pollard 1998: 49). In this respect, the architecture of Neolithic monuments drew on understandings of the world and incorporated elements of that world within the very fabric of the monuments (Richards 1993b, 1996a and b).

References to the ways in which the wider world was structured may also have been symbolised by the types of material that Neolithic people deposited at these structures and the sequences in which certain materials were placed. At many of the monuments considered in the previous chapter, the final phases of use involved the deposition of human remains. At Dunragit the best example was the deposition of the cremated remains of a woman and a sheep in the decay cone of one of the second-phase timber posts of the inner circle (Thomas 2001b: 138). Similarly, at Balfarg a cremation deposit had been inserted into the decayed remains of one of the posts of timber structure 1 (Barclay and Russell-White 1993: 77). A cremation of a human adult was also placed near the edge of the enclosing henge ditch surrounding the second timber structure (Barclay and Russell-White 1993: 88). At Callanish, a chambered cairn, which contained cremated remains, was inserted some time after the construction of the stone circle (Ashmore 1999) and at the Stones of Stenness two human hand bones were found in the upper layers of silting in the ditch terminal (Ritchie 1975–6: 12). This trend for the incorporation of human remains in the later phases may have been accompanied by a transformation in the form of the later phases of these monuments and a change in the type of material used. At sites such as the northern circle at Temple Wood, at Balfarg henge, Meldon Bridge and Machrie Moor, timber monuments were replaced with stone elements. Parker Pearson and Ramilisonina have suggested that this was part of a transformation in the associations of these sites from places associated with the living to places associated with the dead (Parker Pearson and Ramilisonina 1998). This was often accompanied by the cessation of artefact deposition at these sites. For example, at Balfarg henge no artefacts were associated with the stone phases of the monument (Mercer 1977–8: 163). While numerous sherds of pottery and other material were associated with the timber structures and early phases of the henge, at the nearby Balbirnie stone circle virtually no artefacts were associated (Ritchie 1974). There were, however, numerous deposits of cremated bone in the sockets of the circle. Similarly, at Machrie Moor no artefacts were associated with the stone circles and later, in the Early Bronze Age, graves were placed at the centre (Haggarty 1991: 87).

These transformations in materials and associations at the monuments suggest that the architecture and use of the structures may have been connected with overarching notions of the cycles of life and death. The timber structures were associated with gatherings of the living, but once decayed the structures became increasingly more appropriate as places for the deposition of the dead and the sites were closed off to further use. In this way, like the Earlier Neolithic long barrows (Chapter 4), people were using natural symbols and materials to symbolise the lifecycle, but on a much grander scale. The sheer effort invested in these structures underline their role in Neolithic life; it seems likely that the structures themselves played an instrumental part in the formation and maintenance of the ideas that these communities held concerning the natural and cultural environment that surrounded them. Belief about the lifecycles that governed everyday existence would simply have been one of the notions that were incorporated into the design and use of monuments. The pits, postholes, banks and stones of these monuments are the material traces of the practices and beliefs that framed the performances held within these monuments; their use would have created potent experiences, experiences that are difficult to grasp today.

MONUMENTS AND THE EVERYDAY

As well as referencing the sky and the landscape, Later Neolithic monuments also drew on the everyday and on the architecture of domestic structures (Richards 1993b; Bradley 2001). In Orkney, Colin Richards has shown how Later Neolithic houses and monuments drew on the same principles of order (Richards 1993). For example, the spatial arrangement of Maeshowe, with the passageway, cruciform design and side cells, reflects the layout of contemporary houses (Richards 1993b: 155) (Figure 7.1). Indeed the houses and tombs are decorated with similar abstract motifs and settlement and monuments share similar forms of material culture (Bradley et al. 2001; Bradley 2001; Richards 1993b). At the nearby Later Neolithic settlement at Barnhouse the largest and latest building constructed shares many architectural similarities with Maeshowe. Structure 8 was a massively enlarged version of the smaller houses at Barnhouse and was surrounded by a platform of clay and a high wall. The platform

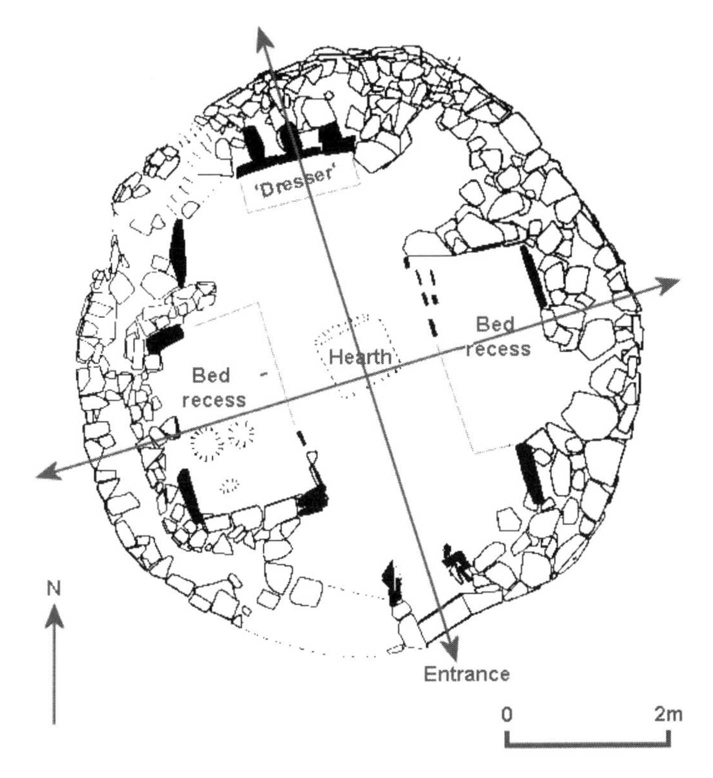

FIGURE 7.1 *The cruciform layout of one of the Neolithic houses at Barnhouse (Source: Richards 1996a: figure 3)*

and wall closely mirrored the form of the clay platform and surrounding ditch and wall at Maeshowe (Richards 1993b). Similarly, the Stones of Stenness shares many architectural similarities with Barnhouse Structure 8, Maeshowe and more standard domestic buildings. Most notably, the Stones of Stenness is centred on a greatly enlarged version of the hearths found within domestic buildings. Moreover, like Structure 8, the standing stones mirror the use of orthostats in the chamber at Maeshowe and both structures are decorated with similar peck markings (Phillips and Bradley 2000; Richards 1993b: 172; Richards 1996b).

As well as sharing principles of order with domestic dwellings, many Later Neolithic monuments actually appear to have been built on top of former domestic dwellings. Excavations on the external platform at Maeshowe by Colin Richards in the 1990s found a stone-lined drain underlying the platform. Richards suggests that the tomb may have been built on top of an earlier domestic structure (Richards 1992b: 448; Richards 2005: 247). At nearby Howe the tomb appears to have replaced two Earlier Neolithic buildings (Ballin Smith 1994). If we examine the 'domestic' dwellings themselves it is obvious that there was no clear division between ritual and domesticity in the Neolithic (Turner 1995).

At the Later Neolithic village of Skara Brae in Orkney one of the dwellings stands out as being of a different character to the others (Richards 1991). House 7 was the oldest standing house at the village and unlike the others was not abandoned or dismantled during the lifespan of the village as a whole. House 7 was also unusual in that it was approached by its own passage and was not connected to the other houses. Unlike the other houses the door of house 7 can also be controlled from the outside (Clark 2000: 90). The finds from this house led Gordon Childe, the excavator, to a very negative view of Neolithic life:

> Hut 7 was discovered exactly as it had been left when its occupants beat a hasty retreat [Childe mistakenly thought that the settlement had been abandoned due to a sandstorm]. The observations made during its excavation accordingly afford a graphic and reliable picture of a 'stone age' interior. The first impression produced was one of indescribable filth and disorder. Scraps of bone and shells were lying scattered promiscuously all over the floor, sometimes masked by broken slates laid down like stepping stones over the morass [filth]. Even the beds were no cleaner; the complete skull of a calf lay in the left hand bed, and the green matter usually associated with drains was observed on its floor. (Childe 1931:40)

Childe's views were coloured by the fact that house 7 was the only one in which he was closely involved in clearing. As Colin Richards has shown the other houses at Skara Brae were comparatively clean and house 7 was the only house where large numbers of artefacts were found (Richards 1991). The items in the beds and in the passageway may have been deliberate offerings as they are reminiscent of the type made in chambered cairns (Davidson and Henshall 1989: 58). For example, the broken slates Childe mentions covering deposits of 'morass' are found in chambered tombs covering deposits of bone or bits of pottery. Under the right-hand bed of the house a grave

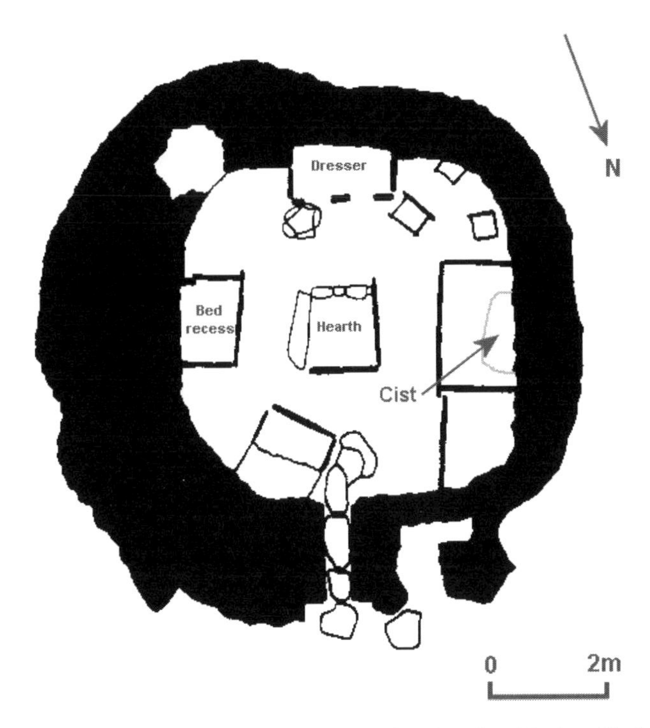

FIGURE 7.2 *House 7 at Skara Brae. A cist was found in the right-hand bed recess (Source: Richards 1991: figure 2.2)*

containing two adult females was found (Childe 1931: 140–2) (Figure 7.2). The covering stone of the grave would have been clearly visible from inside the house. As Richards notes, 'the presence of the dead within hut 7 throws considerable light on the many sanctions imposed on entry and exit' (Richards 1991: 36). The cist may also explain why practices more common in chambered tombs were carried out within the house. A cist was also found at house 2 at Barnhouse (Richards 1993b). Entry to the deepest confines of the most elaborate and architecturally distinct house at Barnhouse involved stepping over a cist, which probably originally contained human remains (Richards 1993b: 159) (Figure 7.3). House 7 and house 2 at Skara Brae and Barnhouse demonstrate the blurred divides between ritualised and everyday activity in these Later Neolithic villages. Outwith Orkney a similar overlap between the domestic and the ritual is found. Balbirnie stone circle surrounds a feature that appears to be an enlarged version of a hearth more common in domestic buildings (Ritchie 1974; Simpson 1996; Childe 1931). However, this was not a house but a place where the dead were deposited. At Beckton Farm in Dumfries and Galloway, two Later Neolithic pits with the remains of a cremation pyre in which a human and animals had been burnt was found amongst a settlement consisting of two hut-structures and a large number of pits and hearths (Pollard 1997). Sherds of the same Grooved Ware vessel were found amongst the cremation pyre, in one of the huts and in more mundane contexts across the site (Pollard 1997: 86; Jones 1997: 90–1). At Beckton, traces of the living and the dead, the domestic and the ritual were intermingled.

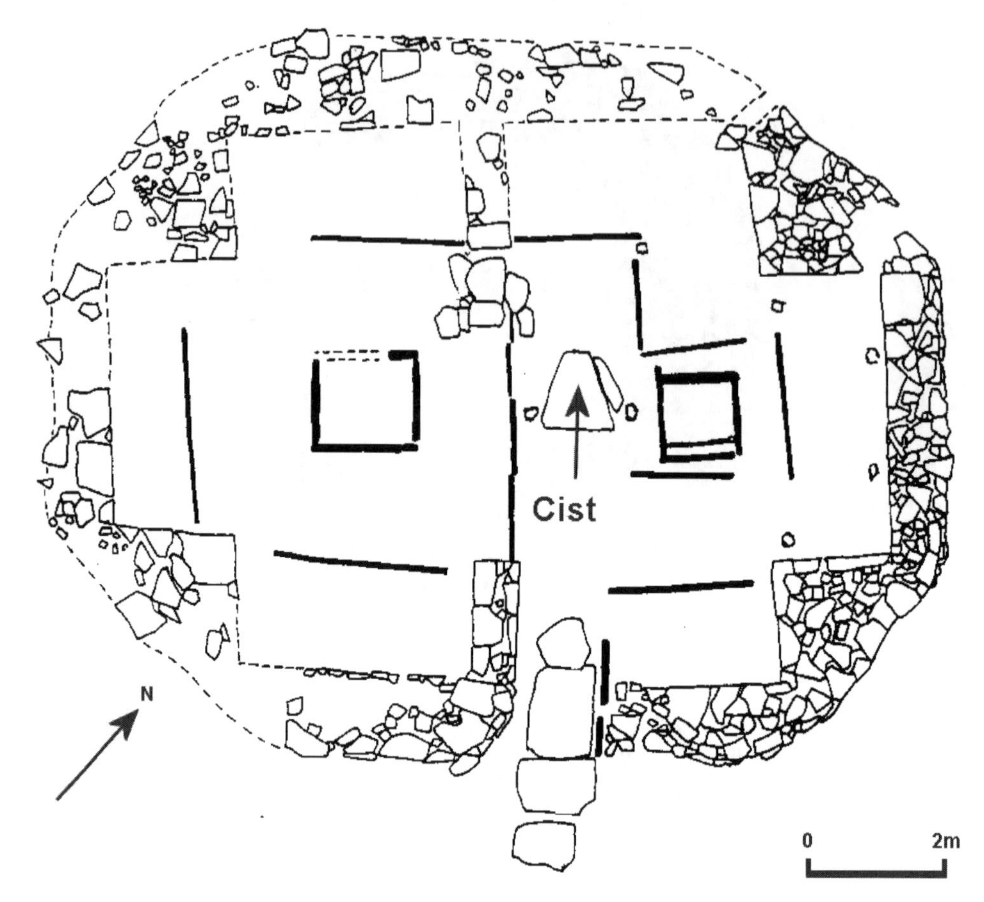

FIGURE 7.3 *House 2 at Barnhouse. A cist had to be walked over in order to gain access to the left-hand side of the building*
(Source: Richards 1993a: figure 9.5)

Like the houses and tombs in Orkney, there are also parallels between domestic and monumental architecture in other parts of Neolithic Scotland. The similarities between the houses found at Beckton and much larger-scale Later Neolithic monuments such as the Balfarg henge are striking (see Figures 6.4 and 7.4). The Beckton houses were small hut-like structures defined by wooden stakes. The pressure of the walls and water falling off the walls created a ditched feature around the hut. Similarly at Balfarg, the site was defined by a ditch, although it was deliberately constructed in this case. Grooved Ware pottery and food consumption were closely involved in the activities at both sites (albeit on a more massive and formal level at Balfarg). In this way, the architecture of the henge at Balfarg drew inspiration from the domestic architecture and the activities carried out there may simply have been formalised exaggerations of everyday activities. At times the function of monumental sites and domestic structures overlapped. The most explicit example of this is at Raigmore in Inverness, where human bodies were cremated on the hearth of a house that had gone out of use (Simpson 1996).

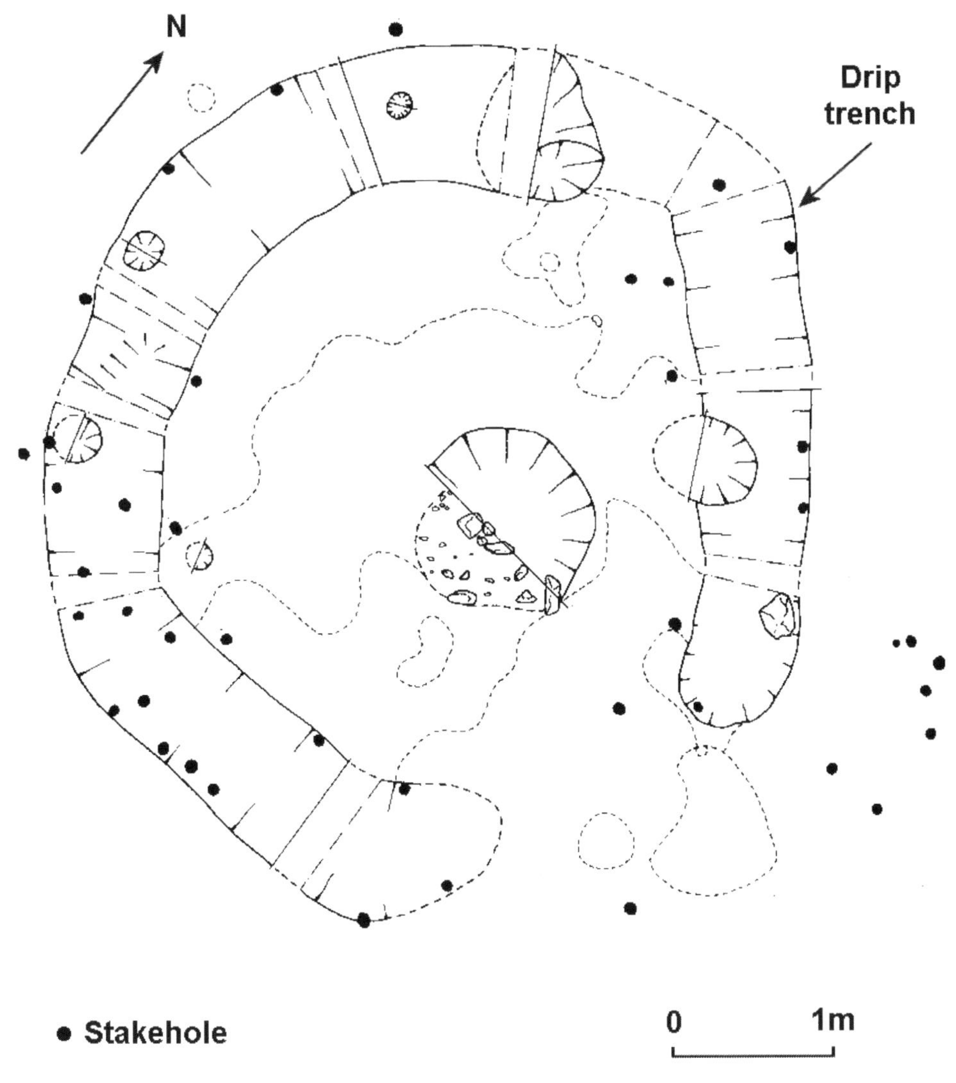

FIGURE 7.4 *One of the houses or 'huts' at Beckton Farm, Lockerbie. Compare with figure 6.4, Balfarg henge*
(Source: Polland 1997: figure 5)

Like Balfarg, many of the forms of Later Neolithic monuments can be seen to be much-enlarged versions of domestic structures (Bradley 2001), much in the same way that some of the Earlier Neolithic monuments may too have drawn on domestic architecture (see Chapter 3). The parallels between house architecture and monuments may suggest that the Later Neolithic enclosures symbolised the unity of the social groups who built and used them (Bradley 2001: 81). The metaphor of the house and group unity is common. For example, the Malays of Langkawi imagine the audiences gathered at communal feasts as an expanded house and one of the origin myths of the Lio in Indonesia tells how the first human beings all lived in one building on top of a mountain, a building in which there were no leaders or differences amongst the inhabitants (Carsten and Hugh-Jones 1995: 27; Howell 1995: 154). Given how houses and monuments both drew on the same principles of order and architecture, it is not unreasonable to suggest that the participants in the ceremonies held at these monuments may have been organised in relation to the ways in which people were classified and ordered in the everyday domestic world and that the gathered audience may have seen themselves as part of a single community, re-joined momentarily through participation in communal ceremony. The ceremonies conducted may have been one of the ways in which these classifications were renewed and maintained through the public presentation of widely accepted themes. In the past, Later Neolithic society has been linked to the development of hierarchical chiefdoms where power was increasingly focused in the hands of a small number of elites (see, for example, Renfrew 1979). The great henge monuments and stone circles were seen as the power base and territorial centre of these chiefdoms. Monuments, in this view, were seen as the means by which unbalanced power relations were both created and maintained in the Later Neolithic. However, small-scale societies are more commonly structured in less hierarchical ways. Age and gender divisions are the main categories by which small-scale societies are structured (Whitehouse 1992: 147). The relationship between the form of Later Neolithic monuments and domestic structures suggests that the gatherings at these monuments may have been organised according to the divisions found more commonly in the domestic domain. Any more hierarchical power relations would probably have been fleeting and present only in limited circumstances. The many modifications that occurred at monuments like Dunragit, Balfarg and Cairnpapple suggests that the ideas and ideologies behind monument construction were often subject to change.

EATING, DRINKING AND THE MAINTENANCE OF SOCIAL RELATIONS

One of the ways in which monuments acted as a means of negotiating and forging social relations between groups of people may have been through feasting. Unfortunately in much of Scotland interpreting the role of Neolithic monuments through the analysis of artefacts is severely hampered by taphonomic factors. Often materials such as unburnt human and animal bone have not survived in the acidic soils of lowland Scotland. However, there is some evidence that these monuments were part of the large-scale feasting ceremonies that it has been suggested took place in monuments in southern England (Richards and Thomas 1984). At Balfarg large numbers of Grooved Ware vessels were recovered from the various monuments allowing the role of food consumption at these sites to be interpreted (Richards 1993c). At the Balfarg henge, food appears to have been prepared around a large hearth (Richards 1993c: 187). At least six Grooved Ware vessels were used and animal bone was burnt there, perhaps the by-product of large-scale food preparation. High phosphate concentrations around this area might also suggest the butchering of animals. The food preparation activities formed a prelude to the main monument-building stages as no material was incorporated in the later henge ditch (Mercer 1977–8: 114). In contrast, at the henge around timber structure 2 at Balfarg Riding School, food preparation and consumption was very much part of the actual use of the monuments. Here, fragments of the largest Grooved Ware vessels were found in the henge ditch, while smaller vessels, more suitable for serving food, were found within the timber structure itself (Richards 1993c: 192). It would appear that food was brought to the edges of the site marked by the ditch in large containers before being served into small bowls and consumed inside the timber structure. In this respect, the use of the monuments here involved formalised ways of consuming food, perhaps creating divisions between those who were serving the food and those who were allowed to consume it within the centre of the monument. At times this consumption was obviously on a large scale: some of the pottery sherds recovered from the ditch were from massive vessels, some of which had been constructed using baskets and mats as supports for their massive bulk (Henshall 1993: 102).

Near the Stones of Stenness, a large hearth found to the north may also have been used for the large-scale preparation of food for consumption in the nearby stone circle (Richards 2005: 207–11). Between the hearth and the Stones of Stenness lay the sockets for two standing stones. Richards argues that food may have passed through the pair of standing stones on its way to being consumed within the stone circle. At the circle itself, animal bones and pottery sherds continued to be deposited long after the ditch began to silt up, indicating that activity was carried out at the monument for some considerable length of time (Ritchie 1975–6: 17). Feasting on a large scale is one of the prime ways in which groups of people renew and reinforce social relations and obligations (Richards and Thomas 1984: 215). In this way, social relations may have been forged through the everyday activities of eating food, framed within the more formal surroundings of monuments.

MONUMENTS AND THE NEOLITHIC ECONOMY

As outlined in Chapter 6, one of the most compelling aspects of the monument landscapes of Scotland is the longevity of use of these landscapes. The longevity of activity in these landscapes can be further demonstrated by the pollen data associated with these complexes. Palaeoenvironmental data is an underused resource in the reconstruction of past landscapes. Yet Scotland is well furnished with detailed pollen data, although the programmes of research are not always tied to archaeological analyses as well as they could be. Consequently, there are only four detailed pollen records from sources close to monumental complexes in Scotland. All four of these cores demonstrate a great time depth to human activity in these locations. This is especially true if we compare these with the nearest pollen cores taken on sites away from these landscapes (see Tipping 1994 for pollen maps of Scotland and core locations).

At North Mains a pollen core was taken 300 metres to the west of the excavation of the henge and provides highly relevant information on the use of the landscape surrounding the monuments at North Mains (Hulme and Shirriffs 1985). The charcoal curve in the pollen sample, probably indicative of human activity, began in the early fifth millennium BC (5000–4000 BC), well before the beginnings of the Neolithic in

Scotland, and may indicate activity in the Later Mesolithic in the North Mains area. Cereal-type pollen was detected from extremely early deposits, as the cereal-type pollen curve commences at the mid-fifth millennium BC (c. 4690–4350 BC; figure 6.7). This coincided with the appearance of arable weed pollen and an increase in grasses and possible pastoral indicators. Immediately before the cereal curve, clear indications of tree clearance and the possible use of fire to achieve this are recorded in the pollen sample. Tipping (1994: 19–20) has highlighted the difficulties in differentiating between cultivated cereals and natural wild grasses. While it is difficult to say to what extent agricultural activity was being carried out in the North Mains area, the simultaneous appearance of the possible cereal-type pollen, arable and pastoral weed pollen, tree clearance and indications of fire are convincing as an indication of very early agricultural activity of some sort (Hulme and Shirriffs 1985: 111). Even if the cereal-type pollen is not definitely of the cultivated variety the pollen core at least indicates relatively intense activity in the North Mains landscape (Tipping 1994: 19–20). This is in contrast to the three nearest pollen diagrams to the site. At Carn Dubh, Perthshire, for example, a pollen core was obtained from a small upland peat basin which demonstrated tree clearance from around the beginning of the fourth millennium (around 4000 BC) (Tipping 1995). However, the clearances were small in scale, probably for low-intensity grazing as no cereal-type pollen was associated with this activity. Indeed, the only sustained cereal cultivation was in the Middle to Late Bronze Age, coinciding with radiocarbon dates for roundhouses, field systems and clearance cairns found in the area (Tipping 1995: 73). At Flanders Moss, Perthshire, similarly very little sustained activity was indicated during the Neolithic period (Turner 1965). Like Carn Dubh, no traces of cultivation were recorded until the Later Bronze Age and no major tree clearance occurred until this period. From sites more distant, two pollen cores are also useful, if not close comparisons. In Argyll, at Dubh Lochan, near Loch Lomond (Stewart et al. 1984), an elm decline was noted around the mid fourth millennium BC. However, the pollen core indicated even less impact on the vegetation by human activity than that found at Carn Dubh and Flanders Moss. In contrast at Black Loch, Ochil Hills, Fife, a pollen sample from a low-lying area, surrounded by agricultural land, indicated a decline in elm around 4000 BC accompanied by an increase in charcoal, possible cereal-type pollen and an increase in grassland (Whittington et al. 1990). This perhaps indicates agricultural activity at the beginning of the Neolithic. However, these impacts were not sustained and the fluctuations in the pollen levels perhaps indicate that activity was of a shifting nature (Whittington et al. 1990: 43). These disturbances became more sustained in the Later Neolithic/Early Bronze Age when tree clearance became more widespread and long term.

The intensity and longevity of activity at North Mains is matched by evidence from a pollen core obtained in the vicinity of Callanish, from a peninsula adjacent to the main stone setting (Bohncke 1988). The core indicates disturbances in the vegetation from the Early Mesolithic period onwards. For example, in the seventh and sixth millennium BC (7000–5000 BC) reductions in woodland and increases in charcoal levels occurred, suggesting that Mesolithic people may have been creating clearings in the woodland to attract game (Bohncke 1988). Human activity continued to occur throughout the fifth millennium BC and into the fourth millennium. Cereal-type pollen and low levels of *Plantago lanceolata* began to appear around 4000 BC, presumably indicating some level of agricultural activity in the Callanish area. At the same time charcoal values reached 'enormous' levels and grass replaced the areas of woodland that appear to have been cleared at this time (Bohncke 1988: 453). Some of this activity seems to have receded in the later fourth millennium. However, at around 3000 BC a decline in birch, a reappearance of cereal-type pollen and *Plantago lanceolata* and a distinct increase in charcoal seems to indicate a second major phase of agricultural activity and clearance. The date for the beginning of this second phase almost exactly coincides with the dates for the building of the stone circle and chambered cairn at Callanish (Figure 6.34). A few centuries later in the last centuries of the Neolithic/beginning of the Bronze Age, further clearances occurred and arable and pastoral activity continued. In the later phases of the Bronze Age, the local clearances at Callanish were augmented by more regional episodes of clearance and agriculture as human activity seems to have expanded. Callanish appears to have become an area of predominantly pastoral land by this time, with less than 10 per cent tree pollen, reduced from between 40 and 50 per cent in the Earlier Neolithic and around 30 to 40 per cent in the Later Neolithic. The evidence for extensive and long-term agricultural activity and human impact at Callanish contrasts strongly with the few nearby pollen cores from the Isle of Lewis. For example, nearby at Little Loch the core showed a dramatically different environment and vegetation history to that of the Callanish area (Birks and Marden 1979). Very few unambiguous indicators of human activity were recorded throughout prehistory. The only cereal-type pollen dated from the Early Medieval period.

Perhaps the most convincing and best example of the uniqueness and longevity of human activity at a ceremonial complex in Scotland is from Machrie Moor on the island of Arran (Hughes 1988) (see Chapter 1). Here, a pollen core was obtained a short distance from the main concentration of monuments on the moor (Robinson and Dickson 1988). As noted in Chapter 2, there are a number of nearby pollen cores from the adjacent mainland that give a good index or comparison to the Machrie diagram. The Machrie Moor pollen core indicated disturbances and changes in the natural vegetation as early as the eighth millennium BC (8000–7000 BC), in the Earlier Mesolithic, thousands of years before the first monuments were built. Evidence of cereal cultivation has also been identified in the last centuries of the fifth millennium BC, accompanied by abundant evidence for the use of pasture by grazing animals. At this time, evidence for human interference with the woodland was widespread with fluctuations in oak, alder and pine pollen, possibly indicating shifting clearance and/or coppicing or pollarding. This is accompanied by an increase in open areas and an expansion in heath. There were occasional lulls in woodland reduction in the Later Neolithic and the Early Bronze Age, but agricultural activity continued and in the Early Bronze Age agricultural activity appears to have markedly increased. Activity continued to increase into the Late Bronze Age: 'it is difficult to conceive of a landscape which would produce such a spectrum. There must have been very extensive agricultural land use around the whole valley basin' (Robinson and Dickson 1988: 232). Robinson and Dickson marvelled at the incompleteness of the forest canopy throughout prehistory and the 'duration and intensity of human activity on the island' (1988: 233). These two phenomena were undoubtedly connected: even at its maximum, woodland accounted for only 45 per cent of the total pollen in the Machrie Moor area; this is unusual when compared with other areas during this period and natural explanations for this seem unlikely (Boyd and Dickson 1987; Robinson and Dickson 1988: 230). It was only after the end of the Bronze Age that agricultural activity decreased and blanket peat began to develop and the landscape became the marginal landscape that exists today.

As highlighted in Chapter 2, the remarkable and intensive activity indicated at Machrie through thousands of years of prehistory can be contrasted with most of the pollen diagrams from the adjacent mainland (Hughes 1988). The only pollen core where substantial activity was recorded was at Aros Moss, Kintyre, where possible Mesolithic impacts on the vegetation were detected in the pollen core. Sudden drops in tree pollen accompanied by rises in grassland at Aros Moss may indicate small-scale clearance, similar to that at Machrie Moor (Robinson and Dickson 1988). After a decline in elm, evidence for pastoral activity was present along with evidence for repeated phases of clearance. Cereal-type grains, the earliest of which was radiocarbon-dated to the middle of the first half of the fourth millennium BC, have also been found at this location (Edwards and McIntosh 1988; Tipping 1994: 19).

A core taken from Blackshouse Burn offers a more schematic outline than those above (Ramsay 1998). Unfortunately, there are few nearby pollen cores to be used as comparisons. The Blackshouse core indicated disturbances as early as those recorded at Machrie Moor and Callanish. Disturbances in the woodland were indicated from the Early Mesolithic onwards. In the eighth millennium BC similar disturbances to those recorded at Machrie Moor were recorded. The disturbances involved a reduction in the woodland and an increase in heather, grasses and sedges – all plants which prefer open conditions. No regeneration was recorded after the initial decline and the landscape became increasingly open until grassland dominated the vegetation. The lack of regeneration suggests that grazing animals used the area for many thousands of years after the initial decline in woodland (Ramsay 1998: 38).

ENVIRONMENTAL IMPACT AND THE CREATION OF MONUMENTS

In all four of the pollen diagrams associated with monumental complexes the longevity of activity indicated is remarkable and surprisingly consistent; this is unlikely to be coincidental. Each seems to demonstrate disturbances in the vegetation long before the beginnings of the Neolithic and agriculture. This is especially true of the Callanish, Machrie Moor and Blackshouse Burn pollen diagrams which show impacts on the vegetation from the Early Mesolithic onwards. The longevity and intensity of activity indicated in these diagrams is in direct contrast to nearly all of the available pollen samples from the surrounding regions, which show little evidence of sustained or intensive activity, often until the Bronze Age or later. The only exceptions are Aros Moss where reasonably early cereal-type pollen grains have been dated and where some Mesolithic activity might be indicated, and Black Loch where there are some signs of agricultural activity around the beginnings of the fourth millennium BC. The Aros Moss diagram itself is located close to some major and unusual monuments. Excavations at Balloch Hill (Peltenberg 1982) suggest that this hilltop site was a form of causewayed enclosure, one of the few identified in Scotland (Mercer 1981: 195). Shallow interrupted ditches, one of which contained a leaf-shaped arrowhead, were found and inside Earlier Neolithic pottery and lithics (including Arran pitchstone) and a light timber structure were located. The Black Loch pollen diagram is also close to a hilltop site where Earlier Neolithic pottery has been uncovered, perhaps suggesting that this location also had a major Earlier Neolithic monument in its vicinity (Cowie 1993: 28). However, even these two pollen cores do not indicate as intensive or long-lasting activity as the four diagrams associated with the extensive monumental complexes outlined above. The environmental evidence from the Scottish ceremonial complexes mirrors that from Cranbourne Chase, Dorset. Cranbourne Chase is the setting for the spectacular 10-kilometre-long Dorset Cursus, and numerous other large-scale Neolithic monuments (Barrett et al. 1991). Recent environmental research has indicated that large parts of the woodland in the area were cleared well before the beginnings of the Neolithic (French et al. 2003). Open grassland was present from an early date and its development may be linked to Mesolithic exploitation of the area (French et al. 2003: 229). The evidence seems to closely mirror that of Callanish, Machrie Moor and Blackshouse Burn.

The link between monument complexes and sustained agricultural and human activity might lend weight to the suggestion that these Later Neolithic monumental complexes were constructed by communities who intensified agricultural production in relation to areas of good land, as Niall Sharples has suggested (Sharples 1992). In this view, monuments were a by-product of investment in the land and the outcome of a community involved in the intensification of agricultural production, a view since repeated (Telford 2002). However, the location of monument complexes on routeways provides alternative perspectives and makes the exceptional evidence of clearance and early activity at these locations more understandable. Clearance and activity identified in the pollen cores may not have been necessarily due to the local exploitation of these areas as these were areas were eminently suitable for facilitating communications *between* separate populations. The impact on the environment may be due to the movement of people through these landscapes as much as it was a product of a local population. This may be why places such as Kilmartin, Machrie Moor and Dunragit became the focus of monumental complexes and intense activity: it was not necessarily due to the agricultural potential of these areas, or their location at the centre of the settlement distribution, but to their location at the centre of converging land and sea routes. This is not to say that these places were empty ceremonial landscapes devoid of subsistence activities, but suggests that their use was more complex and involved both ceremonial and subsistence activities.

Given the quantity of raw materials required to build some of these Later Neolithic monuments and the possible link between monuments and the large-scale consumption of food, it is hardly surprising that the pollen records from monumental complexes show such intensive and long-term impacts on the environment. If these places were the focus for dispersed groups of people, many of whom may have lived some distance from these areas, then it is possible to interpret the agricultural activity in these locations as part of a more complex organisation of the Neolithic economy. The construction of monuments may have been only an intermittent and minor part of the use of these landscapes. At Blackshouse Burn, Lelong and Pollard have suggested that the monuments constructed here may have been built during seasonal gatherings at Blackshouse, gatherings that existed well before the main period of monument building: 'With groups from different settlements using different parts of these expansive uplands, gathering at the summer grazings may have been a central social event' (Lelong and Pollard 1998: 49).

The large-scale gathering of dispersed populations in these places for agricultural and social purposes as well as monument building may explain the exceptional pollen data for these areas. Monument building might then have been only a phase or limited event in a longer-term tradition of social gathering. As well as the pollen evidence, many of the monumental complexes also have physical traces of agricultural activity. At North Mains, for example, fossil soils under the bank were thought to represent cultivation and grazing of the area before monument construction began, corroborating the pollen core evidence which suggested intensive and long-term activity (Romans and Robertson 1983; Hulme and Shirriffs 1985). At Callanish, cultivation ridges underlay the monument structures, again providing physical evidence in support of the evidence for agricultural activity in the pollen data (Ashmore 1995: 30; Bohncke 1988). On Arran, agricultural field systems dating to the Neolithic have been found and on the moor itself agricultural activity including manuring and cereal growing was carried out around the site of the timber circles (Barber 1997; Donnelly et al. 1999; Haggarty 1991). This evidence tallies with the pollen core evidence for intensive and long-term agricultural activity on the moor and around (Robinson 1988). At Blackshouse Burn woodland failed to regenerate after the early clearances in the Earlier Mesolithic, probably due to the subsequent use of the area for grazing (Ramsay 1998). The evidence is consistent with these areas having been used for the communal grazing of animals and for the cultivation of crops, activity that often extended beyond the main phases of monument building. In this respect, like the monuments, the surrounding landscapes themselves may have been formed through the gathering and labour of dispersed groups of Neolithic people. Monuments, then, were an important part of the landscape, but were only a minor component of a landscape that probably drew its significance from the historical use of these areas in the seasonal gatherings of humans and animals engaged in agricultural and social activity.

The products of communal grazing and agriculture may have been used at particular times to enable such great monuments to be built, but this was not always the case. Surplus produce created during the gatherings could be used to support the labour force required to build such great monuments at certain times, perhaps in periods of crisis or to celebrate significant events. In this way, Neolithic 'economy' and monumental landscapes may have been intimately linked, but not in the way that Sharples, Renfrew and others have suggested, where monuments were merely the by-product of economic intensification by a resident group (Sharples 1992; Renfrew 1973, 1976, 1979; Telford 2002). Instead, complexes may have been situated in areas that were traditionally used by dispersed populations during particular seasons; at times labour may have been invested and expended for the express purpose of monument building, but at other times less spectacular activities would have dominated the goings-on at these locations.

MONUMENT COMPLEXES AND SETTLEMENT

It is important to recognise that these landscapes were not simply used for the construction of monuments. The use of these landscapes for activities other than monument construction can be demonstrated by the more ephemeral traces of Neolithic activity found in the proximity of the large-scale monuments. For example, at Balfarg Riding School small concentrations of lithics have been found in the fields surrounding the complex (Downes and Richards 1993). This does not suggest that settlement was particularly dense in the area of the complex, but small lithic concentrations seem to characterise the majority of settlement locations in lowland Neolithic Scotland (Sheridan and Sharples 1992). More extensive evidence of activity has been found in the vicinity of Dunragit. Dunragit is adjacent to the extensive dune system of the Luce Sands, where numerous Neolithic and Bronze Age artefacts have been recovered over the last few centuries (Idle and Martin 1975; Cowie 1996; McInnes 1963–4; Wilson 1875–6, 1880–1, 1898–9). Wilson, for example, in the 1870s found extensive flint scatters and evidence for the working of flint on the dunes (Wilson 1875–6). The dunes contain flint nodules, an important source of flint in southwest Scotland. Flints with evidence of working and stone axes have been found across the six-mile stretch of the sands (Wilson 1875–6 1880–1, 1898–9). Some of the flint found was very fine and may have been imported into the area. Large numbers of artefacts have been recovered from the Luce Sands: Cowie notes that over 8,500 objects are held within the National Museum alone and more than 2,000 flints including 160 leaf and lozenge arrowheads were found by Wilson (Cowie 1996: 14). During an archaeological survey of part of the dunes in the 1990s, Cowie found substantial evidence of flint knapping throughout the area surveyed. Some of the flint was larger than the local pebble source and may have been imported from Ireland. Possible Mesolithic lithics have also been recovered from the dunes by McInnes (1963–4). Again, the evidence suggests a long duration for activity in the Dunragit area with a long history as a place of exchange and gathering for the fundamental raw materials that enabled Neolithic life. These traditions may have contributed through the use of this area to the construction of monuments as symbols of the ties that bound distant communities together.

At Machrie Moor, as noted in Chapter 2, there are significant and probably fairly dense remains of what may be contemporary activity including a possible house structure, field systems and lithic finds in the vicinity of the monument complex (Barber 1997; see also Chapter 2). Fieldwalking by Fiona Gorman and members of Arran Heritage Museum in the 1980s and 1990s has also found evidence for Neolithic and earlier activity with extensive scatters of lithics found in close proximity to the monuments on Machrie Moor. These include a dense Mesolithic site with over 500 microliths and 250 cores (Gorman et al. 1993a, 1995) and a scatter of probably Neolithic date with 37 flint and 77 pitchstone tools with secondary working and a fragment of polished axe (Gorman et al. 1993b, 1993c). Collections of flakes and tools were also found in the early twentieth century nearby around the Tormore area, including leaf-shaped arrowheads, scrapers, knives and blades (PSAS 1907–8). More recently, flakes of pitchstone and a fragment of a flint axehead were found after forestry operations, at nearby Torr Righ Beag (NMS 1993). At least some of the flint found by Fiona Gorman and Arran Heritage Museum was probably imported from Ireland (Fiona Gorman, pers comm.). Arran was also the main source for pitchstone in the Neolithic and Early Bronze Age and this material is found as far afield as Orkney, Ireland and the Borders and has been found at many of the ceremonial complexes outlined above. This is unlikely to have been due to the properties of the material itself as in many areas where pitchstone is found local flint is available. Instead it may mark the importance of Arran in terms of the major routes across Scotland (Thorpe and Thorpe 1984, Simpson and Meighan 1999). Like Dunragit and the Luce Sands, the use of Machrie Moor was not simply for the construction of monuments; the area may have been an arena for exchange and redistribution of lithic material long before monuments were constructed in the landscape.

In the Kilmartin Glen, Neolithic stone tools and settlement evidence have also been found. In the nineteenth century, Mapleton reported that several deposits of flint had been found in the Kilmartin area when areas of deep moss were drained along with material on the surrounding hills. The flint must have been imported as it is not found locally (Mapleton 1869–70: 151). Mapleton also found deposits of flint in a pit, near a cup-and-ring-marked outcrop at Cairnbaan (1869–70: 154). Again, the flint was probably imported and was said to resemble flint from Ireland. Flint arrowheads and other implements along with working debris have also been found at Auchnashelloch (Campbell and Sandeman 1961–2: no. 271). Structural remains may also be present in the Kilmartin Valley. At Corlarach, recent excavations for an electricity line found a clay surface beneath a layer of deep silt (Abernethy 1998a). The surface contained stone-built features, flints and a worked stone anvil. At Badden, structural remains were also found during excavations at the location of the findspot of a decorated cist slab (Campbell et al. 1960–1). Excavations revealed an area of boulders around 5.2 by 2.4 metres in extent under the plough-soil. Among the stones were patches of dark earth, charcoal and some flints, including a scraper. The site apparently resembled a dwelling site rather than a funerary monument and may have been a house structure similar to those found on Orkney (Campbell et al. 1963: 46; Richard Bradley, pers. comm.). Lithics have also been recovered in the Kilmartin valley itself at another cist cemetery at Poltalloch (Creegan 1981). Flint and pitchstone artefacts and hammerstones may indicate that this was a settlement site (Creegan 1981: 24). Flint, chert and pitchstone artefacts have also been located close to the Ballymeanoch henge and stone alignment at Monadh an Tairbh (Abernethy 1995, 1996, 1997, 1998b; Craw 1929–30).

In the Upper Clyde Valley there are extensive lithic scatters and traces of domestic and other activity in the environs of the monumental structures. To the east of Blackshouse Burn lies another expanse of upland moorland, known as Biggar Common (Johnston 1997). Excavations here have revealed settlement and ritual structures from the Mesolithic period onwards. Like the landscapes outlined above the use of these places can be traced to well before the beginnings of the Neolithic. For example, underneath an Earlier Neolithic long mound on Biggar Common a Mesolithic (sixth Millennium BC) stake-built structure was excavated. Under the mound possible traces of cultivation have also been found associated with remains of cereals, fires and Earlier Neolithic carinated bowls. Activity at this site continued into the Later Neolithic with the deposition of a fine axe and leaf point made of Yorkshire flint in a pit in the mound. Concentrations of lithics and pottery have also been found in the vicinity of the long barrow (Johnston 1997). In one area numerous stakeholes and postholes, some of which may have formed a bow-ended structure, and over 1,300 sherds of Earlier Neolithic pottery and a large number of stone tools were found. Like many of the landscapes outlined above, the lithic material found on the Common includes imported items: almost 10 per cent of the artefacts recovered were of flint obtained from the coast and over 7 per cent of Arran pitchstone. A number of Group VI (Langdale, Cumbria) axe fragments were also found.

Further excavations on Biggar Common also recovered lithic scatters and structural features (Ward 1993a). Finds include a large assemblage of Earlier Neolithic pottery, Grooved Ware pottery, chert and pitchstone artefacts, and flakes of Cumbrian stone axes. These finds were associated with postholes, pits and charcoal spreads. Flakes of Cumbrian axes are a recurring feature of lithic scatters in the Upper Clyde Valley. A Cumbrian Group VI axe flake has also been found at Bizzberry Hill, along with a small discrete assemblage of chert including cores (Ward 1999a). Further Cumbrian axe flakes and lithics have also been found at Brownsbank Farm near a possible Earlier Neolithic mortuary structure (RCAHMS 1978: no. 274; Ward 1999b, 2000a). Near Blackshouse Burn itself, lithics including a dense Mesolithic site have been found during fieldwalking (Lelong et al. 1999). Numerous scatters have also been found in the Cornhill area (Ward 1991, 1993b, 1994, 1995a, 1996, 1997a and b, 1998b, 1999e). Finds in this area include a pitchstone leaf arrowhead, microliths and Earlier Neolithic pottery. Further lithic scatters have been found at numerous other locations (Fowell 2002; MacFadzean et al. 1984a, b and c; Archer 2000; Ward 1992, 1999d), including scatters in the Biggar Gap, the floodplain which connects the Tweed and the Clyde (Ward 2000b). Scatters have also been found around the henge at Weston (Ward 1998a, 1999c) These include a number of Mesolithic sites and scatters associated with Earlier Neolithic sherds pitchstone, hazelnut shells and flakes of group VI axes.

THE RELATIONSHIP BETWEEN SETTLEMENT, AGRICULTURE AND MONUMENTS

It would seem that these landscapes were not empty ceremonial landscapes (Bradley 1978: 103). Like the pollen evidence, the artefacts and structural remains found in these landscapes suggest extensive activity stretching back into the Mesolithic period. Activities in these landscapes undoubtedly included the exchange of important raw materials and the construction of monuments, but more everyday activities including settlement also occurred in these landscapes. Occupation traces are particularly dense on the Luce Sands around Dunragit. Cowie has attributed the number of finds at Luce Sands to the 'biased opportunities' that sand-dune environments may offer for the retrieval of finds (Cowie 1996: 95). However, the quantity or quality of finds is not paralleled by fieldwalking projects where finds are just as likely to be brought to the surface by agricultural operations (Bradley 2000b: chapter 9; Sheridan and Sharples 1992). Lithic scatters are also abundant in the vicinity of Machrie Moor.

Despite the number of finds, it seems unlikely that the agricultural potential of these areas can be seen as a reason for the location of these complexes as has been suggested in the past (Bradley and Chapman 1986; Sharples 1992; Telford 2002). The soils of the Luce Sands are of very low fertility and are unlikely to have yielded crops other than on a very short-term basis without manuring (Cowie 1996: 79). The area around Dunragit itself is relatively fertile due to modern drainage, but not markedly so in relation to other areas in the region (Bown 1982). Similarly, while Machrie Moor was obviously cultivated in prehistory it seems unlikely that it was the most productive area in the region, indeed the use of the area culminated in its barren appearance today through soil degradation and peat development, which seems to have put a stop to activity in the area by the end of the Bronze Age (Robinson and Dickson 1988). Callanish is also located in an area of very poor arable land (Sharples 1992: 326). However, the pollen and archaeological evidence suggest that these landscapes were utilised for cultivation and pasture and this may not have been by the local community alone. As argued above, communal grazing and cultivation may have been an integral part of the use of these places during seasonal gatherings. Indeed, the overuse of these areas may have led to the eventual degradation of these landscapes. The use of these areas by distant communities is strengthened by the number of imported stone types present in the lithic scatters and excavated features found in the landscapes above (Cumbrian tuff, pitchstone, Irish flint, and so on). This is despite the fact that places such as Dunragit and Arran have good-quality local stone sources. The quantity of imported materials around ceremonial complexes is not matched by fieldwalking projects elsewhere in Scotland (Bradley 2000b; Bradley 2005). Again, this suggests that monumental complexes cannot be assessed in local terms only and were not simply built and used by a local population

MONUMENTS AND THE 'EXOTIC'

The use of these monumental complexes for diverse social gatherings by dispersed groups is perhaps underlined by the many references to distant and exotic places that monument complexes contain. Bradley (1984: 38, 1993: 110) has noted how the largest monument complexes often contain structures which are unusual or entirely absent in the surrounding region, and more commonly found in distant places. This is certainly true of some of the Scottish monument complexes. Kilmartin contains the only known cursus monuments in Argyll and the henge monument is one of the very few known in western Scotland and again the only example in Argyll. The rock art also includes motifs more commonly found in Orkney and Ireland (Twohig 1981: chapter 4). Similarly in Orkney some of the pottery motifs and the designs found in the Later Neolithic passage graves are very similar to those found in Ireland with little recorded instances in northern and western Scotland between these two distributions (Twohig 1981: 12, map 1). The possible causewayed enclosures at Machrie Moor, Balloch Hill and the Upper Clyde Valley are of a type of monument whose distribution is concentrated in the south of England (Oswald 2001). The chambered cairn at Callanish is of a form more commonly found in northern Scotland or Orkney (comparable with the simplest Orkney-Cromarty types of cairn: Henshall 1963, 1972). The Meldon Bridge and Dunragit style of enclosure are found in regions separated by great distances (Gibson 2002).

Similarly, there is a striking relationship between the largest monumental complexes and concentrations of stone axes, many of non-local materials (Bradley 1984: 54; Stone and Wallis 1951). Some of these areas also include evidence of actual axe production. In the vicinity of Dunragit more stone axes have been found in the parishes that encompass Luce Sands and Dunragit than in any other parish in Dumfries and Galloway (Williams 1970; Murray 1994: figure 11.1). Moreover, in the Luce Sands area, significant numbers of axe flakes and amounts of debitage have been found. At Star, Luce Sands, at least forty-nine fragments of Group VI (Great Langdale, Cumbria) material, all of which show signs of having been axes, along with three whole Group VI axes, have been recovered. A further fifty-seven fragments and chips of Group VI material have been found at Torrs, Luce Sands, and twenty fragments from Knockdoon, directly south of Dunragit on the dunes. Williams mentions the presence of 'polishing workshops' in the Luce Sands area at Star (Williams 1970: 112). One of the most interesting antiquarian finds on the Luce Sands was a hollowed axe-polishing slab, which was found with a partly polished axe of local schist lying within it (Wilson 1880–1: 263). The identified exotic axes are mainly of Cumbrian form, with smaller numbers of Irish axes (Williams 1970: 113). It would have been possible to travel fairly easily from Cumbria by boat to the Luce Sands area as southwest Scotland is visible from this area and some of the main sea routes lead to southwest Scotland from Cumbria via the Isle of Man (see Figure 2.3).

Like the Luce Sands area, the Upper Clyde Valley contains a remarkable concentration of axe heads from elsewhere in Britain and Ireland (Lelong and Pollard 1998: 50; Clough and Cummins 1988). It is also remarkable how many lithic scatters in the Upper Clyde Valley have been found in association with fragments of Group VI Cumbrian polished stone axes. In Arran, Hughes (1988: figure 2) has shown that many more axe heads have been found on the island than surrounding areas, despite the small amount of arable land available on the island (most axes are found after ploughing). A considerable concentration of axes has also been found around the Twelve Apostles stone circle and the Holywood cursus monuments in Dumfries and Galloway (Burl 1976: 102; Williams 1970: 214). There is also a concentration of broken mace heads around the Stenness-Brodgar monuments (Stone and Wallis 1951: 136; Simpson and Ransom 1992). As mentioned above, the presence of many non-local stone types in lithic scatters around monument complexes is notable. The relationship between stone axe/exotic material concentrations and monumental complexes extends outside Scotland too. For example, around the great henge and stone circles at Avebury in southern England a great concentration of stone axes has been identified (Stone and Wallis 1951: 133). Similarly in Yorkshire, artefacts of non-local material are concentrated around a number of cursus monuments and other monument types are centred on the massive monolith at Rudston (Thorpe and Richards 1984: 71).

In the past these concentrations have been seen as evidence for the role of these monument complexes in the processes of exchange (see, for example, Wainwright 1989: 107). However, as early as 1951 Stone and Wallis pointed out that while the distributions suggest that exotic artefacts were brought into these landscapes, there is little evidence for the subsequent onward movement of these artefacts to other regions (Stone and Wallis 1951). As Bradley and Edmonds put it, there is much more evidence for the 'consumption' of exotic artefacts than actual exchange (Bradley and Edmonds 1993: 51). Indeed, it is odd that more axes were apparently dropped in the vicinity of the monuments than actually made it on their journeys to distant communities. It seems more likely that the deposition of stone axes in the vicinity of the monuments was part of the practices involved in gathering at these locations, perhaps brought during the seasonal gatherings at these places. Julian Thomas's observation on how ritual practice may have 'spilled out' into the surroundings of monuments reminds us that the monuments were only a small part of a wider landscape that was at times the focus for intense activity (Thomas 1999a: 182).

The location of monument complexes in places that were easily accessible from a number of regions and able to draw on a large catchment of people suggests that the distinctive form and properties of some of these axes may have been potent and recognisable symbols of the origins of the people who carried these objects to these places rather than being merely artefacts of trade. As Levi-Strauss and other anthropologists have noted, the movement of artefacts is deeply implicated in the classification and circulation of people (Bradley and Edmonds 1993: 12). Harding has highlighted how the presence of some exotic materials around complexes is not understandable as part of exchange networks, but may indicate the actual movement of people (Harding 2000). In this way, the distribution of stone axes around monumental complexes indicates that people circulated and moved through these areas on a regular basis and these places were perhaps crucial to the ways in which people and communities negotiated their place in the networks of contact in Neolithic Scotland. Stone axes may have been deposited in the vicinity of monuments as part of the negotiation of access to the landscapes in which monumental complexes were situated and as part of the dialogue and exchanges that occurred through the meeting of different communities. In this respect it is important to remember that processes of exchange are a form of diplomacy, concerned with the creation and manipulation of social relationships (Bradley and Edmonds 1993: 12). While the concentration of axes around ceremonial complexes is not direct evidence of exchange it seems likely that the bringing and depositing of stone axes around monumental complexes were part of complex mediations in the social relations between communities in the vicinity of great monuments. This is not to say that some of these stone axes were not used in the more mundane activities carried out in the vicinity of these monumental landscapes. The cutting down of timber, the digging of pits and food gathering would have been part of the events of gathering in such places. It is just that many of these tools were then deposited in the landscape surrounding the monuments, perhaps as part of ceremonies implicated in the relationships between people: marriage or kinship ceremonies or as part of competing systems for control and status (Bradley and Edmonds 1993: 12).

Conclusion

The longevity of use of the areas in which ceremonial complexes were located, highlighted by the sequences of monument development in the previous chapter, is reinforced by the pollen records associated with these complexes. Unique sequences of human impact have been found at sites such as Blackshouse Burn, North Mains, Machrie Moor and Callanish. These pollen cores demonstrate activity stretching back well before any monuments were built, into the Mesolithic period. Activity was often continuous at these locations from an early date and there was little regeneration of woodland after the early clearances at these places. This mirrors evidence from Cranbourne Chase in England, one of the largest monument complexes in the south, where substantial clearings were present long before the beginnings of the Neolithic. Many of the complexes demonstrate great continuity as the foci for large-scale monument building throughout the period and were often significant places subsequently (Barnatt 1989: 151). In this respect, it is important to note Ingold's observation that 'places do not have locations but histories' (Ingold 2000: 219). The monumental complexes outlined above have undoubtedly the longest histories of any place in Scotland and were undoubtedly central to the maintenance of Neolithic society.

The use of these landscapes was not necessarily due to the quality of the land or the quantity of resources in these areas (although undoubtedly these were used), but reflected the openness of these locations to a wide catchment of people, who may have used these locations during regular, perhaps seasonal aggregations. Monument complexes were not empty ceremonial landscapes. Many may have begun life as more mundane, yet nonetheless significant, places where people gathered to graze their animals, grow crops, to hunt, gather food and exchange ideas and people in marriage and kinship. At significant transitional times in Neolithic society monuments were built as a means of maintaining and renewing social bonds and relationships that had grown over generations of activity. The earlier histories of these places as places where people met to graze animals remind us that monuments were often just elaborations of a landscape that has already gained significance.

The Neolithic economy and the places in which monumental complexes were built were interlinked, but not perhaps in the ways that have been suggested in the past (Renfrew 1979; Sharples 1992; Telford 2002). These locations were where food was consumed in feasting, where stone axes were used and deposited, where monuments were built and animals grazed and where people met and interacted. The economy of the area at times may have been directly related to the need to provide during periods of monument building; at other times these landscapes were more stable. Complexes were at the centre of a network of paths that led across the landscape. In this respect, Neolithic society was maintained and renewed through community interaction at these places. It is unlikely that these places were dominated by any one social grouping. The power structures of the Later Neolithic are likely to have been quite fluid (Thomas 1999a: 178–81; Harding 2000). Hierarchies amongst the gatherings may have been present, but are likely to have melted away once people dispersed. Social relations would have been constantly reworked over time.

The aggregation of dispersed groups of people in these locations was often reflected in the architecture of the monuments themselves. The use of materials, the architectural styles and the construction methods used seem to indicate the participation of people from a range of locations. Similarly, the presence of so many 'exotic' stone axes probably reflects the movement of people into the area. The enclosure-like form of many Later Neolithic monuments was designed to frame the activities of the gathering population at particularly significant times. Circular spaces were the dominant form of Later Neolithic monumentality, perhaps adopted to discourage the division of the group into hierarchies of power. Instead, the architecture emphasised the group and the relationship between monumental and domestic architecture might suggest that the gathering groups were structured according to the age and gender divisions more commonly found in the household. The architecture of the monuments also drew on aspects of the natural world and the sequences of construction, and the materials used may have reflected ideas about lifecycles and natural processes. In this way, monumental architecture was implicated in people's understandings of the natural and social world around them.

CHAPTER EIGHT

The Early Bronze Age: deconstructing and rebuilding the past

Introduction

This final chapter describes the end of the Neolithic and the beginnings of the Bronze Age. The Early Bronze Age (c. 2500–1600 BC) marks a time when a variety of material cultures and practices were introduced to Britain. Many of the characteristic objects and practices of this period are closely related to styles and habits that originated on mainland Europe. Consequently, the Early Bronze Age seems to indicate a period of escalated contact between the British Isles and the Continent. Traditionally these links and changes were seen as the direct result of immigration or a series of population movements of people from the European mainland (Childe 1935; Piggott 1954; Clarke 1970). Consequently, considerations of this period have been dominated by approaches aimed at identifying the origin of these hypothetical immigrants, through detailed analyses of forms of material culture (principally forms of pottery). Typologies of pots and artefacts were built up in order to suggest the sequences by which people and objects moved to the British Isles. In more recent years, interpretations have highlighted the possibility of more insular sequences of change and suggested that many of the objects associated with this period were adopted and transformed by indigenous groups (for example, Burgess and Shennan 1976; Thorpe and Richards 1984). The discovery of a recent rich burial of a middle-aged man near Stonehenge, who seems to have originated from Central Europe, has, however, re-ignited the idea that some of the changes that occurred at this time happened due to the movement of people as well as ideas (Fitzpatrick 2003). In Scotland little has been done to examine this issue, therefore this chapter will focus on how the Neolithic world was transformed at this time through contact with more distant places and on how regional traditions and practices became more evident in the archaeological record.

Monuments in the Early Bronze Age in Scotland were mainly built to house the dead. Bodies were often contained in stone-defined cists (coffin-like constructions) (Figure 8.1). These in turn were often covered by cairns or earthen barrows, usually of circular form, marking the position of the internments. These monuments were markedly different to the chambered cairns of western Neolithic Scotland (see chapter 5) in that they were not designed to be accessible once constructed; the cairns

FIGURE 8.1 *An Early Bronze Age cist burial (Source: Shepherd 1986: front cover illustration)*

or barrows sealed the remains of the dead indefinitely. Human bodies were also deposited in different ways; remains were not usually mixed together and individual burials were placed within single graves. In this respect, the Early Bronze Age is said to mark a time when notions of individuality changed and funerary activity became as important as ancestor rituals (Barrett 1988; Parker Pearson 1999). Individual identities were maintained in the grave and this could reflect a more hierarchical social organisation in the Early Bronze Age when power structures within communities became more permanent (Thomas 1999a: chapter 3). A whole host of new objects were introduced in the Early Bronze Age. These seem to be primarily associated with display; prestige and authority in the Early Bronze Age may have been garnered through the ability to control the exchange of these exotic goods (Armit 1996; Parker Pearson 1999). The raw materials used included jet, amber, gold and a number of other precious materials. A variety of objects were also made and distributed using the new technologies of metalworking. Metalworking required the ability to access long-distance networks, as the raw materials were concentrated in different parts of Britain, Ireland and mainland Europe.

One important characteristic of the archaeological record of the Early Bronze Age in Scotland is that regional traditions of monumentality and material culture are prominent during this time (Barclay 1998; Bradley 2000b; Bradley 2005; Shepherd 1986). It is tempting to link this to growing regional identities or a more concrete expression of regional identity in the Early Bronze Age. These regional expressions of material culture included the construction of distinctive monumental forms in different parts of the country. In northeast Scotland, for example, recumbent stone circles, small stone circles with massive stones placed in the southwest, were built (Bradley 2005; Burl 1969–70; Shepherd 1986). Further to the west a similar form of architecture, the Clava Cairns, was constructed. These resembled earlier passage-grave-style monuments, but were used in markedly different ways and were surrounded by stone circles (Bradley 2000b). In northern Scotland, megalithic settings of stones in parallel or fan-shaped arrangements were constructed. These form a peculiar regional phenomenon with the closest parallels located in Dartmoor in southern England (Burl 1993). Elsewhere, less regionally distinct (but understudied) forms of cairn and other styles of burial monument were constructed. In Aberdeenshire, new types of material culture, closely similar to styles found on the European mainland were also adopted and deposited in burial cists that are a regular feature of the archaeological record of this part of Scotland. Beaker pottery, a style of pottery that originated on mainland Europe, is the most typical find on Early Bronze Age sites in this area (Clarke 1970; Shepherd 1986). Elsewhere, more local and traditional styles of pottery and artefacts were maintained or developed and European practices seem to have been less readily adopted. For example, in Orkney and Shetland few bronze artefacts have been found and Beaker pottery is rare. In many areas, Food Vessel pots, the other dominant ceramic form in Early Bronze Age Britain and Ireland, rather than Beakers were deposited with the dead. Food Vessels have more in common with indigenous Neolithic forms of pottery vessel than Beakers (Bradley 2002: 57–8). This does not mean that the inhabitants of these places were not aware of the developments happening elsewhere, only that they chose not to embrace these new objects and practices.

Reworking the past

One of the most distinctive and recurrent aspects of the Early Bronze Age in Scotland is the way in which Neolithic monuments were reused and at times rebuilt, augmented or reconstructed. This has been noted in the Western Isles and at a number of Later Neolithic enclosures, but is part of a much wider phenomenon. A number of authors have emphasised the continuities across the Neolithic and Early Bronze Age (for example Burgess 1980; Parker Pearson 1999: 77). In contrast, it is argued here that the use and modification of older monuments in the Early Bronze Age in many areas of Scotland was part of a deliberate attempt to break from the traditions of the Neolithic world. While there was continuity in aspects of Early Bronze Age society, monuments were increasingly associated with individuals and particular lineages; the original ideas and ideologies behind monument construction seem to have been undermined. For example, on Skye and the Western Isles, Ian Armit has noted how earlier Neolithic monuments were often substantially altered in the Earlier Bronze Age (Armit 1996). In many of the excavated chambered tombs on the islands, Beaker burials were inserted into the cairns and the chambers were often blocked off at the same time. Armit suggests the communal monuments of the Neolithic were transformed into monuments that were no longer accessible and contained only the remains of a few individuals; these actions may signify a 'desire to suppress the former active role of ancestors in everyday life' (Armit 1996: 95). Through reuse and modification, the former function and associations of the Neolithic monument were transformed.

Richard Bradley has noted similar processes elsewhere in Scotland (Bradley 1992, 1998: chapter 9). In the southwest, Neolithic rock art was quarried and reused in cist burials in the Early Bronze Age (Bradley 1992). The rock art designs on the quarried stones were inverted and the designs were placed facing the dead rather than open to larger audiences in the open air (Bradley 1992: 173). Bradley suggests that this was part of a subversion of the original meanings and functions of the rock art to now focus on the significance of a particular individual who was contained within the grave. Bradley has also outlined how Later Neolithic circular enclosures were reused and closed off in the Early Bronze Age (Bradley 1998: chapter 9). For example, at Temple Wood, the open stone circle was closed off and transformed into a burial monument over an extended period of time. The first part of this process occurred when the stones of the circle were joined with upright panels of rock that were rebated into the side of the stones, built in the same manner as Early Bronze Age cists (Scott 1988–9: 88). At around the same time a number of burials associated with Beaker pottery were introduced. Some of the early burials were placed at the edge of the perimeter, but soon the central area was used too. This process occurred over a number of centuries with the last burials belonging to the Mid to Late Bronze Age. The perimeter wall and much of the interior was, by then, covered with a rubble cairn; an open enclosure became a closed monument used for burial (Bradley 1998: 136). A very similar process happened at the stone circle at Balbirnie, Fife, and a number of Early Bronze Age graves were also placed in the central space of the henge at Cairnpapple Hill (Bradley 1998; Ritchie 1974). At Cairnpapple Hill, these graves included some elaborate constructions. One was a massive rock-cut grave, surrounded by an oval setting of stones, with a standing stone almost 2.5 metres high at the west end. In the grave a body was laid out full-length and was accompanied by a number of grave goods, including Beaker pots and a set of wooden objects. This grave was later augmented by the incorporation of two cist burials in a small kerb cairn, which were added around the position of the North Grave. Finally, a much larger kerb cairn containing two cinerary urns was constructed over the smaller cairn. The series of burials at Cairnpapple reduced the open area of the henge and changed the use of the enclosure from a gathering space to one increasingly subsumed by burial monuments. These new additions incorporated elements of the original monument as raw materials, which suggests that the original functions and uses of the enclosure were no longer appropriate (Bradley 1998: 142).

The changes that occurred at these Later Neolithic enclosures seem to suggest that these monuments were appropriated for the commemoration of an individual person rather than for the performance of wider group identities (Bradley 1998: 146). The display of particular individuals in elaborate burials in sites that were formerly used by the wider community suggests that positions of authority and seniority were increasingly symbolised in more concrete forms in the Early Bronze Age. The use of the older sites may have been part of an attempt to harness the former power and significance invested in these sites to legitimise the changes that were occurring in Bronze Age society. The very fabric of Neolithic society may have been altered at this time. These changes can be seen as part of a more fundamental and widespread transformation in Early Bronze Age society. Past constructions were regularly reused; most of the earlier traditions of monuments were used and altered and their significance seemingly transformed at this time. Earlier and Later Neolithic monuments and sites were treated in a number of different ways. Some were dismantled or obscured; others were reconstructed or transformed into new constructions. All of these practices suggest that the Neolithic world and the physical remains of that world were reinterpreted in the Early Bronze Age to conform more closely to new conceptions and ideologies.

Cairns and houses in western and southern Scotland

Like the chambered cairns in the Western Isles, many of the monuments in the Clyde tradition of chambered cairns also show evidence of reuse in the Early Bronze Age. In many cases this included the closure of the monument after the addition of a small number of burials. For example, at Cairnholy I, the forecourt and entrance were blocked with a fan-shaped setting of substantial stone slabs (Piggott and Powell 1948–9) (Figure 8.2). The blocking of the chamber was associated with Beaker and Food Vessel pottery and a number of final burials in the compartments of the

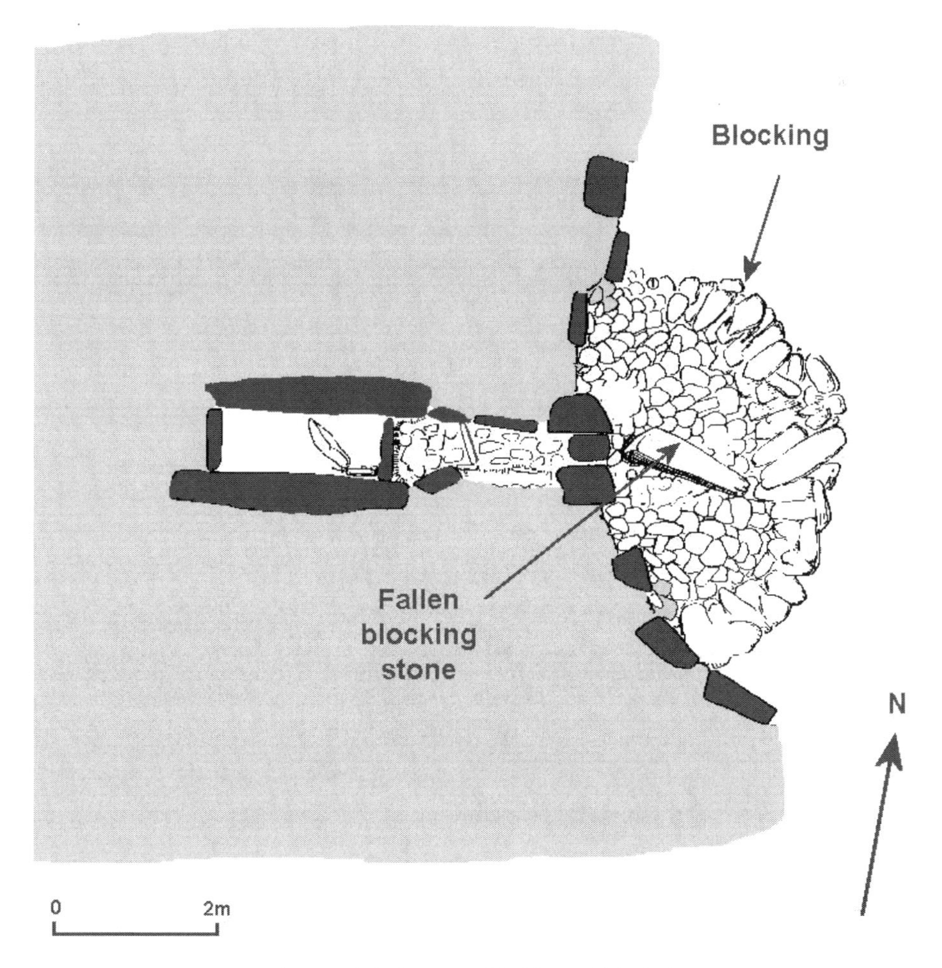

Figure 8.2 *Forecourt blocking at Cairnholy (Source: Piggott and Powell 1948–9: figure 4)*

monument (Piggott and Powell 1948–9: 134). A similar sequence of blocking occurred at Cairnholy II.

Similarly, at Mid Gleniron I carefully built drystone walling was added to the entrance (Corcoran 1969a). The closure activity was associated with Beaker pottery. Kerbstones marked the outer edge of the forecourt blocking, thus obscuring the original façade and entrance (Figure 8.3). At Mid Gleniron II, the entrance was also blocked when the original façade kerb was continued across and blocking was added to the forecourt (Corcoran 1969a: 59). At Brackley, Kintyre, the monument was also reused for burial (Scott 1955–6). Blocking material, which contained sherds of a Food Vessel and jet beads, sealed the chamber and the cremation of an adult on a layer of paving inside. Like Cairnholy and Mid Gleniron, large slabs of stone in a fan-shaped arrangement were also placed outside the entrance, further preventing access. A semi-circular arrangement of blocking was also placed at Dalineun covering a cist constructed in front of the entrance to the chambered cairn (Ritchie 1971–2). The blocking obscured the entrance and altered the original shape of the chambered cairn, sealing the chamber within which the cremation of an adult and an immature individual were also placed. Additionally, in the centre of the cairn, behind the

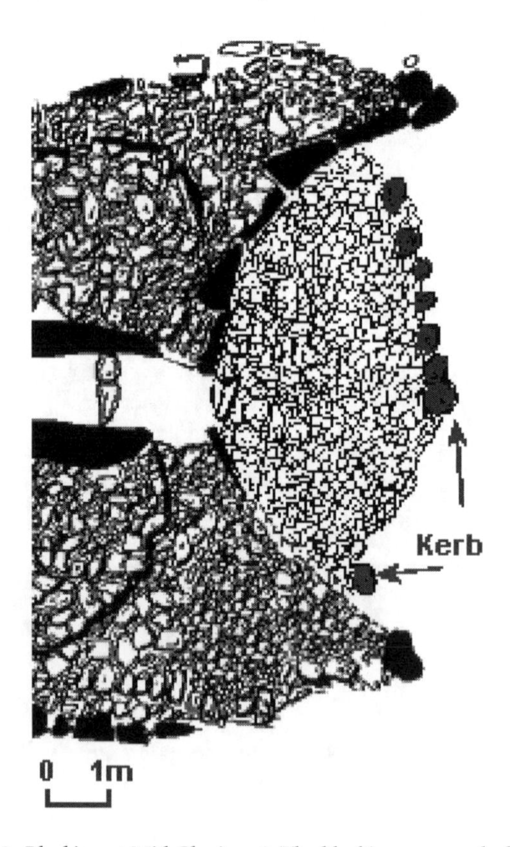

FIGURE 8.3 *Blocking at Mid Gleniron I. The blocking was marked by kerbstones, making it difficult to differentiate between the blocking and the body of the cairn (Source: Corcoran 1969a: figure 3)*

chamber, a large pit was dug into the cairn material through to the natural ground surface below. Within this pit, a massive cist with a cremation and a Food Vessel was constructed. Three Beaker vessels were deposited in the chamber and blocking. At Beacharra, Kintyre, the process of blocking was even more dramatic and necessitated the partial destruction of the monument: 'the final stage of blocking involved the deliberate demolition of courses of dry stone walling which otherwise would have protruded above the blocking' (Scott 1964: 150). In this way, the very fabric of the original monument was altered during the closure of the chamber. Even Neolithic settlement sites were altered in the Early Bronze Age. At Auchategan (Figure 8.4) two cist burials were inserted into the remains of two Earlier Neolithic houses (Marshall 1977–8) (Figure 8.5). The stone walling of one of the houses was reused to construct a semicircular cairn for one of the cists (Marshall 1977–8: 64).

The appropriation of earthen monuments in eastern Scotland

Earthen barrows in eastern Scotland were also reused in the Early Bronze Age. The architecture of these monuments meant that these mounds were already sealed, but

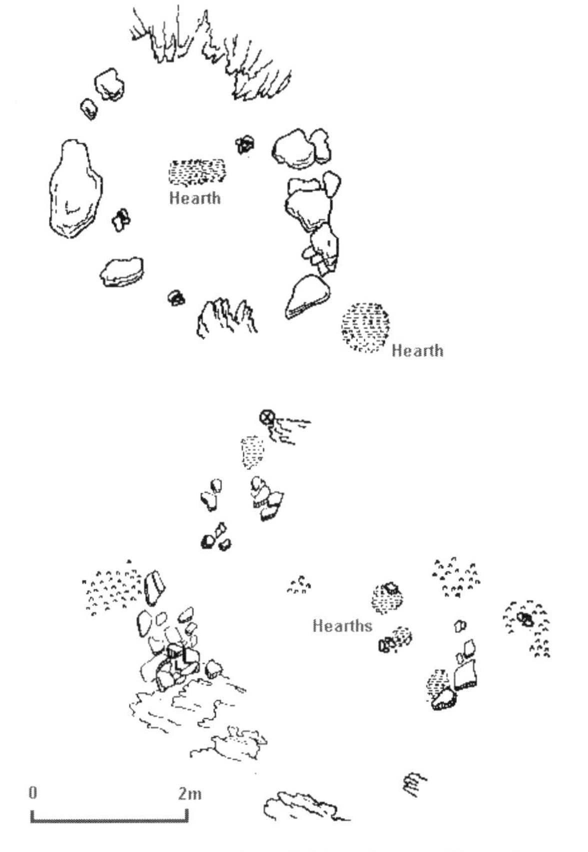

Figure 8.4 *Auchategan, Cowal: Neolithic settlement. Houses/huts were defined by boulder walls and were associated with interior and exterior hearths (Source: Marshall 1977–8: figure 3)*

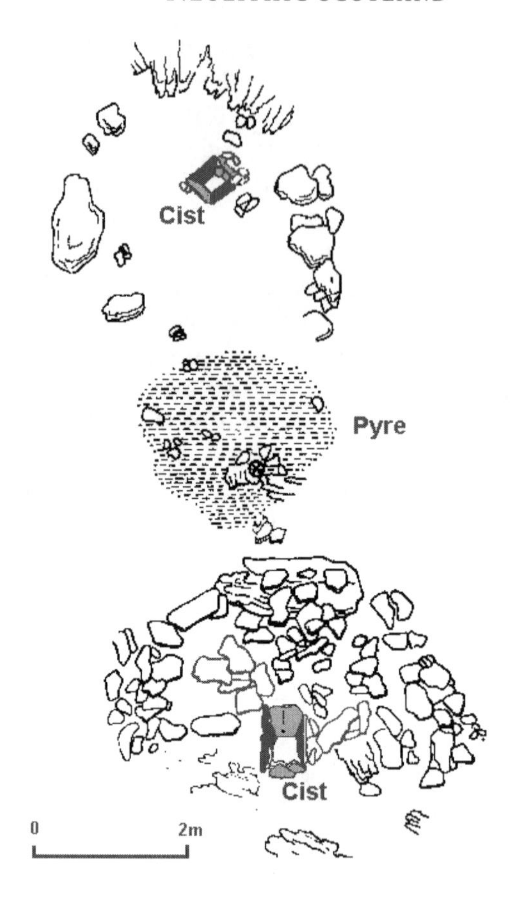

FIGURE 8.5 *Early Bronze Age phase at Auchategan (Source: Marshall 1977–8: figure 14)*

in many cases burials were still inserted into the monuments. For example, a cremation of an adult female was inserted in a pit in the top of the mound at Pitnacree (DES 2003a: 167) (Figure 8.6). The burial was not accompanied by grave goods, but was marked by a standing stone. At Dalladies, three cist burials and a cremation were also inserted into the mound, placed in a line on top (Piggott 1971–2: 35).

The reconstruction of chambered cairns in northern Scotland

Orkney-Cromarty-style chambered cairns were also modified and deconstructed in the Early Bronze Age. At Embo, in Sutherland, the roof of the chambered cairn was dismantled to allow the insertion of a burial (Figure 8.7). The builders of the cist: 'entered the chamber from above, dismantling the roofing. It is probable that the cist stones are reused corbel stones, and the fact that the capstone was unnecessarily large suggests that it was the original capstone of the chamber' (Henshall and Wallace 1962–3: 15). The roof was reinstated after the cist was constructed using different materials to the lower body of the cairn (Henshall and Ritchie 1995: 75). The passage and entrance were also blocked after the cist had been constructed (Henshall and

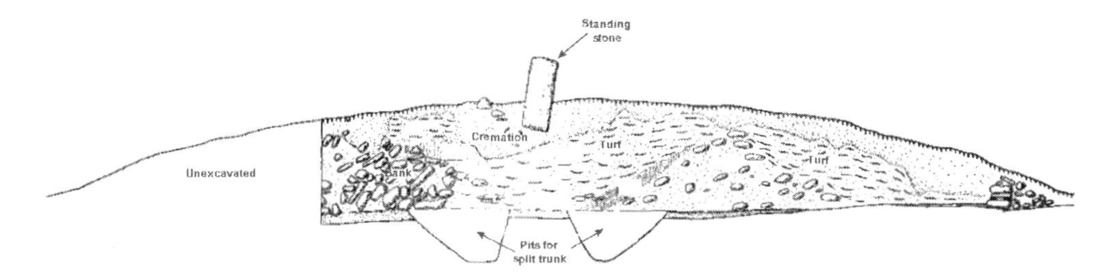

FIGURE 8.6 *Early Bronze Age reuse of Pitnacree mound. A cremation was inserted on top of the mound and marked by a standing stone*
(Source: Coles and Simpson 1965: plate XVII)

Wallace 1962–3: 15). In the northern chamber, a cremation was deposited in the chamber when the cairn was already in a ruinous state. Additionally, between the two chambers a great hollow for a large cist was constructed. This held the remains of two children, a Food Vessel, a Beaker and a bronze object. At some later stage, six further cremations were deposited around the edge of the chambered cairn.

At Ord North, Sutherland, a chambered cairn was also partly dismantled and reused for burial (Sharples 1981). Within the chamber the cremated remains of an adult female and a child associated with Food Vessel sherds were deposited in the remnants of the collapsed roof of the chamber. The roof may have been deliberately destroyed to gain access to the chamber (Davidson and Henshall 1995: 60; Sharples 1981: 28). Similarly, at Tulloch of Assery A in Caithness, a burial was also made on top of the collapsed roof (Sharples 1986). Chambers were also blocked at Tulloch of Assery B and Kilcoy, in Sutherland (Bradley 2000b: 223; MacGregor and Loney 1997; Sharples 1986).

CEREMONIAL COMPLEXES

Many of the elements of the Neolithic ceremonial complexes discussed in chapters 6 and 7 continued in use in the Early Bronze Age. Again this was often for burial and the monuments were often significantly altered for this purpose. At Kilmartin, for example, the Earlier Neolithic chambered cairn at Nether Largie South was incorporated in a linear setting of Early Bronze Age burial cairns and the chamber itself was reused for burial and sealed (Greenwell 1864–6; RCAHMS 1999: no. 19). Many of the cairns in the cemetery covered elaborate cist burials, the stones of which were carved with designs that imitate the form of bronze flat axes (Craw 1928–9, 1929–30a, and b, 1930–1). Cemeteries of cists, cairns and single cists were also constructed across the Kilmartin Valley. At Poltalloch, for example, at least ten cists were built and eight cist burials were located around the positions of the cursus and timber circle at Upper Largie (Barclay 1983; Craw 1928–9; Ellis 2000; Mercer 1987b; Terry 1997; RCAHMS 1999: no. 104). Ballymeanoch henge was also reused for cist burials at this time (RCAHMS 1999: no. 22). Similarly, at North Mains, burials were placed in the centre of the circle in the Early Bronze Age (Barclay 1983). The earthwork elements of the

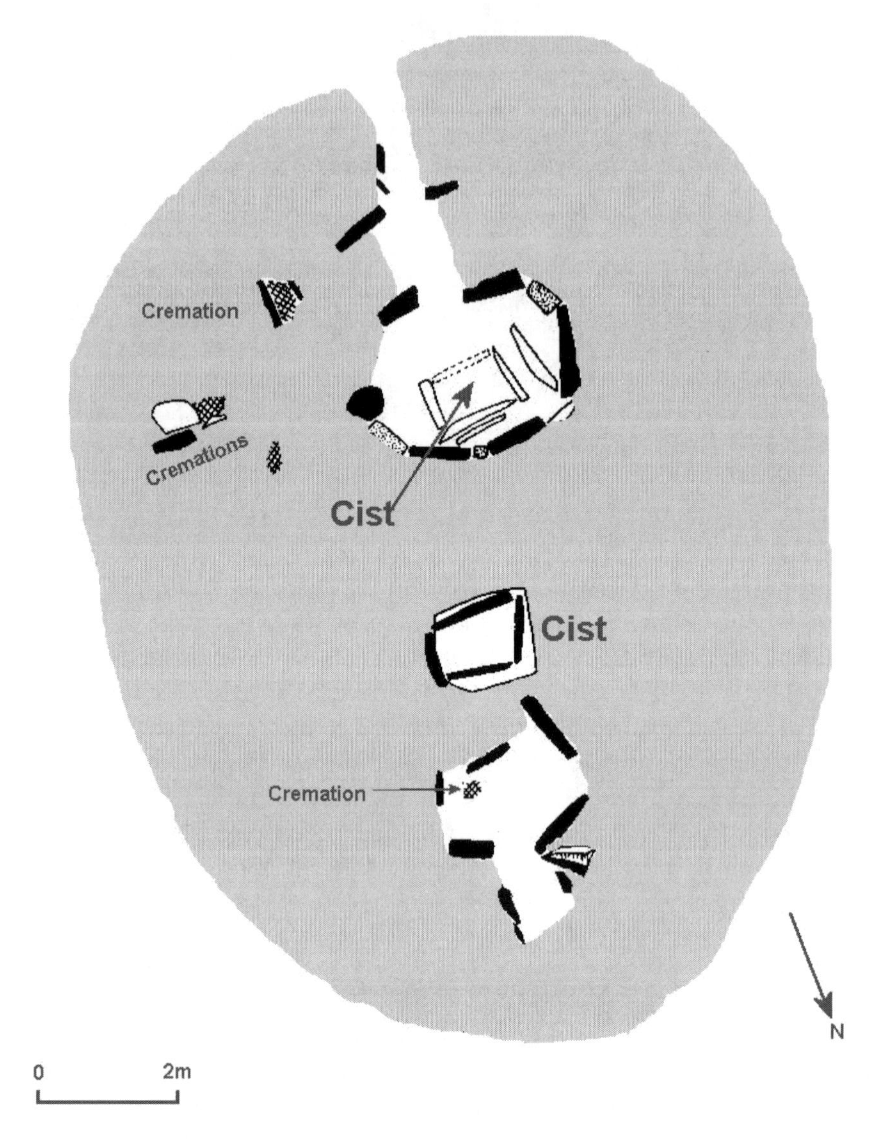

FIGURE 8.7 *Embo, Sutherland*
(Source: Henshall and Wallace 1962–3: figure 2)

henge, the ditch and bank were also dug at this time, perhaps closing the site of the timber circle to further use (DES 2003b: 167). Most of the stone circles at Machrie Moor were reused in a similar manner. Cist burials were constructed in the centre of most of the stone circles (Bryce 1862; Haggarty 1991).

At Callanish, the use of the site in the Early Bronze Age may have been more dramatic and destructive. Outside the chambered cairn, sherds of Beaker pottery and deposits of black earth seem to represent burials that were cleared out of the tomb in the Early Bronze Age (Ashmore 1999). This may have been associated with the cultivation or 'ritual cleansing' of the stone circle area in the same period (Ashmore 1995: 36). However, activity continued at Callanish in other more traditional ways. The stone avenues at Callanish, for example, may be a later addition to the original circle as these have many peculiar design and layout features (Burl 1993: 180). The irregularity of the layout of the avenues suggests that some of the rows at least were added at different times and were not part of a coherent single-phase plan (Fig.6.33). At Cnoc an Tursa, Edinburgh University found a series of Early Bronze Age deposits on top of the outcrop, including burials in a ring cairn and Early Bronze Age artefacts (Geraint Coles, pers. comm.). Large deposits of quartz were found associated with the ring cairn and the outcrop, a phenomenon common in Early Bronze Age monuments elsewhere (Bradley 2000b, in press; Burl 1969–70). It seems possible that the focus of the site was reorientated in the Early Bronze Age towards the outcrop. The new layout incorporated a lunar alignment that sets over the distant hills above Cnoc an Tursa every 18.6 years, silhouetting the moon within the circle as it passes a notch in the horizon (Ashmore 1995: 40). Lunar alignments are much more common in the Early Bronze Age than in the Neolithic (Bradley 2000: 225; Ruggles 1999: 139–41). It may be that some of the most distinctive elements of Callanish were only added in the Early Bronze Age, continuing the tradition of stone erection, but altering the focus of the site. Stone avenues were a feature of Early Bronze Age monumental building elsewhere and were often added to existing monuments (Baines et al. 2004; Burl 1993: 59, 66, 83; Cleal et al. 1995; Mercer 1987a; Ritchie 1919–20).

THE FORMULATION OF EARLY BRONZE AGE SOCIETY

The treatment of Neolithic monuments in the Early Bronze Age can be summarised as follows. Monuments were *obscured* or *concealed*, *closed*, *quarried* or *destroyed*, *recycled* and *inverted*, *marked*, *reconstructed* and *augmented*, or *incorporated*. These treatments of older monuments overlapped and the different processes occurred in combination at individual sites. All of these processes, however, suggest that the Neolithic past was a medium through which Early Bronze Age society was formulated. The acts of obscuring, building upon, destroying and incorporating suggests the past was interpreted and confronted to varying degrees in the Early Bronze Age. Monuments by their very definition are meant to endure, but original builders have little control over how they are utilised by subsequent generations (Barrett 1999; Bradley 2002). Monuments have been likened to fragments of memory (Cummings 2003) or seen as reminders (Holtorf 2003) that help perpetuate particular views of society (Bradley 2002: 12). In the Early Bronze Age it would seem that these memories and views of society were distorted and the material traces of the past were transformed to make them more acceptable to new understandings of the world. These memories can be a powerful resource, as Connerton notes: 'the control of a society's memory largely conditions the hierarchy of power' (Connerton 1989: 1). The subsequent use of Neolithic monuments in the Early Bronze Age suggests that formerly communal burial monuments were converted into the cemeteries of a restricted number of individuals, while open-air enclosures seem to have become more closely associated with particular people and lineages (Barrett 1994: chapter 5). The reworking and at times rebuilding of Neolithic monuments suggests that the histories associated with these places were subverted and modified, perhaps to legitimise new forms of authority (Longden 2003). In the chambered cairns and enclosures the most significant act was the blocking off of the areas in which people formerly gathered. Forecourts and chambers were blocked and the interior spaces of enclosures were increasingly filled with burials and barriers to movement. The public performance of ritual is intimately linked with the creation and maintenance of memory (Connerton 1989). The blocking of the very areas in which such rituals were formerly enacted suggests that these practices were actively discouraged and physically prevented. The Early Bronze Age was lived within a world full of monuments of the past. These were not ignored, but were instead used in a transformative process where previous understandings of the world were drawn upon and were active in shaping present world views (Barrett 1999). In this way, the transition from a society where large-scale monuments were built to promote social cohesion to one where more fluid social groups emerged becomes more understandable when we recognise that the changes were filtered, legitimised and at times contrasted through reference to the Neolithic world (Barrett 1994; Bradley 1984: chapter 4; Thomas 1999a: 162).

LAND, SOCIETY AND THE SOCIAL GEOGRAPHY OF EARLY BRONZE AGE SCOTLAND

The distribution and form of Bronze Age monuments suggests that the Early Bronze Age may have been a society dominated by smaller social groupings in which personal power was more permanent than in the Neolithic (Thomas 1999a: 197). Part of this transition may have involved a greater connection between land and kin groups (Barrett 1994). This is evident in the way in which places increasingly became the focus for burial of a single individual or a small number of individuals over time. Concepts of inheritance rather than notions of communal ancestry may have become dominant (Thomas 1999a: 226). Early Bronze Age burial mounds and cairns are much more numerous and evenly distributed than Neolithic monuments. For example, in the Peak District the even distribution of monuments suggests each barrow, and the burials within, belonged to a single lineage or family (Barnatt 1999). In many areas, Early Bronze Age barrows are much more numerous than Neolithic monuments (Bradley 2000b: 226). In Orkney, for example, Early Bronze Age burial mounds have a more widespread distribution than Neolithic monuments, despite reports of mound destruction (Davidson and Henshall 1989: 15). These may suggest that society splintered into smaller affiliations at the end of the Neolithic and that in the Early Bronze Age there emerged a closer identification between particular groups and distinct parts of the landscape.

The social geography of Scotland also seems to have been significantly altered during this period. Certain areas seem to have become isolated, while others forged links with more distant areas. The new practices associated with single burial and new forms of material culture, such as the Beaker pot, impacted most heavily in Aberdeenshire, where a large percentage of the Beakers from Scotland are concentrated (Clarke 1970: figure XI). Many of the Beakers in Aberdeenshire also have close parallels with Continental forms and most of the metalworking moulds for flat axes (one of the earliest widely distributed metal objects) found in Britain and Ireland are located here (Callander 1903–4; Shepherd 1986). Individual burial was also of a rigidly standard form here, with males and females buried in differing but recurring patterns of orientation and burial goods were of a limited and habitual type (Greig et al. 1989). In contrast, in other areas of Scotland burial in the Early Bronze Age was of a much less consistent form. Single burial was common, but often, in areas outside Aberdeenshire, burials were deposited with Food Vessels rather than Beakers and burial traditions were much more varied (McAdam 1970). In Orkney, the changes and material culture associated with the Early Bronze Age is much harder to identify. Traditionally this has been linked to worsening climate or a 'prehistoric recession' on the islands when the Orkneys became isolated from the rest of the British Isles (Øverik 1985; Ritchie 1995). Ritchie, for example, has cited climactic deterioration around 2000 BC as the cause for the isolation of the islands, making sea travel across the Pentland Firth much more difficult (Ritchie 1995: 87). This seems unlikely as there are strong indications that the Orkney Isles were well aware of the changes associated with the Early Bronze Age, but chose only to adopt those that suited them. For example, cist burials are common on the island, but many have peculiar characteristics. There are a number of instances where cists have been found to contain multiple burials: at Innertown, for example, three skeletons were found in a single cist in a natural mound (Watt 1876–7) and at Holm three burials were found together (Marwick 1927–8); at West Puldrite earlier burials were pushed to one side to allow the incorporation of further burials (Corrie 1928–9). These burials were a subversion of the idea of a single burial cist; the practices may instead refer back to those found at Neolithic burial monuments (Richards 1988). Multiple burials in cists in Aberdeenshire were very rare and were usually confined to the presence of a child accompanying an adult (Shepherd 1986). This suggests that communities in the Orkney Isles were aware of the practices and ideas behind single burial, but chose to adapt this practice to comply with more traditional concepts of death and ancestry. The adaptation of Early Bronze Age practices to local concerns is further suggested by the contents of some Orcadian cists. In a good number of burials steatite urns have been found. The source material for these urns is on Shetland (Turner 1998). If worsening climate made the seas more difficult to navigate it is then perhaps strange that Orcadians at this time chose to open long-distance contacts with the Shetland Isles, contact that is not easily identifiable in the preceding Neolithic period (Fojut 1993; Henshall 1963: chapter 5; Turner 1998). Rather than maintaining links with mainland areas the islands may have chosen instead to initiate closer contacts between the two archipelagos. People in the Northern Isles were very much aware of the changes occurring further to the south and east, as evidenced in the uptake of cist burial, but perhaps chose to adhere to more traditional practices through the continuation of more customary burial practices.

CONCLUSION

The ways in which Neolithic monuments were altered and reused in the Early Bronze Age suggests that changes in society were made in relation to traditional ways of living. Monuments were closed off, rebuilt, hidden and marked. Their modification created something new out of the fragments of the past. New ideologies emerged emphasising membership of smaller social groupings. In some regions authority and prestige were increasingly marked by access to exotic practices and materials. In others, people adhered to more established ideas and habits, only adopting aspects of the new ideology that fitted into customary ways. Places that had formerly been used for communal gathering became the burial places for small numbers of people or particular lineages; territory and land was progressively defined through reference to burial mounds and cist cemeteries. The social geography of Scotland was also altered at this time when the North Sea, rather than the Atlantic coast, became the dominant route by which innovative forms of material culture and practices emerged. The Early Bronze Age in Scotland can be characterised as a time when the regions within Scotland could have had more in common with distant places than immediately adjacent areas. Practices and material culture in Aberdeenshire, for example, became more closely related to those found in lowland Europe and areas in England such as Yorkshire than to places closer by (Clarke 1970; Tuckwell 1975). The islands of Britain faced east rather than west and some regions became isolated from one another. In many ways, Later Neolithic society became fractured and diluted through contact with more distant lands.

Conclusion: timber, stone, earth and fire

In the opening chapters I outlined the differences between eastern and western Scotland and suggested that the Mesolithic-Neolithic transition may have followed different trajectories in these areas. Distinctions were drawn between the geography of the highland west and the lowland areas of the east. Differences in the nature of the Mesolithic-Neolithic transition undoubtedly had an effect on the ensuing Earlier Neolithic. The variability of the evidence indicates that the Mesolithic-Neolithic transition may have been complex and differences in the nature of the transition may have meant that divergent ways of life would have been present in the following centuries of the Earlier Neolithic. The archaeology of Earlier Neolithic Scotland reflects contact with widely separate regions of the European mainland and these separate traditions of architecture can be interpreted in differing ways. The use of timber and stone in the traditions of east and west did not merely reflect the availability of different natural resources in these parts of Scotland, but related to different ceremonial practices that probably ultimately related to different, but often overlapping, conceptions of the world around. It is difficult to discuss a single, definitive Neolithic of Scotland, as suggested by the title of this book. Instead, we can perhaps think of a series of regional Neolithics, each of which describes a loosely defined area (in the past and the present) that contained some sense of a shared lifestyle and identity, which would have been undergoing constant revision.

In Chapters 3 to 5 I outlined the various regional traditions of Earlier Neolithic monumental architecture and suggested that these might represent different interpretations of the world and reflect varying ritual practices and lifestyles. In Chapter 3 I linked the burning of timber structures with the creation of memories and suggested the architecture of these monuments drew on images of the house and were related to everyday life, perhaps as a means of memorialising events that occurred in particular places. I also linked these structures with the onset of the Neolithic and the increasing importance of previous generations to the continuance of society. The process of burning may have been the means by which memories of previous generations and past events were celebrated and retained. This is similar in some ways to the interpretation of the changing form of chambered cairns in western Scotland (Chapter 5). Through an analysis of the architecture of the various traditions of chambered cairns in western Scotland, it is possible to suggest that Neolithic people increasingly used dead bodies and bones as a way of remembering the past. The final form of these cairns hide, in many cases, the varied and changing history of these sites. The original form of many cairns was small and at times inaccessible. It was only at a later date that these monuments were enlarged and made more accessible with areas built specifically for public display. Thus, death became increasingly ritualised. The development of new styles of monument in the west indicates a growing emphasis on notions of ancestry and inheritance in Neolithic life. The manipulation of human bone within the chambers involved a deliberate blurring of the past and the present. I linked this desire to connect with the past with the introduction of farming, drawing on the work of Meillassoux who noted important distinctions in the conception of time between hunter-gatherers and farmers and highlighted the larger emphasis farming communities placed on ancestry.

In Chapter 4 the occurrence of split tree trunks under long and round barrows was associated with the use of tree symbolism in eastern Scotland. These monuments overlap in distribution with the burnt timber structures but used natural symbols in differing ways as the basis for understandings of the world around. In eastern Scotland, life in the Earlier Neolithic would have been surrounded by trees and it is not surprising that these formed part of the ritual practices performed at monumental sites. The split tree trunks may have been a symbol used in rituals that highlighted processes of life and death. At times parts of big trees were used as substitutes for human bodies and were perhaps symbols of what humans should aspire to with age, representing a potent symbol of vitality. Trees were fundamental to Neolithic life and may have been seen as what enabled life to continue. The use of the big tree connected an object of great age with the people who used the tree, perhaps as a means of transferring the characteristics of the old, mature tree to the humans who used it. The tree may have also been a medium through which the past and the ancestors were contacted.

Similar themes and emphases can be drawn out of all these traditions of monumental architecture, in particular the stress on remembering and the importance of the past. The word 'monument' itself suggests the commemorative and enduring qualities of these sites (Bradley 1993), yet it was not the physical structures themselves that enabled the processes of remembering but the practices held there. These monuments would have formed the backdrops and stages for elaborate ritual performances and ceremonies. In Chapter 4 I outlined how drama is essential to ritual. In anthropological studies similarities between ritual and theatre have been outlined (Bell 1992; Connerton 1989; George 1991; Tambiah 1979; Turner 1982). While this is a valid comparison, one of the distinctive differences between theatre and ritual is the fact that ritual does not distinguish between audience and performer (Turner 1982: 112). All the participants essentially share the same set of beliefs and practices and rituals are a way of affirming and reinforcing these shared values. This underlines the basic tenet or purpose of ritual: to ensure and maintain social unity and to enable the reproduction of the social order. Rituals are undertaken at times when the social order is threatened; at these times ritual acts as a form of redress (Turner 1968: 271). Ritual performances can be designed to highlight and privilege certain performers, but the product of ritual is always unity, not division, and is achieved through collective or communal enactment (Tambiah 1979: 118). To complete a ritual is to overcome divisions that threaten the make-up of society (Turner 1968: 270). All of these traditions of architecture were the physical manifestations of activities that were designed to emphasise the solidarity of the gathering group and these monuments may have been instrumental to the maintenance of Neolithic society. The effort expended in building these structures, often requiring highly disproportionate levels of labour in comparison to everyday houses and structures, reinforces the emphasis that was laid upon these monuments in Neolithic Scotland. Monuments were an integral and essential part of Neolithic life. They mark a distinctive period in prehistory, as monumental architecture became less common in the subsequent Bronze and Iron Ages. In this way, they must occupy a crucial position in our attempts to understand the Neolithic.

Earlier Neolithic Scotland was a place and time of change, where new lifestyles associated with the new technologies of farming were rapidly adopted. Traditions of architecture emerged that utilised the natural symbols and materials of the landscape as stone, wood and earth were manipulated to create great monuments to the past. These were places where social relations were structured and renewed and these monuments allow us glimpses of the transformations in society that occurred at this time. The Earlier Neolithic was a period when new ways of coping with the world around materialised and new understandings of the processes that governed everyday life were formed. The practices introduced at this time radically altered the natural environment through the clearance of forest and the introduction of new animals and plant types. In this respect, the process of 'Neolithicization' created an entirely new Scotland.

THE END OF THE NEOLITHIC

Distinctions between Earlier and Later Neolithic Scotland are not always easy to identify. In some cases the monuments of the Later Neolithic were built on an even grander scale than previously, however the large enclosures of the Later Neolithic were often built in places that were already significant in the economic, social and ritual cycles of the Earlier Neolithic. Ceremonial or monumental complexes have often been seen as a feature of the Later Neolithic, associated with particular forms of hierarchical political structures. However, both the archaeological record and the palaeoenvironmental record, as demonstrated in Chapters 6 and 7, suggest that activities in these landscapes were particularly long-lived and it is clear that the histories of these landscapes are amongst the lengthiest of any in the British Isles.

Chapter 6 argued that the interpretation of these complexes must acknowledge their placement at locations where networks of land and sea-routes converged. Monument complexes could undoubtedly draw on a wide catchment of people, who may have used these places during regular, perhaps seasonal aggregations. In this way, Neolithic society may have been maintained and renewed through community interaction at these locations. Consequently monument complexes perhaps formed a more important and complex role in the Neolithic period than we have previously imagined. The power structures of the Neolithic may have been relatively unstable and prone to change; social relations may have been constantly reworked during gatherings at these monumental landscapes. The monuments in these landscapes and the landscapes themselves were the product of the aggregation and participation of dispersed groups of people intent on maintaining wider social bonds and connections. The surviving monuments in these landscapes only hint at their wider significance during the Neolithic. Chapter 7 suggested that many complexes may have begun life as places where people gathered to graze their animals, grow crops, to hunt, gather food, and exchange ideas and people in marriage and kinship. The monuments built were often just elaborations of a landscape that had already gained significance through other activities. It is clear that in order to fully appreciate and interpret the monumental landscapes of the Later Neolithic it is essential to look at how earlier constructions and landscapes of the Earlier Neolithic and the Mesolithic were modified and augmented at this time. By the time monuments such as the Stones of Stenness and Blackshouse Burn were constructed, the landscapes around them had undergone millennia of change through both human and animal action. The landscapes of the Later Neolithic were already significantly altered from those that existed at the beginning of the Neolithic.

In the Early Bronze Age, society was also transformed through the manipulation of the material remains of the past. Neolithic monuments were disassembled and reassembled, appropriated and manipulated. Often monuments were altered to become burial monuments that marked the internment of small numbers of individuals. Monuments also became more widely distributed and may have been more closely identified with particular families or lineages. This may have anticipated Middle to Later Bronze Age society where the division of the land through the construction of field systems and more permanent domestic structures became prevalent across the whole of Scotland and was no longer restricted to island communities in the north and west. In this way, change occurred over long periods of time and was filtered through what had come before.

THE FUTURE OF THE PAST

In 1985 Ian Kinnes suggested that 'Scottish prehistory depends upon a persistent sense of the marginal: geographically, culturally and economically. Perceptions are coloured by a recurrent need to derive innovation from without and then to resort to the parochial for explanation and understanding' (Kinnes 1984: 15). In this book I have tried to outline the wider context of Scottish prehistory, by escaping the modern borders of Scotland through the use of parallels and examples from outside. At the same time I have tried to ensure that my interpretations have come from a critical analysis of Scottish archaeology itself. Neolithic Scotland was not isolated, but part of a larger island archipelago where people and material culture moved around on a regular basis. Any account of the archaeological remains from this area must try to take account of this, as Neolithic society in this region was dynamic and open to influences from a range of geographical areas.

Kinnes' paper seems to have been written at a time when interest in Scottish prehistory was at a standstill. This, thankfully, is no longer the case. Major, innovative projects of research have since been completed and many are ongoing. Work on Scottish sites by Gordon Barclay, Richard Bradley, Colin Richards and Julian Thomas (to name but a few) has revolutionised our understandings of the Neolithic in this area. However, more remains to be done. The cropmark record in large parts of lowland Scotland (especially Aberdeenshire and Moray) remains largely unexplored, and research into these areas would be a significant contribution to our understanding of regional differences. In the west, the landscapes between stone burial monuments deserve closer scrutiny as there is great unrealised potential for extending beyond the study of chambered cairns that has dominated research into these areas. Tim Phillips' work on the Black Isle, where fieldwalking was combined with landscape studies of burial monuments, demonstrates the ways in which this might be achieved. Further work on what fieldwalking material represents through excavation may also be fruitful. Colin Richards' work on Orkney, where an abundance of Neolithic settlements was unexpectedly found through this approach, highlights the possible rewards of such studies (Richards 2005).

In general, many aspects of the Neolithic and Early Bronze Age remain poorly dated and at times poorly understood. Questions about the onset of the Neolithic, for example, are hampered by the lack of cereal assemblages and skeletal material with closely defined contexts. In some respects this is a issue of survival, but the potential for closer integration between environmental and archaeological analysis is highlighted by projects such as Chapelfield Cowie, where new techniques of analysis helped elucidate much greater levels of detail than would have been previously possible on such a truncated site (Atkinson 2002). More dates on cereal assemblages and skeletal remains from chambered cairns, would, for example, provide a check on the associations made with poorly contextualised material and particular archaeological features. Interpretations must be made on securely researched archaeological evidence. However, it is easy to be pessimistic. Overall, the study of the Scottish Neolithic is fairly healthy, and hopefully this can only be improved. Wider syntheses such as this one will hopefully combine in the future with greater detailed regional sequences to produce fuller considerations of the Neolithic. Interpretive syntheses must exist alongside scientific analyses and traditional corpuses to enable this. In the future, it should be possible to have a more detailed and illuminating past.

Bibliography

Abernethy, D. (1995), 'Monadh An Tairbh (Kilmichael Glassary parish), flint scatter', *Discovery and Excavation in Scotland*: 64.

Abernethy, D. (1996), 'Monadh An Tairbh (Kilmichael Glassary parish), flint scatter', *Discovery and Excavation in Scotland*: 22.

Abernethy, D. (1997), 'Monadh An Tairbh (Kilmichael Glassary parish), flint scatter', *Discovery and Excavation in Scotland*: 21.

Abernethy, D. (1998a), 'Corlarach and Kilchoan (Kilmartin parish), lithics; ?prehistoric settlement', *Discovery and Excavation in Scotland*: 20.

Abernethy, D (1998b), 'Longwalk (Kilmichael Glassary parish), flint scatter', *Discovery and Excavation in Scotland*: 20.

Alexander, D. (1997), 'Excavation of pits containing decorated Neolithic pottery and early lithic material of possible Mesolithic date at Spurryhillock, Stonehaven, Aberdeenshire', *Proceedings of the Society of Antiquaries of Scotland*, 127: 17–27.

Alexander, D. (2000), 'Excavations of Neolithic pits, later prehistoric structures and a Roman temporary camp along the line of the A96 Kintore and Blackburn bypass, Aberdeenshire', *Proceedings of the Society of Antiquaries of Scotland*, 130: 11–76.

Alldritt, D. M. (2002), 'The plant remains', in J. A. Atkinson, 'Excavation of a Neolithic occupation site at Chapelfield Cowie, Stirling', *Proceedings of the Society of Antiquaries of Scotland*, 132: 139–92.

Anderson, J. (1865–6), 'On the chambered cairns of Caithness, with results of recent explorations', *Proceedings of the Society of Antiquaries of Scotland*, 6: 442–51.

Anderson, J. (1866–8), 'On the horned cairns of Caithness: their structural arrangement, contents of chambers &c', *Proceedings of the Society of Antiquaries of Scotland*, 7: 480–512.

Anderson, J. (1870–1), 'Notice on the excavation of "Kenny's Cairn", on the Hill of Bruan, Carn Righ, near Yarhouse; the Warth Hill cairn, Duncansbay; and several smaller sepulchral cairns in Caithness', *Proceedings of the Society of Antiquaries of Scotland*, 9: 292–7.

Anderson, J. (1886), *Scotland in Pagan Times: the Bronze and Stone Ages*, Edinburgh: David Douglas.

Anthony, D. W. (1990), 'Migration in archaeology: the baby and the bathwater', *American Anthropologist*, 92: 895–914.

Archer, E. (2000), 'Chesterhall Farm, South Lanarkshire (Wiston and Roberton Parish)', *Discovery and Excavation in Scotland*: 88.

Argenti, N. (1999), 'Ephemeral monuments, memory and royal sempiternity in a grassfields kingdom', in A. Forty and S. Küchler (eds) (1999), *The Art of Forgetting*, Oxford: Berg, 21–52.

Armit, I. (1996), *The Archaeology of Skye and the Western Isles*, Edinburgh: Edinburgh University Press.

Armit, I., Cowie, T. G. and Ralston, I. (1994), 'Excavation of pits containing Grooved Ware at Hillend, Clydesdale District, Strathclyde Region', *Proceedings of the Society of Antiquaries of Scotland*, 124: 113–27.

Armit, I. and Finlayson, B. (1992), 'Hunter-gatherers transformed: the transition to agriculture in northern and western Europe', *Antiquity* 66: 664–76.

Armit, I., Murphy, E., Nelis, E. and Simpson, D. (eds) (2003), *Neolithic Settlement in Ireland and Western Britain*, Oxford: Oxbow.

Ashbee, P. (1966), 'The Fussell's Lodge long barrow excavations 1957', *Archaeologia*, 100: 1–80.
Ashmore, P. (1995), *Calanais: the standing stones*, Isle of Lewis: Urras nan Tursachan.
Ashmore, P. (1996), *Scotland in the Neolithic and Early Bronze Age*, Edinburgh: Historic Scotland.
Ashmore, P. (1999), 'Radiocarbon dating: avoiding errors by avoiding mixed samples', *Antiquity*, 73: 124–130.
Atkinson, J. A. (2002), 'Excavation of a Neolithic occupation site at Chapelfield Cowie, Stirling', *Proceedings of the Society of Antiquaries of Scotland*, 132: 139–92.
Atkinson, R. J. C. (1956), *Stonehenge*, London: Hamish Hamilton.
Atkinson, R. J. C. (1965), 'Wayland's Smithy', *Antiquity*, 39: 126–33.
Atkinson, R. J. C., Piggott, C. M. and Sanders, N. K. (1951), *Excavations at Dorchester, Oxon.*, Oxford: Ashmolean.
Austin, P. (2000), 'The emperor's new garden: woodland, trees and people in the Neolithic of southern Britain', in A. S. Fairbairn (ed.), *Plants in Neolithic Britain and Beyond*, Oxford: Oxbow Books, 63–78.
Baines, A., Brophy, K. and Pannett, A. (2004), 'Battle Moss: making sense of stone rows in northern Scotland', *Scottish Archaeological News*, 44: 6.
Ballin Smith, B. (1994), *Howe: Four Millennia of Orkney Prehistory, Excavations 1978–1982*, Edinburgh: Society of Antiquaries of Scotland Monograph Series, 9.
Barber, J. W. (1977–8), 'The excavation of the holed-stone at Ballymeanoch, Kilmartin, Argyll', *Proceedings of the Society of Antiquaries of Scotland*, 109: 104–13.
Barber, J. W. (1988), 'Isbister, Quanterness and the Point of Cott: the formulation and testing of some middle range theory', in J. Barrett and I. Kinnes (eds), *The Archaeology of Context in the Neolithic and Early Bronze Age: Recent Trends*, Sheffield: Sheffield University Press, 57–62.
Barber, J. W. (1997), *The Archaeological investigation of a Prehistoric Landscape: Excavations on Arran 1978–1981*, Edinburgh: Scottish Trust for Archaeological Research.
Barclay, A. and Harding, J. (eds) (1999), *Pathways and Ceremonies: The Cursus Monuments of Britain and Ireland*, Oxford: Oxbow.
Barclay, G. J. (1983), 'Sites of the third millennium BC to the first millennium AD at North Mains, Strathallan, Perthshire', *Proceedings of the Society of Antiquaries of Scotland*, 113: 122–281.
Barclay, G. J. (1989), 'The cultivation remains beneath the North Mains Strathallan barrow', *Proceedings of the Society of Antiquaries of Scotland*, 119: 59–61.
Barclay, G. J. (1996), 'Neolithic buildings in Scotland', in T. Darvill and J. Thomas (eds), *Neolithic Houses in Northwest Europe and Beyond*, Oxford: Oxbow, 61–5.
Barclay, G. J. (1997), 'The Neolithic', in K. J. Edwards and I. B. M. Ralston (eds), *Scotland: Environment and Archaeology 8000 BC–AD 1000*, Chichester: Wiley, 127–50.
Barclay, G. J. (1998), *Farmers, Temples and Tombs: Scotland in the Neolithic and Early Bronze Age*, Edinburgh: Historic Scotland.
Barclay, G. J. (1999), 'Cairnpapple revisited: 1948–1998', *Proceedings of the Prehistoric Society*, 65: 17–46.
Barclay, G. J. (2000), 'Between Orkney and Wessex: the search for the regional Neolithics of Britain', in A. Ritchie (ed.), *Neolithic Orkney in its European Context*, Cambridge: McDonald Institute for Archaeological Research, 275–85.
Barclay, G. J. (2001a), '"Metropolitan" and "parochial"/"core" and "periphery": a historiography of the Neolithic of Scotland', *Proceedings of the Prehistoric Society*, 67: 1–18.
Barclay, G. J. (2001b), 'Neolithic enclosures in Scotland', in T. Darvill and J. Thomas (eds), *Neolithic Enclosures in Atlantic Northwest Europe*, Oxford: Oxbow, 144–54.
Barclay, G. J. (2003), 'Neolithic settlement in the lowlands of Scotland: a preliminary survey', in I. Armit, E. Murphy, E. Nelis and D. Simpson (eds), *Neolithic Settlement in Ireland and Western Britain*, Oxford: Oxbow, 71–83.
Barclay, G. J., Brophy, K. and MacGregor, G. (2002), 'Claish, Stirling: an Early Neolithic structure in its context', *Proceedings of the Society of Antiquaries of Scotland*, 132: 65–138.
Barclay, G. J. and Brophy, K. (2004), 'A rectilinear timber structure and post-ring at Carsie Mains, Meikleour, Perthshire', *Tayside and Fife Archaeological Journal*, 10: 1–22.

Barclay, G. J., Carter, S. P., Dalland, M. M., Hastie, M., Holden, T. G., MacSween, A. and Wickham-Jones, C. J. (2001), 'An Early Neolithic settlement at Kinbeachie, Easter Ross', *Proceedings of the Society of Antiquaries of Scotland*, 131: 57–85.

Barclay, G. J. and Maxwell, G. S. (1991), 'Excavation of a Neolithic long mortuary enclosure within the Roman legionary fortress at Inchtuthil, Perthshire', *Proceedings of the Society of Antiquaries of Scotland*, 121: 27–44.

Barclay, G. J. and Maxwell, G. S. (1998), *The Cleaven Dyke and Littleour: Monuments in the Neolithic of Tayside*, Edinburgh: Society of the Antiquaries of Scotland Monograph Series, 13.

Barclay, G. J. and Russell-White, C. J. (1993), 'Excavations in the ceremonial complex of the fourth to third millennium BC at Balfarg/Balbirnie, Glenrothes, Fife', *Proceedings of the Society of Antiquaries of Scotland*, 123: 43–110.

Barclay, G. J. and Wickham-Jones, C. R. (2002), 'The investigation of some lithic scatters in Perthshire', *Tayside and Fife Archaeological Journal*, 8: 1–11.

Barnatt, J. (1989), 'Stone circles of Britain: taxonomic and distributional analyses and a catalogue of sites in England, Scotland and Wales', *British Archaeological Reports British Series*, 215.

Barnatt, J. (1999), 'Taming the land: Peak District farming and ritual in the Bronze Age', *Derbyshire Archaeological Journal*, 119: 19–78.

Barrett, J. (1988), 'The living, the dead and the ancestors: Neolithic and Early Bronze Age mortuary practices', in J. Barrett and I. Kinnes (eds), *The Archaeology of Context in the Neolithic and Early Bronze Age: Recent Trends*, Sheffield: Sheffield University Press, 30–41.

Barrett, J. (1994), *Fragments from Antiquity*, Oxford: Blackwell.

Barrett, J. (1999), 'The mythical landscape of the British Iron Age', in W. Ashmore and A. B. Knapp (eds), *Archaeologies of Landscape*, Oxford: Blackwell, 253–63.

Barrett, J., Bradley, R. and Green, M. (1991), *Landscape, Monuments and Society: The Prehistory of Cranbourne Chase*, Cambridge: Cambridge University Press.

Bell, C. (1992), *Ritual Theory, Ritual Practice*, Oxford: Oxford University Press.

Beveridge, B. (1911), *North Uist: Its Archaeology and Topography*, Edinburgh: William Brown.

Birks, H. H. (1972), 'Studies in the vegetational history of Scotland', *Journal of Ecology*, 60: 183–217.

Birks, H. J. B. and Madsen, B. J. (1979), 'Flandrian vegetational history of Little Loch Roag, Isle of Lewis', *Journal of Ecology*, 67: 825–42.

Bloch, M. (1998), 'Why trees, too, are good to think with: towards an anthropology of the meaning of life', in L. Rival (ed.), *The Social Life of Trees: Anthropological Perspectives on Tree Symbolism*, Oxford: Berg, 39–55.

Bloch, M. and Parry, J. (1992), *Death and the Regeneration of Life*, Cambridge: Cambridge University Press.

Bohncke, S. J. P. (1988), 'Vegetation and habitation history of the Callanish area, Isle of Lewis, Scotland', in H. H. Birks, H. J .B. Birks, P. E. Kaland and D. Mae (eds), *The Cultural Landscape – Past, Present and Future*, Cambridge: Cambridge University Press, 445–62.

Bonnemère, P. (1998), 'Trees and people: some vital links. Tree products and other agents in the life cycle of the Ankave-Anga of Papua New Guinea', in L. Rival (ed.), *The Social Life of Trees: Anthropological Perspectives on Tree Symbolism*, Oxford: Berg, 113–31.

Bonsall, C., Sutherland, D. G., Russell, N. J., Coles, G., Paul, C., Huntley, J. and Lawson, T. J. (1994), 'Excavations in Ulva Cave, Western Scotland 1990–91: a preliminary report', *Mesolithic Miscellany*, 15(1): 8–21.

Boyd, W. E. and Dickson, J. H. (1987), 'A post-glacial pollen sequence from Loch a'Mhuillin, north Arran: a record of vegetation history with special reference to the history of the endemic Sorbus species', *New Phytologist*, 106: 221–44.

Bowen, E. G. (1972), *Britain and the Western Seaways*, London: Thames and Hudson.

Bown, C. J. (1982), *South-West Scotland: Soil and Land Capability for Agriculture*, Aberdeen: Macaulay Institute.

Bradley, R. (1978), *The Prehistoric Settlement of Britain*, London: Routledge.

Bradley, R. (1984), *The Social Foundations of Prehistoric Britain: Themes and Variations in the Archaeology of Power*, London: Longman.

Bradley, R. (1992), 'Turning the world – rock carvings and the archaeology of death', in N. Sharples and A. Sheridan (eds), *Vessels for the Ancestors: Essays in Honour of Audrey Henshall*, Edinburgh: Edinburgh University Press, 168–76.

Bradley, R. (1993), *Altering the Earth*, Edinburgh: Society of Antiquaries of Scotland Monograph Series, 8.

Bradley, R. (1998), *The Significance of Monuments*, London: Routledge.

Bradley, R. (2000a), *Tomnaverie Recumbent Stone Circle: Excavation and Field Survey, 2000: Interim Report*, University of Reading, unpublished.

Bradley, R. (2000b), *The Good Stones: A New Investigation of the Clava Cairns*, Edinburgh: Society of Antiquaries of Scotland.

Bradley, R. (2001), 'The birth of architecture', in W. G. Runciman (ed.), *The Origin of Human Social Institutions*, Oxford: Oxford University Press, 69–92.

Bradley, R. (2002), *The Past in Prehistoric Societies*, London: Routledge.

Bradley, R. (2003), 'Neolithic expectations', in I. Armit, E. Murphy, E. Nelis and D. Simpson (eds), *Neolithic Settlement in Ireland and Western Britain*, Oxford: Oxbow, 218–22.

Bradley, R. (2005), *The Moon and the Bonfire: An Investigation of Three Stone Circles in Northeast Scotland*, Edinburgh: Society of Antiquaries of Scotland Monograph.

Bradley, R. and Chapman, R. (1986), 'The nature and development of long-distance relations in the Late Neolithic of Britain and Ireland', in C. Renfrew and J. F. Cherry (eds), *Peer Polity Interaction and Socio-political Change*, Cambridge: Cambridge University Press, 127–36.

Bradley, R and Edmonds, M. (1993), *Interpreting the axe trade: production and exchange in Neolithic Britain*, Cambridge: Cambridge University Press.

Bradley, R., Phillips, T., Richards, C. and Webb, M. (2001), 'Decorating the houses of the dead: incised and pecked motifs in Orkney chambered tombs', *Cambridge Archaeological Journal*, 11: 45–67.

Brewer, W. F. (1995), 'What is recollective memory?', in D. C. Rubin (ed.), *Remembering our Past: Studies in Autobiographical Memory*, Cambridge: Cambridge University Press, 19–66.

Broodbank, C. (2000), *An Island Archaeology of the Early Cyclades*, Cambridge: Cambridge University Press.

Brophy, K. (1999a), 'The cursus monuments of Scotland', in A. Barclay and J. Harding (eds), *Pathways and Ceremonies: The Cursus Monuments of Britain and Ireland*, Oxford: Oxbow,120–9.

Brophy, K. (1999b), *The Cursus Monuments of Scotland*, University of Glasgow: unpublished Ph.D. thesis.

Brophy, K. (2000), 'Water coincidence? Cursus monuments and rivers', in A. Ritchie (ed.), *Neolithic Orkney in its European Context*, Cambridge: McDonald Institute for Archaeological Research, 59–70.

Bryce, J. (1862), 'An account of excavations within the stone circles of Arran', *Proceedings of the Society of Antiquaries of Scotland*, 4: 499–524.

Bryce, T. H. (1901–2), 'On the Cairns of Arran', *Proceedings of the Society of Antiquaries of Scotland*, 36: 74–181.

Bryce, T. H (1902–3), 'On the Cairns of Arran – a record of further explorations during the season of 1902', *Proceedings of the Society of Antiquaries of Scotland*, 37: 36–67.

Bryce, T. H. (1908–9), 'On the Cairns of Arran no. III – with a notice of a megalithic structure at Ardnadam, on the Holy Loch', *Proceedings of the Society of Antiquaries of Scotland*, 43: 337–70.

Bryce, T. H. (1939–40), 'The so-called heel-shaped cairns of Shetland, with remarks on the chambered tombs of Orkney and Shetland', *Proceedings of the Society of Antiquaries of Scotland*, 74: 23–36.

Burgess, C. (1980), *The Age of Stonehenge*, London: Dent.

Burgess, C. and Shennan, S. (1976), 'The Beaker phenomenon: some suggestions', in C. Burgess and R. Miket (eds), *Settlement and Economy in the Third and Second Millennia BC*, 309–31.

Burl, A. (1969), 'Henges: internal features and regional groups', *Archaeological Journal*, 126: 1–28.

Burl, A. (1969–70), 'The recumbent stone circles of north-east Scotland', *Proceedings of the Society of Antiquaries of Scotland*, 102: 56–81.

Burl, A. (1976), *The Stone Circles of the British Isles*, London: Yale University Press.

Burl, A. (1980), 'Machrie Moor, Arran, Argyle, Strathclyde region: stone circles', *Proceedings of the Prehistoric Society*, 46: 365.

Burl, A. (1984), 'Report on the excavation of a Neolithic mound at Boghead, Speymouth Forest, Fochabers, Moray, 1972 and 1974', *Proceedings of the Society of Antiquaries of Scotland*, 114: 35–73.

Burl, A. (1993), *From Carnac to Callanish: the Prehistoric Stone Rows and Avenues of Britain, Ireland and Brittany*, New Haven: Yale University Press.

Burl, A. (1995), *A Guide to the Stone Circles of Britain, Ireland and Brittany*, New Haven: Yale University Press.

Burrow, S. (1997), *The Neolithic Culture of the Isle of Man: A Study of the Sites and Pottery*, BAR British Series 263.

Calder, C. S. T. (1936–7), 'A Neolithic double-chambered cairn of the stalled type and later structures on the Calf of Eday, Orkney', *Proceedings of the Society of Antiquaries of Scotland*, 71: 115–56.

Calder, C. S. T. (1949–50), 'Report on the excavation of a Neolithic temple at Stanydale in the parish of Sanduting, Shetland', *Proceedings of the Society of Antiquaries of Scotland*, 84: 185–205.

Calder, C. S. T. (1955–6), 'Report on the discovery of numerous stone age house-sites in Shetland', *Proceedings of the Society of Antiquaries of Scotland*, 89: 340–97.

Callander, J. G. (1903–4), 'Notice of a stone mould for casting flat bronze axes and bars found in the parish of Insch, Aberdeenshire', *Proceedings of the Society of Antiquaries of Scotland*, 38: 487–505.

Callander, J. G. and Grant, W. G. (1933–4), 'A long stalled chambered cairn or mausoleum (Rousay type), near Midhowe, Rousay, Orkney', *Proceedings of the Society of Antiquaries of Scotland*, 68: 320–50.

Callander, J. G. and Grant, W. G. (1934–5), 'A long stalled cairn, the Knowe of Yarso, in Rousay, Orkney', *Proceedings of the Society of Antiquaries of Scotland*, 69: 325–51.

Callander, J. G. and Grant, W. G. (1935–6), 'A stalled chambered cairn, the Knowe of Ramsay, at Hullion, Rousay, Orkney', *Proceedings of the Society of Antiquaries of Scotland*, 70: 407–419.

Callander, J. G. and Grant, W. G. (1936–7), 'Long stalled cairn at Blackhammer, Rousay, Orkney', *Proceedings of the Society of Antiquaries of Scotland*, 71: 297–308.

Cameron, K. (2002), 'The excavation of Neolithic pits and Iron Age souterrains at Dubton Farm, Brechin, Angus', *Tayside and Fife Archaeological Journal*, 8: 19–76.

Campbell, E. (1996), 'Dunadd (Kilmichael Glassary parish), ?cursus', *Discovery and Excavation in Scotland*: 22.

Campbell, M. and Sandeman, M. L. S. (1961–2), 'Mid Argyll: an archaeological survey', *Proceedings of the Society of Antiquaries of Scotland*, 95: 1–125.

Campbell, M., Scott, J. G. and Piggott, S. (1960–1), 'The Badden cist slab', *Proceedings of the Society of Antiquaries of Scotland*, 94: 46–61.

Campbell, M., Scott, J. G. and Piggott, S. (1963), 'The Badden cist slab', *Proceedings of the Society of Antiquaries of Scotland*, 94: 46–61.

Card, N. and Downes, J. (2000), 'Crossiecrown, Orkney (Kirkwall and St. Ola parish) Neolithic/Bronze Age settlement', *Discovery and Excavation in Scotland*: 64–5.

Carruthers, M. and Richards, C. (2000), 'Stonehall, Orkney (Firth parish), Neolithic settlement', *Discovery and Excavation in Scotland*: 64.

Carsten, J. and Hugh-Jones, S (eds) (1995), *About the House: Levi-Strauss and Beyond*, Cambridge: Cambridge University Press.

Cartwright, K. S. G. and Findlay, W. P. K. (1958), *Decay of Timber and its Prevention*, London: Her Majesty's Stationery Office.

Case, H. (1969), 'Neolithic explanations', *Antiquity*, 43: 176–86.

Case, H. J. (1973), 'A ritual site in north-east Ireland', in G. Daniel and P. Kjaerum (eds), *Megalithic Graves and Ritual*, Moesgard: Jutland Archaeological Society, 173–96.

Childe, V. G. (1931), *Skara Brae: A Pictish Village in Orkney*, London: Kegan Paul, Trench and Trubner and Co.

Childe, V. G. (1935), *The Prehistory of Scotland*, London: Kegan Paul, Trench, Trubner and Co.

Childe, V. G. (1942), *What Happened in History*, Hamondsworth: Penguin.

Childe, V. G. (1949), 'The origin of Neolithic culture in northern Europe', *Antiquity*, 23: 129–35.

Childe, V. G. (1951–2), 'Re-excavation of the chambered cairn of Quoyness, Sanday, on behalf of the ministry of works in 1951–2', *Proceedings of the Society of Antiquaries of Scotland*, 86: 121–39.

Childe, V. G. (1954–6), 'Maes Howe', *Proceedings of the Society of Antiquaries of Scotland*, 88: 155–72.
Childe, V. G. and Grant, W. G. (1938–9), 'A Stone-Age settlement at the Braes of Rinyo, Rousay, Orkney', *Proceedings of the Society of Antiquaries of Scotland*, 78: 6–31.
Childe, V. G. and Grant, W. G. (1946–7), 'A Stone-Age settlement at the Braes of Rinyo, Rousay, Orkney', *Proceedings of the Society of Antiquaries of Scotland*, 81: 16–42.
Church, M. (2002), 'Carbonised plant macrofossils', in K. Cameron, 'The excavation of Neolithic pits and Iron Age souterrains at Dubton Farm, Brechin, Angus', *Tayside and Fife Archaeological Journal*, 8: 19–76 (51–68).
Clark, G. (1977), 'The economic context of dolmens and passage graves in Sweden', in V. Markolic (ed.), *Ancient Europe and the Mediterranean*, Warminster: Amis and Phillips, 35–49.
Clarke, D. L. (1970), *Beaker Pottery of Great Britain and Ireland*, Cambridge: Cambridge University Press.
Clarke, D. V. and Sharples, N. (1985), 'Settlements and subsistence in the third millennium BC', in C. Renfrew (ed.), *The Prehistory of Orkney*, Edinburgh: Edinburgh University Press, 54–82.
Clarke, D. V. (2003), 'Once upon a time Skara Brae was unique', in I. Armit, E. Murphy, E. Nelis and D. Simpson (eds), *Neolithic Settlement in Ireland and Western Britain*, Oxford: Oxbow, 84–92.
Cleal, R. M. J., Walker, K. E. and Montague, R. (1995), *Stonehenge in its Landscape: Twentieth-Century Excavations*, London: English Heritage.
Clough, T. H. M. and Cummins, W. A. (1988), *Stone Axe Studies*, London: Council for British Archaeology.
Clouston, J. S. (1884–5), 'Notice of the excavation of a chambered cairn of the Stone Age, at Unstan, in the Loch of Stennis, Orkney', *Proceedings of the Society of Antiquaries of Scotland*, 19: 341–5.
Clutton-Brock, J. (1979), 'Report of the mammalian remains other than rodents from Quanterness', in C. Renfrew (ed.), *Investigations in Orkney*, London: Thames and Hudson, 112–134.
Coles, G. M. (1993), 'Cnoc an Tursa (Uig parish): excavation', *Discovery and Excavation in Scotland*: 110–11.
Coles, G. M. and Rees, T. (1994), 'Cnoc an Tursa (Uig parish): excavation', *Discovery and Excavation in Scotland*: 96.
Coles, J. M. (1966–7), 'Further discoveries at Brackmont Mill, Brackmont Farm at Tentsmuir, Fife', *Proceedings of the Society of Antiquaries of Scotland*, 99: 60–92.
Coles, J. M. (1971), 'The early settlement of Scotland: excavations at Morton, Fife', *Proceedings of the Prehistoric Society*, 37: 284–366.
Coles, J. M. and Simpson, D. D. A. (1965), 'The excavation of a Neolithic round barrow at Pitnacree, Perthshire, Scotland', *Proceedings of the Prehistoric Society*, 31: 34–57.
Collins, A. E. P. (1976), 'Dooey's cairn, Ballymacaldrack, County Antrim', *Ulster Journal of Archaeology*, 39: 1–7.
Connerton, P. (1989), *How societies remember*, Cambridge: Cambridge University Press.
Cook, M. (2000), 'Excavation of Neolithic and Bronze Age settlement at Lamb's Nursery, Dalkeith, Midlothian', *Proceedings of the Society of Antiquaries of Scotland*, 130: 93–114.
Cooney, G. (1986), 'Irish Neolithic settlement and its European context', *The Neolithic of Europe: the World Archaeological Congress* (University of Southampton).
Cooney, G. (1997), 'Images of settlement and the landscape in the Neolithic', in P. Topping (ed.), *Neolithic Landscapes*, Oxford: Oxbow, 23–31.
Cooney, G. (2000a), *Landscapes of Neolithic Ireland*, London: Routledge.
Cooney, G. (2000b), 'Coping with death, changing the landscape: people, place and histories in the Irish Neolithic', in A. Ritchie (ed.), *Neolithic Orkney in its European Context*, Cambridge: McDonald Institute for Archaeological Research, chp. 21.
Cooney, G. (2003), 'Rooted or routed? Landscapes of Neolithic settlement in Ireland', in I. Armit, E. Murphy, E. Nelis and D. Simpson (eds), *Neolithic Settlement in Ireland and Western Britain*, Oxford: Oxbow, 47–55.
Coppock, J. T. (1976), *An Agricultural Atlas of Scotland*, Edinburgh: John Donald.
Corcoran, J. X. W. P. (1960), 'The Carlingford Culture', *Proceedings of the Prehistoric Society*, 26: 89–148.
Corcoran, J. X. W. P. (1964–6), 'Excavation of three chambered cairns at Loch Calder, Caithness', *Proceedings of the Society of Antiquaries of Scotland*, 101: 1–76.

Corcoran, J. X. W. P. (1969a), 'Excavation of two chambered cairns at Mid Gleniron Farm, Glenluce, Wigtownshire', *Transactions of the Dumfries and Galloway Natural History and Antiquarian Society*, 41: 29–90.

Corcoran, J. X. W. P. (1969b), 'The Cotswold-Severn group', *Megalithic Enquiries in the West of Britain*, Liverpool: Liverpool University Press, 13–72, 73–106.

Corcoran, J. X. W. P. (1969c), 'Excavation of two burial cairns at Mid Gleniron Farm, Glenluce, Wigtownshire', *Transactions of the Dumfries and Galloway Natural History and Antiquarian Society*, 41: 91–9.

Corcoran, J. X. W. P. (1972), 'Multi-period construction and the origins of the chambered long cairn in western Britain and Ireland', in F. Lynch and C. Burgess (eds), *Prehistoric Man in Wales and the West*, Bath: Adams and Dart, 31–64.

Cormack, W. F. (1962–3), 'Burial site at Kirkburn, Lockerbie', *Proceedings of the Society of Antiquaries of Scotland*, 96: 107–35.

Cormack, W. F. (1986), 'Glecknabae (N. Bute): Mesolithic core', *Discovery and Excavation in Scotland*: 26.

Corrie, J. M. (1928–9), 'A short cist at West Puldrite, in the parish of Evie and Rendall, Orkney', *Proceedings of the Society of Antiquaries of Scotland*, 63: 190–5.

Cowie, T. G. (1993), 'A survey of the Neolithic pottery of eastern and central Scotland', *Proceedings of the Society of Antiquaries of Scotland*, 123: 13–42.

Cowie, T. G. (1995), 'Neolithic pottery', in J. Kendrick (ed.), 'Excavation of a Neolithic enclosure and an Iron Age settlement at Douglasmuir, Angus', *Proceedings of the Society of Antiquaries of Scotland*, 125: 29–67 (44–7).

Cowie, T. G. (1996), 'Torrs Warren, Luce Sands, Galloway: a report on archaeological and palaeoecological investigations undertaken in 1977 and 1979', *Transactions of the Dumfries and Galloway Natural History and Archaeology Society*, 71: 11–106.

Cowie, T. and MacSween, A. (1999), 'Grooved Ware from Scotland: a review', in R. Cleal and A. MacSween (eds), *Grooved Ware in Britain and Ireland*, Oxford: Oxbow, 48–65.

Cowley, D. C. and Brophy, K. (2001), 'The impact of aerial photography across the lowlands of Scotland', *Transactions of the Dumfries and Galloway Natural History and Archaeology Society*, 75: 47–72.

Craw, J. H. (1928–9), 'On a jet necklace from a cist at Poltalloch, Argyll', *Proceedings of the Society of Antiquaries of Scotland*, 63: 154–89.

Craw, J. H. (1929–30), 'Excavations at Dunadd and at other sites on the Poltalloch Estates, Argyll', *Proceedings of the Society of Antiquaries of Scotland*, 64: 111–46.

Craw, C. (1930–1), 'Further excavations of cairns at Poltalloch, Argyll', *Proceedings of the Society of Antiquaries of Scotland*, 65: 269–80.

Creegan, E. R. (1981), 'Excavations on the cist cemetery at Poltalloch, Argyll, 1960–2', *Glasgow Archaeological Journal*, 8: 19–28.

Cressey, M. (1995), 'Charcoals', in J. Kendrick (ed.), 'Excavation of a Neolithic enclosure and an Iron Age settlement at Douglasmuir, Angus', *Proceedings of the Society of Antiquaries of Scotland*, 125: 29–67 (51).

Cummings, V. (2003), 'Building from memory', in H. Williams, *Archaeologies of Remembrance: Death and Memory in Past Societies*, London: Kluwer Academic/Plenum, 25–43.

Cummings, V. and Whittle, A. (2004a), *Places of Special Virtue: Megaliths in the Neolithic Landscapes of Wales*, Oxford: Oxbow.

Cummings, V. and Whittle, A. (2004b), 'Tombs with a view: landscape, monuments and trees', *Antiquity*, 77: 255–66.

Cunliffe, B. (2001), *Facing the Ocean*, Oxford: Oxford University Press.

Daniels, S. (1988), 'The political iconography of woodland in later Georgian England', in D. Cosgrove and S. Daniels (eds), *The Iconography of Landscape: Essays in the Symbolic Representation, Design and Use of Past Environments*, Cambridge: Cambridge University Press, 43–82.

Darvill, T. (1995), *Billown Neolithic Landscape Project, Isle of Man*, Bournemouth University: School of Conservation Sciences, Research Report 1.

Darvill, T. (1998), *Billown Neolithic Landscape Project, Isle of Man*, Bournemouth University: School of Conservation Sciences, Research Report 4.

Darvill, T. (1999), *Billown Neolithic Landscape Project, Isle of Man*, Bournemouth University: School of Conservation Sciences, Research Report 5.
Darvill, T. (2000), 'Neolithic Mann in context', in A. Ritchie (ed.), *Neolithic Orkney in its European Context*, Cambridge: McDonald Institute for Archaeological Research, chp. 32.
Darvill, T. (2002), 'Billown Down', *Archaeometry*, 44: 42.
Darvill, T. (2003), 'Billown and the Neolithic of the Isle of Man, in I. Armit, E. Murphy, E. Nelis and D. Simpson (eds), *Neolithic Settlement in Ireland and Western Britain*, Oxford: Oxbow, 112–19.
Darvill, T. and Thomas, J. (eds) (2001), *Neolithic Enclosures in Atlantic Northwest Europe*, Oxford: Oxbow.
Davey, P. (ed.) (1999), *Recent Archaeological Research on the Isle of Man*, British Archaeological Reports, 278.
Davey, P. and Innes, J. (2003), 'The Early Neolithic and the Manx environment', in I. Armit, E. Murphy, E. Nelis and D. Simpson (eds), *Neolithic Settlement in Ireland and Western Britain*, Oxford: Oxbow, 20–7.
David, A., Cole, M., Housley, T., Linford, N., Linford, P. and Martin, L. (2004), 'A rival to Stonehenge? Geophysical survey at Stanton Drew, England', *Antiquity*, 78: 341–58.
Davidson, J. L. and Henshall, A. S. (1982), 'Staney Hill (Birsay and Harray parish): long cairn', *Discovery and Excavation in Scotland*: 17–18.
Davidson, J. L. and Henshall, A. S. (1989), *The Chambered Cairns of Orkney: An Inventory of the Structures and their Contents*, Edinburgh: Edinburgh University Press.
Davidson, J. L. and Henshall, A. S. (1991), *The Chambered Cairns of Caithness: An Inventory of the Structures and their Contents*, Edinburgh: Edinburgh University Press.
Davidson, J. L. and Henshall, A. S. (1995), *The Chambered Cairns of Sutherland: An Inventory of the Structures and their Contents*, Edinburgh: Edinburgh University Press.
Davidson, J. M. (1951–2), 'Report on some discoveries at Glenluce Sands, Wigtownshire', *Proceedings of the Society of Antiquaries*, 86: 43–69.
Davies, M. (1946), 'The diffusion and distribution pattern of the megalithic monuments of the Irish Sea and north channel coastlands', *Antiquaries Journal*, 26: 38–60.
Davies, D. (1988), 'The evocative symbolism of trees', in D. Cosgrove and S. Daniels (eds), *The Iconography of Landscape*, Cambridge: Cambridge University Press, 32–42.
De Boer, W. (1997), 'Ceremonial centres from the Cayapas (Esmereldas, Ecuador) to Chillicothe (Ohio, USA)', *Cambridge Archaeological Journal*, 7: 225–53.
De Valera, R. (1960), 'The court cairns of Ireland', *Proceedings of the Royal Irish Academy*, 60: 9–140.
Denison, S. (1997), 'News', *British Archaeology*, 29: 5.
DES (1992), 'Mumrills (Polmont parish)', *Discovery and Excavation in Scotland*: 11.
DES (2003a), 'Pitnacree, Perth and Kinross', *Discovery and Excavation in Scotland*: 167.
DES (2003b), 'North Mains henge (burial A)', *Discovery and Excavation in Scotland*: 167.
Directors of the Chamber of Commerce and Manufacture in Glasgow (1792), *Prospectus of the Advantages to be Derived from the Crinan Canal*, Glasgow: William Reid and Co.
Donnelly, M., McLellan, K. and Sneddon, D. (2000), *Arran Ring Main Water Pipeline*, Glasgow: Glasgow University Archaeological Research Division.
Douglas, M. [1966] (2000), *Purity and Danger: An Analysis of Concepts of Pollution and Taboo*, London: Routledge.
Downes, J. and Richards, C. (1993), 'The fieldwalking exercise', in G. J. Barclay and C. J. Russell-White, 'Excavations in the ceremonial complex of the fourth to third millennium BC at Balfarg/Balbirnie, Glenrothes, Fife', *Proceedings of the Society of Antiquaries of Scotland*, 123: 43–110 (162–5).
Downes, J. and Richards, C. (1998), 'Crossiecrown, Quanterness (Kirkwall and St Ola parish) Neolithic/Bronze Age settlement', *Discovery and Excavation in Scotland*: 70–1.
Dunne, C. M. (2003), 'Neolithic structure at Drummenny Lower, Co. Donegal: an environmental perspective', in I. Armit, E. Murphy, E. Nelis and D. Simpson (eds), *Neolithic Settlement in Ireland and Western Britain*, Oxford: Oxbow,164–71.
Durno, S. E. (1956), 'Pollen analysis of peat deposits in Scotland', *Scottish Geographical Magazine*, 72: 177–87.

Durno, S. E. (1976), 'Postglacial change in vegetation', in E. L. Birse and J. S. Robertson (eds), *Plant Communities and Soils of Lowland and Southern Upland Regions of Scotland*, Aberdeen: University of Aberdeen, 20–36.

Edmonds, M. (1995), *Stone Tools and Society: Working Stone In and Bronze Age Britain*, London: B. T. Batsford.

Edmonds, M. (1999), *Ancestral Geographies of the Neolithic*, London: Routledge.

Edmonds, M., Sheridan, A. and Tipping, R. (1993), 'Survey and Excavation at Creag na Caillich, Killin, Perthshire', *Proceedings of the Society of Antiquaries of Scotland*, 122: 77–112.

Edwards, K. J. (2004), 'People, environmental impacts and the changing landscape of Neolithic and Bronze Age times', in I. A. G. Shepherd and G. J. Barclay, *Scotland in Ancient Europe*, Edinburgh: Society of Antiquaries of Scotland, 55–69.

Edwards, K. J. and Hirons, K. R. (1984), 'Cereal pollen grains in pre-elm decline deposits: implications for the earliest agriculture in Britain and Ireland', *Journal of Archaeological Science*, 11: 71–80.

Edwards, K. J. and McIntosh, C. J. (1988), 'Improving the detection rate of cereal-type pollen grains from Ulmus decline and earlier deposits from Scotland', *Pollen et Spores*, 30: 179–88.

Edwards, K. J. and Ralston, I. (1984), 'Postglacial hunter-gatherers and the vegetation history of Scotland', *Proceedings of the Society of Antiquaries of Scotland*, 114: 15–35.

Edwards, K. and Whittington, G. (1997), 'Vegetation change', in K. J. Edwards and I. B. M. Ralston (eds), *Scotland: Environment and Archaeology, 8000 BC–AD 1000*, Chichester: Wiley, 63–82.

Ellis, C. (2000), 'Upper Largie, Argyll and Bute (Kilmartin parish): timber circle; sub-rectangular enclosure; cist', *Discovery and Excavation in Scotland*: 16.

Erdoğu, B. (2003), 'Visualizing Neolithic landscape: the early settled communities in Western Anatolia and eastern Aegean islands', *European Journal of Archaeology*, 6: 7–23.

Evans, C., Pollard, J. and Knight, M. (1999), 'Life in woods: tree-throws, "settlement" and forest cognition', *Oxford Journal of Archaeology*, 18 (3): 241–54.

Evans, J. D. (1973), 'Islands as laboratories for the study of culture process', in C. Renfrew (ed.), *The Explanation of Culture Change: Models in Prehistory*, London: Duckworth, 517–20.

Evens, E. D., Grinsell, L. V., Piggott, S. and Wallis, F. S. (1962), 'Fourth report of the sub-committee of the south-western group of museums and art galleries on the petrological identification of stone axes', *Proceedings of the Prehistoric Society*, 28: 209–65.

Fairbairn, A. S. (ed.) (2000), *Plants in Neolithic Britain and Beyond*, Oxford: Oxbow Books.

Fairhurst, H. (1977), 'Shiskine, stone circle (four poster)', *Discovery and Excavation in Scotland*: 9.

Fairweather, A. D. and Ralston, I. B. M. (1993), 'A Neolithic timber hall at Balbridie, Grampian Region, Scotland: the building, the date, the plant macrofossils', *Antiquity*, 67: 313–23.

Fitzpatrick, A. (2003), 'The Amesbury Archer', *Current Archaeology*, 184: 146–52.

Fleming, A. (1972), 'Vision and design', *MAN*, *7*: 57–73.

Fojut, N. (1993), *A Guide to Prehistoric and Viking Shetland*, Lerwick: *Shetland Times.*

Forty, A. and Küchler, S. (eds) (1999), *The Art of Forgetting*, Oxford: Berg.

Fowell, K. (2002), 'The Sills (Pettinain parish)', *Discovery and Excavation in Scotland*: 114.

Fraser, D. (1983), *Land and Society in Neolithic Orkney*, BAR British Series 117.

French, C., Lewis, H., Allen, M. J., Scaife, R. G. and Green, M. (2003), 'Archaeological and palaeo-environmental investigations of the Upper Allen Valley, Cranbourne Chase, Dorset (1998–2000): a new model of the Earlier Holocene landscape development', *Proceedings of the Prehistoric Society*, 69: 201–34.

George, D. E. R. (1991), *Balinese Ritual Theatre*, Cambridge: Chadwick-Healey.

Gerritsen, F. (1999), 'To build or to abandon. The cultural biography of late prehistoric houses and farmsteads in the southern Netherlands', *Archaeological Dialogues*, 6 (2): 78–114.

Giambelli, R. A. (1998), 'The coconut, the body and the human being: metaphors of life and growth in Nusa Penida and Bali', in L. Rival (ed.), *The Social Life of Trees: Anthropological Perspectives on Tree Symbolism*, Oxford: Berg, 133–58.

Gibson, A. (1986), *Neolithic and Early Bronze Age Pottery*, Risborough: Shire.

Gibson, A. (1998), *Stonehenge and Timber Circles*, Stroud: Tempus.

Gibson, A. (2002), 'The Later Neolithic palisaded enclosures of Britain', in A. Gibson (ed.), *Behind Wooden Walls: Neolithic Palisaded Enclosures in Europe*, BAR International Series 1,013, 5–23.
Gifford, E. and Gifford, J. (2004), 'The Ferriby ship experiment', *Current Archaeology*, 191: 499–505.
Gorman, F., Lambie, E. and Bowd, C. (1993a), 'Machrie, Arran (Kilmory parish): knapping site', *Discovery and Excavation in Scotland*: 79.
Gorman, F., Lambie, E. and Bowd, C. (1993b), 'Machrie, Arran (Kilmory parish): fieldwalking', *Discovery and Excavation in Scotland*: 80.
Gorman, F., Lambie, E. and Bowd, C. (1993c), 'Machrie, Arran (Kilmory parish): stone axe', *Discovery and Excavation in Scotland*: 79.
Gorman, F., Murray, B. and Lambie, E. (1995), 'Machrie, Arran (Kilmory parish): Mesolithic site', *Discovery and Excavation in Scotland*: 72.
Greenwell, W. (1864–66), 'An account of excavations in cairns near Crinan', *Proceedings of the Society of Antiquaries of Scotland*, 6: 336–51.
Greig, M. K., Gerig, C., Shepherd, A. N. and Shepherd, I. A. G. (1989), 'A beaker cist at Chapelden, Tore of Troup, Aberdour, Banff and Buchan District, with a note on the orientation of beaker burials in northeast Scotland', *Proceedings of the Society of Antiquaries of Scotland*, 119: 73–82.
Groeger, J. A. (1997), *Memory and Remembering: Everyday Memory in Context*, Harlow: Addison Wesley Longman.
Grogan, E. (1996), 'Neolithic houses in Ireland', in T. Darvill and J. Thomas (eds), *Neolithic Houses in Northwest Europe and Beyond*, Oxford: Oxbow, 41–60.
Grogan, E. (2002), 'Neolithic houses in Ireland: a broader perspective', *Antiquity*, 76: 517–25.
Guttmann, E. (2005), 'Midden cultivation in prehistoric Britain: arable crops in gardens', *World Archaeology*, 37 (2): 223–38.
Haggarty, A. (1991), 'Machrie Moor, Arran: recent excavations at two stone circles', *Proceedings of the Society of Antiquaries of Scotland*, 121: 51–94.
Haldane, A. R. B. (1997), 'The drove roads of Scotland', Edinburgh: Birlinn.
Halliday, S. (2002), 'Excavations at a Neolithic enclosure at Castle Menzies, Aberfeldy, Perthshire', *Tayside and Fife Archaeological Journal*, 8: 10–18.
Hanson, W. and Maxwell, G. (1983), *Rome's Northwest Frontier: The Antonine Wall*, Edinburgh: Edinburgh University Press.
Harding, J. (2000), 'Later Neolithic ceremonial centres, ritual and pilgrimage: the monument complex of Thornborogh, North Yorkshire', in A. Ritchie (ed.), *Neolithic Orkney in its European Context*, Cambridge: McDonald Institute for Archaeological Research, chp. 2.
Harding, J. (2003), *The Henge Monuments of the British Isles*, Stroud: Tempus.
Hedges, J. W. (1984), *Tomb of the Eagles: A Window on Stone Age Tribal Britain*, London: Murray.
Henshall, A. S. (1963), *The Chambered Tombs of Scotland*, Edinburgh: Edinburgh University Press.
Henshall, A. S. (1972), *The Chambered Tombs of Scotland*, Edinburgh: Edinburgh University Press.
Henshall, A. S. (1983), 'The Neolithic pottery from Easterton of Roseisle', in A. O'Connor and D. V. Clarke (eds), *From the Stone Age to the 'Forty-Five'*, Edinburgh: John Donald, 19–44.
Henshall, A. (1993), 'The Grooved Ware', in G. J. Barclay and C. J. Russell-White, 'Excavations in the ceremonial complex of the fourth to third millennium BC at Balfarg/Balbirnie, Glenrothes, Fife', *Proceedings of the Society of Antiquaries of Scotland*, 123: 43–110 (94–108).
Henshall, A. S. and Ritchie, J. N. G. (1995), *The Chambered Cairns of Sutherland: An inventory of the Structures and their Contents*, Edinburgh: Edinburgh University Press.
Henshall, A. S. and Ritchie, J. N. G. (2001), *The Chambered Cairns of the Central Highlands: An Inventory of the Structures and their Contents*, Edinburgh: Edinburgh University Press.
Henshall, A. S. and Wallace, J. C. (1962–3), 'The excavation of a chambered cairn at Embo, Sutherland', *Proceedings of the Society of Antiquaries of Scotland*, 96: 9–36.
Herne, A. (1988), 'A time and a place for the Grimston bowl', in J. C.Barrett and I. A. Kinnes (eds), *The Archaeology of Context in the Neolithic and Bronze Age: Recent Trends*, Sheffield: University of Sheffield, 9–29.
Hodder, I. (1990), *The Domestication of Europe*, Oxford: Blackwell.

Hodder, I. (1994), 'Architecture and Meaning: The Example of Neolithic Houses and Tombs', in M. Parker Pearson and C. Richards (eds), *Architecture and Order: Approaches to Social Space*, London: Routledge, 73–86.

Hodder, I. (1998), 'The domus: some problems reconsidered', in M. Edmonds and C. Richards (eds), *Understanding the Neolithic of North-west Europe*, Glasgow: Cruithne Press, 84–101.

Hodder, I. and Shand, P. (1988), 'The Haddenham long barrow: an interim statement', *Antiquity*, 62: 349–53.

Holtorf, C. (2003), 'Dyster star dősen', in H. Williams, *Archaeologies of Remembrance: Death and Memory in Past Societies*, London: Kluwer Academic/Plenum, 281–9.

Howell, S. (1995), 'The Lio house: building, category, idea, value', in J. Carsten and S. Hugh-Jones (eds), *About the House: Levi-Strauss and Beyond*, Cambridge: Cambridge University Press, 149–69.

Hughes, I. (1988), 'Megaliths: space, time and the landscape – a view from the Clyde', *Scottish Archaeological Review*, 5: 41–58.

Hulme, P. D. and Shirriffs, J. (1985), 'Pollen analysis of a radiocarbon-dated core from North Mains, Strathallan, Perthshire', *Proceedings of the Society of Antiquaries of Scotland*, 115: 105–13.

Idle, E. T. and Martin, J. (1975), 'The vegetation and land use history of Torrs Warren, Wigtownshire', *Transactions of the Dumfries and Galloway Natural History and Archaeology Society*, 51: 1–11.

Ingold, T. (2000), *The Perception of the Environment*, London: Routledge.

Johnston, D. A. (1997), 'Biggar Common, 1987–1993: an early prehistoric funerary and domestic landscape in Clydesdale, South Lanarkshire', *Proceedings of the Society of Antiquaries of Scotland*, 127: 185–253.

Jones, A. (1997), 'The ceramics', in T. Pollard, 'Excavation of a Neolithic settlement and ritual complex at Beckton Farm, Lockerbie, Dumfries and Galloway', *Proceedings of the Society of Antiquaries of Scotland*, 127: 69–121 (89–95).

Jones, A. (1998), 'Where eagles dare: landscape, animals and the Neolithic of Orkney', *Journal of Material Culture*, 3 (3): 301–24.

Jones, A. (1999), 'Local colour: megalithic architecture and colour symbolism in Neolithic Arran', *Oxford Journal of Archaeology*, 18 (4): 339–50.

Jones, O. and Cloke, P. (2002), *Tree Cultures*, Oxford: Berg.

Jordan, D. (1995), 'The palaeochannel', in J. Kendrick (ed.), 'Excavation of a Neolithic enclosure and an Iron Age settlement at Douglasmuir, Angus', *Proceedings of the Society of Antiquaries of Scotland*, 125: 29–67 (43–4).

Keen, I. (1990), 'Ecological community and species attributes in Yolngu religious symbolism', in R. G. Willis (ed.), *Signifying Animals: Human Meaning in the Natural World*, London: Unwin Hyman, 85–102.

Kendrick, J. (ed.) (1995), 'Excavation of a Neolithic enclosure and an Iron Age settlement at Douglasmuir, Angus', *Proceedings of the Society of Antiquaries of Scotland*, 125: 29–67.

Kiely, J. (2003), 'A Neolithic house at Cloghers, Co. Kerry', in I. Armit, E. Murphy, E. Nelis and D. Simpson (eds), *Neolithic Settlement in Ireland and Western Britain*, Oxford: Oxbow, 182–7.

Kinnes, I. (1984), 'Microliths and megaliths: monumental origins on the Atlantic fringe', in G. Burenhult (ed.), *The Archaeology of Carrowmore, Co. Sligo*, Stockholm: Institute of Archaeology, 367–7.

Kinnes, I. (1985), 'Circumstance not context: the Neolithic of Scotland as seen from the outside', *Proceedings of the Society of Antiquaries of Scotland*, 115: 15–57.

Kinnes, I. (1992a), *Non-megalithic Long Barrows and Allied Structures in the British Neolithic*, British Museum Occasional Paper 52.

Kinnes, I. (1992b), 'Balnagowan and after: the context of non-megalithic mortuary sites in Scotland', in N. Sharples and A. Sheridan, *Vessels for the Ancestors: Essays in Honour of Audrey Henshall*, Edinburgh: Edinburgh University Press, 83–103.

Küchler, S. (1987), 'Malangan: art and memory in a Melanesian society', *Man*, 22: 238–55.

Küchler, S. (1999), 'The place of memory', in A. Forty and S. Küchler, *The Art of Forgetting*, Oxford: Berg, 53–72.

Lacaille, A. D. (1934–5), 'The small flint knives of Orkney', *Proceedings of the Society of Antiquaries of Scotland*, 69: 251–2.

Lacaille, A. D. (1954), *The Stone Age in Scotland*, Oxford: Oxford University.

Lane, A. and Campbell, E. (2000), *Dunadd: An Early Dalriadic Capital*, Oxford: Oxbow.

Lelong, O., Barrowman, C. and Donnelly, M. (1999), 'Carmichael estate', *Discovery and Excavation in Scotland*: 82.

Lelong, O. and Pollard, T. (1998), 'The excavation and survey of prehistoric enclosures at Blackshouse Burn, Lanarkshire', *Proceedings of the Society of Antiquaries of Scotland*, 128: 13–53.

Lethbridge, T. C. (1952), *Boats and Boatmen*, London: Thames and Hudson.

Lievers, M., Roberts, J. and Peterson, R. (2000), 'The Cairn at East Finnercy, Dunecht, Aberdeenshire', *Proceedings of the Society of Antiquaries of Scotland*, 130: 183–95.

Logue, P. (2003), 'Excavations at Thornhill, Co. Londonderry', in I. Armit, E. Murphy, E. Nelis and D. Simpson (eds), *Neolithic Settlement in Ireland and Western Britain*, Oxford: Oxbow, 149–55.

Loney, H. and MacGregor, G. (1997), *Excavation at Kilcoy South, Chambered Cairn*, Glasgow: Glasgow University Archaeology and Research Division.

Longden, G. (2003), 'Iconoclasm, belief and memory in Medieval Wales', in H. Williams (ed.), *Archaeologies of Remembrance: Death and Memory in Past Societies*, London: Kluwer Academic/ Plenum, 171–92.

Loveday, R. and Petchey, M. (1982), 'Oblong ditches: a discussion and some new evidence', *Aerial Archaeology*, 8: 17–24.

MacArthur, J. (1861), *The Antiquities of Arran with a Historical Sketch of the Island*, Glasgow.

MacSween, A. (1992), Orcadian Grooved Ware, in N. Sharples and A. Sheridan (eds), *Vessels for the Ancestors: Essays in Honour of Audrey Henshall*, Edinburgh: Edinburgh University Press, 259–71.

MacFadzean, H., MacFadzean, M., and MacFadzean, D. (1984a), 'Broadfield Farm (Wandel parish)', *Discovery and Excavation in Scotland*: 28.

MacFadzean, H., MacFadzean, M., and MacFadzean, D. (1984b), 'Lamington quarry (Wandel parish)', *Discovery and Excavation in Scotland*: 28.

MacFadzean, H., MacFadzean, M., and MacFadzean, D. (1984c), 'Thankerton (Covington parish)', *Discovery and Excavation in Scotland*: 28.

MacSween, A. (1995), 'Grooved Ware from Scotland: aspects of decoration', in I. Kinnes and G. Varndell (eds), *Unbaked Urns of Rudely Shape: Essays on British and Irish Pottery for Ian Longworth*, Oxford: Oxbow Monograph 55, 41–48.

Malone, C. (2001), *Neolithic Britain and Ireland*, Stroud: Tempus.

Manby, T. G. (1965), 'The distribution of rough-out "Cumbrian" stone axes', *Transactions of the Cumberland and Westmorland Antiquarian and Archaeology Society*, 65: 1–37.

Manby, T. G. (1970), 'Long barrows of northern England; structural and dating evidence', *Scottish Archaeological Forum*, 2: 1–28.

Mapleton, R. J. (1869–70), 'Report on Prehistoric remains in the neighbourhood of the Crinan Canal, Argyllshire', *Journal of the Ethnological Society London*, 2.

Marsden, P. (1997), *Ships and Shipwrecks*, London: English Heritage.

Marshall, D. N. (1977–8), 'Excavations at Auchategan, Glendaruel, Argyll', *Proceedings of the Society of Antiquaries of Scotland*, 109: 36–74.

Marshall, D. N. and Taylor, I. D. (1976–7), 'The Excavation of the Chambered Cairn at Glenvoidean, Isle of Bute', *Proceedings of the Society of Antiquaries of Scotland*, 109: 1–39.

Marwick, E. W. (1975–6), 'The Stone of Odin', in J. N. G. Ritchie, 'The Stones of Stenness, Orkney', *Proceedings of the Society of Antiquaries of Scotland*, 107: 1–60 (28–34).

Marwick, H. (1927–8), 'Cist burials in Holm, Orkney', *Proceedings of the Society of Antiquaries of Scotland*, 62: 263–8.

Masters, L. (1973a), 'The Lochhill long cairn', *Antiquity*, 47: 96–100.

Masters, L. (1973b), 'Slewcairn', *Discovery and Excavation in Scotland*: 31.

Masters, L. (1974), 'Slewcairn', *Discovery and Excavation in Scotland*: 43–4.

Masters, L. (1975), 'Slewcairn', *Discovery and Excavation in Scotland*: 27–8.

Masters, L. (1976), 'Slewcairn', *Discovery and Excavation in Scotland*: 39.

Masters, L. (1977), 'Slewcairn', *Discovery and Excavation in Scotland*: 20.

Masters, L. (1978), 'Slewcairn', *Discovery and Excavation in Scotland*: 5.

Masters, L. (1979), 'Slewcairn', *Discovery and Excavation in Scotland*: 6.

Masters, L. (1980), 'Slewcairn', *Discovery and Excavation in Scotland*: 4.

Masters, L. (1987), 'Chambered tombs and non-megalithic barrows in Britain', in J. D. Evans, B. Cunliffe and C. Renfrew (eds), *Antiquity and Man: Essays in Honour of Glyn Daniel*, London: Thames and Hudson, 161–77.

Masters, L. (1997), 'The excavation and restoration of the Camster Long chambered cairn, Caithness, Highland 1967–80', *Proceedings of the Society of Antiquaries of Scotland*, 127: 123–83.

McAdam, E. (1974), *Some Aspects of Early Bronze Age Cists in Scotland*, Department of Archaeology, University of Edinburgh: unpublished MA dissertation.

McCarroll, D., Garrard, L. and Dackombe, R. (1990), 'Lateglacial and Postglacial environmental history', in V. Robinson and D. McCarroll (eds), *Isle of Man: Celebrating a Sense of Place*, Liverpool: Liverpool University Press, 55–76.

McCartan, S. B. (1999), 'The Manx Early Mesolithic: a story in stone', in P. Davey (ed.), *Recent Archaeological Research on the Isle of Man*, British Archaeological Reports, 278 (5–11).

McCormick, F. and Buckland, P. C. (1997), 'Faunal change', in K. J. Edwards and I. Ralston (eds), *Scotland: Environment and Archaeology, 8000 BC–AD 1000*, Chichester: John Wiley and Sons, chp. 6.

McCullagh, R. (1988–9), 'Excavations at Newton, Islay', *Glasgow Archaeological Journal*, 15: 23–52.

McGrail, S. (1998), *Ancient Boats in North-West Europe*, London: Longman.

McInnes, J. (1963–4), 'The Neolithic and Early Bronze Age pottery from Luce Sands, Wigtownshire', *Proceedings of the Society of Antiquaries*, 97: 40–81.

McSparron, C. (2003), 'The excavation of a Neolithic house in Enagh Townland, Co. Derry', in I. Armit, E. Murphy, E. Nelis and D. Simpson (eds), *Neolithic Settlement in Ireland and Western Britain*, Oxford: Oxbow, 172–5.

Megaw, J. V. S. and Simpson, D. D. A. (1979), *An Introduction to British Prehistory: From the Arrival of Homo Sapiens to the Claudian Invasion*, Leicester: Leicester University Press.

Meillassoux, C. (1972), 'From reproduction to production', *Economy and Society*, 1: 93–105.

Mellars, P. (1987), *Excavations on Oronsay: Prehistoric Human Ecology on a Small Island*, Edinburgh: Edinburgh University Press.

Mercer, J. (1967–8), 'Stone tools from a washing-limit deposit of the highest Post-Glacial transgression, Lealt Bay, Isle of Jura', *Proceedings of the Society of Antiquaries of Scotland*, 100: 1–46.

Mercer, J. (1972–4), 'Glenbatrick waterhole, a microlithic site on the Isle of Jura', *Proceedings of the Society of Antiquaries of Scotland*, 105: 9–32.

Mercer, J. (1978–80), 'Lussa Wood 1: the Late Glacial and Early Post-Glacial occupation', *Proceedings of the Society of Antiquaries of Scotland*, 110: 1–32.

Mercer, R. J. (1977–8), 'The excavation of a Late Neolithic Henge-type enclosure at Balfarg, Markinch, Fife, Scotland', *Proceedings of the Society of Antiquaries of Scotland*, 111: 63–171.

Mercer, R. J. (1981), 'Excavations at Carn Brea, Illogan, Cornwall, 1970–3: a Neolithic fortified complex of the third millennium BC', *Cornish Archaeology*, 20: 1–204.

Mercer, R. J. (1987a), *Archaeological Field Survey in Northern Scotland: Volume III 1982–3*, University of Edinburgh Occasional Paper No. III.

Mercer, R. J. (1987b), 'The excavation of a cist-group at Upper Largie quarry', *Glasgow Archaeological Journal*, 14: 25–38.

Mercer, R. J. (1992), 'Cumultative cairn construction and cultural continuity in Caithness and Orkney', in N. Sharples and A. Sheridan (eds), *Vessels for the Ancestors: Essays in Honour of Audrey Henshall*, Edinburgh: Edinburgh University Press, 49–61.

Mercer, R. J. (2003), 'The early farming settlement of south western England in the Neolithic', in I. Armit, E. Murphy, E. Nelis and D. Simpson (eds), *Neolithic Settlement in Ireland and Western Britain*, Oxford: Oxbow, 56–70.

Mercer, R. J., Barclay, G. J., Jordan, D. and Russell-White, C. J. (1988), 'The Neolithic Henge-type enclosure at Balfarg: a re-assessment of the evidence for an incomplete ditch circuit', *Proceedings of the Society of Antiquaries of Scotland*, 118: 61–7.

Miller, J. and Ramsay, S. (2002), 'The plant macrofossils', in G. J. Barclay, K. Brophy and G. MacGregor, 'Claish, Stirling: an Early Neolithic structure in its context', *Proceedings of the Society of Antiquaries of Scotland*, 132: 65–138 (90–6).

Mills, C. (1991), 'The burnt timbers', in G. J. Barclay and G. S. Maxwell, 'Excavation of a Neolithic long mortuary enclosure within the Roman legionary fortress at Inchtuthil, Perthshire', *Proceedings of the Society of Antiquaries of Scotland*, 121: 27–44 (37–8).

Mitchell, F. (1992), 'Notes on some non-local cobbles at the entrances to the passage-graves at Newgrange and Knowth, County Meath', *Journal of the Royal Society of Antiquaries of Ireland*, 122: 128–45.

Mithen, S (ed.) (2000), *Hunter-gatherer Landscape Archaeology: The Southern Hebrides Mesolithic Project 1988–98*, Cambridge: McDonald Institute.

Moore, D. G. (2003), 'Neolithic Houses in Ballyharry Townland, Islandmagee, Co. Antrim', in I. Armit, E. Murphy, E. Nelis and D. Simpson (eds), *Neolithic Settlement in Ireland and Western Britain*, Oxford: Oxbow, 156–63.

Morgan, F. M. (1959), 'The excavation of a long barrow at Nutbane, Hants', *Proceedings of the Prehistoric Society*, 25: 15–51.

Morris, R. W. B. (1970–1), 'The petroglyphs at Achnabreck, Argyll', *Proceedings of the Society of Antiquaries of Scotland*, 103: 33–56.

Muckelroy, K. (1978), *Maritime Archaeology*, Cambridge: Cambridge University Press.

Mullin, D. (2003), *The Bronze Age Landscape of the Northern English Midlands*, BAR British Series 351.

Murray, J. (1994), *The Role of Monuments in the Neolithic of the South of Scotland*, Department of Archaeology, University of Edinburgh: unpublished Ph.D. thesis.

Name Book (1864), *Original Name Books of the Ordnance Survey, Book 2*: 38.

Nelson, C. J. (2003), *West Lindsaylands and Brownsbank: Two Geophysical Surveys in the Upper Clyde Valley, and their Possible Neolithic Context*, Department of Archaeology, University of Glasgow: unpublished undergraduate dissertation.

Niblett, R. (2001), 'A Neolithic dugout from a multi-period site near St Albans, Herts, England', *International Journal of Nautical Archaeology*, 30.2: 155–95.

Nichols, H. (1967), 'Vegetational change, shoreline displacement and the human factor in the Late Quaternary history of southwest Scotland', *Transactions of the Royal Society of Edinburgh*, 67: 145–87.

NMS (1993), 'Torr Righ Beag, Isle of Arran (Kilmory parish): lithic findspot', *Discovery and Excavation in Scotland*: 80.

O'Drisceoil, C. (2003), 'Archaeological excavation of a Neolithic settlement at Coolfore, Co. Louth', in I. Armit, E. Murphy, E. Nelis and D. Simpson (eds), *Neolithic Settlement in Ireland and Western Britain*, Oxford: Oxbow, 176–81.

O'Kelly, M. J. (1989), *Early Ireland: An Introduction to Irish Prehistory*, Cambridge: Cambridge University Press.

Oswald, A. (2001), *The Creation of Monuments: Neolithic Causewayed Enclosures in the British Isles*, Swindon: English Heritage.

Øverik, S. (1985), 'The second millennium and after', in C. Renfrew (ed.), *The Prehistory of Orkney*, Edinburgh: Edinburgh University Press, 131–49.

Parker Pearson, M. (1999), 'The Earlier Bronze Age', in J. Hunter and I. Ralston (eds), *The Archaeology of Britain from the Upper Palaeolithic to the Industrial Revolution*, London: Routledge, 77–94.

Parker Pearson, M. and Ramilisonina (1998), 'Stonehenge for the ancestors: the stones pass on the message', *Antiquity*, 72: 308–26.

Parker Pearson, M. and Richards, C. (1994), *Architecture and Order: Approaches to Social Space*, London: Routledge.

Peltenberg, E. J. (1982), 'Excavations at Balloch Hill', *Proceedings of the Society of Antiquaries of Scotland*, 112: 142–214.

Phillips, T. (2002), *Landscapes of the Living, Landscapes of the Dead: The Location of the Chambered Cairns of Northern Scotland*, BAR British Series 328.

Phillips, T. (2003), 'Landscapes and seascapes in Orkney and northern Scotland', *World Archaeology*, 35 (3): 371–84.

Phillips, T. and Bradley, R. (2000), 'Pick-dressing on the Neolithic monuments of Orkney', *Scottish Archaeological Journal*, 22.2: 103–10.

Philpot, J. H. (1897), *The Sacred Tree or the Tree in Religion and Myth*, London: Macmillan.

Pierpoint, S. J., Barnatt, J. and Lambert, N. (1980), 'A chambered tomb at Machrie Water, Arran', *Glasgow Archaeological Journal*, 7: 112–13.

Piggott, S. (1947–8), 'Excavations at Cairnpapple Hill, West Lothian, 1947–8', *Proceedings of the Society of Antiquaries of Scotland*, 82: 68–123.

Piggott, S. (1954), *The Neolithic Cultures of the British Isles*, Cambridge: Cambridge University Press.

Piggott, S. (1958), *Scotland Before History*, Edinburgh: Nelson.

Piggott, S. (1971–2), 'Excavation of the Dalladies long barrow, Fettercairn, Kincardineshire', *Proceedings of the Society of Antiquaries of Scotland*, 104: 23–47.

Piggott, S. (1983), 'The National Museum of Antiquities and archaeological research', in A. O'Connor and D. V. Clark (eds), *From the Stone Age to the 'Forty-five': Studies Presented to R. B. K. Stevenson*, Edinburgh: John Donald, 4–8

Piggott, S. and Powell, T. G. E. (1948–9), 'The excavation of three Neolithic chambered tombs in Galloway, 1949', *Proceedings of the Society of Antiquaries of Scotland*, 83: 103–61.

Pitts, M. (2004), 'Rare henge builders' homes revealed', *British Archaeology*, 76: 9.

Platenkamp, J. D. M. (1992), 'Transforming Tobelo ritual', in D. de Coppet (ed.), *Understanding Rituals*, London: Routledge, 74–96

Plint, R. G. (1962), 'Stone axe factory sites in the Cumbrian Fells', *Transactions of the Cumberland and Westmorland Antiquarian and Archaeology Society*, 62: 1–26.

Pollard, J. (2000), 'Neolithic occupation practices and social ecologies from Rinyo to Clacton', in A. Ritchie (ed.), *Neolithic Orkney in its European Context*, Cambridge: McDonald Institute for Archaeological Research, 363–70.

Pollard, T. (1997), 'Excavation of a Neolithic settlement and ritual complex at Beckton Farm, Lockerbie, Dumfries and Galloway', *Proceedings of the Society of Antiquaries of Scotland*, 127: 69–121.

Ponting, G and Ponting, M. (1977), *The Standing Stones of Callanish*, private publication.

Powell, T. G. E. (1973), 'Excavation of the megalithic chambered cairn at Dyffryn Ardudwy, Merioneth, Wales', *Archaeologica*, 104: 1–50.

PSAS (1907–8), 'Donations to and purchases for the Museum and Library, with exhibits', *Proceedings of the Society of Antiquaries of Scotland*, 42: 64.

Radley, A. (1993), 'Upper Largie (Kilmartin parish)', *Discovery and Excavation in Scotland*: 75.

Ralston, I. B. M. (1982), 'A timber hall at Balbridie farm', *Aberdeen University Review*, 168: 238–49.

Ramsay, S. (1998), 'Pollen', in O. Lelong and T. Pollard, 'The excavation and survey of prehistoric enclosures at Blackshouse Burn, Lanarkshire', *Proceedings of the Society of Antiquaries of Scotland*, 128: 13–53 (37–40).

RCAMS (1928), *Ninth Report, with an Inventory of Monuments and Constructions in the Outer Hebrides, Skye and the Small Isles*, Edinburgh; The Royal Commission on the Ancient and Historical Monuments and Constructions of Scotland.

RCAMS (1946), *Twelfth Report, with an Inventory of the Ancient Monuments of Orkney and Shetland*, Edinburgh: The Royal Commission on the Ancient and Historical Monuments of Scotland.

RCAHMS (1978), *Lanarkshire: An Inventory of the Prehistoric and Roman Monuments*, Edinburgh: The Royal Commission on the Ancient and Historical Monuments of Scotland.

RCAHMS (1984), *The Archaeological Sites and Monuments of North Kincardine, Kincardine and Deeside District, Grampian Region*, The Archaeological Sites and Monuments of Scotland Series No. 21, Edinburgh: The Royal Commission on the Ancient and Historical Monuments of Scotland.

RCAHMS (1987), *The Archaeological Sites and Monuments of East Rhins, Wigtown District, Dumfries and Galloway Region*, The Archaeological Sites and Monuments of Scotland Series No. 26, Edinburgh: The Royal Commission on the Ancient and Historical Monuments of Scotland.

RCAHMS (1997), *Eastern Dumfriesshire: An Archaeological Landscape*, Edinburgh: The Royal Commission on the Ancient and Historical Monuments of Scotland.

RCAHMS (1999), *Kilmartin: Prehistoric and Early Historic Monuments*, Edinburgh: The Royal Commission on the Ancient and Historical Monuments of Scotland.

Renfrew, A. C. (1973), 'Monuments, mobilisation and social organisation in Neolithic Wessex', in C. Renfrew (ed.), *The Explanation of Culture Change: Models in Prehistory*, London: Duckworth, 539–58.

Renfrew, C. (1976), 'Megaliths, territories and populations', in S. De Laet (ed.), *Acculturation and Continuity in Atlantic Europe*, Bruges: De Tempel, 198–229.

Renfrew, C. (1979), *Investigations in Orkney*, London: Thames and Hudson.

Richards, C. (1986), 'Unstan (Stenness parish)', *Discovery and Excavation in Scotland*: 22.

Richards, C. (1988), 'Altered Images: a re-examination of Neolithic mortuary practices in Orkney', in J. Barrett and I. Kinnes (eds), *The Archaeology of Context in the Neolithic and Early Bronze Age: Recent Trends*, Sheffield: Sheffield University Press, 42–56

Richards, C. (1991), 'Skara Brae: revisiting a Neolithic village in Orkney', in W. Hanson and E. A. Slater (eds), *Scottish Archaeology: New Perceptions*, Aberdeen: Aberdeen University Press, 24–43.

Richards, C. (1992a), 'Doorways into another world: the Orkney–Cromarty chambered tombs', in N. Sharples and A. Sheridan (eds), *Vessels for the Ancestors: Essays in Honour of Audrey Henshall*, Edinburgh: Edinburgh University Press, 62–76.

Richards, C. (1992b), 'Barnhouse and Maes Howe', *Current Archaeology*, 131: 444–48.

Richards, C. (1993a), *An Archaeological Study of Neolithic Orkney: Architecture, Order and Social Classification*, University of Glasgow: unpublished Ph.D. thesis.

Richards, C. (1993b), 'Monumental choreography: architecture and spatial representation in Late Neolithic Orkney', in C. Tilley (ed.), *Interpretative Archaeology*, Oxford: Berg: 143–80.

Richards, C (1993c), 'Contextual analysis of the Grooved Ware at Balfarg', G. J. Barclay and C. J. Russell-White, 'Excavations in the ceremonial complex of the fourth to third millennium BC at Balfarg/Balbirnie, Glenrothes, Fife', *Proceedings of the Society of Antiquaries of Scotland*, 123: 43–110 (185–92).

Richards, C. (1996a), 'Henges and water: towards an elemental understanding of monumentality and landscape in Late Neolithic Britain', *Journal of Material Culture*, 1: 313–36.

Richards, C. (1996b), 'Monuments as landscape: creating the centre of the world in Late Neolithic Orkney', *World Archaeology*, 28: 190–208.

Richards, C. (1998), 'Centralising tendencies? A re-examination of social evolution in Late Neolithic Orkney', in M. Edmonds and C. Richards (eds), *Understanding the Neolithic of North-Western Europe*, Glasgow: Cruithne Press, 516–32.

Richards, C. (2004), 'Rethinking the great stone circles of northwest Britain', http://www.orkneydigs.org.uk/dhl/papers/cr.

Richards, C. (2005), *Dwelling Amongst the Monuments: The Neolithic Village of Barnhouse, Masehowe Passage Grave and Surrounding Monuments at Stenness, Orkney*, Cambridge: McDonald Institute for Archaeological Research.

Richards, C. and Thomas, J. (1984), 'Ritual activity and structured deposition in Later Neolithic Wessex', in R. Bradley and J. Gardiner (eds), *Neolithic Studies: A Review of Some Current Research*, British Archaeological Reports British Series 133, 189–218.

Richards, M. P. (2003), 'Explaining the dietary isotope evidence for the rapid adoption of the Neolithic in Britain', in M. Parker Pearson (ed.). *Food, Culture and Identity in the Neolithic and Early Bronze Age*, British Archaeological Reports International Series 1,117, 31–6.

Richards, M. P. and Hedges, R. E. M. (1999), 'A Neolithic revolution? New evidence of diet in the British Neolithic', *Antiquity*, 73: 891–7.

Rideout, J. S. (1997), 'Excavations of Neolithic enclosures at Cowie Road, Bannockburn, Stirling, 1984–5', *Proceedings of the Society of Antiquaries of Scotland*, 127: 29–68.

Ritchie, A. (1983), 'Excavation of a Neolithic farmstead at Knap of Howar, Papa Westray', *Proceedings of the Society of Antiquaries of Scotland*, 113: 40–121

Ritchie, A. (1995), *Prehistoric Orkney*, London: Historic Scotland.

Ritchie, A. (ed.) (2000), *Neolithic Orkney in its European Context*, Cambridge: McDonald Institute for Archaeological Research.
Ritchie, J. (1919–20), 'The Stone Circle at Broomend of Crichie, Aberdeenshire', *Proceedings of the Society of Antiquaries of Scotland*, 54: 154–72.
Ritchie, J. N. G. (1969–70), 'Excavation of the chambered cairn at Achnacreebeag', *Proceedings of the Society of Antiquaries of Scotland*, 102: 31–55.
Ritchie, J. N. G. (1971–2), 'Excavation of a chambered cairn at Dalineun, Lorn, Argyll', *Proceedings of the Society of Antiquaries of Scotland*, 104: 48–62.
Ritchie, J. N. G. (1974), 'Excavation of a stone circle and cairn at Balbirnie, Fife', *Archaeological Journal*, 131: 1–32.
Ritchie, J. N. G. (1975–6), 'The Stones of Stenness, Orkney', *Proceedings of the Society of Antiquaries of Scotland*, 107: 1–60.
Ritchie, J. N. G. (1985), 'The ritual monuments', in C. Renfrew (ed), *The Prehistory of Orkney*, Edinburgh: Edinburgh University Press.
Ritchie, J. N. G. (1997), *The Archaeology of Argyll*, Edinburgh: Edinburgh University Press.
Rival, L. (1993), 'The growth of family tree: understanding Huaorani perceptions of the forest', *MAN*, 28: 635–52.
Rival, L (ed.) (1998a), *The Social Life of Trees: Anthropological Perspectives on Tree Symbolism*, Oxford: Berg.
Rival, L. (1998b), 'Trees, from symbols of life and regeneration to political artefacts', in ibid.,1–35.
Robinson, D. E. and Dickson, J. H. (1988), 'Vegetational history and land use: a radiocarbon-dated pollen diagram from Machrie Moor, Arran, Scotland', *New Phytologist*, 109: 223–51.
Robinson, M. A. (2000), 'Coleoptera evidence for the elm decline, Neolithic activity in woodland, clearance and the use of the landscape', in A. S. Fairbairn, *Plants in Neolithic Britain and Beyond*, Oxford: Oxbow Books, 85–91.
Romans, J. C. C. and Robertson, L. (1983), 'Soils', in G. J. Barclay, 'Sites of the third millennium BC to the first millennium AD at North Mains, Strathallan, Perthshire', *Proceedings of the Society of Antiquaries of Scotland*, 113: 122–281 (260–9).
Rowley-Conwy, P. (2002), 'Great sites: Balbridie', *British Archaeology*, 64: 22–4.
Rowley-Conwy, P. (2004), 'How the west was lost: a reconsideration of agricultural origins in Britain, Ireland, and southern Scandinavia', *Current Anthropology*, 45: 83–113.
Ruggles, C. L. N. (1999), *Astronomy in Prehistoric Britain and Ireland*, London: Yale University Press.
Saville, A. (1999a), 'An exceptional polished flint axe-head from Bolshan Hill, near Montrose, Angus', *Tayside and Fife Archaeological Journal*, 5: 1–6.
Saville, A. (2000), 'Orkney and Scotland before the Neolithic period', in A. Ritchie (ed.), *Neolithic Orkney in its European Context*, Cambridge: McDonald Institute for Archaeological Research, 91–100.
Saville, A. (ed.) (2004), *Mesolithic Scotland and its Neighbours*, Edinburgh: Society of Antiquaries of Scotland.
Scarre, C. (2002), 'A pattern of islands: the Neolithic monuments of north-west Brittany', *European Journal of Archaeology*, 5: 24–41.
Schacter, D. L. (1995), *Memory Distortion: How Minds, Brains and Societies Reconstruct the Past*, London: Harvard University Press.
Schulting, R. J. and Richards, M. P. (2002), 'The wet, the wild and the domesticated: the Mesolithic–Neolithic transition on the west coast of Scotland', *European Journal of Archaeology*, 5 (2): 147–89.
Scott, J. G. (1955–6), 'The chambered cairn at Brackley, Kintyre', *Proceedings of the Society of Antiquaries of Scotland*, 89: 22–54.
Scott, J. G. (1964), 'The chambered cairn at Beacharra, Kintyre', *Proceedings of the Prehistoric Society*, 30: 134–58.
Scott, J. G. (1969), 'The Neolithic period in Kintyre', in T. G. E. Powell (ed.), *Megalithic Enquiries in the West of Britain*, Liverpool: Liverpool University Press.
Scott, J. G. (1988–9), 'The stone circles at Temple Wood, Kilmartin, Argyll', *Glasgow Archaeological Journal*, 15: 53–125.

Scott, J. G. (1992), 'Mortuary structures and megaliths', in N. Sharples and A. Sheridan (eds), *Vessels for the Ancestors: Essays in Honour of Audrey Henshall*, Edinburgh: Edinburgh University Press, 104–19.

Scott, L. (1951), 'The colonisation of Scotland in the second millennium BC', *Proceedings of the Prehistoric Society*, 17: 16–82.

Scott, W. L. (1934–5), 'The chambered cairn of Clettraval, North Uist', *Proceedings of the Society of Antiquaries of Scotland*, 69: 480–536.

Scott, W. L. (1947–8), 'The chambered tomb of Unival, North Uist', *Proceedings of the Society of Antiquaries of Scotland*, 82: 1–49.

Sharpe, L. and Hamer, J. (1999), 'Craigie Burn (Libberton parish) geophysical survey of ?henge', *Discovery and Excavation in Scotland*: 84–5.

Sharples, N. (1981), 'The excavation of a chambered cairn, the Ord North, at Lairg, Sutherland, by J. X. W. P. Corcoran', *Proceedings of the Society of Antiquaries of Scotland*, 111: 21–62.

Sharples, N. (1985), 'Individual and community: the changing role of megaliths in the Orcadian Neolithic', *Proceedings of the Prehistoric Society*, 51: 59–74.

Sharples, N. (1986), 'Radiocarbon dates from three chambered tombs at Loch Calder, Caithness', *Scottish Archaeological Review*, 4: 2–10.

Sharples, N. (1992), 'Aspects of regionalisation in the Scottish Neolithic', in N. Sharples and A. Sheridan, *Vessels for the Ancestors: Essays in Honour of Audrey Henshall*, Edinburgh: Edinburgh University Press, 322–31.

Sharples, N. and Sheridan, A. (1992), *Vessels for the Ancestors: essays in Honour of Audrey Henshall*, Edinburgh: Edinburgh University Press.

Shepherd, I. A. G. (1986), *Powerful Pots: Beakers in North-east Prehistory*, University of Aberdeen: Anthropological Museum.

Sheridan, A. (2000), 'Achnacreebeag and its French connections: vive the "auld alliance"', in J. C. Henderson (ed.), *The Prehistory and Early History of Atlantic Europe*, BAR International Series 861: 1–15.

Sheridan, A. and Sharples. N. (1992), 'Introduction: the state of Neolithic studies in Scotland', in N. Sharples and A. Sheridan (eds), *Vessels for the Ancestors: Essays in Honour of Audrey Henshall*, Edinburgh: Edinburgh University Press, 1–12.

Sherratt, A. (1990), 'The genesis of megaliths', *World Archaeology*, 22: 147–67.

Sherratt, A. (1996a), 'Why Wessex? The Avon route and river transport in later British prehistory', *Oxford Journal of Archaeology*, 15: 211–34.

Sherrat, A. (1996b), 'Linking Wessex with the three rivers Avon', *British Archaeology*, 20: 6.

Simpson, D. (1996), 'Excavation of a kerbed funerary monument at Stoneyfield, Raigmore, Inverness, Highland, 1972–3', *Proceedings of the Society of Antiquaries of Scotland*, 126: 53–86.

Simpson, D. and Meighan, I. (1999), 'Arran pitchstone', *Archaeology Ireland*, 13: 26–30.

Simpson, D. and Ransom, R. (1992), Maceheads and the Orcadian Neolithic, in N. Sharples and A. Sheridan (eds), *Vessels for the Ancestors: Essays in Honour of Audrey Henshall*, Edinburgh: Edinburgh University Press, 221–43.

Simpson, D. D. A. and Coles, J. M. (1990), 'Excavations at Grandtully, Perthshire', *Proceedings of the Society of Antiquaries of Scotland*, 120: 33–44.

Smith, A. N. (1995), 'The excavation of Neolithic, Bronze Age and Early Historic features near Ratho, Edinburgh', *Proceedings of the Society of Antiquaries of Scotland*, 125: 69–138.

Smith, C. A. and Lynch, F. M. (1987), *Trefignath and Din Dryfol: The Excavation of Two Megalithic Tombs in Angelesey*, Carmbridge Archaeological Association.

Snow, C. H. (1903), *The Principal Species of Wood: Their Characteristic Properties*, London: John Wiley and Sons.

Speak, S. and Burgess, C. (1999), 'Meldon Bridge: a centre of the third millennium BC in Peebleshire', *Proceedings of the Society of Antiquaries of Scotland*, 129: 1–118.

Stevanović, M. (1997), 'The age of clay: the social dynamics of house destruction', *Journal of Anthropological Archaeology*, 16: 334–95.

Stewart, D. A., Walker, A. and Dickson, J. H. (1984), 'Pollen diagrams from Dubh Lochan, near Loch Lomond', *New Phytologist*, 98: 531–49.

Stone, J. E. S. (1949), 'Some Grooved Ware pottery from the Woodhenge area', *Proceedings of the Prehistoric Society*, 15: 122–7.

Stone, J. F. S. and Wallis, F. S. (1951), 'Third report of the sub-committee of the south-western group of museums and art galleries on the petrological determination of stone axes', *Proceedings of the Prehistoric Society*, 17: 99–158.

Strachan, I., Ralston, I. and Finlayson, B. (1998), 'Neolithic and later prehistoric structures, and early medieval metal-working at Blairhall Burn, Amisfield, Dumfriesshire', *Proceedings of the Society of Antiquaries of Scotland*, 128: 55–94.

Stuart, J. (1862–4), 'Notice of excavations in the chambered mound of Maes-Howe, in Orkney, and the runic inscriptions on the walls of its central chamber', *Proceedings of the Society of Antiquaries of Scotland*, 5: 247–9.

Sturt, F. (2005), 'Fishing for meaning: lived space and early Neolithic of Orkney', in V. Cummings and A. Pannett (eds), *Set in Stone: New Approaches to Neolithic Monuments in Scotland*, Oxford: Oxbow.

Svensson, M. (2002), 'Palisade enclosures – the second generation of enclosed sites in the Neolithic of Northern Europe', in A. Gibson (ed.), 'The Later Neolithic palisaded enclosures of Britain', *Behind Wooden Walls: Neolithic Palisaded Enclosures in Europe*, BAR International Series 1,013, 5–23 (28–58).

Switsur, V. R. (1981), 'Natural radiocarbon measurements 15, Cambridge University', *Radiocarbon*, 23: 81–93.

Tambiah, S. J. (1979), 'A performative approach to ritual', *Proceedings of the British Academy*, 65: 113–69.

Taylor, C. (1979), *Roads and Tracks of Britain*, London: Orion (2nd edn).

Telford, D. (2002), 'The Mesolithic inheritance: contrasting Neolithic monumentality in eastern and western Scotland', *Proceedings of the Prehistoric Society*, 68: 289–315.

Terry, J. (1997), 'Upper Largie (Kilmartin parish), prehistoric ritual and funerary complex', *Discovery and Excavation in Scotland*: 19–20.

Thomas, J. (1988), 'Neolithic explanations revisited: the Mesolithic–Neolithic transition in Britain and southern Scandinavia', *Proceedings of the Prehistoric Society*, 54: 59–66.

Thomas, J. (1991), *Rethinking the Neolithic*, Cambridge: Cambridge University Press.

Thomas, J. (1998), 'Towards a regional geography of the Neolithic', in M. Edmonds and C. Richards (eds), *Understanding the Neolithic of North-west Europe*, Glasgow: Cruithne Press, 37–60.

Thomas, J. (1999a), *Understanding the Neolithic*, London: Routledge.

Thomas, J. (1999b), Dunragit Excavations Project 1999–2002, http://orgs.man.ac.uk/research/dunragit/dunragit_1999.htm

Thomas, J. (1999c), 'The Holywood cursus complex, Dumfries: an interim account 1997', in A. Barclay and J. Harding (eds), *Pathways and Ceremonies: The Cursus Monuments of Britain and Ireland*, Oxford: Oxbow, 107–18.

Thomas, J. (2000), 'The identity of place in Neolithic Britain: examples from southwest Scotland', in A. Ritchie (ed.), *Neolithic Orkney in its European Context*, Cambridge: McDonald Institute for Archaeological Research, chp. 6.

Thomas, J. (2001a), Dunragit Excavations Project 1999–2002, http://orgs.man.ac.uk/research/dunragit/dunragit_2001.htm

Thomas, J. (2001b), 'Neolithic enclosures: reflection on excavations in Wales and Scotland', in T. Darvill and J. Thomas (eds), *Neolithic Enclosures in Atlantic Northwest Europe*, Oxford: Oxbow, 132–43.

Thomas, J. (2002), Dunragit Excavations Project 1999–2002, http://orgs.man.ac.uk/research/dunragit/dunragit_2002.htm

Thorpe, I. J. and Richards, C. (1984), 'The decline of ritual authority and the introduction of Beakers into Britain', in R. Bradley and J. Gardiner (eds), *Neolithic Studies: A Review of Some Current Research*, BAR British Series 133, 67–84.

Thorpe, O. W. and Thorpe, R. S. (1984), 'The distribution and sources of archaeological pitchstone in Britain', *Journal of Archaeological Science*, 11: 1–34.

Tipping, R. (1994), 'The form and fate of Scotland's woodlands', *Proceedings of the Society of Antiquaries of Scotland*, 124: 1–54.

Tipping, R. (1995), 'Holocene landscape change at Carn Dubh, near Pitlochry, Perthshire, Scotland', *Journal of Quaternary Science*, 10: 59–75.

Tipping, R., Edmonds, M. and Sheridan, A. (1993), 'Paleoenvironmental investigations directly associated with a Neolithic axe "quarry" on Beinn Lawers, near Killin, Perthshire, Scotland', *New Phytologist*, 123: 585–97.

Tolan-Smith, C. (1996), 'And then came farmers to the North', *British Archaeology*, 11: 7.

Topping, P. (1996), 'Structure and ritual in the Neolithic house: some examples from Britain and Ireland', in T. Darvill and J. Thomas (eds), *Neolithic Houses in Northwest Europe and Beyond*, Oxford: Oxbow, 157–70.

Toren, C. (1995), 'Seeing the ancestral sites: transformations in Fijian notions of the land', in E. Hirsch and M. O'Hanlo (eds), *The Anthropology of Landscape: Perspectives on Place and Space*, Oxford: Clarendon, 163–83.

Tresset, A. (2003), 'French connections II: of cows and men', in I. Armit, E. Murphy, E. Nelis and D. Simpson (eds), *Neolithic Settlement in Ireland and Western Britain*, Oxford: Oxbow, 18–29.

Tringham, R. (1991), 'Households with faces: the challenge of gender in prehistoric architectural remains', in J. M. Gero and M. W. Conkey (eds), *Engendering Archaeology: Women and Prehistory*, Oxford: Basil Blackwell, 93–131.

Tuckwell, A. (1975), 'Patterns of burial orientation in the round barrows of east Yorkshire', *The Bulletin of the Institute of Archaeology, University of London*, 12: 95–123.

Turner, J. (1965), 'A contribution to the history of forest clearance', *Proceedings of the Royal Society of London*, 161: 343–54.

Turner, V. (1995), *The Ritual Process: Structure and Anti-structure*, New York: Aldine de Gruyter.

Turner, V. (1998), *Ancient Shetland*, Edinburgh: Historic Scotland.

Turner, V. W. (1968), *The Drums of Affliction*, Oxford: Clarendon.

Turner, V. W. (1982), *From Ritual to Theatre: The Human Seriousness of Play*, New York: Performing Arts Journal Publications.

Turnock, D. (1974), *Problem Regions of Europe: Scotland's Highlands and Islands*, Oxford: Oxford University Press.

Twohig, E. S. (1981), *The Megalithic Art of Western Europe*, Oxford: Clarendon.

van Beek, W. E. A. and Banga, P. M. (1992), 'The Dogon and their trees', in E. Croll and D. Parkin (eds), *Bush Base, Forest Farm: Culture, Environment and Development*, London: Routledge: 57–75.

van de Noort, R. (2003), 'An ancient seascape: the social context of seafaring in the Early Bronze Age', *World Archaeology*, 35.3: 404–15.

Vyner, B. E. (1984), 'The excavation of a Neolithic cairn at Street House, Loftus, Cleveland', *Proceedings of the Prehistoric Society*, 50: 151–95.

Wainwright, G. J. (1979), *Mount Pleasant, Dorset: Excavations 1970–1*, London: Society of Antiquaries.

Wainwright, G. J. (1989), *The Henge Monuments: Ceremony and Society in Prehistoric Britain*, London: Thames and Hudson.

Walker, I. C. (1968), 'Easterton of Roseisle: a forgotten site in Moray', in J. M. Coles and D. D. A. Simpson (eds), *Studies in Ancient Europe*, Leicester: Leicester University Press: 95–115

Ward, T. (1991), 'Cornhill (Culter parish)', *Discovery and Excavation in Scotland*: 65–6.

Ward, T. (1992), 'Biggar Common (Biggar parish)', *Discovery and Excavation in Scotland*: 65.

Ward, T. (1993a), 'Biggar Common (Biggar parish)', *Discovery and Excavation in Scotland*: 87.

Ward, T. (1993b), 'Cornhill (Culter parish)', *Discovery and Excavation in Scotland*: 88.

Ward, T. (1994), 'Cornhill (Culter parish)', *Discovery and Excavation in Scotland*: 72.

Ward, T. (1995a), 'Cornhill (Culter parish)', *Discovery and Excavation in Scotland*: 87.

Ward, T. (1995b), 'Cornhill (Culter parish)', *Discovery and Excavation in Scotland*: 87.

Ward, T. (1996), 'Cornhill (Culter parish)', *Discovery and Excavation in Scotland*: 99.

Ward, T. (1997a), 'Cornhill (Culter parish)', *Discovery and Excavation in Scotland*: 76.

Ward, T. (1997b), 'Cornhill (Culter parish)', *Discovery and Excavation in Scotland*: 76.

Ward, T. (1998a), 'Weston Farm (Carnwath parish)', *Discovery and Excavation in Scotland*: 90.
Ward, T. (1998b), 'Cornhill (Culter parish)', *Discovery and Excavation in Scotland*: 90.
Ward, T. (1999a), 'Bizzberry Hill (Biggar parish)', *Discovery and Excavation in Scotland*: 82.
Ward, T. (1999b), 'Brownsbank Farm (Biggar parish)', *Discovery and Excavation in Scotland*: 82.
Ward, T. (1999c), 'Weston Farm (Carnwath/Dunsyre parishes)', *Discovery and Excavation in Scotland*: 83.
Ward, T. (1999d), 'Carwood Farm (Biggar parish)', *Discovery and Excavation in Scotland*: 82.
Ward, T. (1999e), 'Cornhill (Culter parish)', *Discovery and Excavation in Scotland*: 83.
Ward, T. (2000a), 'Brownsbank Farm (Biggar parish)', *Discovery and Excavation in Scotland*: 84.
Ward, T. (2000b), 'Heavyside Farm (Biggar Gap)', *Discovery and Excavation in Scotland*: 84.
Ward, T. (2001), 'Brownsbank Farm (Biggar parish)', *Discovery and Excavation in Scotland*: 90.
Warren, G. (2000), 'Seascapes: people, boats and inhabiting the later Mesolithic in western Scotland', in R. Young (ed.), *Mesolithic Lifeways: Current Research from Britain and Ireland*, Leicester: University of Leicester: 97–104.
Warren, G. (2003), 'Sands of Forvie', *Discovery and Excavation in Scotland*: 155.
Warren, G. (2004), 'The start of the Neolithic in Scotland', in G. J. Barclay and I. A. G. Shepherd (eds), *Scotland in Ancient Europe: the Neolithic and Early Bronze Age of Scotland in their European Context*, Edinburgh: Society of Antiquaries of Scotland, 91–102.
Watt, W. G. T. (1876–7), 'Notice of the discovery of a cist, with three skeletons at Innertown, near Stromness', *Proceedings of the Society of Antiquaries of Scotland*, 12: 301–2.
White, J. (1995), *Forest and Woodland Trees in Britain*, Oxford: Oxford University Press.
Whitehouse, R. (1992), *Underground Religion: Cult and Culture in Prehistoric Italy*, University of London: Accordia Research Centre.
Whittington, G. and Edwards, K. J. (1997), 'Climate change', in K. J. Edwards and I. B. M. Ralston (eds), *Scotland: Environment and Archaeology 8000 BC–AD 1000*, Chichester: John Wiley and Sons, 11–22
Whittington, G., Edwards, K. J. and Cundill, P. R. (1990), *Paleoenvironmental Investigations at Black Loch, in the Ochil Hills of Fife, Scotland*, University of Aberdeen: O'Dell Monograph 22.
Whittle, A. (1977), *The Earlier Neolithic of Southern England and its Continental Background*, BAR British Series 35.
Whittle, A. (1985), 'Scourd of Brouster and early settlement in Shetland', in B. Smith (ed.), *Shetland Archaeology*, Lerwick: *Shetland Times.*
Whittle, A. (1986), *Scord of Brouster: An Early Archaeological Settlement on Shetland*, Oxford: Oxford University Committee for Archaeology Monograph No. 9.
Whittle, A. (1991), 'Wayland's Smithy, Oxfordshire: excavations at the Neolithic tomb in 1962–3 by R. J. C. Atkinson and S. Piggott', *Proceedings of the Prehistoric Society*, 57.2: 61–101.
Whittle, A. (1996), *Europe in the Neolithic*, Cambridge: Cambridge University Press.
Whittle, A. (1997), *Sacred Mound, Holy Rings: Silbury Hill and the West Kennet Palisade Enclosures: A Later Neolithic Complex in North Wiltshire*, Oxford: Oxbow Monograph 74.
Wickham-Jones, C. R. (1990a), *Rhum: Mesolithic and Later Sites at Kinloch Excavations 1984–6*, Edinburgh: Society of Antiquaries of Scotland Monograph Series No. 7.
Wickham-Jones, C. R. (1990b), 'Survey of mesolithic sites', *Discovery and Excavation in Scotland*: 44.
Wickham-Jones, C. R. (1994), *Scotland's First Settlers*, Edinburgh: Historic Scotland.
Wickham-Jones, C. R. (2004), 'Structural evidence in the Scottish Mesolithic', in A. Saville (ed.), *Mesolithic Scotland and its Neighbours*, Edinburgh: Society of Antiquaries of Scotland, 229–42.
Wickham-Jones, C. R. and Collins, G. H. (1977–8), 'The sources of flint and chert in northern Britain', *Proceedings of the Society of Antiquaries of Scotland*, 109: 7–21.
Williams, E. (1989), 'Dating the introduction of food production into Britain and Ireland', *Antiquity*, 63: 510–21.
Williams, J. (1970), 'Neolithic axes in Dumfries and Galloway', *Transactions of the Dumfries and Galloway Natural History and Archaeology Society*, 47: 111–22.
Williams, H. (ed.) (2003), *Archaeologies of Remembrance: Death and Memory in Past Societies*, London: Kluwer Academic/Plenum.
Williams, M. (2003), 'Tales from the dead', in ibid., 89–112.

Wilson, G. (1875–6), 'Notice on a collection of stone implements and other antiquities from Glenluce, Wigtownshire, now presented to the museum', *Proceedings of the Society of Antiquaries*, 11: 580–7.

Wilson, G. (1880–1), 'Notice on a collection of implements and ornaments of stone, bronze, from Glenluce, Wigtownshire', *Proceedings of the Society of Antiquaries*, 15: 262–77.

Wilson, G. (1898–9), 'List of antiquities of Glenluce, Wigtownshire, with descriptive notes', *Proceedings of the Society of Antiquaries*, 33: 170–85.

Woodman, P. (1978), 'A re-appraisal of the Manx Mesolithic', in P. Davey (ed.), *Man and Environment in the Isle of Man*, British Archaeological Reports No. 54 (i), 119–40.

Woodman, P. (2000), 'Getting back to basics: transition to farming in Ireland and Britain', in T. D. Price (ed.), *Europe's First Farmers*, Cambridge: Cambridge University Press, 219–59.

Woodman, P., Anderson, E. and Finlay, N. (1999), *Excavations at Ferriter's Cove 1983–95: Last Foragers, First Farmers in the Dingle Peninsula*, Wicklow: Wordwell.

Woodman, P. and McCarthy, M. (2003), 'Contemplating some awful(ly interesting) vistas: importing cattle and red deer into prehistoric Ireland', in I. Armit, E. Murphy, E. Nelis and D. Simpson (eds), *Neolithic Settlement in Ireland and Western Britain*, Oxford: Oxbow, 31–5.

Wordsworth, J. (1991), 'Balmachree (Petty parish): several pits containing Neolithic/EBA pottery', *Discovery and Excavation in Scotland*: 41.

Index

Aberdeenshire, 231–2
Achnacreebeag, 113–15
Aegean, 43
agriculture, 137, 210–11, 214
Aldwincle I, 72
alignments, 197–8
ancestry, 132–4, 137
Anderson, J., 118–19
Aros Moss, 208–9
Auchategan, 225
axes, 183, 215–17

Badden, 212
Balbirnie, 146, 222
Balbridie, 48
Balfarg, 141–6, 195, 204–5
Ballyharry, 53
Balvraid, 122
Barnhouse, 199–200
Beakers, 20, 221, 231
Beckton Farm, 59, 201–2
Biggar Common, 61, 213
Blackshouse Burn, 148–9, 151–3, 195–7, 208
Blarihall Burn, 62
boats, 24, 26, 29, 43–4, 185–7
bones (human), 134
Brittany, 133
Bryce, T. H., 104, 123
burning, 56–7, 70

Cairnholy, 111–13, 223–4
Cairnpapple Hill, 147–8, 222
Caithness, 118–21
Calf of Eday, 116–7
Callanish, 168–73, 197, 206–7, 227–8
Camster Long, 119–21, 131
carinated pottery, 15
Carsie Mains, 181–2
cattle, 22, 35–6
cereals, 14, 21, 32–3, 206–8
chambered cairns, 17, 102–38
Chapelfield Cowie, 59, 237
chiefdoms, 204
Childe, V. G., 200–1
cists, 219, 231
Claish, 47–8
Clava cairns, 220–1
clearance, 14, 33–6, 205–11
Cloghers, 51–2
Clyde cairns 104, 113
communication, 192–3, 209
Coolfore, 51
Corcoran, J. X. W. P., 105
Cowie Road, 49
Cranbourne Chase, 209
Craonaval, 124
cremation, 100–1, 136
cursus, 15–17, 45, 139–40, 150, 155, 157–8, 163

Dalladies, 83–6, 226
decay, 99–101
Deer's Den, 61
Dooey's Cairn, 90–1
Douglasmuir, 49
drama, 57–8, 234–5
Drummenny, 55
Dryffyn Ardudwy, 127
Dubton Farm, 62
Dunragit, 155, 195–7, 211

Early Bronze Age, 219–32
economy, 217–18
Embo, 121, 226
Enagh Townland, 52
environment, 12, 208–11
exotic, 214–17, 220
exposure platforms, 72–4, 92–4

feasting, 204–5
Fertile Crescent, 8

Ferriter's Cove, 35–6
field systems, 37–40, 162
fieldwalking, 32–4, 237
Food Vessels, 221
Fussell's Lodge, 72–3, 75–8

Glecknabae, 34
grazing, 210–11, 214
Grooved Ware, 19, 204–5
group construction, 194–5

Hebridean tombs, 123–4
henges, 18, 142–8, 150–1, 168
Highland, 28
Holywood, 46, 158
houses, 37–40, 51–6, 68–70, 199–204
Howe, 178
human body, 98–9

Impressed Ware, 15, 19
Inchtuthil, 48
individual burial, 220–2, 229–31
Ireland, 35–7, 51–6
islands, 24–44
Isle of Man, 29–33

Kilmartin Glen, 162–8, 212–13, 227
Kinbeachie, 61
Kinnes, I., 236–7
Kirkburn, 46

Lamb's Nursery, 59
Leadketty, 181
lifecycles, 69, 96–7, 198
lithics, 20–1, 32–3, 211–13
Lochhill, 82–3
Long barrow, 17, 71–101
Luce Sands, 211, 214

Machrie Moor, 34–35, 37, 160–2, 197, 207–8, 211–12, 227
Maeshowe, 175–8
megaliths, 102–38
Meillassoux, 137
Meldon Bridge, 153–4, 196
memory, 45, 57–8, 69–70, 137, 229, 234
Mesolithic, 7, 24–44, 173
metalworking, 220
Mid Gleniron, 105–11, 224
Midhowe, 135
monumental landscapes, 139–93, 194–219
motorways, 190

Newgrange, 184, 195
North Mains, 146–7, 205–6
Notgrove, 126
Nutbane, 90

oak, 57
Orkney-Cromarty, 115–18

Papa Westray North, 117
passage graves, 113–14
Pipton, 127
Pitnacree, 73–4, 78–9, 226
pits, 32, 62–4, 66–8, 141, 160
platforms, 118, 121
pollen, 32–5, 36, 205–11

Raigmore, 202
recumbent stone circles, 220
Rhum, 33–4
Ring of Brodgar, 178–80
ritual, 57–8, 66, 70, 99, 132
rock art, 168, 178
routeways, 26, 29–30, 183–93, 216–17

scorching, 136
Scord of Brouster, 40
sea 9, 24–44, 184–7
settlement, 22–3, 211–14
shell middens, 34
Skara Brae, 200–1
Slewcairn, 80–2
stalled cairns, 115–16
Stenness-Brodgar complex, 173–80
stone circles, 146, 159, 170–3, 173–5, 177–8
stone rows, 170–2, 221, 229
Stonehenge, 195
Stones of Stenness, 173–5, 205
Street House, 89
subsistence, 21–2

Temple Wood, 164–7, 222
Thornborough, 184, 190–1
timber buildings, 24–44, 142–3, 146–8, 151–7, 181–2
timber halls, 48–9, 59, 69, 181–2
trans-isthmian routes, 184–6
trees, 71, 94, 96–101
Twelve Apostles, 159, 216
Ty Isaf, 127

Upper Clyde Valley, 148–53, 213–15

Vementry, 123
viewing platforms, 195–6

Wales, 42
Wayland's Smithy, 86–8
Wessex, 183–4
West Lindsaylands, 149–50
woodland, 12, 14, 94–6

Zetland, 123–4